Is Art History Global?

EDITED BY

JAMES ELKINS

University College Cork
Coláiste na hOllscoile Corcaigh

Routledge
Taylor & Francis Group
New York London

Routledge is an imprint of the
Taylor & Francis Group, an informa business

Routledge
Taylor & Francis Group
270 Madison Avenue
New York, NY 10016

Routledge
Taylor & Francis Group
2 Park Square
Milton Park, Abingdon
Oxon OX14 4RN

Printed in the United States of America
10 9 8 7 6 5 4 3 2 1

International Standard Book Number-10: 0-415-97785-1 (Softcover) 0-415-97784-3 (Hardcover)
International Standard Book Number-13: 978-0-415-97785-2 (Softcover) 978-0-415-97784-5 (Hardcover)

Visit the Taylor & Francis Web site at
http://www.taylorandfrancis.com

and the Routledge Web site at
http://www.routledge-ny.com

Contents

Series Preface

It has been said and said that there is too much theorizing in the visual arts. Contemporary writing seems like a trackless thicket, tangled with unanswered questions. Yet it is not a wilderness; in fact it is well posted with signs and directions. Want to find Lacan? Read him through Macey, Silverman, Borch-Jakobsen, Žižek, Nancy, Leclaire, Derrida, Laplanche, Lecercle, or even Klossowski, but not — so it might be said — through Abraham, Miller, Pontalis, Rosaloto, Safouan, Roudinesco, Schneiderman, or Mounin, and of course never through Dalí.

People who would rather avoid problems of interpretation, at least in their more difficult forms, have sometimes hoped that "theory" would prove to be a passing fad. A simple test shows that is not the case. The table below shows the number of art historical essays that have terms like "psychoanalysis" as keywords, according to the *Bibliography of the History of Art.* The increase is steep after 1980, and in three cases — the gaze, psychoanalysis, and feminism — the rise is exponential.

Another sampling shows that citations of some of the more influential art historians of the mid-twentieth century, writers who came before the current proliferation of theories, are waning.

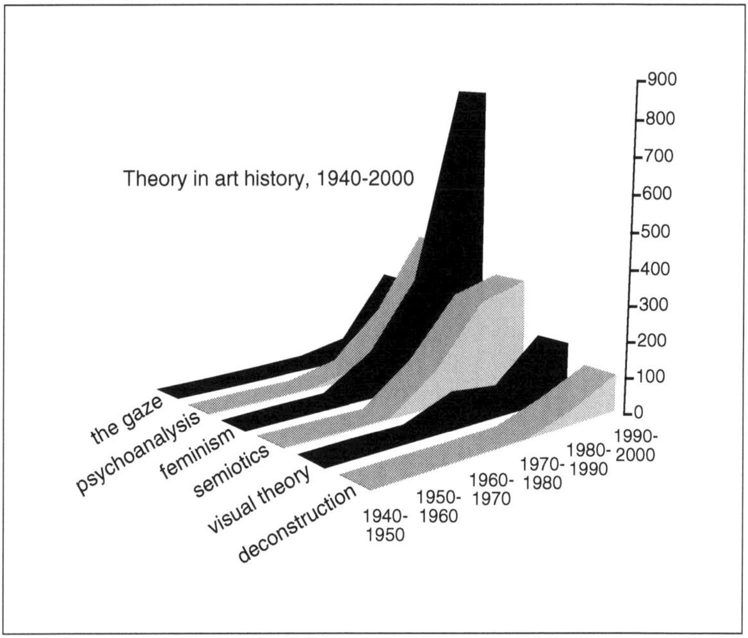

Figure 1 Theory in art history, 1940–2000.

In this second graph there is a slight rise in the number of references to Warburg and Riegl, reflecting the interest they have had for the current generation of art historians, but the graph's surprise is the precipitous decline in citations of Panofsky and Gombrich.

Most of art history is not driven by named theories or individual historians, and these graphs are also limited by the terms that can be meaningfully searched in the *Bibliography of the History of Art*. Even so, the graphs suggest that the landscape of interpretive strategies is changing rapidly. Many subjects crucial to the interpretation of art are too new, ill-theorized, or unfocused to be addressed in monographs or textbooks. The purpose of *The Art Seminar* is to address some of the most challenging subjects in current writing on art: those that are not unencompassably large (such as the state of painting), or not yet adequately posed (such

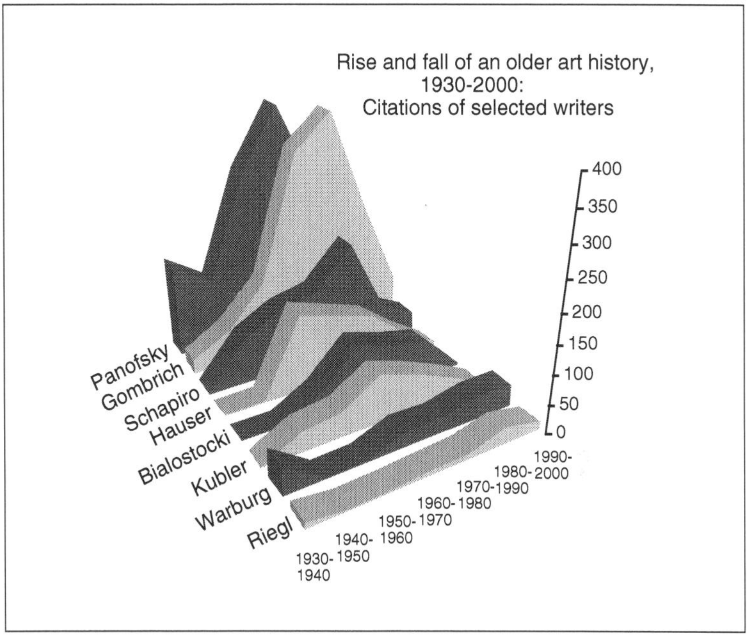

Figure 2 Rise and fall of an older art history, 1930–2000: Citations of selected writers.

as the space between the aesthetic and the anti-aesthetic), or so well known that they can be written up in critical dictionaries (the theory of deconstruction). The subjects chosen for *The Art Seminar* are poised, ready to be articulated and argued.

Each volume in the series began as a roundtable conversation, held in front of an audience at one of the three sponsoring institutions — the University College Cork, the Burren College of Art (both in Ireland), and the School of the Art Institute of Chicago. The conversations were then transcribed, and edited by the participants. The idea was to edit in such a way as to minimize the correctable faults of grammar, repetitions, and lapses that mark any conversation, while preserving the momentary disagreements, confusions, and dead ends that could be attributed to the articulation of the subject itself.

In each volume of *The Art Seminar*, the conversation itself is preceded by a general introduction to the subject and one or more "Starting Points," previously published essays that were distributed to participants before the roundtable. Together the Introductions and "Starting Points" are meant to provide the essential background for the conversation. A number of scholars who did not attend the events were then asked to write "Assessments"; their brief was to consider the conversation from a distance, noting its strengths and its blind spots. The "Assessments" vary widely in style and length: some are highly structured, and others are impressionistic; some are under a page, and others the length of a commissioned essay. Contributors were just asked to let their form fit their content, with no limitations. Each volume then concludes with one or more "Afterwords," longer critical essays written by scholars who had access to all the material including the "Assessments."

In that way *The Art Seminar* attempts to cast as wide, as fine, and as strong a net as possible, to capture the limit of theorizing on each subject at the particular moment represented by each book. Perhaps in the future the subjects treated here will be colonized, and become part of the standard pedagogy of art: but by that time they may be on the downward slide, away from the centers of conversation and into the history of disciplines.

1

Introduction

Art History as a Global Discipline

James Elkins

What is the shape, or what are the shapes, of art history across the world? Is it becoming global — that is, does it have a recognizable form wherever it is practiced? Can the methods, concepts, and purposes of Western art history be suitable for art outside of Europe and North America? And if not, are there alternatives that are compatible with existing modes of art history?

The book you are about to read takes off from problems like these. Since the Art Seminar roundtable in spring 2005, world art history and the globalization of the discipline have attracted increasing interest. Several books are in press at the same time as this one. A volume called *World Art Studies,* edited by Wilfried van Damme and Kitty Zijlmans (who also contributes an Assessment to this book) is forthcoming, and, in the odd logic of publishing, it contains a brief essay of mine, in which I contemplate the results of this project. At the moment, in autumn 2006, the subject is still entrancingly disorganized. It is not quite a field of study, even given the inception of programs in Leiden and East Anglia that aim to teach "world art studies." A sign of the relative novelty of the subject is the fact that despite extensive efforts, we could not find anyone who would contribute the kind of synoptic, historical Introduction that other volumes in this series have — one that would survey the history of art history's awareness of its geographic spread. This Introduction has no such ambitions; it was originally one of the essays that were precirculated among the panelists of the roundtable; some others are presented in Section 2. All I aim to do here is set out ten informal talking points: five reasons why art history might be considered to comprise several different practices, which vary from one place to another; and then five more reasons why art history can be considered as a single, fairly cohesive enterprise — not one that is homogeneous certainly, and not one that is distributed evenly around the world, but a field that shares some basic concepts and purposes. In the first case, art history would not be global because it would be several enterprises that happen to share a name — either that, or the current diffusion of Western models of art history would be weakening and melting into many local practices. In the second case, art history would be global, or on its way to becoming so. (I will note in passing that a global art history would be very approximately comparable to science. A field like physics, for example, can be said to share a rigorously defined set of assumptions and protocols no matter where it is practiced. A worldwide practice of art history would have a looser, less quantitative version of that kind of coherence: it would be a field some of whose assumptions, founding texts, interpretive protocols, and institutional forms are compatible wherever they are taught.)

The ten points, five on each side, are not meant to cover the field or even to introduce the writers who have contributed to this volume; I mean only to offer hooks on which to hang the conversation. This book is full of scholarly references to a bewilderingly wide range of cultures and literatures. I thought it would be best, in the absence of a historical introduction, to start with these two loose and open-ended lists. At the end I'll say something of my own stake in all this.

I

I begin, then, with five arguments against the idea that art history is, or could become, a single enterprise throughout the world.

1. *What counts as "art history" in many countries is newspaper art criticism.*

   In smaller and developing countries, newspaper art criticism normally serves as art history, so that reviews and exhibition brochures compose the written self-description of the country's art. In Paraguay there is a brilliant critic named Ticio Escobar: he knows postcolonial theory and visual culture, and in a country like Germany or France he could be employed in an art history department. But he writes cultural criticism and art theory, somewhat along the lines of Homi Bhabha or Nestor García Canclini, rather than art history. When I visited Paraguay in 2002, there were no art historians, and the only newspaper art criticism was being written by Olga Blinder, a painter at the Instituto del Arte Superior in Asunción. Her essays range over the history of Paraguayan modernism, and so they constitute an ad hoc history, but one focused mainly on personal appreciations of painters. There is also a book on Paraguayan modernism (and another), but it is mainly a collection of biographical facts and critical descriptions. There is no developed field of art historical research. The available texts could be said, without injustice, to be either biographical appreciations or postcolonial cultural criticism that does not have the history of fine art as its primary focus.

   Around 2002 the Getty Research Institute funded a translation project, intended to produce English translations of major art historical texts from around the world.

I was at one of the preliminary meetings, and one of the issues that became apparent right at the outset was a disagreement over what might count as art history. Several of us at the meeting said that when it came to art of the past two centuries, the project should really concentrate on newspaper art criticism and on essays of the kind that appear in exhibition brochures. We wondered how many countries don't have art history as a discipline at all — Paraguay was one — and how many countries would understand art criticism to be art history. (That meeting was inconclusive, and in the end the translation project focused on major, indisputably art historical texts.)

2. *Art history, as a named discipline and a department in universities, is principally known in North America and Western Europe.*

One way to measure the presence or absence of art history in different parts of the world is to look at the number of universities that have departments of art history. There is no definitive list, and even if there were, the results would be blurred by the existence of art schools and art academies, which often have art historians on staff, although it can be impossible to determine which have degrees in art history and which are artists or critics. A country may have one or more universities that have history of art departments, and other universities that offer a few courses in art history in various departments. In Colombia, for instance, Andrés Gratán of the Pontifica Universidad Javeriana informed me that there are six other universities in Bogotá that have art history courses, and also two in Cali, two in Medellín, and one each in Santa Marta, Cartagena, and Bucaramanga. That list includes a couple of art academies, and most of the universities he named do not have art history departments; instead they have departments of Communication or Design with art historians on staff. It would be necessary to visit in order to determine how many of the instructors are trained in art history.

At the University College Cork in 2004–6 we assembled a database of nearly eight hundred institutions worldwide that have art history departments, centers, or programs. At present it is the world's largest database of universities that use "art history" or its cognates to identify academic units. Even though that criterion is subject to discussion — for example, it misses most of the institutions Gratán named because they do not have art history departments — we have some indications that the list is nearly complete. Art historians from Finland, Jordan, Singapore, Germany, and Denmark wrote us during 2004–5, giving definitive lists of institutions in their countries that offer art history, and their lists have corresponded well with ours. On that admittedly insecure ground I have drawn some tentative conclusions about how widespread art history is as a named discipline. (The full results will appear in a book on canons in art history, edited by Anna Brzyski, which is currently in press.)

The approximate number of institutions with departments of art history in Ireland and the United Kingdom is 97. The number for continental Europe, including Turkey (which has 10 universities with art history departments), is 193. German-speaking countries have 50 institutions and the United Kingdom and Ireland roughly double that, which indicates — against a claim sometimes made in central Europe — that most art history is written in English, not German. Eastern Europe and southeastern Europe have relatively few institutions with art history departments: our database has two in Slovakia (one, the

Slovak Academy of Sciences, is very active), two in Romania, and two in Bulgaria.

The number for the United States and Canada is 226, so it appears there is more art history being taught in the States than in all of Europe. (Another caveat here is that smaller colleges in North America are likely to incorporate art departments, so that what would in Europe be art colleges and academies are counted disproportionately.) For South America and Central America the number is 48, although here as in Africa and parts of Asia the numbers are low largely because of the institutions' sporadic Internet presence. The actual number might be more on the order of 80. For Africa our database has 79 institutions, a number that is raised by a recent publication by the University of Maryland, which gives addresses for sub-Saharan countries, but lowered by the very uneven web presence of African institutions. I was amazed to discover that as of spring 2006 the Ahmadu Bello University in Nigeria, the country's largest with 32,000 students, had no official web page. Our database has 17 universities with art history departments in Australia and New Zealand; 65 in China, Japan, and Korea; 36 in southeast Asia excluding Australia; and another half-dozen in central Asia, where the low numbers partly reflect the Islamic tradition, and partly, in central Asia, the influence of the Soviet system that placed art academies and art history outside of universities.

This survey is incomplete in the ways I have mentioned, and also in that it has no entries for countries that I assume may have universities with art history departments, such as Belarus, Moldova, and Andorra in Europe; or Guinea, Liberia, Togo, Burundi, the Democratic Republic of the Congo, and Somalia in Africa. But the University College Cork database is fairly accurate and reasonably exhaustive, and it suggests that as a discipline and as a unit within universities, art history is very much a North American and western European phenomenon.

3. *Art history is closely affiliated with senses of national and regional identity.*

It is a not-so-harmless truism that art historians' interests have traditionally been driven by their senses of what visual art in their own cultures seem most important. Hans Belting's wonderful little book *The Germans and Their Art: A Troublesome Relationship* chronicles, in a merciless fashion, the dependence of generations of German art historians on changing ideas of Germany. In the decades immediately after the Second World War, for example, the question of the nature of German art could hardly be raised, he says, because of the partitioning of the country. At other times, German art history was driven by notions of the essential Germanness of certain centuries, especially the late middle ages, or the supposed Germanness of artists such as Dürer or Holbein. (Oskar Bätschmann has also written some excellent pages on this subject.) Belting's book is a salutary read for anyone who assumes that art historians are driven by purely personal passions, unconnected to politics, or by a disinterested sense of historical veracity. Senses of nationalism or ethnicity have been the sometimes explicit impetus behind art historical research from its origins in Vasari and Winckelmann. The current interest in transnationality, multiculturalism, and postcolonial theory has not altered that basic impetus but only obscured it by making it appear that art historians are now free to consider themes that embrace various cultures or all cultures in general.

A few years ago, I was working on a book called *Stories of Art*, which is intended as a response to E.H. Gombrich's ubiquitous and very Eurocentric *Story of Art.* In the course of researching my book, I looked up as many introductory surveys of art history as I could find. In the second half of the twentieth century, Gombrich's book was the world's best seller, followed by Helen Gardner's and — at a distant third — by Horst Janson's. (In India and China, pirated and sometimes lightly rewritten editions may be more common than the copyrighted originals.) A number of countries have produced their own introductory art history textbooks, and I have seen examples printed in the last quarter-century in Paraguay (as I mentioned), Egypt, Romania, Iran, Japan, India, Cambodia, the Czech Republic, Australia, and Turkey. Those books tend to be deeply nationalistic in motivation, and their nationalism can strongly affect their content. Burhan Toprak's *Sanat Tarihi* (1960), a Turkish textbook, tells the history of art from Prehistory to gothic architecture and the Mérode altarpiece. Perhaps Chartres and the Mérode altarpiece seemed too Christian or too European for the author, because he veers aside and ends his survey with two chapters on Hindu art and Japan. That arrangement may seem imbalanced, but my argument in *Stories of Art* is that it is better understood as a contrast with texts like Gombrich's, which are just as nationalist or regionalist in their own different ways.

A slippery problem lies in wait here, because it may be impossible to read a book like Toprak's as a viable, independent history of art rather than as a certain *excerpt* from the history of art: in other words, it may be not so much habit that makes Gombrich more congenial, as much as the structure of art history itself, which may be based on purposes that are themselves European and North American. That treacherous problem aside, the patent nationalism of individual art histories is another cogent argument against the notion that art history is global.

4. *Art history seems to be dissolving into image studies or visual studies.*

Given the rapid increase in the proliferation of art historical research on all subjects, it can appear that art history is growing in such a way that it will soon encompass all visual practices, and lose the sense of itself as a discipline. There was an interesting exchange of essays in 2003 in the *Journal of Visual Culture*, in which nine scholars responded to something Mieke Bal had written, celebrating the dissolution of disciplinary boundaries. Some of the respondents, including me, were roundly criticized by Bal in her reply for allegedly trying to police the boundaries of art history. Bal is at one extreme of the spectrum of ideas about disciplinarity and de-disciplinarity, but her exhilaration at the destruction of disciplines could be in line with the majority opinion.

An increasing amount of work tries to mix art history with neighboring disciplines (for example, the journals *Representations, Res, Critical Inquiry, Kritische Berichte*). Also, a rapidly growing number of journals are associated with visual studies, for instance the *Journal of Visual Culture, Parallax, Invisible Culture* (that is published on the web at Rochester), *Cultural Studies, Third Text,* and even *Screen* and *diacritics.* Scholars with an interest in postcolonial studies, such as John Clark, and those whose work is informed by interests outside art history, such as Craig Clunas, can come — by very different routes — to a way of writing that works very differently from art history.

All this could be taken as a sign that art history as we might recognize it is on the verge of disappearing. Certainly there are a number of departments worldwide that are currently threatened by visual studies. It is another question whether that means the study of painting, sculpture, and architecture will be edged out, first by film studies, video, and new media, and then by the study of advertising, television, and eventually such things as graffiti and tattoos. There are universities where that is exactly what is happening, and the question is whether that is the wave of the future, or a fad that can be resisted. If visual studies becomes ubiquitous, then art history may get a bit lost, whether or not it is a coherent enterprise at the moment.

5. *My last reason to wonder about the worldwide coherence of the discipline is that there are different kinds of publications for different art historians.*

This is an especially vexed question. It's true that there are certain publications that have less to do with what gets called "theory," for example, *The Journal of the Warburg and Courtauld Institutes, Journal of Architectural Historians, Acta historiæ artium*, the *Annual Report of the American Academy in Rome, The Burlington Magazine, Antike Kunst, Artibus Asiae, Ars Orientalis*, the *Zeitschrift des Kunsthistorisches Institut in Florenz, Hesperia, Master Drawings, Oud Holland, Studies in Iconography, Antichità viva, Antologia di Belle Arti, Archivo Español de Arte*, the *Römisches Jahrbuch für Kunstgeschichte, Dumbarton Oaks Papers, History of European Ideas, Bollettino d'Arte*, and *Storia dell'arte*.

It is also true that some journals seem to be more invested in what gets called "theory": for instance *October, Representations, Critical Inquiry*, the French journal *Critique*, the *Journal of Aesthetics and Art Criticism*, the *Zeitschrift für Kunstgeschichte, Kritische Berichte, Qui parle, SubStance, Heresies, diacritics, boundary 2*, or *Glyph*.

These two lists are excerpted from my book *Our Beautiful, Dry, and Distant Texts: Art History as Writing,* in which I argue that the difference between "theory" and "practice" names a divide within the discipline, and that it can be observed in something as simple as a checklist of periodicals. Despite a lot of effort on the part of "theorists" to claim that there is no distinction between those who explicitly use theories and those who say they don't, the bibliographic division is a real one, and it reflects a disciplinary division. In the larger universities in western Europe and North America, this may seem like a pseudo-problem because there may not be any people who describe themselves as not using "theory": but in smaller universities and countries, the distinction is very real, and it affects the social interactions of the discipline as well as the choice of publications.

(I have suggested to some intransigent theory-types that if they believe there is no difference between these kinds of journals they try publishing something in, say, *The Burlington Magazine.* It's not that easy to do.)

It is also true that some theories are limited in their appeal; they become briefly popular, and then they disappear. Semiotics was revived at least four different times in the past century: once by the Prague linguistic school, again by Meyer Schapiro, by Hubert Damisch in the 1970s, and then by a number of scholars in the 1990s, including Mieke Bal. Anthropological theories of liminality, derived from Victor Turner, were very popular in the mid-1980s. I remember Norman Bryson chaired a session in one of the College Art Association meetings called "What Use Is Deconstruction Anyway?" and a similar session was chaired by T.J. Clark on the question of De Man's relevance for art history.

I would not deny that the discipline is fragmented by infatuations with more or less evanescent theories. But there is also a counter-argument, and so now I'll turn to the second part of my Introduction: five arguments in favor of the idea that art history is, or could become, a single coherent enterprise throughout the world.

II

1. *It can be argued, against the previous claim, that some of the best scholarship in the field is done by writers who know a lot about theories, and conversely that scholars who are not conversant with theories run the risk of producing texts that are out of touch.*

   This is a delicate subject, so I'll give just a few examples. Clark's *Farewell to an Idea* is, I think, one of the best books on modern art that has been produced in the last few decades. It seems to engage theories in an elliptic and idiosyncratic way, but it is actually built around deeply considered responses to Hegel, poststructuralism in general (and semiotics in particular), and especially Paul De Man. Although it may not appear so, Michael Fried is another example: his books include encounters with phenomenology, psychoanalysis, and a range of philosophers from Kierkegaard and Wittgenstein to Robert Vischer. In medieval art history there is Michael Camille; any assessments of his relation to Meyer Schapiro, for example, would have to take on board Camille's understanding of poststructuralism and especially Derrida.

   If I were to go on in this vein, the claim would be that art history is potentially unified because the writers in fullest command of relevant theories are also those who are in fullest command of the possibilities of the discipline. There might be a parallel here to a discipline like physics, although I don't want to make too much of it: in physics, a researcher who does not know the most recent theories can presumably go on working, but her results will fail to attract the attention of physicists who were working on the current issues in the field. Emphasizing theories — even evanescent ones — as evidence that art history is potentially a coherent field around the world is also a way of saying that it is the methods of art history, and not its subject matter, that effectively unify the field.

2. *The distinction between art history and art criticism still holds.*

Depending on your point of view regarding what David Carrier calls "artwriting," you might want to argue that art history and criticism are blurred or that their boundaries cannot be drawn with any useful degree of precision. I would argue that it is both easy and useful to distinguish the two, and that they can be separated using institutional, contextual, and commercial criteria.

Institutionally, art criticism is wholly excluded from universities. There are classes on the *history* of art criticism — on Baudelaire for example, or on the reception of the New York School — but nothing on how to write art criticism. That subject is occasionally taught in art schools, but its rigorous exclusion from universities is a sign that it differs clearly from art history. Contextually and commercially, art history is produced for different venues. Criticism can be found, of course, in magazines and newspapers, but art history is seldom found there. (The two do mix, at a grossly adulterated level, on television.)

There is much more to be said about this; volume 4 in this series, *The State of Art Criticism,* investigates it at length. In this context I'll just note that the same separation I assumed in the first point, at the beginning of this Introduction, can also be used to urge that art history *is* unified because wherever it exists it can be distinguished from art criticism.

3. Art history remains focused on a specific canon of artists.

I wonder if an informal poll of art historians might not show that most of us think that there is effectively no longer a canon in art history, if only because the discipline is expanding so quickly and so unpredictably. "Canon" is an odd-sounding word in art history because we have avoided the major debates about the canon (what were called the "canon wars") that sprang up in departments of literature and languages in the United States and Canada in the 1980s. The issue then was how to make room for women writers and writers from outside the West by displacing canonical figures like Plato or Sophocles. Art history avoided the canon wars by relying on the very large survey textbooks, which were simply enlarged to include artists of color, women artists, outsider artists, and postcolonial artists, without ever really displacing any artists that had composed the "canon."

It is helpful in this regard to distinguish between *intensive* and *extensive* scholarship. If the growth of the discipline were characterized by extensive scholarship, art historians would be studying new artists, new media, and new kinds of visual practices at an increasing rate. If the discipline's growth were due more to intensive scholarship, the field would be getting larger because there are increasing numbers of studies of the major artists — that is, the canon. In 1999 I got a special printout of two decades of entries of the *Bibliography of the History of Art,* one of the two largest databases in the discipline, from Michael Rinehart, who was then its editor. The printout arranges the scholarly output of the discipline according to the artists who were being written about. I collated the list and found that art history is still quite intensive: there is a canon of artists who are still studied disproportionately more than the many artists who have only been studied recently.

Here is the top-ten list for art history. The most frequently cited artists are as follows:

1.	Picasso	757
2.	Dürer	616
3.	Rubens	600
4.	Michelangelo	537
5.	Leonardo	526
6.	Raphael	460
7.	Rembrandt	442
8.	Titian	418
9.	Goya	391
10.	Palladio	377

In terms of media, note that this top-ten list includes only painting, sculpture, and architecture. As the list continues, it is clear that painting is really the canonical medium: it goes on past Van Gogh, Turner, and Cézanne to Tiepolo, Constable, and Lotto … almost all the artists in the top one hundred are "dead white males"; all are European and North American; and virtually all are painters.

Looking at things the other way around, it is possible to count the number of artists who are cited only once, those who are cited just twice, and so forth, so for example:

Cited once	c. 10,000
Cited twice	c. 5,000
Cited three times	c. 1,400
Cited four times	1,105
Cited five times	715

In this count it becomes apparent that the discipline is also growing extensively, with nearly 20,000 different artists cited four or fewer times.

In statistical terms, there is a broad middle region between these seldom-cited artists and the "outliers" like Picasso: that is the canon of art history, and it corresponds well with the contents of the large introductory art history textbooks. The full results will appear in the essay I mentioned in Brzyski's volume; all I mean to suggest here is that art history's exponential growth has been as much intensive as extensive, and it is still effectively unified by a canon of representative interests.

4. Art history is guided by a stable series of narratives.

The same claim can be made about art history's narratives, such as the story of the rise of illusionism told in Gombrich's *Art and Illusion*, and the familiar sequences of formal elements that lead from Greece and Rome through medieval uses to Renaissance "survivals" and postmodern "appropriations." Such narratives have been questioned by feminist art historians and augmented by postcolonial theory, queer theory, and disciplines such as literary theory, but they still give sense and structure to introductory texts.

It has been argued that specialized monographs in art history owe little to these large-scale narratives, but I am not so sure. The reason for studying a particular artwork or an individual artist must have to do with that artist's importance in the larger scheme of things. As art historians, I think we are still dependent on a relatively small number of plots. Books with titles like *Modern Cambodian Art* or *Modern Art in Tibet* will sometimes begin with promises not to be beholden to Western historiography or examples, but in my experience the authors soon find themselves deeply indebted not only to the inevitable Western comparisons (so-and-so Philippine painter is influenced by Bernard Buffet, and so forth) but also to the Western storylines of naturalism or antinaturalism, or even the Wölfflinian stories about successions of "classical" and "baroque" periods.

The grip of our accustomed narratives is best demonstrated by the few books that try to break the mold.

Stan Abe's *Ordinary Images,* a book about provincial Taoist bas-reliefs in China, includes anomalous examples on purpose, perhaps in order to upset the reader's expectations that the material will fit into neat style categories or period sequences. The result, for me, is sometimes a sense of a new kind of historical account, but more often a feeling of incompletion, as if the narrative has not quite ended where it should. Another example would be Georges Didi-Huberman's work on Aby Warburg, *l'Image survivante*: it creates an alternate narrative for art history — one that is founded on Warburg's *Pathosformel* and Didi-Huberman's Lacanian interpretation of it — but I wonder if his approach will seem like a fruitful alternative for many historians. The grip of the familiar narratives is still very strong.

5. *Art history depends on Western conceptual schemata.*

Perhaps the most surprising fact about worldwide practices of art history is that there may be no conceptually independent national or regional traditions of art historical writing. Chinese art history, for example, demands expertise in very different kinds of source materials and formal concepts, but its interpretive strategies remain very Western. Chinese art historians, both in China and in universities in the West, study Chinese art using the same repertoire of theoretical texts and sources — psychoanalysis, semiotics, iconography, structuralism, anthropology, identity theory. They frame and support their arguments in the same ways Western art historians do: with abstracts, archival evidence, summaries of previous scholarship, and footnoted arguments.

I think it can be argued that there is no non-Western tradition of art history, if by that is meant a tradition with its own interpretive strategies and forms of argument.

Art historians in different countries vary in what they study, and there is a wide latitude in the kinds of interpretive methods that are employed. (Most scholarship, I think, still takes iconography as its principal or default model.) But there is no such thing as an independent narrative or scholarly approach to the writing of the history of art that can be understood *as* a history of art. There are ways of writing about art's history that developed in India from the seventh century, and in China from the Han Dynasty; but those texts are not recognizable *as* art history, and a simple proof of their distance from current practice is that no art historian who chose to emulate those texts could get a permanent position in a university. None of the Chinese specialists I know who teach in Western universities were hired because of their ability to deploy indigenous historiographic methods; but part of their qualifications would normally be the ability to negotiate the principal Western methods such as formal analysis and iconography.

This can also be put in more general terms. In 2000 I discovered that the basics of Western art history, such as formal analysis, periodization, and iconography, along with Chinese translations of Wölfflin, Panofsky, and Gombrich, were being taught in art academies in Beijing, Hangzhou, and Nanjing, where they were applied to both Chinese and non-Chinese art. Is that a sensible development? Shouldn't indigenous Chinese terms and methods be used to explicate Chinese art? Those questions, so apparently straightforward and self-evident, lead into thickets of problems — as the discussions in this book will show.

Some of the most ambitious books in art history in recent years attack this question of the Westernness of art history from widely differing perspectives. There is Hans Belting's *Bild-Anthropologie,* which expands art history in the direction of a Continental sense of anthropology; John Clark's *Modern Asian Art,* which looks at east Asian art using institutional critique to evade some traditional Western categories; and most ambitious of all, David Summers's *Real Spaces,* which was one of the occasions for the roundtable in this book. All these books raise fundamental questions concerning the alternatives to art history as we know it, but by doing so, and still remaining clearly Western, they also demonstrate an underlying unity in art history.

Any one of these five reasons could be used to urge that art history is, or could become, a truly global enterprise. For better or worse, art history would then be thought of as a field whose subject matter changes with its location but whose assumptions, purposes, critical concepts, and narrative forms remain fairly consistent around the world.

III

My own feeling is that, by and large, these last five arguments are more compelling than the first five, and art history *is* becoming a global enterprise. One of the most interesting things about that possibility, I think, is that it creates an *obligation.* I'll close with a few words about that, even though it is not a theme that is developed in this book, and — as far as I can guess — may not be widely held by historians outside contributors to this book. To the extent that art history can be spoken of as a single problematic, it follows that what happens in art history in Austria, say, or in Russia, can have consequences for art history in, say, Ecuador or Singapore. That doesn't mean the *subject matter* of a monograph written in one country will be of immediate interest elsewhere, but that the *methods,* the *form* of the text, and the *questions* it raises may well be important for scholars in very different places. I don't think the subjects of art history need to be shared: an Irish art historian specializing in medieval church architecture may not need to know about medieval Slovenian altars. But I do think that it is important to share the methods of art history: ideally an Irish or a Slovenian art historian will need to know Cao Yiqiang's account of renascences, or Shigemi Inaga's interpretations of orientalisms. This would not be true if the common ground in art history is standard-issue iconography, or style analysis, because then I would not feel obligated to check to see *how* artworks are being interpreted in other places. But it will be true if the connections between local practices of art history reach deeper into the discipline. If world art studies deserves the name, then an art historian working in Estonia, for example, should not be able to afford to ignore what is being written by art historians in Argentina, Peru, or China: not because the Estonian art historian needs to know about Argentine modernism, Peruvian Moche pottery, or Chinese tomb reliefs, but because the Estonian art historian may need to know about the new interpretive methods and senses of history that are being tried on those very different kinds of objects.

At the same time I don't mean that it would be bad if art history divided into local practices: in fact it should be a matter of concern if art history does *not* divide into local practices. Primadi Tabrani's *Bahasa Rupa* is a book written in 2005 in Indonesian; it uses Marshall McLuhan and a mixture of Western sources to talk about twentieth-century southeast Asian painting and the southeast Asian qualities of Borobudur. As far as I can tell, that book wouldn't seem like art history if it were translated. (I suspect it would read like very idiosyncratic art criticism.) But I think it would matter if *Bahasa Rupa* came out sounding like a natural extension of western European art history (because that would be strange), and it would also matter if it sounded like nothing that could count as a plausible art history (because that would raise the question of what way of talking about those same objects and authors *could* sound like plausible art history).

A worldwide set of practices identifiable as art history poses a fascinating challenge. No one can read everything, but a worldwide endeavor, especially one whose coherence is contested and problematic, requires worldwide reading. For me, that obligation is one of the principal reasons this subject is so interesting: no matter how art history develops (or dissolves), and even aside from the pressing political problems of the spread of Western practice, I think art history increasingly imposes an obligation to read widely and continuously, outside of any specialization.

That is just by way of introduction. It is a very different matter to ask what, exactly, constitutes art history's common language, and what historical, political, linguistic, and economic consequences that commonality might have: those are questions for the rest of this book.

2
Starting Points

Notes on Art History in Latin America

Andrea Giunta

"Is art history global?" The question implies much more than a simple affirmative or negative answer. It alludes to an intention to transcend an entire group of problems — which, it is worthwhile to point out, have never been among art history's central debates — with the aim of arriving at a kind of *entente*, from which we can move forward toward the future. There are objectives underlying this question that are not explicitly articulated; however, given that I will be answering in the affirmative, a second question immediately arises: "What does art history do for us?"

I

To begin, I will recall some of James Elkins's arguments, in some cases to develop different alternatives, and in others to furnish material that will confirm his affirmations. I will refer to examples taken from the field of art history in Latin America, with the understanding that I am participating in the Art Seminar as a quasi-representative of that region.

Elkins says that "there is no developed field of art historical research … in countries like Paraguay. Art criticism serves as art history." One of his examples is Ticio Escobar, who writes cultural criticism and art theory, "somewhat along the lines of Homi Bhabha or Nestor García Canclini." It is true that Escobar has focused his work around cultural critique, although he has written art history.[1] But here another figure that is central to cultural critique in Latin America, Nelly Richard, should be added to the scholars Elkins names. Through critical essays (which she unhesitatingly calls cultural criticism), Richard quite intentionally intervenes in what appears to be an agreement concerning the international distribution of knowledge about Latin America. She states that there seems to be an agreement holding that academia in North America produces theory at the same rate that Latin America produces works, books, and descriptions about its own production. In a polemical meeting of the Latin American Studies Association held in Guadalajara in April 1997, following the launch of the Latin American branch of Subaltern Studies, Richard openly proposed that Latin America can produce theory.[2] This position is also, in my view, the place where Escobar's production is inscribed, between art history and cultural critique.

I would now like to consider some descriptive aspects regarding art history in Latin America. With regard to art history departments in Latin America — another of Elkins's points — their number is without a doubt considerably much smaller than in the United States or in Europe. Careers in art history exist in very few places in Latin America. In the UNAM in Mexico City art history forms part of general postgraduate studies, but it does not yet exist as an undergraduate degree, and the same thing happens throughout almost all of Latin America. In Argentina, art history was established in the University of Buenos Aires in 1962. In other universities such as Rosario or La Plata it is part of the system of artistic formation.[3]

I would also like to point out that the Latin American academic system is inscribed within the European tradition rather than the North American system. In other words, while a North

American student can hold a major in art history with approximately twelve credits of his or her BA coming from within the art history department, a student at the University of Buenos Aires takes all his or her credits exclusively from the art history department. This provides students with a more encyclopedic background, and they emerge equipped with a historic archive that a student with a BA in art history from a North American university lacks. In this sense, it can be held that history of art in Latin America is a local inscription of Western art history's methodology as well as its established narrative.

Regarding another of the aspects pointed out by Elkins, it's true that in Latin America academic journals are as scarce in the field of theory as they are in the field of more traditional art history. In this sense, I believe that the best indication of scholarly production in the visual arts is conferences, whose proceedings are usually published immediately after they are held.[4] The instability of the academic field, and the lack of sustained sources for funding publications, leads to the custom of using conference fees for the production of publications. You could say that the most regular publications, which bring historical and theoretical perspectives together in a single volume, are congress proceedings.

II

I now turn to the arguments in favor of a global history of art, or, to put it more precisely, in favor of a history of art that, based on certain overall contributions to the discipline, allows aspects of our culture to be recognized that are not revealed by other disciplines.

Here it is appropriate to introduce some personal background. I studied at the University of Buenos Aires between 1978 and 1983, during the military dictatorship. Personal safety was threatened during that period, and so was thought. In other words, the very possibility of thinking (and with this I refer to critical thought) and of creating knowledge was jeopardized. In Argentina at that time, "research" was a word practically devoid of meaning in art history. Only a few professors carried out research or published books. Such productions were scarce, and no book disagreed with any other: there were no conflicting theories.

In 1983, when I completed my last course at the university, democracy had been regained. Debates began to take place at the university, and there were changes in the curricula; little by little, a fragile system for financing research appeared. It was a grant scheme that for the first time made a monthly salary possible for those engaged in research. A group of students from my generation entered into what would later be known as the grant system. Above and beyond all the negative consequences that institutionalization can engender, this had an immediate effect on a generation that abounded in projects, and that saw before itself the possibility to do research, to think, to debate, and to write.

Those who dedicated their efforts to the colonial era were able to find references within the local environment, but that was not the case for those who took on issues from an era that had been, up until that point, excluded from programs of study. Before the study plan reforms were approved in 1986, in the art history degree at the Philosophy and Letters Faculty at the University of Buenos Aires, the history of pre-Hispanic and Precolumbian art was not taught, and neither was nineteenth- and twentieth-century Latin American art, nor twentieth-century Argentinean art, nor contemporary art from the postwar period. Naturally, courses like Sociology of Art or Communications Media and Theory didn't exist either. The subject matter of these courses had been considered subversive under the repressive dictatorial system. It is true that art history took on a vindictive, nationalistic character at that moment. To write the history of art — either constructing something that had been nonexistent, or reevaluating texts that we questioned — was a way of recovering our own memory and past. In my case, that it exactly what happened: the first research project I undertook as a grantee was on a period that I had lived through — the traumatic years of the dictatorship.

However, the immediate political context was not the only reason that research as a whole was oriented toward Argentinean art. There were also material conditions: the grants weren't large, traveling or residing abroad was unthinkable, and in many cases there was also a language barrier. Very few people spoke English, and then there were those of us who could read English with some difficulty. "Practicality" was a consideration in the evaluation of possible grants. It was unthinkable that one of the grants be given to a candidate who proposed to study Etruscan, Renaissance, or North American art — first, because none of these subjects could be studied using the resources in Buenos Aires, and second, because the grants were insufficient to cover travel costs. For beginning researchers, coming from a university that was not much more than a "university of shadows" and from a discipline that was marginalized and practically without a tradition in academia, it was impossible to imagine that we might ever apply for international grants or participate in international congresses.

From this it can be deduced that we were concerned with more than the topics themselves. Our interests in art history were not just about completing a narrative or incorporating areas that had been excluded from previous narratives. It went beyond that. There was also an intense dispute about the legitimacy of art history within the field of social science. Art history was a discipline whose tradition was not recognized as such by scholars in history, literature, or philosophy. Art history was considered entertainment for rich girls or well-traveled women who, once their children married, returned to the university to complete the accumulation of symbolic capital that they had suspended in order to have children. As a result, options did not exist, as they did in other disciplines with greater prestige and longer history, to travel, attend other universities, or enroll in postgraduate studies in other countries.

We had to find books that we could take as models for what we wanted to do. Books that, we would later realize, had also been conceived in a specific generational context. They were books by T.J. Clark, Thomas Crow, and Serge Guilbaut, and later we discovered books by Tom Cummins and others. There were some translations of such books, and later we also began to read in English. One of the books that had been prohibited during the dictatorship, but circulated clandestinely, was Nicos Hadjinicolaou's *Historia del arte y lucha de clases* (*Histoire de l'art at lutte des clases*, 1973) published in Spanish by a historic Mexican publishing house called Siglo XXI. Other books by Hadjinicolaou followed, such as his *L'ouvre d'art face à ses significations* (also in a Spanish edition by Siglo XXI in 1981). Years later, when we were integrated into a more international academic world, we would find out that all these people were linked in some way, that some had been professors of others, or had written under the direction of others, and that in different ways, they had some relation to UCLA during the sixties.

We found many of the things we were looking for in these books: a meticulous reading of texts and of works; a good archival labor; the reevaluation of hypotheses; and especially the idea of a study focused on one specific work of art, with just a few paintings whose interpretation exploded upon the page. Works were regarded not only in terms of style or biography, but also in terms of political history, and of their institutional and social background. It was a kind of art history that didn't sacrifice the discipline's precise instruments, such as the reading of the painting's surface, brushstrokes, technique, or iconography. Paintings were pored over for 400 pages, and their previous reception history submitted to a critical gaze and rewritten; the texts were passionate and illuminating, much more so than the traditional taxonomic classification into schools, styles, periods of work, and catalogues raisonné that we had memorized in the form of more or less senseless names and dates. In these new books, art history itself was being rewritten — and that was precisely what we wanted to do.

These books, which we read, underlined, and lent one another endlessly, were adopted and disputed as a point of departure for our own works. They formed our generation: they were our long-distance professors. After having penetrated their pages looking for every one of their clues, we formulated our critiques, and we evaluated what the books did and didn't do. And in this way we went along delineating the manner in which to produce an art history that would be nourished by all possible means, so that it might be not only a practice or a profession, but a field of work from which it would be possible to engage in debate with other fields of social science — a field capable of taking on problems that could not be handled in disciplines.

These readings had other important effects. The archival work involved had a great impact on us. We saw it entailed not only journalistic research, but work in personal and institutional archives, involving letters, records, contracts, and so forth. At the time, there were no archives linked to our discipline in Buenos Aires. It isn't that the repositories didn't exist; it was that no one had thought of them as sources of information for art history. Many personal and institutional archives were conceived of as archives, recovered, classified, conserved, and opened to the public as a result of research that developed from the second half of the 1980s onward.[5] Museum archives were also seen as spaces for research; they had rarely been consulted prior to that moment. During the 1990s the process of conservation and institutionalization of archives in Buenos Aires and other parts of Latin America continued, and today a monumental archiving project is being carried out in the Museum of Fine Arts in Houston (under the direction of Mari Carmen Ramirez) that could be considered the culmination of this process of archival growth: it is, in a sense, the evidence of our growing consciousness of the value of such resources in Latin America, and so it is ultimately a product of Latin American interests.

You could say that Argentine art history had to be national in order to be international. That is so because we eventually became integrated in university environments and in congresses on account of our research on Argentine art. One fundamental turning point was the 1992 art history congress in Zacatecas. It was made possible thanks to Rita Eder's incredible talent for uniting disparate projects. Eder, at the time director of the Aesthetics Research Institute at the UNAM, organized the congress of the Art History Association with support from the J.P. Getty Foundation. The congress was notable for its central goal of bringing established figures from the field of art history together along with nonexperts and unknowns — like me — whose abstracts had been reviewed and accepted and who received economic support that permitted us to attend the congress. We had all been brought together basically to discuss Latin America. There, an entire generation of beginners found themselves face to face with the authors of the books they had read. A detailed account of that encounter, and what it meant for art history in Latin America, needs to be written. Friendships and working networks were forged that still remain active today. There we met Hadjinicolaou, García Canclini (who was exiled in Mexico), Aracy Amaral, Nelly Richard, Ida Rodríguez Prampolini, Jorge Alberto Manirque, Fausto Ramirez, Juan Acha, and Gerardo Mosquera; for us, they were all practically mythical figures. We also met colleagues from other Latin American countries, closer to our own generation: Natalia Majluf, Renato González Mello, Jaime Cuadriello, Cuauhtemoc Medina, Justo Pastor Mellado, Gabriel Peluffo Linari, Gustavo Buntinx, Clara Bargellini, Graciela Schmilchuk, Alexandra Kennedy Troya. There were also many people whom we couldn't speak with at the time because they didn't speak Spanish and we didn't speak English, like David Brian Howard or Serge Guilbaut, and others we hadn't yet heard of, like Olivier Debroise, James Oles, and Francisco Reyes Palma. It was a kind of coming out for our generation: we were present as a group at an international congress, and to our surprise, we received recognition as the discipline's up-and-coming generation. Expectations for renovation were in the air; there was a need to hear new voices, separated from those that had come before by a generation that had been decimated. After that conference, practically our entire generation began to carry out research abroad, even while we continued working with Argentine art. We were interested in archives outside Argentina because it was clear that part of the art history we were determined to write was to be found in the archives of the North Americans, Europeans, and Latin Americans. The archives at the MoMA, the OEA, the AAA, the Rockefeller Foundation, the Getty Foundation, the Saõ Paulo Biennial, and the Picasso Museum in Paris (just to cite some of the places I visited while researching my PhD dissertation) all held documents that we needed. Those archives were not of interest because they could serve some style history; they gave us evidence of material relationships, institutional circuits, trips, and networks: Nelson Rockefeller was involved in the founding of Saõ Paulo's Museum of Modern Art; Clement Greenberg and Alfred Barr had visited Argentina; the *Guernica* had been exhibited at the second Saõ Paulo biennial; and many Spanish republicans had come to Argentina in exile. (In 1963 there were more than thirty Argentinean artists living in Paris, and in 1966 many of them moved to New York.)

Other international connections involved South America. During Pinochet's dictatorship the CAYC (Centro de Arte y Comunicación, Center of Art and Comunication) in Buenos Aires had become a center for the Chilean avant-garde; meanwhile, artists in the Argentinean group *Nueva Figuración* (New Figuration) had exhibited in Río de Janeiro, and had an effect there. Many Argentineans had studied with Torres García or with Gurvich, and the Argentinean artist León Ferrari spent the years between 1976 and 1991 in exile in Saõ Paulo. We could not work on the history of Argentine art without understanding these regional and international maps, with their maze of correspondence, trips, friendships, magazines, and institutions. At that moment, the history of Argentinean art ceased to be merely a national history.

III

So art history, and not art criticism, is what is taught in universities, even if it is hardly equivalent in quantity to the production of the academic system in the United States or Europe. It is worth noting here that art history was viewed disparagingly in critical circles. Traditional critics and the institutional world assumed an entrenched position against art historians. In part that was because historians were considered to be boring academics; but it was also because our research uncovered hidden connections and networks of power.

In the past fifteen years, art history in Argentina has begun to question its canon, and to investigate how it was imported, transmitted, adopted, and assimilated. In the current state of affairs, art history is bent on investigating problems, without any vindictive, hagiographic, or recuperative intention, but rather to focus on issues we consider important. Today it is difficult for a student to justify her choice of a thesis simply by saying it is a subject that has not yet been studied; what's relevant is the issue that the student proposes to investigate, the question that he wants to answer. Art history is nourished by contributions from feminism, postcolonialism, literary theory, and all the instruments that enable us to diagram issues that lie beyond the discipline. At the same time local art history nourishes itself, unhindered by the new developments. In a sense local art history never felt the discipline's trauma.

Contemporary Argentine art history bases itself upon a Western conceptual scheme. That is trivially so because art history is a discipline established in the West, but more deeply the case because Latin America is an active part of the establishment of the idea of the West. The main question would be what purpose art history serves now that it has emerged from the process of reestablishment;

that is, what is it about the cultural processes in Latin America that it will allow us to reveal what other disciplines cannot.

That is a general picture of the current state of art history in Latin America; I will conclude with several more specific points.

First, there is the lack of interest in a generalized or global history of Latin American art. In my courses on Latin American Art from the nineteenth and twentieth century I do not use global art histories as textbooks. (Instead, I prepare reading lists.)

Second, research tends to concentrate on particular issues. Case studies are based as much on intensive archival work as they are on interpretative analysis, and they focus on such issues as the function of history and landscape painting in the constitution of nation-states (for example the work of Laura Malosetti Costa, Roberto Amigo, Natalia Majluf, Gabriel Peluffo Linari); the development of projects for modernity including the representation of the city and the nude figure (for instance Diana Wechsler, Laura Malosetti Costa); the study of images and ideas of artists' travels as they are shown in exhibitions and magazines (in my own work); the function and power of images in relation to the public, the church, and the state (Gabriela Siracusano, Jaime Quadriello, Marta Penhos); the development of zones of contact; and the emergence of different regional maps.[6]

It would generally be agreed that images have the power to inaugurate and configure. The history of art is well able to address those problems, given that it has both indigenous instruments of interpretation, and also others that have arisen in the friction between disciplines. In this sense, I would venture to affirm that it is not important for art historians in Latin America to ask themselves whether or not the history of art is global in terms of its methods. The problem lies in utilizing the history of art, with all of its methods and all of those borrowed from other disciplines, to reveal the multiple meanings that can be found crystallized, trapped beneath the dense surfaces of the objects.

Notes

1. Specifically a history of Paraguayan art in two volumes, the first dedicated to indigenous and colonial art and the second to the twentieth century. The first volume seeks to establish the parameters of indigenous visual culture, and with this approach he continuously turns to terminology from the fields of aesthetics, anthropology, history, and art history: abstraction, meanings, mythic content, functions, conquest, colonization, colonies, baroque, and so on. While Escobar avoids organizing the second volume according to European artistic movements (that is, he challenges these categorizations, his discussion also assumes an internalization of the story of modern art. Movements such as Action painting, Pop, *art informel,* and others are continuously in question; he evaluates and sometimes minimizes or critiques their impact. Viewed in relation to art history or criticism, this project of Escobar's appears small in comparison with his principal undertaking, the Museo del Barro, in which he achieves an exemplary coalescence of all the aspirations that someone who writes about art can have with regard to art's social function.
2. See Castro-Gómez y Eduardo Mendieta (Coordinadores), *Teorías sin disciplina. Latinoamericanismo, poscolonialidad y globalización en debate* (México, D.F. and San Francisco: University of San Francisco and Miguel Angel Porrúa, 1998).
3. Two institutes in particular are important in art history: the Investigaciones Estéticas department at the UNAM in Mexico City, and the Instituto Payró in Buenos Aires. Since the late 1980s, the activities of the Centro Argentino de Investigadores de Artes have also been linked to research at the Instituto Payró.
4. The proceedings published by the IIE, the Instituto Payró, the CAIA, and the colloquia on art history held in Brazil together constitute an up-to-date bibliography from which it is possible to assess the current status of scholarship. These meetings brought together a wealth of 30–40 local researchers, with some from other countries on the continent.
5. In this connection I would cite the critic Jorge Romero Brest's archive of material from art biennials from the Americas at the I.T.D.T. In 1993 a foundation, Espigas, began a documentation project for Argentine art that today constitutes an essential repository.
6. For example, Laura Malosetti Costa, *Los primeros modernos: Arte y sociedad en Buenos Aires a comienzos del siglo XIX* (Buenos Aires: Fondo de Cultura Económica, 2001); Roberto Amigo, *Tras un inca: Los funerales de Atahualpa de Luis Montero en Buenos Aires* (Fundación Telefónica-Fundación Espigas, 2001); Natalia Majluf, *Aguinaldo para las señoras del Perú y otros ensayos* (Lima: Institut français d'études andines and IFEA, Museo de Arte de Lima, 2003); Diana Wechsler, *Papeles en conflicto: Arte y crítica entre la vanguardia y la tradición, Buenos Aires (1920–1930),* Serie Monográfica no. 8, Instituto de Teoría e Historia del Arte "Julio E. Payró" (Buenos Aires: FFyL-UBA); Jaime Quadriello, *Las glorias de la República de Tlaxcala o la conciencia como imagen sublime* (Mexico City: UNAM, 2004); Gabriela

Siracusano, *El poder de los colores: De lo material a lo simbólico en las prácticas culturales andinas, Siglos XVI-XVIII* (Buenos Aires: Fondo de Cultura Económica, 2005); and Marta Penhos, *Ver, conocer, dominar: Imágenes de sudamérica a fines del siglo XVIII* (Buenos Aires: Siglo XXI, 2005).

On David Summers's *Real Spaces*

James Elkins

Far and away the most pressing problem facing the discipline is the prospect of world art history. [1] And yet the first thing that needs to be said about that troublesome expression is that there is no consensus about its meaning or even its value. The common alternates and near-synonyms for world art history are also problematic: multiculturalism carries with it the air of a compromised relativism;[2] visual culture is currently an unstable field, subject to intensive debates;[3] and global art has the unfortunate connotation of conceptual imperialism, as if art history is already adequate to all possible occasions.[4] It remains unclear how a world art history might be related to its neighboring disciplines. It has been proposed that art historians take anthropological theories as models; but it has also been urged that art history define itself by its difference from anthropology.[5] It has been said that art history should remain distinct from visual studies, but it has also been predicted that the two fields will end up entwined.[6] It has been suggested that literary theory is the best resource for the expanding discipline, but it has also been claimed that literary theory is a wrong direction for art history.[7]

Despite this conceptual disarray it remains absolutely essential for art history to ask about its limits and its future, and those questions inevitably lead to the problem of world art history. It is a cardinal virtue of *Real Spaces* that Summers dares, as few art historians have, to tackle the problem of world art history in a single book. In 2000 John Onians organized a conference at the Clark Art Institute on the theme of art historical writing that keeps to the local and particular, as opposed to writing that tries, in Onians's phrase, "to put the world in a book."[8] The conference began with speakers whose work "expanded" local subjects into specialized monographs, and progressed to the most "compressed" attempts to address the problem of world art in its totality. I was on the final panel, along with Onians, Summers, and David Freedberg; we were said to have tried "to put the world in a book." Each of us, except for Summers, denied the charge.[9] The panel would have been more representative and problematic if it had included Marilyn Stokstad and other authors of one-volume freshman world art survey texts, because then it would have been apparent that Summers's book is unique: it is the only recent attempt to write about the entirety of world art history without relying on chronology as a central ordering principle, and as such — aside from all the issues I will raise in this review — it is crucially important for the current state of the discipline.

Real Spaces is Summers's magnum opus, the intermittent and concerted project of about twenty years' work. It has been circulating in manuscript for some time; I had seen an earlier version that stood a good foot and a half high on my desk. The book is compact by comparison and its argument is cogent and polished. Even so, *Real Spaces* has a complex structure, so it is best to begin with a tour of its contents. Afterward I will turn to larger questions of the book's relation to existing writing on world art, and to the general project of a world art history.

Summers divides *Real Spaces* into seven chapters, six of which introduce concepts that can be made applicable, according to the argument, to art produced anywhere in the world. The first chapter is "Facture," understood as an indication that an object has been made. *Real Spaces* proceeds throughout at a high level of abstraction: at times it is nearly a conceptual lexicon for art, and it never strays far from etymological analyses of the Greek and Latin roots of common terms. "Facture" itself, Summers writes, "is the past participle of the Latin *facio, facere,* to make or to do; it thus has the same derivation as 'fact,' which might be defined as something evidently done. Understood in this way, 'fact' and 'facture' are closely related; *to consider an artifact in terms of its facture is to consider it as a record of its own having been made*" (74). Throughout the book Summers points out when words used in apparently unrelated contexts are etymologically linked to facture; Monet's painting *Impression: Sunrise,* for example, "has the *effect* (another facture word) of instantaneity" (623). In that way facture, like Summers's other critical terms, becomes a versatile critical tool.

In the chapter on facture, Summers considers concepts of form, seriality, diachronicity, "distinction" (defined as "effort superfluous to function," 88), refinement, ornament, play (it "explores the absolutely possible," 102), difficulty and facility, "notional" limitations ("abstract and generalized dimensional relations," 107), and models (objects that resemble others "by virtue of relation alone," 114). Some of these concepts, including facture itself, are given wholly new definitions; others, including ornament, are adjusted in relation to the existing literature; and still others, such as diachronicity, are taken over without important changes. As he proceeds, Summers builds interdependence among the concepts. The development is rigorous and not well suited to the abbreviations of a review. Speaking of notionality, for example, he remarks that "*[a]s pure, thinkable relation, the notional is to the actual size of one artifact or another as ratio and proportion are to measure*"; later in the chapter he proposes that "[m]ovement is from real spatial to notional … , abstraction from size to ratio *as* notional, possible elaboration at the level of the notional, and back to social space" (108, 115).

The other six thematic chapters are just as involved. It may be helpful to potential readers if I simply list the chapters and their leading concepts, before returning to the discussion of world art history and the consequences of this approach to art.

Chapter 2, "Places," turns on the proposal that "places, as real social spaces, provide the possibility for the actual statement of relations of difference" (123). The chapter discusses the concepts of difference (emphasizing its spatial meanings), sex (understood not as biological difference but as setting apart, the "basis on which social spaces are divided within a group," 127), centers and diasporas, shrines ("from the Latin *scrivium,* a cupboard or box for books or papers," therefore stressing "housing, preserving, or keeping," 139), precincts, boundaries, paths, alignments and orientations, and the idea of a periphery and division of land outside the *sanctum.*

Chapter 3, "The Appropriation of the Centre," takes Egyptian, Akkadian, Roman, Khmer, Chinese, and French examples to articulate the change from cultures in which rulers appropriated the center, to those that tend toward "inclusive and non-hierarchical" arrangements based on a notional framework of metric space. Of the book's chapters, this is the one that most resembles a history, in that it depends on a series of case studies.

Chapter 4, "Images," opens with a realignment of discussions on the origins of images, proposing that "images are fashioned in order to make present in social spaces what for some reason is not present" (252). They are therefore substitutive, and it is important to study their "conditions of presentation" and "the relations of those conditions to our own spatiotemporality" (253). There are meditations on traces (marks "continuous with their cause," 255), "images of traces" (256), and abstraction (which is taken in an Aristotelian, not a Platonic sense). Summers then discusses "real metaphor," a central concept for the book as a whole; it is a way of pointing to the actual spatial origins of metaphor, and the role of art in enacting the primary significance of linguistic metaphor. Shape, contour, resemblance, and others terms are brought to bear to explain how the metaphoric relation is recognized as such. Monumental, sometimes aniconic images are contrasted with images small enough to be manipulated. An especially important category of manipulable images are votive objects, whose "fundamental values ... are proximity" (280). He then turns to icons (where a "real metaphor is specified by powerful materials or resemblant elements") and effigies (which work through a "causal or indexical relation to what they reproduce," 284); and he uses those ideas to open a meditation on iconoclasm, masks, theater, character, and comedy. The final portion of the chapter discusses "metric naturalism," defined as "the making of resemblance according to measure and ratio" (312). The chapter concludes with sections on mental images and planarity, automata, the facingness of images, virtuality, the imaginative completion of images, and the origins of notions of succession and narrative.

Chapter 5, "Planarity," follows the development of planar orders "as they shape and enable all kinds of routine, second-natural practices and activities" (344). Concepts that follow on from planarity include order (which is one of the basic relations between parts of an image, but is also "*analogous* to the order of the parts of something to which the image refers," 358), measure and proportion, hierarchy, framing and division, symmetries, oppositions, profiles and frontal figures, harmony, ratio, grids, and maps. Of the chapters in this book this one is closest in its interests to Rudolf Arnheim.[10]

Chapter 6, "Virtuality," concerns the capacity to complete images by seeing three dimensions in two, or by perceiving what is absent from what is given. Virtuality raises the problem of illusion, and for Summers it also conjures several concepts he had introduced earlier in the book: effigies (because virtual forms "are evidently of or from what they represent," 431), narratives (because any such reference implies a temporal gap), and doubting or skepticism. The chapter includes discussions of relief space, ground lines, occlusion, foreshortening, the viewer's space, stage space, functional light, modeling, skenographia, linear perspective, and quadratura. Of all the chapters except the last, this one is most specific to Western art and least amenable to world art history, although Summers's opening examples come from Egypt and China. In that respect it is similar in structure, but not in purpose or interpretation, to Gombrich's *Art and Illusion.*

In this sampling of the book's contents I have omitted the introduction and the final chapter, which frame the project and contain Summers's large-scale claims regarding history, art, and interpretation. It is in the nature of a book as ambitious as *Real Spaces* that part of it can be explained in the terms it sets out, and part requires a shift in terminology. First I will consider the issues raised by *Real Spaces*, following the order of the words in the book's title: "Real," "Spaces," "Western art history," and "Western modernism." This may seem capricious given that the book changed titles several times in draft, but I find it accurately consolidates the principal issues. Then I will set out the principal currently theorized possibilities for a world art history, including Summers's, and I will do so target-fashion, beginning with the most conservative options and moving outward and away to the most distant possibilities. First, an exposition of the book's concepts by way of its title.

1. *Real.* The underlying philosophy of Real Spaces is realist: "the world we find ourselves sharing in common," Summers argues, has been shaped and interpreted in different ways, but it remains a common ground (12–13). His realism is articulated with the help of classical rhetoric and modern empiricism, and it has affinities with phenomenology, existentialism, and cognitive psychology. His direct precedents and models range from Ernst Mach and Robert Vischer to Maurice Merleau-Ponty, Gaston Bachelard, and George Lakoff, but *Real Spaces* owes its deepest

debt, I think, to Heidegger — and that is so despite the fact that Summers chooses only to mention Heidegger in passing (22–23).

In my reading there are two deep currents of indebtedness to Heidegger. The first is the emphasis on embodied knowledge of the world. Art is encountered and experienced through fundamental properties of the body and the "conditions of human corporeality" including handedness, uprightness, "tangibility, manipulability, portability, possessability," distance, heft, and cardinality (41, 43). Formulations such as "[t]hings 'stand' (or do not stand) in relation to our standing, 'face' in being faced by us" are fairly directly indebted to Heidegger's relativization of truth to embodied human experience (37).[11] "Real metaphor" is a foundation for the understanding of embodied experience, because it is the "metaphor underlying metaphor," the actual human transaction that produces art and its meaning (257).[12]

I suspect that, given this foundation, Summers's dependence on Plato and Aristotle is subject to a misreading: the ubiquitous citations are only partly intended to function as appeals to "the fundamental statements of the Western 'problem of knowledge'" (319). In another sense, Summers means his classical sources as exemplars of preexisting "specific social spatial relations" such as "the relation of a viewer to imitative painting, that is, of painting of descriptive forms in space and light, and the relation of a spectator in a theater to drama" (319). Real metaphors precede and condition the philosophic formulations that are properly taken as authoritative for the Western tradition. This is not the normal way for a classically minded scholar to use philosophy (it is not, for example, what George Steiner means to do with his citations), although it is not far from the usual scientific move that subsumes philosophy into a series of partly mistaken insights into the empirical facts of experience. Summers's approach makes sense if it is read alongside Heidegger's critique of Western metaphysics, because both involve rethinking things and objects, ontology and being, in terms that answer to the specifically human experience in the world.[13]

It is tricky to decide when it is relevant to mention Heidegger. He may matter least when he is most directly cited, and on the other hand when his influence is indirect and systemic, and therefore matters most, it may serve no clear critical purpose to mention him at all. The reception of Heidegger (including the refusal of Heidegger) varies widely from writers whose work is deeply informed by his texts (for example, Stephen Melville) to those who adapt his ideas for rhetorical purposes (for instance, Germano Celant). One of the challenges for the current generation of art historians — and this is one of the threads that binds Summers's book to those it might not seem to resemble — is to come to terms with Heidegger's place in current understandings of historical art. At the least, a range of contemporary art historical and theoretical writings that are in search of embodied truths about the world might become more self-reflective if they posed their encounter with Heidegger instead of passively embodying it. Heidegger's thought has limitations and side effects in writing on art: it opens the door to pathos, as Derrida has shown so acutely; and it can limit discourse to what are taken to be the *Ur*-conditions of human experience — conditions often too general to have much grip on the specifics of artworks.[14] I will give an example of both limitations after I consider the next concept, which is also the next word in the book's title.

2. *Spaces.* Summers's book is a compendium of different senses of space. The index to *Real Spaces* distinguishes coordinate space, metaoptical space, metric space, personal space, real space, social space, viewer space, and virtual space. In the text Summers also mentions Henri Lefebvre's "social space" and a half-dozen others and observes that it would require "another large book to sort out the disputed critical history of the idea of space in the twentieth century" (21).[15] Summers's central methodological purpose, he says at one point, is to replace "the lingering formalist notion of

the 'visual arts' by what I call the spatial arts" (41). He makes a basic distinction between real spaces and virtual spaces; the latter are "always representations of space," although he notes that the word virtual comes less from its cyberspace connotations than from virtue (*virtus*, *virtù*), so it has an embodied power in its own right (43).

The dissection and classifications of kinds of space is a common opening move in a wide variety of art historical texts. And yet outside of a certain tradition of Kantian philosophy, the concept of space is not a given: it exists in history, as a foundational post-Renaissance Western concept.[16] The concept of space is entangled in the self-definition of post-Renaissance art, and at the same time, and despite its branching history, it has retained and perhaps expanded the role Kant assigned it as ground or possibility of experience.[17] It is inextricably entangled, therefore, in currently viable Western concepts of art and experience.

The problem this poses for a world art history is acute. Should the concept of space be used at all for pre-Renaissance and non-Western art? Should art historians continue dividing and defining kinds of space and assigning them to diverse historical settings? Can the concept of space serve as a master trope for an art historical inquiry like *Real Spaces?* Let me suggest three reasons why it may be problematic to treat the concept of space as a ground for art historical inquiries.

First, it is not clear how many of the "real spaces" Summers describes would be common to all observers, and how many are reports on his own experience. His opening example of real space is the Aztec *Coatlicue* sculpture in the Museo Nacional de Antropología, Mexico City (45–50). Summers notes that "the block tilts slightly forward and looms over anyone standing beside it, so that the simplest personal address to the image is filled with threat and portent." After considering the sculpture's symbolism Summers concludes with a description of the surrounding city of Tenochtitlan and the image of Tlahltecuhtli on the base of the statue, noting that the *Coatlicue* "embodies ... a larger ritual, social, political, and finally cosmic planar order" (50). Given that the position of the *Coatlicue* in the temple precinct of Tenochtitlan is not known, the "address" of the sculpture *to* its original viewers is uncertain, and Summers's account has to rest on *Coatlicue's* planarity and on the assumption that structures in the city were organized analogously. The viewer's "personal address" *to* the sculpture is also open to question because it might vary from one person to the next. My own experience is more in line with an astonishing photograph taken by Leo Katz in 1943, showing the *Coatlicue* looming darkly above the rubble of other broken pieces recovered from the temple site; the picture is taken from below, looking up, and from a corner instead of from the front or a side.[18] The effect is not of planes but of motion, and a different — still hypothetical — account of the "real spaces" of the sculpture could be built from that starting point, leading to different conclusions. Another example of the same issue, more amenable to detailed discussion, concerns representations of the body that use grids and modules. Summers mentions Indian sculpture that uses the palm (*thalam*) as a module, and Egyptian reliefs that employ grids and cubits as their units (410, 444). He mentions both in the chapter on planarity, and takes them as examples of grids; but the two sculptural practices are significantly different even in regard to modules and grids. The rules of proportionality of sculpture given in Indian texts such as the *Viṣṇudharmottara Purāṇa* are exacting, and so are the confusing imbricated iterations of grids, Royal cubits, fingerbreadths, and other lengths in Egyptian practice.[19] Both are eloquent systems for conceptualizing the body, and neither is easily reducible to grids or planarity. If I were to write an account of the Indian or Egyptian sculptures, I might well end with a wholly different sense of their "real spaces."

Second, there are objects whose reception can be said to depend on *ignoring* spatial characteristics, or on not cognizing or articulating spatial properties. Medieval Swedish runic stones are an example. Unlike similar stones in Denmark, the Swedish stones are decorated with incised serpents. At first the serpents look compressed, because their coils overlap one another like Borromean rings, with no deep space implied and no *fondo* (back plane) as in classical reliefs. I take it that the absence of sculpted relief and the very simplicity of the rendering of the overlapping coils are indications that these designs are not to be understood as existing in space, whether it is understood as compressed or symbolic.[20] Nor is any particular "real space" implied by the stones themselves, which were originally set as boundary markers at the edges fields. The stones do not face the viewer (or potential trespasser) in a confrontational manner, and they do not imply any distinct social spaces. Instead the complexity of the knotted serpents' bodies can be taken as evidence that the original viewers were asked to follow the coils, visually disentangling the serpents' bodies, counting their unexpected legs, arms, tails, and supernumerary heads, while also reading the runic inscriptions that are carved on their flanks. In that process of seeing and reading, space — real or virtual — is not at stake, and an analysis beginning from spatial concepts or metaphors would run in the wrong direction. How much of visual art is nonspatial in this specific sense?

A third reason to question a history that depends on the concept of space is that space is involved in our consciousness in ways we cannot conceptually manage. An interesting example of this entanglement is in the book *Western Historical Thinking*, which opens with Peter Burke's list of ten "historiographical assumptions or principles" that characterize Western historical writing. Burke's final proposal is that "Western historians have characteristic views of space." The book is organized around papers presented at a conference in Bielefeld in 1994, and fifteen responses follow Burke's ten principles of Westernness. In the Afterword, Burke notes that only one of his fifteen respondents even mentioned his tenth thesis on space; I take that as a sign that the Westernness of space is nearly buried in Western historical consciousness.[21]

As David Paxman argues in *Voyage into Language: Space and the Linguistic Encounter, 1500–1800,* spatial metaphors have even guided linguists' sense of the structure of language. The evolving concepts of space have also been incorporated into language, where they have had effects on Westerners' ideas of the world and of their languages. A writer who wishes to base a historical inquiry on the concept of space has to take into account the aftereffects of the age of exploration on what appear to be natural uses of the word *space.*[22] These historical and philosophic puzzles cannot be solved by turning to current scholarship in comparative linguistics or cognitive science, because those literatures are also in some disarray.[23] For all these reasons it seems prudent to assume that space, as a concept, is a problematic starting point for an art historical analysis that means to bridge Western and non-Western cultures.

3. *World art history* ... All art has "a certain universality," Summers writes, "even though social spaces and artifacts are formed in specific ways" (38). The question, for a world art history modeled on Summers's, is whether that universality (given, for the sake of argument, that it exists) can make effective contact with the "specific ways" that it is formed. Summers gives the example of the temple platforms at Teotihuacán, Mexico:

> We will never know when and in what ceremonies the great temple platforms of Teotihuacán were ascended, only that there were such occasions, that ascensions took place, and that any significance must have been fitted to climbing and pausing, rising from level to level, finally to reach a summit. We may repeat these movements ourselves, with the most minimal sense, however, of the occasions for which this might have been done by the first builders of the site.[57]

The treacherous thing about emphasizing universal elements of embodied experience is that they can be at once nonspecific and uncognized. If I ride an elevator in a skyscraper, my experience is about ascending by stages to reach a summit, but I probably won't think of it that way. I might listen to the sounds of the elevator's cables, or watch the numbers change floor by floor. The abstract idea of ascent may not have much to do with my experience. At Teotihuacán the Temple of the Sun has eight terraces and slopes with at least six different gradients, so that the experience is more than just an ascent with pauses. The open question for the account in *Real Spaces* is whether an experience of the temple's actual structure is added on to a basal experience of "climbing and pausing," or whether the eight terraces decisively overwrite the more general concept of ascent.[24]

There are many opportunities to test the grip of abstraction on the concrete experience of historical objects. The western portion of the cave under the Temple of the Sun at Teotihuacán was deliberately narrowed, and lowered ceilings were put in place to force people to kneel down. The cave's structure is unexpectedly complex, and even though the rituals performed there are lost, a close-grained phenomenological description might well yield interesting results: but not if it were confined to general observations about centrality, axiality, and centers of power.[25] A few pages after the description of Teotihuacán, Summers mentions the green stone "massive offerings" that were planted underground at the Olmec site of La Venta in Tabasco. He takes the offerings as evidence of the importance of facture, because it was "not sufficient" that the stones were simply buried; they also had to be "refined" and "distinguished" by smoothing (86–87). La Venta is far more complex than it may seem from the account in *Real Spaces;* the green stone assemblies were packed under adobe tiles, floated over green stone mosaics, and surrounded by basalt columns. The sand matrix that supported the stones was laid down in dozens of distinct tones of pink, red, yellow, white.[26] The site is archaeologically complex, and those details could be used to support Summers's concept of facture, but they could equally well be used to urge that facture, refinement, and distinction are in themselves too general to capture what happened at La Venta. Ascent, planarity, centrality, axiality, and facture may be the ground bass of experience, but they may be pitched so low that they are effectively inaudible.

One more point before I leave the subject of world art history. History itself — its chronologies, its institutional habits — is in question throughout *Real Spaces.* Whenever he implies that a concept can be used to speak about art throughout the world, he risks — as he knows very well — losing historical specificity. I recognize both the allure and the problematics of this conditional release from art history.[27] *Real Spaces* is intermittently nonhistorical, but not ahistorical: it is historically grounded, but sometimes misaligned from historical narratives. On a superficial reading, *Real Spaces* may appear deficient in historical narrative, but the deeper question is the degree to which art historical writing calls for analyses like the ones in *Real Spaces.* Accounts of Teotihuacán cannot avoid mentioning axiality and ascent, and those may be the only available approximations to a universal language that can link one account, one culture, to the next. Outside of art history, there are encyclopedic, nonhistorical treatments of aesthetic and critical terms, such as Karl Aschenbrenner's survey of the concept of coherence, or dictionaries such as the *Encyclopedia of Aesthetics.*[28] Such books are at times detached from the forms and purposes of art historical narrative. In other cases, nonhistorical conceptual analyses can be closely tied to art historical concerns; examples include Julius Weinberg's essay on the concept of abstraction, Wolfgang Peitz on the origin of the fetish, and Summers himself on concepts such as *figura serpentinata* and contrapposto.[29] It is conceivable that even though the day-to-day writing of art history calls for analyses such as Summers's, the reverse is not true, and art historical writing may not take nourishment even from those conceptual analyses that grew out of art historical writing. The point cannot be argued, but it can be observed: it will be interesting to see if Summers's book is taken as a facilitator for world art history. The reception of other conceptually based works, including George Kubler's *Shape of Time* and E.H. Gombrich's *Sense of Order*, remain problematic in that regard.[30] Art history seems to engender conceptual meditations and abstractions, but not always to take them as nourishment.

4. ... *and the rise of Western modernism.* To finish the discussion of the book's title: Summers's final chapter, on Western modernism, hinges on a contentious thesis: modernism was made possible by a shift from "an assumed world of forms" as in the Aristotelian tradition, "to one of forces" (551). Forces operate in a kind of space Summers calls "metaoptical": a preexisting, "notional," "boundless," "universalizable co-ordinate metric" framework that is "ananthropomorphic" and "neither scaled nor shaped to our physical selves" (564, 557, 657).[31] He calls on a long roster of writers to make his point, including Hobbes, Hume, Kant, Rousseau, Adam Smith, Marx, Darwin, and Freud. Several of his readings — especially one of Freud's *Beyond the Pleasure Principle* — are in themselves partial and open to further argument (564–65, 572–73). The chapter then ranges through seminal concepts of modernism, including the sublime, caricature, photography, and cubism. Specialists consulting these pages (and I suspect that the book's fate will be to attract selective readings) may not find accounts that are complete or connected to current discussions. The section on the sublime, for example, stresses the concept of infinity and relies on Burke, Kant, Samuel Monk's study of the sublime, and Marjorie Nicholson's wonderful book *Mountain Gloom and Mountain Glory* — the latter two published in 1935 and 1959 respectively.[32] There is, of course, no reason why an account needs to be up to date, but Summers's omission of the fairly enormous literature on the modern and postmodern sublime means that readers will have to create their own links to the contemporary literature.[33] Still, what matters for *Real Spaces* is not how the subject looks today, but how it looks when it takes its place in Summers's encyclopedic argument. The sublime, like most subjects, rarely appears in such a context,

and much can be learned from observing the forms Summers is compelled to give it in order to fit it into place. The chapter closes with an extended discussion of the Rothko Chapel, to show that it resonates with spatial configurations that have been discussed throughout the book.[34]

It would be tempting, from the standpoint of some contemporary scholarship, to say that *Real Spaces* is a dead end, a sensitive and informed but ultimately — against its author's own wishes — Eurocentric attempt to construct a single intellectual edifice for all world art. But the education of art historians begins with large-scale introductory narratives, and as inadequate as they may be, our stock-in-trade of specialized monographic treatments only postpones the moment when it will be necessary to say what those introductory narratives really *should* look like. It strikes me the problem of world art history is so pressing, and so often evaded in favor of specialized studies, that it may be helpful to set out the principal approaches, Summers's included. Here, as a reference and a spur for further conversation, are five possibilities that have been proposed in recent art history and political history. They are in order of increasing radicalism, from the intellectually conservative option of retaining art history intact, to the radical proposal that art history should dissolve entirely in order to accommodate new cultures and practices. *Real Spaces*, I will suggest, is midway along the scale.

1. *Art history can remain essentially unchanged as it moves into world art.* We could augment our traditional subject matter (high art, mainly Western painting, sculpture, and architecture) by looking at non-Western art, trusting that the new material will produce organic changes in the discipline's interpretive methods and politics. As far as I know, this first option has not been formally proposed or defended, but it is the de facto position of monographic treatments of non-Western art that appear in scholarly journals, as well as specialized write-ups in commercial magazines and auction catalogs.

Eventually, in this account, art history will move toward new narratives, unfamiliar histories, new "central" works. As art historians push outward, considering such things as Indian roadside memorials, sixth-century provincial Chinese stelae, and indigenous elements in postcolonial Mexican church decoration, the new objects and their histories may passively and painlessly make our conversations more global.[35] Such a change would not need to affect our current concerns (we would continue to investigate social contexts, gender, and identity), our common interpretive strategies (from formal analysis to psychoanalysis), or our working concepts (such as realism, intention, narrative, space, and evidence).[36] Much of the discipline's sense of itself would therefore remain intact. Non-Western art would disseminate through the medium of art history like colored ink in water. Of the options in this list, I find this the most potentially destructive of the coherence and interest of art history. It simplifies the current scholarship on globalism and multiculturalism by assuming that art history's inherent flexibility will allow it to re-form itself in any new context. If specialized studies in non-Western art continue to be produced in the numbers they are today, the discipline will once again shut itself off from the most interesting intellectual discussions of the time. What is needed, what Summers's book attempts to provide, is an articulate response to the challenge of organizing the new material, and not a passive archivism or formalism that supposes close attention to the art object is sufficient insurance against Eurocentrism.

2. *Art history can redefine and adjust its working concepts to better fit non-Western art.* This is Summers's position; he is interested in finding "the means to address as many histories as possible nearly enough in their own terms to permit new intercultural discussions" (12). He proposes to retain and adjust the basic critical concepts of art history so that they provide "new frameworks" for understanding other cultures. In this approach there are other histories and "other modernisms" beyond the Western one. Summers is

"not indifferent to the problems raised by imposing presumptive categories of art, culture, and history itself on the lives and accomplishments of others," but he takes the risk in order to be able to "address … a great array of specific cultural choices, patterns, and traditions" (12).

The philosophical ground of this approach can be found outside of art history, in discussions about the "linguistic relativity hypothesis": if languages (and therefore languages of art) are inherently commensurate then it can make sense to write a world art history based on a single language of art.[37] Summers's position is realist in the philosophic sense, because it depends on the conviction that there is a shared basal experience of the world. It would also be possible to defend his position using the philosophy of language, by arguing that languages have shared structures.[38] However Summers's position might be defended, I will hazard the guess that a plurality of art historians will find themselves on the other side of the question. Art historians pay close attention to the languages of different cultures, in order to understand the artworks through the concepts their makers and viewers would have known. Languages of art, in that view, are not commensurate: otherwise there would be less reason to learn foreign languages to study visual art. Summers's book is technically multilingual, since it includes Latin, Greek, Italian, French, and several other languages, but it is overwhelmingly unconcerned with the existence of non-Western languages.

One way to defend and extend Summers's strategy is to consider cases in which there are no relevant surviving non-Western terms. In such cases it can be necessary to analyze indigenous and colonial uses of Western terms. An example is Tom Cummins and Joanne Rappaport's study of colonial Andean culture in southern Colombia using terms in Sebastian Covarrubias's dictionary written in 1611. Cummins and Rappaport note how the reduction (*reducción*) of Andean social spaces on maps and in city planning left traces of Andean concepts. Cities and city plans were articulated according to concepts such as *portada, frontispicio,* and *lienzo,* terms that were defined by Covarrubias as "the front of the house," "the front ... where the main door with its decoration is located," and "continuing, upright wall." The uses of such terms, and images of them, are not simply Spanish but bear witness to "the multiple Andean concepts of space and order that were superimposed in the colonial order."[39] Philosophically this work resembles Summers's, with the important difference that even though Cummins and Rappaport are forced to consider Andean culture through Spanish concepts, they are very attentive to sixteenth-century usages. The level of generality at which Summers operates does not prompt him to consider such sources, and that could be considered a strength because it means scholars like Cummins and Rappaport could begin from Summers's more general models. It could also be seen as a weakness because Summers has not often found it necessary to consider historical variations in his operative concepts.

3. *Art history can go in search of indigenous critical concepts.* In current scholarship, the principal alternate to Summers's approach is to leave the Western words to one side and attempt to locate terms that were in use in the non-Western cultures under study. Such terms can be near-synonyms for English terms, such as Latin *spatium* for space; they can be terms taken to be opposed to Western ones, such as Japanese *ma* for both space or time; they can be terms that approach English terms but also mean very different things, such as Chinese *kong*, which means space in the sense of empty or void but also Buddhist void (*sunyata*); they can be problematically conflated with Western terms, as in Heidegger's own equation of Japanese *kotoba* and German *Ding*; and they can be new terms that have no clear equivalents in Western discourse, such as Chinese *liqi*.[40] This practice of finding non-Western terms can be considered as a natural outgrowth of the nineteenth- and twentieth-century European art historical use of terms such as contrapposto, chiaroscuro, or *tableau*. The practice may seem unproblematic, but

it leads directly to the thorniest questions of multicultural scholarship. To put it in a formula: too many unfamiliar terms, and the text may no longer feel like art history. I will give two examples, both of which move beyond the strategies of *Real Spaces* to engage non-Western languages. Two scholars of Chinese art, Wu Hung and Robert Bagley, were recently involved in a lengthy exchange over Wu's book *Monumentality*, which mined classical Chinese texts for terms such as *liqi* and "classification systems" that can help interpret Chinese artifacts.[41] Bagley accused Wu of inappropriate use of indigenous texts, and of attempting to escape from "scientific archaeology" in order to restore a "traditional Chinese scholarship" accessible only to "cultural insiders."[42] Although their exchange left the issue unresolved, it demonstrates that there is a point beyond which the writing will no longer appear to function, for some readers at least, as Western scholarship. A judicious use of foreign terms has always seemed appropriate in Western art historical writing, but when the fundamental critical terms are non-Western the work can appear to lose its conceptual, cultural, and disciplinary foundation.

A second example is Nancy Munn's work on Australian Aboriginal senses of space. Using a Walpiri concept she tentatively identifies with the word *warri-ngirntiri,* Munn explores an Aboriginal sense of space that sometimes requires long detours around prohibited places. *Warri-ngirntiri* is one of the possible words for such a bypass.[43] The negative spaces defined by such detours are centered on specific people, spirits, places, and events, but they are not "clearly bounded, discrete locations." Rather they are dependent on "mobile actors," people who produce the contours of the *warri-ngirntiri* by avoiding it, either in stories or in the actual landscape. Part of what Munn argues is compatible with Summers's approach, especially the fact that these prohibited places are "center-oriented," with diminishing spheres of influence.[44] But Munn's essay also defines a sense of space that is fundamentally non-Western in its dependence on the specifics of the Aboriginal experience.[45] This third approach is a crossroads: in one direction is the careful recalculation of Western concepts that Summers proposes; in the other is the unknown territory of new linguistic resources. The linguistic relativity hypothesis is the motivating factor in each.

4. *Art history can attempt to avoid Western interpretive strategies.* This is different from the preceding option, and more radical. In addition to finding non-Western concepts to guide the interpretation of artworks, art historians might also try to discard interpretive models based on psychoanalysis, semiotics, linguistics, anthropology, literary criticism, feminism, queer theory, structuralism, and poststructuralism. Because all such models have readily identifiable Western genealogies, it has seemed to some historians that they need to be avoided along with Western terms, categories, and critical concepts. Wu's *Monumentality* is not consistently an example of this category because he adopts some Chinese classificatory schemes and concepts, but remains Western in his interpretive methods and scholarly protocols. There have been some systematic attempts to renounce Western interpretive interests: Cao Yiqiang, for example, is interested in adapting elements of a ninth-century Chinese art historical text by Zhang Yanyuan, called *Record of the Famous Painters of All the Dynasties*; Grant Hardy has proposed that Western historians look at the parallel narrative structure in a classical history text by Ssu-ma Ch'ien; and Masayuki Sato has suggested a rereading of Liu Zhiji's *Comprehensive Historiography*, written in the eighth century.[46]

A consistently non-Eurocentric art history could consider abandoning its traditional reliance on Western interpretive methods. An interesting example is Vinay Lal's *The History of History: Politics and Scholarship in Modern India*, a neo-Gandhian meditation on the Westernness of history in general. For Lal, historical writing as it has been inherited from the West "has immeasurably narrowed the possibilities for conceptualizing alternative modernities."[47] As part of his argument he observes — later this observation is heavily qualified — that writers identified with postcolonial theory and Subaltern studies have continued to use Western methodologies to discuss non-Western subject matter:

> The Subaltern historians are comfortable with Marx, Hegel, Heidegger, Jakobson, Habermas, Foucault, Barthes, and Derrida, but the interpretive strategies of the Indian epics or Purāṇas, the political thinking of a Kautilya, the hermeneutics of devotional poetry, the philosophical exegesis of Nagarjuna, and the narrative frameworks of the *Panchatantra* or the *Kathasaritsagara*, are of little use to them … .[48]

Let me extract this moment from Lal's argument and from his wider purpose, and let it stand for a radical approach to the problem of writing about non-Western art. Multiculturalism itself would have a new meaning if scholars took not only their subject matter but their interpretive methodologies from the cultures they study. There is some writing, mainly in anthropology, that attempts this, but so far no scholarship in art history.[49] A simple test of this is the fact that, as far as I am aware, no North American or European university has hired a specialist in Chinese art whose work follows historiographically Chinese interpretive norms. Scholars are chosen for their expertise in Chinese art and their command of the relevant Western scholarly and interpretive protocols.[50] The same observation could be made regarding Indian art historians.[51] The possibility of non-Western interpretive methods looms on the horizon for a genuinely multicultural world art history. Otherwise the "global community" of art historians will continue to refer, in Hayden White's words, to "congeries of historians from various countries who have adopted the 'standards of practice' of Western professional historians."[52]

Summers's book, which may appear distant from the radical aim of abandoning Western interpretive methods, is actually close to it in several respects. One of the traits that makes Zhang Yanyuan's *Record of the Famous Painters of All the Dynasties* so different from contemporary art history is its author's insistence that painting promotes filial piety and the health of the community. While a Confucian purpose might not seem compatible with academic art history, it is amenable to readings proposed in *Real Spaces,* because the action of artworks in social spaces is one of Summers's main concerns. I am not suggesting *Real Spaces* is a bridge to books like Zhang's, because Summers provides only the first half of the bridge — but *Real Spaces* is at least compatible with Zhang's book in a way that current scholarship on Chinese painting, with its emphasis on politics, identity, and patronage, may not be.

5. *Art history can disperse as a discipline.* Scholarship that is attentive to non-Western concepts and methods is arguably the most promising and intellectually difficult future for a world art history. But there is a final possibility, which may turn out to be the de facto state of affairs: art history may disappear as a field. The notion of interdisciplinarity has already been augmented by transdisciplinarity and subdisciplinarity; following those leads what is currently known as art history might deliquesce, leaving only traces of its former sense of methods and objects. Perhaps, as Gérard Mermoz argues, "a multidisciplinary approach to visual representations" might replace "the mystifying discourse of 'art history.'"[53] This is one of the current ideas in discussions of visual studies or visual culture. Yet despite the threat supposedly posed by anthropology (according to the 1996 *October* "Visual Culture Questionnaire") and aside from the temptations of literary theory, archaeology, postphenomenology, and varieties of poststructuralism, art history has not yet melted into visual culture.[54] The field of visuality and visual practices seems to be opening wider each year, becoming more intriguing and rewarding. As that happens, art history as it is presented in *Real Spaces* is becoming harder to recognize.

The logic of the discipline points to world art history, even if only a few people want to risk discovering what it might look like to "put the world into a book" or — more realistically — to talk across cultures. In that respect Summers's book is exemplary: it holds a dark mirror to the current optimism of postcolonial studies. *Real Spaces* is the most thorough, learned, and soberly reasoned description of what art history might look like if it retains its disciplinary shape and its allegiance to the West. All of us need to come to terms with it in order to conceptualize the discipline's future.

Notes

1. This review originally appeared in *The Art Bulletin* 86 no. 2 (2004): 373–80.
2. The nonpluralistic ideologies concealed in multiculturalism are discussed in Kelly Chien-hui Kuo, "A Euphoria of Transcultural Hybridity: Is Multiculturalism Possible?" *Postcolonial Studies* 6 no. 2 (2003): 223–35; for a trenchant exposé of multiculturalism's putative relativism, see Stanley Fish, "Boutique Multiculturalism, or, Why Liberals Are Incapable of Thinking about Hate Speech," *Critical Inquiry* 23 no. 2 (1997): 378–95.
3. For recent discussions see Mieke Bal, "Visual Essentialism and the Object of Visual Culture," *Journal of Visual Culture* 2 no. 1 (2003): 5–32, and the set of responses by Norman Bryson, Michael Holly, W.J.T. Mitchell, and others, in *Journal of Visual Culture* 2 no. 2 (2003): 229–68; and the newly reformulated journal, *Culture, Theory, and Critique* (Nottingham), beginning with vol. 44 no. 1 (2003).
4. An instructive parallel with art history is provided by essays in *The Post-Development Reader*, edited by Majid Rahnema and Victoria Bawtree (London: Zed, 1997), where the overall project is to construct models for third-world development that are not dependent on Western capitalism. It can be argued that the models are themselves outgrowths of Western philosophic understandings of non-Westernness and nationalism, so that the authors' proposals therefore come out of, and fold back into, Western discourse on capitalism — a pessimistic model for a global art history. Skepticism is registered in Gérard Mermoz, "The Problems of a Universal Art History," in the essay "Art History, §III: Contemporary Issues," *Grove Dictionary of Art*, online, accessed December 26, 2003. Against these reasons for skepticism, see the oddly optimistic globalism in *Frontiers of Transculturality in Contemporary Aesthetics*, edited by Grazia Marchiano and Raffaelle Milani (Turin: Trauben, 2001).
5. The rejection of anthropology was posed most visibly for the discipline by the anonymous rhetorical questions posed in the *October* "Visual Culture Questionnaire," *October* 77 (1996): 25. The potential of anthropology has been put most articulately by Hans Belting in *Bild-Anthropologie: Entwürfe für eine Bildwissenschaft* (Munich: Fink, 2001).
6. The principal moment when art history was dissociated from visual culture was the *October* "Visual Studies Questionnaire," *October* 77 (summer 1996). Art history's proximity to visual studies has been defended in several ways.

Horst Bredekamp has argued, unconvincingly I think, that art history in Germany has long been posed as a field continuous with what is now called visual studies. His argument depends on the fact that early twentieth-century German art historians such as Heinrich Wölfflin made extensive use of transparencies, film, and photography; but that was a *use,* not a study, of photographic media. Bredekamp's argument for the affinity of visual studies and German art history also relies on Walter Benjamin's interests in visual culture; but those have not been part of the methodological apparatus of the field until very recently. The point about Benjamin is made eloquently by T.J. Clark, review of Benjamin, *The Arcades Project,* in *The London Review of Books* 22 no. 12 (June 22, 2000): 3–9. Bredekamp, "A Neglected Tradition? Art History and *Bildwissenschaft,*" *Critical Inquiry* 29 no. 3 (2003): 418–29. A different way of arguing the confluence of art history and visual studies is Douglas Crimp's polemic essay against the *October* position on visual studies; see Crimp, "Getting the Warhol We Deserve," *Social Text 59* vol. 17 no. 2 (summer 1999): 49–66. My own *Visual Studies: A Skeptical Introduction* (New York: Routledge, 2003), 1–30, contains a survey of claims about the relation between the disciplines through fall 2002.

7. Both arguments can be read in Mieke Bal, *Reading "Rembrandt": Beyond the Word-Image Opposition* (Cambridge: Cambridge University Press, 1991), 1–24.
8. The conference was called "Compression vs. Expression: Containing and Explaining the World's Art," and was held April 6–8, 2000.
9. Freedberg had been invited in part for his *Power of Images: Studies in the History and Theory of Response* (Chicago: University of Chicago Press, 1989). My own *Domain of Images: On the Historical Study of Visual Artifacts* (Ithaca NY: Cornell University Press, 1999) is not posed as a history of art but a conceptual analysis.
10. Especially Arnheim, *The Power of the Center: A Study of Composition in the Visual Arts* (Berkeley: University of California Press, 1988).
11. One way to demonstrate direct links would be to focus on metaphors of at-handedness. Summers suggests that "the conditions for our own real spatiality entail the broader definitions of our finding ourselves in the world. ... There is a peculiar, deep, and seemingly absolute certainty about the understandings that take shape around conditions. ... This certainty is different both from what we know from logical inference, or from what we know intuitively. Matters at hand are also true in the sense that we may trust them ..." (38). The expression "matters at hand" as it is used here is very close to Heidegger's definition of *thing* (*Ding*) as opposed to *object;* compare Heidegger, *What Is a Thing?,* translated by W.B. Barton Jr. and Vera Deutsch (Chicago: H. Regnery, 1967).
12. In an essay published in 1991, Summers exposited these concepts with the help of the expression "defect of distance," which was also the working title for the book that became *Real Spaces* (12). He introduced the notion of art as a remedy for the "defect of distance" with a reading of Freud's *fort-da* game, stressing the fact that the alternation of at-handedness and absence in the game models a primordial condition of art, because art substitutes for things and places that are not present. In this interpretation, art becomes a scene of pathos and remembrance, recuperation and loss,

all experienced through the viewer's body, near or in or apart from the art object in "real spaces." Summers's interpretation of the *fort-da* game is not psychoanalytic like Freud's or Jean Laplanche's, or linguistic like Lacan's, but Heideggerian: it turns on what Heidegger called "thrownness" (*Geworfenheit*), our finding ourselves in the world and — in Summers's model — our use of art as a substitute for that inherent "defect." This theme gave the 1991 essay a pathos that Summers has largely removed from *Real Spaces.* Although the 1991 essay and other texts leading up to *Real Spaces* are not my subject here, the strong affect of the expression "defect of distance," together with the conviction that art is born of loss and its imperfect remedy, would have created a very different and perhaps more personal book than the one Summers eventually wrote.

The 1991 essay is Summers, "Real Metaphor: Towards a Redefinition of the 'Conceptual' Image," *Visual Theory: Painting and Interpretation,* edited by Norman Bryson, Michael Holly, and Keith Moxey (New York: HarperCollins, 1991), 231–59. Fragments of that text survive in *Real Spaces,* 11, 26, 257–59, 339–41. The expression "defect of distance" is borrowed from Gabriele Paleotti's *Discourse on Images,* published in 1582. It is mentioned in Summers, "Real Metaphor," 246. For thrownness see the skeptical critique by Simon Critchley, "Enigma Variations: An Interpretation of Heidegger's *Sein und Zeit,*" *Ratio* 15 no. 2 (2002): 154–75.

13. For things and objects, see Heidegger, *What Is a Thing?,* translated by W.B. Barton and Vera Deutsch (Chicago IL: H. Regnery, 1967). For ontology a useful account is Emmanuel Levinas, "Martin Heidegger and Ontology," *diacritics* 26 no. 1 (1996): 11–32.
14. Derrida, *The Truth in Painting,* translated by Geoff Bennington and Ian McLeod (Chicago: University of Chicago Press, 1987), 284–85, 292–93. My criticism here is expanded in *Our Beautiful, Dry, and Distant Texts: Art History as Writing* (University Park: Penn State Press, 1997), 230–45. For an attempt to name the *Ur*-conditions of embodied experience in physical terms, see George Lakoff and Mark Johnson, *Philosophy in the Flesh: The Embodied Mind and Its Challenge to Western Thought* (New York: Basic Books, 1999).
15. Summers juxtaposes and often nearly blends real space and social space, for example in a passage describing a Rembrandt drawing as evidence of the "history of Rembrandt's drawing in real spaces — and, more specifically, its history in *social* spaces …" (52).
16. The history of space and its synonyms is not transhistorical, but is bounded by the late Renaissance; it is significant for example that the word "space" does not appear in any Western architectural treatise before the eighteenth century. Peter Collins, *Changing Ideals in Modern Architecture, 1750–1950* (London: Faber and Faber, 1965), 285.
17. Even phenomenological accounts can be considered as Kantian, in the sense that they depend on Newtonian three-dimensional space as a preexisting referential frame. It has been persuasively argued that even Merleau-Ponty's sense of space is neither Leibnizian (not given apart from the totality of experienced spatial relationships) nor neo-Kantian (that is, experienced in parts and "regions") but Newtonian, "because it is presented as the spatial field or background for all phenomenological contents." Priest, *Merleau-Ponty* (London: Routledge, 1998), 234.

18. Katz, "Art and Archaeology in the Aztec Figure of Coatlicue," *Magazine of Art* 38 (1945): 133–37, photograph on p. 37.
19. Priyabala Shah, *Viṣṇudharmottara Purāṇa, Third Khanda,* vol. 2, *Introduction, Appendices, Indexes.* Gaekwad's Oriental Series, edited by B. J. Sandesara, no. 137 (Baroda, India: Oriental Institute, 1961); Erik Iverson, *Canon and Proportions in Egyptian Art,* second edition fully revised in collaboration with Yoshiaki Shibata (Warminster, England: Aris and Phillips Ltd., 1975).
20. Sven Jannson, *The Runes of Sweden,* translated by Peter Foote (Stockholm: Norstedt, 1962); Claiborne Thomson, *Studies in Upplandic Runography* (Austin: University of Texas Press, 1975).
21. Burke, "Western Historical Thinking in a Global Perspective — Ten Theses," in *Western Historical Thinking: An Intercultural Debate,* edited by Jörn Rüsen (New York: Berhahn, 2002), 15–32, quotations on 28, 27 respectively; and see 196.
22. Paxman, *Voyage into Language: Space and the Linguistic Encounter, 1500–1800* (Burlington VT: Ashgate, 2003). In my reading, Paxman's argument is not entirely coherent because he vacillates between arguing that "spatial experience ... guided those who investigated the properties of language" and that spatial metaphors in language evolved, creating new configurations of meaning in language (1, 16). Nevertheless the possibility remains that metaphors of spatiality in language are influenced by and also guide Westerners' sense of the world.
23. John Lacy, "Space in Language and Thought: Commentary and Discussion," *Ethos, Journal of the Society for Psychological Anthropology* 26 no. 1 (1998): 105–11.
24. More generally for Teotihuacán studies, the question would involve the fit between metaphors of ascent and axiality, on the one hand, and the stratified and only partly symmetric disposition of the portions of the city as a whole, on the other; compare for example Linda Manzanilla, "Social Identity and Daily Life at Classic Teotihuacán," *Mesoamerican Archaeology: Theory and Practice,* edited by Julia Hendon and Rosemary Joyce (Oxford: Blackwell, 2004), 124–47.
25. Doris Heyden, "An Interpretation of the Cave Underneath the Temple of the Sun in Teotihuacán, Mexico," *American Antiquity* 40 no. 2 (1975): 131–47; and her speculative essay, "Caves, Gods, and Myths: World View and Planning at Teotihuacán," in *Mesoamerican Sites and World-Views,* edited by Elizabeth Benson (Washington: Dumbarton Oaks, 1981), 1–39.
26. Philip Drucker, Robert Heizer, and Robert Squier, *Excavations at La Venta Tabasco, 1955,* in the series *Smithsonian Institution Bureau of American Ethnology,* no. 170 (Washington: United States Government Printing Office, 1959).
27. James Herbert, one of the readers of the manuscript of my own book, *The Domain of Images,* pointed out that in order to provide the conceptual analyses of image types, I had been compelled to write a book that is fundamentally nonhistorical. The difference between intermittently historical, nonhistorical, and ahistorical was at issue there, as in *Real Spaces.* Herbert, personal communication, 1998.

28. Aschenbrenner, *The Concept of Coherence in Art* (Dordrecht, the Netherlands: Kluwer, 1985); *Encyclopedia of Aesthetics,* edited by Michael Kelly, 4 vols. (Oxford: Oxford University Press, 1998). Another recent encyclopedia of aesthetics is Li Zehou and Ru Xin, *Mei xue bai ke quan shu* [*Encyclopedia of Aesthetics*], edited by Ming Yu Zhu (Beijing: She hui ke xue wen xian chu ban she [Social Science Archive Publishing House], 1990). I thank Qigu Jiang for assistance with this book.
29. Weinberg, "Abstraction in the Formation of Concepts," *Dictionary of the History of Ideas: Studies of Selected Pivotal Ideas,* edited by Philip Weiner, 5 vols. (New York: Scribner's, 1973), vol. 1, 1–9; Peitz, "The Problem of the Fetish, II: The Origin of the Fetish," *Res* 13 (1987): 23–45 (both of these are cited in *Real Spaces,* 672); and Summers, "Contrapposto: Style and Meaning in Renaissance Art," *The Art Bulletin* 59 (1977): 336–61.
30. It is difficult to assess the impact of books like *The Sense of Order* or *The Shape of Time,* but I propose that they have had little influence in proportion to the breadth of their subjects. The *Arts and Humanities Citation Index* yields relatively few citations of either. Reviews of Kubler's *Shape of Time* are helpfully collected by Kubler himself in "*The Shape of Time* Revisited," *Studies in Ancient American and European Art: The Collected Essays of George Kubler,* edited by Thomas Reese (New Haven CT: Yale University Press, 1985), 424–30. Reviews of Gombrich's *Sense of Order* include Henri Zerner, in *The New York Review of Books* 26 part 28 (June, 1979):18–21, with a response by Gombrich in Ibid., 60–61; and John Kennedy, in *Journal of Aesthetics and Art Criticism* 38 no. 4 (1980): 453–57. I thank Richard Woodfield for these three references.
31. A central text for the difference between embodied place and disembodied ("metaoptical") space is Ed Casey, *Getting Back into Place: Toward a Renewed Understanding of the Place-World* (Bloomington: Indiana University Press, 1993), xv, 41–105; Summers cites the book but only as a "history of the idea of place" (666); Casey's work is in fact antithetical to the final chapter of *Real Spaces* and of the notion of metaoptical space.
32. Monk, *The Sublime: A Study of Critical Theories in Eighteenth-Century England* (New York: Modern Language Association, 1935); Marjorie Nicholson, *Mountain Gloom and Mountain Glory: The Development of the Aesthetics of the Infinite* (Ithaca NY: Cornell University Press, 1959); Nicholson's book was developed from lectures given at Cornell University in 1948.
33. A modernist and contemporary sense of the sublime could be triangulated with the help of Neil Hertz, *The End of the Line: Essays on Psychoanalysis and the Sublime* (New York: Columbia University Press, 1985); Peter De Bolla, *The Discourse of the Sublime: Readings in History, Aesthetics, and the Subject* (London: Basil Blackwell, 1989); *Of the Sublime: Presence in Question,* edited and translated by Jeffrey Librett (Albany: State University of New York Press, 1993); Philippe Lacoue-Labarthe, "On the Sublime," translated by Geoff Bennington, in *Postmodernism, ICA Documents,* edited by Lisa Appignanesi (London: Free Association Books, 1989), 11–18; and the very useful essay by Martin Donougho, "Stages of the Sublime in North America," *MLN* 2 (2001): 909–40.

34. An Epilogue returns to the dual purpose of the book: to adapt Western concepts to meet non-Western art, and to understand what is specific to the West even when Western concepts have changed so much that they no longer constitute a single unified approach to art (625, 653). The latter purpose is an excellent corrective to multicultural initiatives that take the West as a given term.
35. These examples are from, respectively: *Memorial Stones [in India]: A Study of Their Origin, Significance, and Variety,* edited by S. Settar and Gunther Sontheimer (Dharwad, India: Institute of Indian Art History, 1982); Stan Abe, *Ordinary Images* (Chicago: University of Chicago Press, 2002); and Samuel Edgerton, *Theaters of Conversion: Religious Architecture and Indian Artisans in Colonial Mexico* (Albuquerque: University of New Mexico Press, 2001).
36. By "working concepts" I mean also the leading concepts in *Critical Terms for Art History,* edited by Richard Shiff and Robert Nelson (Chicago: University of Chicago Press, 1996).
37. John Lucy, *Language Diversity and Thought: A Reformulation of the Linguistic Relativity Thesis* (Cambridge: Cambridge University Press, 1992); and Peter Carruthers, *Language, Thought, and Consciousness* (Cambridge: Cambridge University Press, 1996). In North America the most famous exemplar of the relativity hypothesis is Benjamin Whorf; it is pertinent that his relativism was inspired by a linguistic universalism, almost as if it were necessary to believe in a common human experience through language in order to proselytize for the importance of individual languages. A concise summary of the evidence against Whorf's position is Einar Haugen, "Linguistic Relativity: Myths and Methods," in *Language and Thought: Anthropological Issues,* edited by William McCormack and Stephen Wurm (The Hague: Mouton, 1977), 11–28, especially 22.
38. For the latter, see Jerry Fodor, "Defending the 'Language of Thought,'" in *Art and Cognition: A Reader,* edited by William Lycan (Cambridge MA: Blackwell, 1990), 282–99; and Noam Chomsky, *Knowledge of Language: Its Nature, Origin, and Use* (New York: Praeger, 1985).
39. Cummins and Rappaport, "The Reconfiguration of Civic and Sacred Space: Architecture, Image, and Writing in the Colonial Northern Andes," *Latin American Literary Review* 26 no. 52 (1998): 174–200, quotations on pp. 182, 193 respectively.
40. In anthropology a distinction is made between *internal* and *external classifications;* I have not adopted it here because it confuses concepts that operate as classificatory systems with Western interpretive strategies, which is the next subject on my list. See Robert Sharer and Wendy Ashmore, *Fundamentals of Archaeology* (Menlo Park CA: Benjamin and Cummings, 1979), 278. For the overinterpreted term *ma* see Arata Isozaki, *Ma: Space-Time in Japan* (New York: Cooper-Hewitt Museum, 1978), and Madeleine Sutter, "Ma: An Investigation into the Making of Exterior Meditative, Physical, and Sequential Space," master's thesis, North Carolina State University, 1999, unpublished; for *kotoba* and Heidegger's essay "Aus einem Gespräch von der Sprache" see Reinhard May, *Heidegger's Hidden Sources: East Asian Influences on His Work,* translated by Graham Parkes (London: Routledge,

1996), together with the review by Gereon Kopf, *Philosophy East and West* 51 no. 1 (2001): 122–25; and for *liqi* ("ritual paraphernalia," or by extension "ritual art") see Wu, *Monumentality in Early Chinese Art and Architecture* (Stanford CA: Stanford University Press, 1995), 18–20.

41. Wu, *Monumentality.*
42. Bagley, review of Wu, *Monumentality,* in *Harvard Journal of Asiatic Studies* 51 (1998): 221–56. The quotations are cited in Wu, "Response to Robert Bagley's Review of My Book, *Monumentality in Early Chinese Art and Architecture* (Stanford University Press, 1995)," *Archives of Asian Art* 51 (1998–99): 92–102, quotations on p. 97.
43. Munn, "Excluded Spaces: The Figure in the Australian Aboriginal Landscape," *Critical Inquiry* 22 (1996): 446–65; the Walpiri term is on p. 451 n. 16.
44. Munn, "Excluded Spaces," 451, 454; in n. 28 she quotes Stanley Tambiah on Thai spaces and Benedict Anderson on Javanese spaces, sources not cited by Summers but compatible with his approach.
45. In concluding this way I am reading against the grain of Munn's essay, since she means to contribute to ongoing Western conversations about spatiality and temporality, and so she ends with a Western example (a design for Central Park) to show the applicability of her more mobile concept of space. Yet I think that conclusion goes against the essay's strongest claims, which are about Aboriginal senses of space that are *not* reducible to, or even compatible with, Western ones.
46. Cao Yiqiang, personal communications, 1999 and 2000. The text in question is Zhang Yanyuan, *Ming hua chi* [*A Record of the Famous Painters of All the Dynasties*], in *Some T'ang and pre-T'ang Texts on Chinese Painting,* translated by William Acker (Leiden, the Netherlands: E. J. Brill, 1954), 59–382. Grant Henry, "Can an Ancient Chinese Historian Contribute to Modern Western Theory? The Multiple Narratives of Ssu-ma Ch'ien," *History and Theory* 33 no. 1 (1994): 20–38; and Sato, "Cognitive Historiography and Normative Historiography," in *Western Historical Thinking,* 128–41, especially 129. In the same volume, Yü Ying-shih considers the revivals of interest in traditional Chinese historiography considered "in its own terms"; see Ying-shih, "Reflections on Chinese Historical Thinking," *Western Historical Thinking,* 152–72, quotation on p. 153.
47. Lal, *The History of History: Politics and Scholarship in Modern India* (Delhi: Oxford University Press, 2003), 208.
48. Lal, *History of History,* 206–7. He then qualifies his criticism by observing that because the "origins of modern social sciences lie in Western intellectual practices … it is not unreasonable that … interpretive models should also be derived from these practices." Even so, "there is still no reciprocity" in "intellectual matters." (Ibid., 207.) I have proposed an analogous critique of Gayatri Spivak's *Critique of Postcolonial Reason: Toward a History of the Vanishing Present* (Cambridge MA: Harvard University Press, 1999) in my *Visual Studies,* 115–16, arguing that Spivak can be read as a writer concerned with multiculturalism but unwilling to forego certain Western interpretive methods (principally Derridean poststructuralism and psychoanalysis).
49. An interesting example in anthropology is Diana Losche, "Skin, Organs, Bone: Narrative, Image, and the Body," *Visual Arts and Culture* 1 no. 2 (1999): 135–48.

50. I thank James Cahill, Marty Powers, Jerome Silbergeld, and Dick Vinograd for conversations on this complicated subject. It has been suggested to me that Wen Fong's scholarship is fundamentally Confucian, and that his many Western preoccupations — which would include connoisseurship, social art historical analyses, and formal concerns — are superadded. Although it is nearly impossible to assess such a claim, it can be observed that the theoretical interests that are brought to bear on Chinese material are Western, even while the overall purpose of the scholarship may not be. This is clearest in earlier essays such as Wen, "Toward a Structural Analysis of Chinese Landscape Painting," *Art Journal* 28 (1969): 388–97.
51. The works of Geeta Kapur are an instructive example; her sense of modernity and its aftermath in *When Was Modernism? Essays on Contemporary Cultural Practice in India* (New Delhi: Tulika, 2000) draws, for example, on Jean-François Lyotard's discussion of the sublime and on Hal Foster's sense of the "anti-aesthetic."
52. He continues: "Can one suppose that the standards honored by the 'global community' are a product of contributions made by non-Western as well as Western historians? Or is it more likely that this 'global community' is an exact counterpart of the 'global community' of physicists or chemists, which is to say, a community made up of those who have accepted standards of practice for their disciplines that developed exclusively in the West?" White, "The Westernization of World History," *Western Historical Thinking*, 111–18, quotation on p. 112.
53. Mermoz, "The Problems of a Universal Art History."
54. Anonymous, "Visual Culture Questionnaire."

The Modality of Spatial Categories

Friedrich Teja Bach

The reservations one might have concerning a globalized art history are readily apparent. Their common denominator is the fear that today, in the era of a politically aggressive globalization, discourse a discipline oriented in this way will be universalistic in the worst sense, so that it could not sufficiently do justice to the differences between the varied forms of artistic and humanistic achievements, and would be — even against the intentions of its advocates — a form of more or less hidden Eurocentrism, or more precisely a centrism of Western cultures, and therefore a form of cultural imperialism.

In addition to this come severe problems on the level of practicability, not the least of which is that of language, or rather languages. After all, a globalized art history would not only be about incorporating the corresponding *termini* and technical terms from non-Western cultures, but would also, considering the cognitive dimensions of images, need to incorporate the very languages "belonging" to those images and forms. Unlike the question, "Are cultural studies global?" the question "Is art history global?" already presupposes a problematic separation of disciplines.

A look at comparable tendencies in adjacent fields of study only heightens such fears. The leading German linguist, Jürgen Trabant, observes in his *Kleine Geschichte des Sprachdenkens* (*A Brief History of Language-Thought,* 2003) that "the current interest of linguistic research clearly lies in universalistic research projects." In the universalistic goals of such projects, even such contrasting approaches as Chomsky's mentalism and the body-linguistics of Georges Lakoff and Mark Johnson reach a common accord. In Trabant's view, this situation is all the more alarming, given that "this scientific universalism coincides with the brutal linguistic glob-*ang*-lization in which the diversity of the world's languages and therewith the 'merveilleuse varieté des operations de notre esprit' is set to perish."

In what follows, I would like to introduce two examples in which I question the *modalities* of the central category of space. As both David Summers's great book *Real Spaces* (2003) and Jim Elkins's review have shown, the founding of art historical inquiries on the concept of space is by no means unproblematic. I will then emphasize the importance of a historicization of the leading question, "Is Art History Global?" and, in closing, present a brief *plaidoyer* for an inclusion of historical deep time in our considerations of the globalization of art history.

I

First of all, then, a few remarks on modalities of space, namely on the dimensions of the infinite and on planarity. As is well known, several American sculptors of the 1960s, most notably artists of Minimal Art, alluded each in their own way to Constantin Brancusi in their engagement with European Modernism. Perhaps the most interesting allusion concerned his most radical work, the *Endless Column* (early version, 1918; monumental version in Tirgu Jiu 1937–38). It is in reference to this that Dan Flavin speaks about the "pretension to infinity" in regard to his own project *The Continuous Icon* 1963, speaking of his own work's "unlimited extension" and its closeness to Brancusi's *Endless Column.* The moment one goes beyond the mere affirmation of an artistic "influence," and takes the conception of both works seriously, it becomes apparent that infinity has a completely different meaning in the two works. Flavin translates the notion of infinity, as it were, into the representational scheme of perspectival endlessness, whereas Brancusi realizes infinity in his column through a rhythmically perfect form whose proportion (unit width x overall height) is precisely determined, and whose title should really not be *Endless Column* but rather *Infinite Column.*

Brancusi's *Infinity Column* is capable of representing infinity by virtue of being precisely restricted — just as Ezra Pound once described his ideal form in marble as "an approach to the infinite by form." Important here is not so much the assessment that both Brancusi's and Flavin's works thematize infinity, but rather that in each of them the difference in what "infinity" means is thematized; it becomes the "dissimilarity of the similar" (Sklovsky).

What has been established here for sculpture can be applied to painting, as well, as Kurt Badt claimed in *Raumphantasien und Raumillusionen*: "The organization of a partial view of a landscape achieving the image of a clearly limited, finite place is the only way to represent the notion of infinity," he wrote:

> Infinity cannot be represented by orthogonals converging in a distance. These, on the contrary, show the finiteness of our view on a limited piece of the earth. A space built upon perspectival qualities is not really conceivable as a fraction of an infinite space. It is rather perspectivally limited, it is a specific, finite space.

II

My second point will consist of some brief remarks on the question of planarity, or "flatness," as it has been termed in Modernist discourses. A phenomenon in modern sculpture that has remained largely unnoticed is the interest artists have taken in the quality of planarity in Early Mediterranean objects. The importance of the category of planarity or flatness and its implications for modernism needn't be addressed at length here; I pursued it in depth in the exhibition "Shaping the Beginning: Modern Artists and the Ancient Eastern Mediterranean" at the Museum on Cycladic Art in Athens (2006).[1]

Scholarship also exists on the formulation of orthogonal space during the transition from Paleolithic to Neolithic, and in its later implementations. Noteworthy among the earlier literature on this subject is the work of Guido Kaschnitz-Weinberg, who, in his essay, "Von der zweifachen Wurzel der statuarischen Form im Altertum" (1944) portrayed the emergence of coordinate space as a new symbolic sphere, concluding that the inability to stand upright in early Paleolithic idols signifies the absence of a coordinate space. According to Kaschnitz-Weinberg, it was not until the early Bronze Age that "the ambition to provide a surface on which the idol can stand becomes clear. This horizontal surface or base is nothing other than an incarnate piece of the new space. ... The idol transforms itself into a statuette." In *Grundstrukturen der Ägyptischen Kunst* (1986), Dietrich Wildung points out that "base slabs and backrests were, as space generating elements, perceived by the sculptor not as makeshift, but as fixed constituent parts of the pictorial concept. They are a part of the design motif, they communicate information on 'space' and 'order.'" (In the recent literature one of course thinks of the chapter "Planarity" in Summers's *Real Spaces.*)

It is particularly interesting for our discussion that for several classic modernist sculptors, planarity appeared in the context of an engagement with the early art of the Mediterranean. Such is the case with Henry Moore, who linked his sculpture *Moon Head* (1964) to the early Cycladic formal language, as Kenneth Armitage did in works like *Diarchy* (1957). And inspirations from Neolithic objects and artworks of early Mediterranean cultures also seem to be fundamental to the planarity of many of Alberto Giacometti's artworks, such as *Standing Man* (1928) and *Three Eyes–Two Arms*

(1931/32), which have parallels with Cycladic and Neolithic sculptures, as I show in the exhibition. The same parallels holds true for the planarity of Giacometti's *horizontal* sculptures, which Rosalind Krauss has rightly designated as his essential contribution to modern sculpture; there Egyptian sacrificial plates seem to have been a major inspiration.

In this context, I am omitting detailed notes; these can be found in the book that accompanied the exhibition. My concern here is not to trace Giacometti's interaction with Neolithic and early Mediterranean art in detail, but to suggest the fundamental *change* which through this reference can be registered in the quality of planarity. In a sculpture *like Tête qui regarde* (1928), planarity is no longer the nearly neutral, *a priori* determination of space, a spatial coordinate, which could simply be demarcated. Rather it becomes almost expressive, becomes activated as a force encountering the viewer: it is not a spatial determinate but a *figural agency*.

III

As Jim Elkins has suggested in his review of *Real Spaces*, it is "problematic to treat the concept of space as a ground for art historical inquiries." When considering the issue of using the problematic — but at the same time seemingly indispensable — notion of space as a category essential for intercultural comparison, it seems to be helpful to extend our understanding of the problem by revisiting earlier canonical discussions of the discipline, and to understand them in their historical contexts. Surely it would be instructive, for example, to discuss the proposal of a "comparative art history" as Dagobert Frey introduced it in his *Grundlegung zu einer Vergleichenden Kunstwissenschaft (Foundation for a Comparative Art History*, 1949, second edition 1970). Frey's subtitle was *Space and Time in the Art of the African-Eurasian High Cultures;* he identified cultures' differences in the configuration of space by using the categories of "Status," "Movement," "Monument," and "Way," an approach that was methodically criticized because of the a priori notion of space used to substantiate it.

Above all, here too it is important to bear in mind the discussion in the 1950s on the theme of space and place (for example Hedwig Conrad-Martius, *Der Raum*, 1958; Kurt Badt, *Raumphantasien und Raumillusionen*, 1960), following Heidegger's lecture "Bauen, Wohnen, Denken" ("Building, Living, Thinking," 1951). Especially for the 1950s, the problematization of a universalistic, abstract notion of space can be relatively clearly understood in the recognition that the crisis at the time was felt to be rooted in a "violent self-assertion of the constructive," as Blumenberg argued in 1957. The problematic dimensions of these debates of the 1950s are particularly informative. These debates — which largely dispensed of a performative concept of space that was conceived of not only in terms of things but more importantly in terms of human presence — responded, in German-speaking regions, to the disaster of a geopolitical space discourse.

IV

Despite the fundamental problems irrefutably bound up with the concept of space, it seems likely that the category is in many ways indispensable. The example of Giacometti should above all bring to our attention that for conceptual approaches which work with extremely heterogenic cultural materials, or are even aimed at the structuring of such heterogeneity, the question of the appropriateness of the basic categories is central, but so, too, is the question of the identity and difference of the *modalities* of such categories. Even when the planarities of Cycladic figures or Egyptian sacrificial stones, on the one hand, or that of Giacometti, on the other hand, seem to be early and late forms of fundamentally comparable planarities, the appearance, the modality of planarity, is still fundamentally different.

The example of planarity in the works of Giacometti and in the early Mediterranean civilizations also brings out another easily overlooked dimension of the issue at hand: the problem of historical deep time. We mainly consider the globalism of art history in geographic terms, meaning that we are concerned not only with

European "art" but also the "art" of Australia, Asia, South and North America, Africa, the Arctic, the Caribbean, and so forth. Even so, a merely additive expansion of the field of art history would be fundamentally unjust to the question of its globality. The dimension of time, which has become so topical in the art of the twentieth century, needs to be taken more seriously. In addition to geographic space, the issue of globality — of the wholeness of art — also implies the dimension of deep time. Nevertheless the expression *longue durée* is to be avoided, because it suggests a continuity of phenomena which, far from being guaranteed, would first have to be introduced as a question; and it threatens to overlook the possibility of a *leap* in time, presenting as real that which actually has the character of a cultural projection, a phantasm. Certainly, questions of deep time demand special discretion. Unlike that which is Other in a geographical sense, that which is chronologically distant has no political advocates who could shelter it from appropriation or defend its difference.

Unlike art theory, art history as a discipline deals in a factual as well as a historical sense with the specific. The antagonism, however, between universalization and particularization is, at the same time, a necessary foundational conflict, and in that conflict a paradox manifests itself: namely, that it is only the attempts at universalization that make each particularity recognizable. It is only in the tension of universalizing tendencies that the value of the nonidentical, the nonintegrable, becomes ascertainable. One of the conditions for an auspicious globalization of art history would thus be that this tension-filled relationship between universalization and particularization, between the general and the specific, remains productively in suspension.

Notes

1. The central thesis of this exhibition is that, due to the prevailing focus of attention on African and Oceanic art in the discussion of "Primitivism in Twentieth-Century Art," the significance of the "archaic" (as represented in the "primitive art" of the early cultures of the Eastern Mediterranean)

for modern artists has not yet been fully recognized. The exhibition and its catalogue discuss this significance for individual artists like Henry Moore, Alberto Giacometti, Constantin Brancusi, Pablo Picasso, and Henri Matisse as well as in general categories like origin, simplicity, flatness, block, "truth to the material," sign and structure (spiral, pyramid and grid), and in motif-groups like woman-vase, the eye and the gaze, the bull. See Friedrich Teja Bach, *Shaping the Beginning: Modern Artists and the Ancient Eastern Mediterranean* (Athens: Goulandris Foundation, Museum of Cycladic Art, 2006).

Is a Truly Global Art History Possible?

Ladislav Kesner

Is the prospect of global (world) art history "the most interesting," or "far and away the most pressing" problem facing art history today, as James Elkins suggests? It is not easy to share this sense of urgency, especially when the "prospect of world art history" is compared to issues such as the purpose of the discipline vis-à-vis the continuing and deepening erosion of tradition, the trivialization of knowledge and values, or whether practices of art history sufficiently address the enormous gap between the potential of artworks to offer unique experiences and the mostly meager outcomes of actual encounters with them.

The simple question "Is art history global?" admits two readings. It can be taken as a direct question, open to dispassionate analytical dissection. But it can also be pronounced in a critical and more or less aggressively interrogating manner, suggesting a priori that art history isn't global, and instigating a sense of guilt — in the way that discourse on multiculturalism and globalization, spurred by the spirit of social activism and political correctness, has been attacking humanistic disciplines, curricula, and cultural institutions. This is not to imply that art history should not be interrogated, or that it should avoid difficult, soul-searching examinations of its practices. Quite the contrary. But it seems to me that in the past two decades or so art history has paid enough attention to the tenets of postcolonialism and globalization, and that it should reserve its capacity for self-scrutiny and reflection for other issues, including the ones I have just mentioned. The discourses of postcolonialism, multiculturalism, and globalization may have contributed to changing the shape of art history, but at least in their more aggressive forms they are largely incompatible with the humanistic concerns of art history — concerns that may be considered outdated by some, but certainly not all its practitioners. I will give a number of reasons for insisting that art history should go only so far in criticizing itself for not being sufficiently "global."

I

Such a view might seem wholly at odds with the personal experience of someone who has worked mostly on one aspect of world art (Chinese art), mainly from within the context of one small art historical environment (the Czech Republic), and who has been confronted with art history's deeply entrenched antiglobal shape. (I take "environment" here to subsume the whole spectrum of institutionalized practices concerned with presenting, interpreting, and teaching art — not simply scholarship and writing.) In Czech art history, as undoubtedly in some other such local art histories, non-European or world art has been traditionally relegated to the realm of ethnology or area studies — and this despite the fact that the Czech Republic has considerable collections of Asian art and a glorious tradition of Egyptology. A few brief personal observations might be in place to highlight the contours of the situation.

Fewer than twenty years ago, one of my first scholarly articles, on Chinese tomb sculpture, caused a great deal of debate when I submitted it to the main Czech academic art-historical journal, *Umění*. The issue was not whether it met the qualitative standards of the journal, but whether the flagship of art historical research in the country should publish a piece on Chinese art in the first place (ironically, the same journal had already published two articles on Chinese art in the 1950s). In the early 1990s, as a curator of Chinese art in the National Gallery, I became involved in museum management and served as deputy director of the National Gallery for some time, mainly to be able to influence institutional policies and budget structuring; I wanted to open permanent galleries of Asian art in the face of the silent but unyielding opposition of other departments. This finally happened in 1999, thirty-seven years after the National Gallery had established its Department of Asian Art! The galleries are located in a Baroque chateau, far on the outskirts of Prague and outside the established tourist routes. The location provides a succinct spatial metaphor for the marginal place afforded to non-Western traditions in the Czech art historical scene. As I write this in winter 2006, it seems likely that the galleries of Asian arts will be relocated to a more central, but also much smaller space. The National Gallery's collection of Asian art is as representative in its scope and quality as the collection of European art, but the Asian art will be allocated some 3% of the total floor space of all permanent galleries of the foremost national institution entrusted with presentation of art.

Lectures on world art are only sporadically included in the curricula of university art history departments in Prague and other cities. There is no specialist on world art in any of the four art history departments in the Czech Republic that currently offer PhD degrees, and there is no specialist on non-Western art among some thirty scholars who staff the Institute of Art History at the Czech Academy of Sciences. The fact that no specialist on world or non-Western art has ever served on editorial boards (or grant committees, or other power and money-allocating structures) perpetuates the status quo. A near-total ignorance of world art is proudly displayed by members of the art historical community as a badge of their professional status.

The discipline of art history in Czech Republic is anything but "global" in its scope, sense of purpose and value judgments. On the contrary, it remains entrenched in the most embarrassing, obsolete Eurocentric practices. What does that say about the state of art history as such? Not much, but it shows the state of the discipline in one particular context. The charges of Eurocentrism and a concomitantly insufficient grasp of world art can be justifiably leveled against the practices of art history in some less developed local contexts, but they don't pertain to international scholarship more generally.

This brings me to a viable sense in which the concept of "global art history" might be used. It is not so much the contrast between "Western" art history and the ways art is discussed and reflected upon outside the West, but rather the contrast between the shape of that portion of the discipline that addresses international audiences, versus the shape of those portions that are concerned with various local contexts and audiences for art history. One of the main differences between the former and the latter is the extent to which they are able to acknowledge and embrace world art. The boundaries between "global art history" and local environments are fluid and permeable, sustained largely by language — English as the *lingua franca* of the international discipline, as opposed to the respective languages of local art histories. The very choice of one's language often conditions the approaches and outcomes even more fundamentally than the limitations any given language necessarily imposes on the description or interpretation of art. Writing in English (or in one's native language, but with the view that it will be translated into English), one at least implicitly intends to address the international community — the competitive global market — and this may put different priorities into play than writing in one's native language, in which case one implicitly acknowledges that the readership will only consist of members of given local art historical community, or those able to read the language in question. The latter alternative is not necessarily less demanding or inferior; it just brings different demands.

One of the reasons that local incarnations of art history persist and even flourish is the lingering myth of the special "national qualities" of local art that only the cultural insider, or someone who is thoroughly suffused with the *Geist* of the culture, is able to comprehend and explicate.[1] On the other hand, there may be implicit fear that some local, less well-known artists or even certain themes would not be sufficiently interesting for global art historical community. There is also the pragmatic difficulty of being able to write sufficiently well in English, or of having one's writing translated into English, as well as a fact that a substantial fraction of the art historical audience in local contexts may not be able or willing to read scholarship in English. The choice of the language and the audience is then closely related to publishing opportunities: the competitive pressures in the publication venues of the international scene are very high, and so it is often a safer bet to publish in local venues, in one's native language. It is beyond the scope of my imminent concerns here to examine to what extent such a distinction between the global and local art historical environments can be seen as extending the differences between the shapes of the disciplines in America and in Europe, as Erwin Panofsky observed long time ago,[2] or how art historical practices are affected by nationalistic justifications and motivations.[3]

The global-versus-local structure of art history is not only applicable to scholarship and writing; it is also sustained by other practices, especially curatorial practices. Art is often displayed according to national schools, and there is often an artificial separation between national or local art, on the one hand, and global art, on the other, for reasons which may range from a resurgence of nationalism or a politically sponsored "antiglobalism" to very sound museum marketing concerns. (Tourists, after all, can be legitimately expected to be interested above all in highlights of locally specific art.)

The prospect for a more intercultural art history in local contexts is thus decisively predetermined by institutional structures and traditions, which have naturally much to do with the personal interests of scholars and others within the academic and museum environment. Taking the Czech context as an example, one can see factional interests working in tandem. While the discipline of art history stubbornly resists opening its scope to include non-European art, specialists in area studies such as Sinology (some of them visibly nourishing Hegelian assumptions of the totality of culture, and proposing their knowledge of language as a master code that opens the door to understanding of any cultural form) eagerly concur that visual arts indeed should be studied from within their precincts — a stance that often ends up producing embarrassingly inadequate interpretations. There are, in short, many-sided powerful practical institutional incentives that prevent and will continue to prevent the integration of world art within art history.

II

This brief overview was instrumental in pointing out some real differences between the international shape of the discipline and various local art historical environments and their constraints. In the remaining part of this essay, whenever I invoke "Western art history" I will be referring to art history on the international scene, as opposed to the generally much less global profile of local practices. The sense of urgency of the problem of "global art history" is linked to the worry that the structure of the discipline does not accommodate non-Western, world art traditions. Speaking about Chinese painting, Elkins has observed: "It seems to me that no matter how seriously you take Chinese painting, no matter how long a time you spend studying it, if you are within art history, as it is generally construed you can never take Chinese painting as seriously as you take Western art." And further on he adds: "In order to see [Chinese art] as central … you have to give up large parts of the discipline of art history."[4]

Others argued that the (Euro-American) concept of an art object is itself inadequate and misleading and similar claims have been reiterated many times.[5] Such a sense of the inadequacy of Western art history seems to motivate also David Summers's recently published monumental effort to build a foundation for a more intercultural art history.[6] I shall therefore prefer to pursue an alternative and contrary claim, extending the thought experiment suggested by Elkins. Suppose that one were to follow the advice that in order to take Chinese painting (or any other world art form) as seriously *as* Western, to take it as central to one's expectations vis-à-vis works of art, one would have to renounce significant aspects of the Western art-historical discipline, with its concomitant value judgments, methods, etc. Having thus been relieved of such constraining baggage, what would one learn about Song Dynasty painting, or Khmer sculpture, or Maya Tikal stelae, or Sepik woodcarving, that would satisfy one's curiosity and facilitate possibilities for meaningful understanding? Presumably not much. As the distorting optics of the Western art historical trade is put aside, the very object of the interest entirely disappears — because it was precisely on account of such intellectual and cultural equipment that works of other traditions have been discovered as objects worthy of preservation, care, aesthetic mediation, and scholarly investigation in the first place. Only an extremely limited and narrow range of things relevant for contemporary viewers (as opposed to original audiences) of any work of art could be articulated from outside the scope of modern Western art history and cultural consciousness. In addressing the inadequacy of the structure of Western art history and its habits of looking and interpreting vis-à-vis non-Western art, a careful distinction should be therefore made. It is one thing to admit that the usual plots and structures of the "history of art," especially in general survey books, introductory curricula, and publications aimed at broad audience, do not adequately accommodate non-Western traditions. But that is not the same as assuming that structures and concepts of Western art history somehow stand in the way of enjoying and understanding non-Western art.

In what follows I take advantage of a conceptual scaffolding that Elkins has offered in his review as part of an attempt to systematize "five possibilities that have been proposed in recent art history and political theory" to address the challenge of world art. In my view the global art historical scene can in fact be characterized in a much more straightforward manner. The first of these five options (*art history can remain essentially unchanged as it moves into world art*) is patently not true, because the discipline is continually in flux; while the fifth (*art history can disperse as a discipline*) is highly unlikely. What has been actually going on for several decades now is the third and fourth scenarios: that is, art history has been *redefining and adjusting its working concepts to better fit non-Western art* and it has been *searching for indigenous critical concepts* — and with those two initiatives, the shape of art history is changing. But these scenarios hardly promise some sort of radical innovation of the discipline. There is indeed nothing revolutionary in incorporating native, culturally specific concepts and categories into the study and interpretations of non-European art. Scholarship concerned with non-European art from Africa to Oceania has been practicing this importation with remarkable erudition for a long time, and in the process it has been also redefining and adjusting disciplinary protocols and tools. This has undoubtedly changed the shape of art history without, however, altering its basic structure, which remains essentially Western. The concepts, methods, models of Western art history, and indeed its very purpose (however much it may be open to dispute), enriched and augmented by culturally specific concepts, seem to provide the most viable, user-friendly platform from which to address works of art of any tradition. Those concepts, methods, models, purposes, and their attendant concepts permit a range of essential questions, such as: Why does it look the way it does? What does it meant to people who made and used it? Why was it special or valuable for them? I shall provide one example and one thought experiment to substantiate this claim.

Confronted with a work such as the underground terracotta army of the First Emperor of Qin, and trying to answer some obvious questions — Why would anyone bother to bury 7000 life-size figures under the ground? Why do the soldiers look as they do? — it is possible to omit the surviving contemporaneous metaphysical and religious concepts or ideological and administrative tenets of Qin state. In fact, the category of *mingqi* (special objects made for mortuary use) has been noted and employed by Western scholars since the beginning of their interest in funerary sculpture and mortuary goods in the early twentieth century. Contemporary Chinese scholarship still tends to interpret the significance of the army with reference to the process of substitution (of living people or precious things by models) embodied by the term *mingqi*. Such a category will figure in any formal description of this complex work of art and in any attempt to reconstruct its significance or intentionality; in itself, however, *mingqi* provides only a bare foundation for a conceptual structure needed to get closer to answering the above-mentioned questions. To really understand such a work, the emic category of *mingqi* must be processed in the light of various senses of *substitution* and *representation*, taken from the long tradition of Western philosophical and art historical mediations of such terms. In a similar vein, an awareness of the Western tradition and Western art-historical discourse on representation and naturalism are instrumental in making a thorough assessment of the form of the terracotta soldiers within the real space of their deployment, and in the more nuanced description of their form — a description which would do more than just provide them with the usual unreflective labels *realism* or *naturalism*.[7] An interpretation can also take clues from recent notions of intentionality, or Western notions of ideological role of representation provided by social and structural archaeology.

In Chinese art alone, a long array of examples could be given of older and recent Western scholarship which carefully, often with enormous erudition, makes judicious use of culturally specific categories and concepts ranging from classificatory schemes and philosophical and religious concepts, to technical terms used in painting and in specific ways of looking. Such terms have long been analyzed and transferred into art-historical narratives.[8] A similar claim can be made for the art of Africa, Precolumbian America, and other cultures.

Second, a small thought experiment. If we were to compose a list of critically important concepts and terms for art history (one which should at least try not to ignore world art as unashamedly as the well-known compendium[9]), what non-Western, culture-specific categories and terms — terms potentially applicable to other artistic traditions — should we include? Of several possible candidates from Chinese art and culture, we might choose the concepts *fu gu* (return to the ancient), *da cheng* (Great Synthesis), and *zhi* (intention, but also variously translated as ideal, will, ambition, or "heart's wishes"), all extensively employed in Chinese painting theory and criticism and used by Western scholars of Chinese art. But even they do not seem to provide a range of associations and uses comparable for instance to the notions of "style" or "intention" (to name two included in the well-known anthology). Incidentally, to the best of my knowledge, none of these terms have ever been mentioned or used outside the sphere of Chinese art, either in the recent conceptual analyses of "style" or in the various meditations on postmodern stylistic plurality and the relationship to tradition. Now, is that absence a sign of ignorance and of a much-needed opening out of the discipline, which remains so Eurocentric, or is it rather a sign of the very limited potential applicability of such culturally specific terms outside of their original contexts? One could ask the same question with regard to some well-documented concepts and aesthetic categories of other cultures, such as the distinction between *pachigh* and *karam* in Pakor artifacts, or aesthetic categories in Yoruba or Fang culture, or the Japanese concept of *mono,* or the Indian *rasa.*[10]

What, then, about Elkins's next step, the more radical alternative of a "consistently non-Eurocentric art history" which, instead of merely infusing Western art history with native concepts and categories, would abandon any reliance on Western interpretive methods? Robert Nelson has claimed that "A history of art written from the aesthetic and historical perspective of the thousand-year-old-antiquarian tradition of China, for example, ought to be as valid as one composed according to the tenets of nineteenth-century European historicism, and valid not only for China but also for Europe."[11] This is obviously a mere rhetorical proposition, since the claims to legitimacy of such alternative histories would first have to be fully granted. It remains, nevertheless, difficult to imagine that such narratives, even if they aren't taken as mere curiosities, could ever change the shape and structure of art history precisely because only Western art history — unlike the Chinese antiquarian tradition or other culturally specific discourses on art and images — has been in a position to continually develop and be enriched by contact with other cultures and non-European art. One thus finds little support for Elkins's optimistic view that "the possibility of non-Western interpretive methods looms on the horizon for a genuinely multicultural world art history."

And there is another reason to temper the eager expectation that adopting non-Western art historical methods will ultimately lead to better understanding or to a more open and engaging appreciation of world art. This last reason has to do with the danger inherent in using culturally specific terms to interpret visual (or spatial) objects. As in other artistic traditions, the history of Western and Chinese interpretations of Chinese art yields numerous examples of concepts that are taken to stand for certain social facts, or express some religious, metaphysical, or historical truth. Such concepts speed up the inevitable displacement of the visual by the textual, removing the visual object from immediate consciousness and effectively sealing off the interpretation.[12] In Chinese art, examples of this sort — usually a variant of iconographic logocentrism, grafted onto native hermeneutic tradition — abound. The Chinese cultural tradition, where many paintings or images could have been intended as cryptic messages or visual puns, is very susceptible to such problems.

If, as I believe, the art historian's goal is to provide readers and viewers with conditions for more open-ended hermeneutics or interpretive play, postponing the final displacement of the visual by the verbal, then what is most promising is as complete as possible a knowledge of the relevant cultural contexts, grafted onto Eastern art historical and philosophical traditions.[13] The structure of contemporary Western art history, with its advantage of possessing an articulated interpretive consciousness — it has a historical record of its awareness, which includes an awareness of previous interpretations of cultural objects from many traditions — is much better suited for such a task.[14]

The problem does not seem to be in the structure and protocols of Western art history as such, their insufficiency or limits for interpretation and understanding of world art. The dilemma, rather, is how to transfer the enormous capital of recently specialized, culturally sensitive scholarship on both Western and non-Western traditions — scholarship destined for specialized audiences, with limited circulation and practical impact — into survey books, courses, introduction and general-purpose art historical narratives that serve to educate art historians, other professionals, and the general public. In that latter body of writing, the emphasis is still heavily on the Western art, and non-Western art is barely acknowledged. Some recent examples, such as the Metropolitan Museum of Art's *Timeline of Art History*, might point to possible solutions.[15]

III

A particularly troublesome aspect of discussions on global or world art history has to do with the very definition of artistic or cultural traditions, or cultural groups. I have so far used terms such as "Western art" and "Chinese art," which are also used by James Elkins and David Summers, quite liberally. It is worth noting that critiques of Western art history and discourse from a multiculturalist or postcolonial point of view often smack of essentialism: "Western" art is contrasted with non-Western (global) art, which is typically divided into numerous linguistically or culturally defined entities such as Chinese, Japanese, Pre-Hispanic Mesoamerican, traditional African, and so forth. There is no need to dwell here either on the arbitrariness of such geographical ordering in art historical narratives, because it has been very well pointed out recently by Robert Nelson.[16] Such a structural organization of world art is often based on a more or less articulated belief in the distinctiveness of traditions, but it projects internal coherence at the expense of profound differences within individual traditions. One can of course make a list of comparisons between "Western" and "Chinese" visual arts: on the most general level, there's the distinction between oil painting as the typical medium of Western art and ink painting as the typical medium of Chinese painting; or the different shifts from representational modes of painting to self-expression and deictic strategies; or the observation that in early China visual representations, while used in ritual and religious contexts, were typically not used to depict supernatural beings. It is also tempting to link some of the observable differences in visual arts to deep-seated philosophical, cosmological, and metaphysical patterns or structural differences; such arguments have been made by respected scholars of Chinese culture and thought: there is, for example, the classical distinction between the supposedly analogical and correlative Chinese thinking and the allegedly causal and analytical Western thinking;[17] or the notion of an essential "cosmological gulf" that allegedly separates China from the West.[18] Observations of this kind might be illuminating and helpful in particular cases, especially on the level of philosophical reflection or major conceptual synthesis, but they take us only so far when it comes to the practical considerations of art history. What are the defining characteristics of the enormously diverse artifacts and objects of "Chinese art"? In an exemplary fashion, Craig Clunas, author of the most innovative recent overview of Chinese art, opens his book by stating his reservations about the term "Chinese art," saying he prefers instead to think instead of "art in China."[19]

Essentialist beliefs in the distinctiveness and coherence of culture still flourish in Sinology, as attested by statements such as "[t]his volume tells a great story of how peculiarly, concretely Chinese the notions of 'time' and 'space' are in Chinese culture,"[20] or "[t]he name of the conference implied its organizer's belief in the distinctiveness of Chinese literature as compared to the Western tradition, as well as their wish to understand the essence of this distinctiveness."[21] Such beliefs are rarely formulated so explicitly. But despite the fact that art historians now seldom embrace essentialism based on putative linguistic or national uniqueness — the kind of essentialism to which area specialists subscribe — some of the most interesting recent conceptual treatments of Chinese art — such as Lothar Ledderose's attempt to recast the history of Chinese art as instances of a modular system — effectively do just this.[22]

The essentialist way of categorizing cultures and artistic traditions could even get a new lease on life if it appealed to the results of cognitive research on the influence of the environment on perceptual patterns, rather than to the much discredited notions of *Zeitgeist* or *mentalités*. Moreover, the rather strict environmental determinism current in the 1960s has given way to much more subtle and sophisticated research, powered by the enormous progress of cognitive science. Thus in a series of works, psychologist Richard Nisbett and his colleagues outlined fundamental differences in cognitive processes between East Asians and Westerners and presented a causal chain running from social structure to social practice to attention and perception and cognition. Their model makes space for aesthetic products as one of environmental "affordances" (as they are called in perception and cognitive research) in the environment which influences perception.[23] At the same time, such views point to the difficulties of establishing a sound interface between cognitive psychology and art history. Take Nisbett's observation (underwritten by empirical research) of a presumed basic difference between Eastern holism (in itself extending earlier explanations of the "holistic nature" of Chinese thought) and "the atomistic attitude of Westerners," their propensity to atomize and modularize.[24] How is one to reconcile such an assessment of major cognitive characteristics with Ledderose's recently proposed view of modularity as an essential creative and technological strategy of Chinese visual arts and cultural representation?[25]

In a rather curious twist on this type of scientific research, the art historian John Onians has offered a particular kind of ecological determinism, claiming that principal differences between European and Chinese painting have ecological and biological foundations. His view merits some extended quotation: "European and Chinese artists absorb different things because they see different things," he writes. Trying to explain the critical distinguishing features of Chinese art and of the Greek art that lies at the root of the European tradition, he notes:

> While the Greeks were brought up surrounded by white cliffs and rocks of hard angular limestone and marble, the inhabitants of the great valleys of the Yellow River and the Yangtze in which Chinese culture and Chinese culture grew up were used to landscape in which great streams curved through plains and burst through crumbling mountains of soft loess and where the atmosphere was often full of mists and clouds which circulated to produce a climate favorable to agricultural fertility. All who lived in China would have had brains whose visual cortex was attuned to soft tones, curving shapes and an omnipresence of water, in the earth and in the air.[26]

Ridiculous as it seems in itself, such a view opens the way for some important considerations. The point is not to deny that such culturally specific patterns of perception and visual cognition could be conditioned on a physiological basis. New findings on so-called synaptic neuronal plasticity do provide some relevant facts for art history. They demonstrate, for example, that prolonged exposure to certain forms of visual conditioning lead to subtle reorganizations of synaptic connections, establishing a certain pattern of visual skills. The research describes detailed workings of neuronal plasticity from the micro (molecular) level to the level of the brain's functional systems. It proves that the brain is not only plastic in its early phases (during ontogenesis), but is continually tuned and adjusted in response to visual and other kinds of experience.[27] New research in neurosciences and cognitive sciences thus strongly suggests that the ways we view and interpret objects are enabled by a distinct neuronal architecture and at the same time influence that architecture. Perhaps the perception of images is indeed cognitively penetrable on the level of "minimal," pre-epistemic vision. After all, the very real differences of seeing between, let's say, a connoisseur of Chinese painting and a contemporary nonexpert viewer, ultimately must be physiologically enabled, even though the science is not yet able to demonstrate precisely how this might be.

If the new research is right, then the synaptic plasticity supports the notion of specific cognitive styles, or what Michael Baxandall famously dubbed "period eyes." People who share visual environments and are engaged in distinct social practices, or who have specifiable agendas with respect to objects and images consisting of specific patterns of embodied activities, are considered to share cognitive styles.[28] In other words, cognitive styles are admissible on the level of particular local cultures, within specific temporal horizons, and even within certain strata of society, but are largely incompatible with plotting the space of art history into large geographically, linguistically, and nationally defined entities. They imply the existence of local traditions, or period eyes, connected to very specific places and periods within the large abstract categories such as "Western," "European," "Chinese," or "Latin American" art.

This is directly related to a concern of David Summers's *Real Spaces*, where he stresses that "works of art are achieved among the real forms involving and shaping human uses; as the immediate results of the more or less specialized activities of makers." Similarly, observers of works of art stand in social spatial relationships to these works, and their "observancies" have their own social spatial histories: "It is precisely at this level of habit and expectation that some of the most crucial differences (and similarities) in traditions of images and artifacts are to be located and addressed."[29] Both the making and specific history of works of art are inseparable from the concrete historical circumstances — the real spatial circumstances in which they were made and used. Cultures, for Summers, may thus be defined in terms of systems of real spatial uses as well as in terms of the values and beliefs that are associated with these uses.[30]

What seems to be underestimated, or left out from such an account of art as shaped by the real spatial uses (as opposed, that is, to being prompted by mere pictorial imagination and vision) is the role of perception and visual activities themselves in the making of those real spatial usages. It doesn't matter that most works of art were created outside the tenets of Western representationalist psychology; as Summers rightly observes, a substantial part of these real spatial experiences — habits, skills, or social competences — were actually composed of various perceptual and visual activities. At the very least, all sorts of visual activities are always firmly interlocked with the whole spectrum of human psychosomatic experiences related to objects: approaching, addressing, touching, lifting, carrying, and manipulating art. Perception and vision, as any number of examples can attest, form a central aspect of somatic and bodily experiences, notably those instrumental in handling objects and artifacts.[31] This is especially so, if perception itself is understood not so much within an orthodox representational account, based on a notion of neural processes building up an internal representation of the object in the brain,[32] but rather in accord with one of the available "heterodox accounts" that conceive of perception as a result of the interaction of brain, body, and environment.[33]

In its currently most sophisticated formulation, the concept of enactive or embodied vision elaborated by Kevin O'Regan and Alva Noë, visual experience is described as a "temporally extended pattern of exploratory activity," a form of openness to the environment. Seeing is something we do, not something that happens in our brains and consists of temporally extended pattern of exploratory activity.[34] In such an account, one's thorough knowledge of decorum, one's fluency in codes and in the constraints of usages within the real spatial conditions of artifacts would be to a great extent enabled by one's mastery of what Noë calls "patterns of sensorimotor contingency." Similarly, one's proprioceptive awareness, that is, one's awareness of sensory information about the body itself, is indissolubly linked to perception.[35]

These patterns of sensorimotor contingency, underlying perception-in-action (or perception-as-action) would then form a cognitive skeleton of "habits" and cultural competences; alternatively, the cognitive styles of given culture are substantially shaped by the "deep reservoirs of real spatial experience and habits" that are connected to the use of artifacts and symbolic systems.[36] This would provide an additional reason why they cannot be mechanistically equated with linguistic or national categories such as "Chinese," "Mayan," "African," or "Western," but should be sought on a much more specific level. The main problem would be to define such spatially and temporally specific entities and relate them to ethnic, linguistic, or geopolitically defined groups. I shall return to this thorny question after briefly considering one specific example.

The example at hand is familiar to me not as object of art historical inquiry, but rather from my interest in photographing Baroque limestone statues, which once dotted Central European countryside, until a recent increase of organized crime threatened their disappearance. In trying to capture the spaces inhabited by these statues within the surrounding landscape, I have been trying to understand (to borrow Summers's terminology) the real spatial conditions of these sculptures, how the perception of them intersects with one's visual consciousness of surrounding landscape, and how the very possibilities of meaning and their ontological status are inseparably linked to the spatial framework of their existence. These sculptures are products of a not very remote past, most of them having been made from the eighteenth to the early nineteenth centuries, in a countryside I know very well, by people whose languages I speak, who share my understanding of basic religious and ideological tenets. Unlike most works of art in museum collections, these statues (or, rather, those not taken by the thieves) are to be found *in situ*, in the original "real spaces." These *loci* may have undergone some changes over time, but they have kept their topographies. Nor were these sculptures the objects of complicated activities. In comparison to most museum objects, from prehistoric cave paintings to Japanese *chinso* sculptures, to Gothic altarpieces and countless others, they present a rather uncomplicated case. With a reasonable degree of plausibility, one can infer the kinds of uses made of these sculptures: passing by, circumambulating, paying respect, facing them, glancing at them, perhaps (and only in some instances) addressing them verbally, touching them, laying simple symbolic offerings before them, or lifting candles in front of them. As compared to most works of art these are relatively simple, nonspecific uses and simple symbolic behavior. All such forms of *handling* are inseparably linked and coextensive with forms of *perceiving*. But despite the seeming proximity, the more time I have spent thinking about the ways these sculptures were observed and addressed by their original audiences, the more I feel that they are indeed a product of a different "period eye," and much as the specific real spatiotemporal experiences they induced may seem "closer" or not so distant as the spatiotemporal experiences of observers or users of *Coatlicue*, Shang dynasty bronze *guang*, or Maori tattooing, they are still emphatically not mine. I can never hope to attain cognitively the kind of seeing and habits the original audiences had when such objects entered their consciousness, but only hope to arrive at some approximations of them. And how should such be conceptualized?

If works of art are to be taken as potential guides to other worlds, to other human choices and possibilities (as Summers urges us to do), then these specifics should be respected and not subsumed under essentialist, nationalist, or linguistic categories such as "Western" or "Chinese." Thus the insistence on truly multicultural and global art history, taken to its logical conclusion, would have to insist on granting all objects the spatiotemporal particularity of the specific past from which they have come to us, and to dispense with notions such as "Western," "Chinese," "traditional African," and "Latin American." To Elkins's list of scenarios we should therefore add at least this sixth option: art history as a patchwork of specifically defined local traditions or "period eyes."

Unfortunately this is neither an easy nor perhaps a very practical proposition. The difficult questions it raises mostly have to do to with the problem of how to go about defining all those local and specific spatiotemporal horizons for the production, use, and knowledge of art. First of all, there is a fact of scale and commensurability: an attempt to list for example the characteristics of Maya art would raise some doubts, but the essentialism implicit here seems somewhat less inappropriate than in cases such as "European" or "Chinese" art.[37] This brings up again the problem of how the "deep reservoirs of spatiotemporal experiences" and habits and period eyes relate to traditionally defined cultural groups or cultures and their world views or mentalities. And it becomes progressively less troublesome in the case of other geographically or temporarily restricted traditions, for instance "Yoruba carving," "Dogon world view," "Fang aesthetics," "Haida sculpture," or "Walpiri iconography."

In such cases, I think that charges of essentialism hardly come to mind. A nonspecialist would be likely to assume some cultural continuity and coherence among such groups, and that would be justified by solid anthropological and historical evidence.[38] Perhaps art historians or archaeologists can avoid thinking in terms of nonspatial or ahistorical generative structures, and insist instead that cultural constructs should be defined precisely by the demonstrable differences in their artifacts and images, and by the ways those objects are distributed and handled.[39] But there is still a palpable asymmetry between the notion of the real spatial experiences (habits, or cultural competences) associated with the use of symbolic artifacts and the cognitive styles or "period eyes" of their viewers and users, as the following example will demonstrate. A visitor to a museum in the late nineteenth century, standing in front of a framed painting, will not have behaved in importantly different ways from a viewer in a contemporary, twenty-first-century museum. At the same time the latter will exhibit different patterns of seeing, of attentional and perceptual routines, of ways of coming to terms with the painting. In ways that are experimentally measurable and observable, he or she may be said to possess a different period eye. There are also specific spatiotemporal experiences related to handling, say, a fourteenth-century reliquary commissioned by a high-ranking and devout aristocrat. Such an encounter would also have involved very different patterns of perception-in-action than the visual and somatic experiences involved when the same person would encounter an altarpiece.

In most cases we obviously don't possess enough independent information to infer social practices and patterns of perception and action from the objects themselves.[40] How then can art history reconcile a respect for the radical spatiotemporal uniqueness of many distinct art traditions and local "period eyes" with the need to meaningfully organize this diversity into larger plots and narratives, for the general purposes of presenting, publishing, and teaching about visual arts? (And even for such apparently trivial tasks as labeling shelves in bookstores.) The ideal of truly multicultural art history — and incidentally also of David Summers's book — cannot be fulfilled by a spectrum, where any number of traditions defined in terms of nations, ethnicities, or languages are given their due alongside whatever counts as "Western." Truly intercultural art history, taken to its logical conclusion, will have to resemble a network or a dense mosaic of narrowly defined cultural groups, or local and particular cognitive styles (or period eyes), each with its local spatiotemporal horizon for the production and use of art. However, unlike essentialist categories, which come naturally to hand and can be easily plotted into various periodizations and geographical divisions, it would make no sense to organize the specialized "period eyes."[41] It will always be up to individual interpreters concerned with particular traditions to reconstruct the relevant practices and relate them to their respective cultural groups or *argument gemeinschaften* (in Oskar Bätschmann's phrase).[42]

In the end, the very program of attending to cultural uniqueness as against a leveling essentialism runs the risk of essentialism, especially when it is driven by politics — by the more or less explicit need of a scholar or group of scholars to legitimize some culture as an independent field of study.[43]

IV

If the ethics of the study of art is to be seen in facilitating the enjoyment and understanding of art objects, as well as in finding some insight into the lives and sensibilities of the people who made and used the art, then the topic of global art history will sooner or later face the issue of universals: a concept that enjoys little prestige in contemporary humanities. Appeals to "essential human conditions," a "common humanity," or an "inner spiritual core" may have legitimate roles in particular kinds of rhetoric, but they provide a feeble foundation for thinking about global art history.[44] A different way of engaging universals, that of anthropological research on cross-cultural patterns in art creation and appreciation — I am thinking of the so-called aesthetic universals — was pursued with scientific rigor in 1960s and 1970s, but did not provide much nourishment for art history. Attempts were made to objectively determine the universality of aesthetic values; the investigators typically concluded that there are some universal formal categories such as symmetry, proportion, balance, and repose, and that the aesthetic appeal of a work of art depends partly on the universals of human nature.[45] Not surprisingly, such views were seldom found useful for the interpretation and presentation of works of art. Many anthropologists engaged in study of "ethnoart" agreed that to understand and appreciate the aesthetic dimensions of other cultures one needs to study their images not as isolated aesthetic phenomena but rather in the context of social action and the lives of human actors — which, as is well known, is precisely what influential strands of art history have been doing since the 1970s, and what contextual art history, visual anthropology, and the sociology of perception have been doing ever since.

Presently, the problem of universals in art and the human mind is benefiting from new research in neuroscience and cognitive science; there is emerging interest in the implication of these finds for the social sciences and humanities. Increasingly clear and complex knowledge about the neural substrate of perception and cognition, including visual processing and the modularity of human vision, as well as the processing of emotions, all provide a solid foundation for reconsidering the role of biological universals in perceptual and aesthetic experience. Again, however, art history has so far been largely reticent about these implications — perhaps understandably, since art historians are faced with the unbridled optimism of some neuroscientists who try to spell out the implications of brain research for art and aesthetics.[46]

It is therefore one of the major accomplishments of Summers's project that it is anchored in a humanist study of art, which sees art as opening a way to human understanding. His project reengages the question of universals from a different perspective. His contribution is founded in the belief that there are universal elements of embodied experience that provide the possibility of understanding worlds of art of different cultures; such a purpose shifts the emphasis from universals of human psychology and neurology to the category of space, where they are more immediately accessible by art historians and offer much greater utility. Ironically, this provides only temporary respite from biology and psychology. Summers's insistence that any manifestation of cultural difference is finally rooted in real spatial conditions, which themselves take their "irreducible importance" from conditions of human embodiment, points back to the human body as the nexus of psychosomatic processes. The treacherous problem here, as Elkins elaborates, is that the universal elements of embodied experience evoked by Summers can be both nonspecific and uncognized and in any case they may be exceedingly difficult to specify.

Appeals to universal elements of embodied experience, or to biological or cognitive universals, may not be of much help to the art historian's task of reconstructing the specific historical circumstances of particular works of art, and they are particularly at odds with the normal narrative forms of art historical exposition. But they will become all the more important if and when art historical accounts are no longer aimed at intellectual understanding, but are constructed to enjoin an imaginative empathy in the reader or viewer; in that case understanding will depend on the viewer's deployment of many modes of mental representations.[47] The true difficulties and desiderata of a global art history will then be less a matter of complying with multiculturalists' demands that art historical narratives be amended, or their lacunae filled. The real challenge will be in reconciling a dedication to the uniqueness of diverse art traditions and the culturally specific ways in which art has been created, with a faith in certain universal dispositions of human consciousness: what is needed is an ability to engage both sides, and to embody them as powerfully as possible in art historical narratives and strategies of art presentation.[48]

Notes

1. An example, in the area of the arts of China may be the notion that Chinese art can be better grasped through what James Cahill called an "intuitive, holistic approach, a kind of lyric metacriticism," which experiences the object from inside, rather than by analytical approaches from outside (see *The Barnhart-Cahill-Rogers Correspondence, 1981* [Berkeley CA, 1982], 60.) Analogies to such an approach can be found elsewhere in Western art traditions — for example the long-persisting notion that art of the Slavonic nations allegedly exhibits "distinct qualities" (it is "lyric" or "rustic") necessitating a kind of introspective understanding from within.
2. Panofsky observes that "what made the greatest impression on the stranger when first becoming aware of what was happening in America was this: where the European art historians were conditioned to think in terms of national and regional boundaries, no such limitations existed for the Americans." In this regard his remarks on the role of languages in shaping the art historical practice are very pertinent; see Panofsky, "Three Decades of Art History in the Unites States: Impressions of a Transplanted European," the Epilogue to his *Meaning in the Visual Arts* (New York, 1955), 325–38.
3. Some of these issues have been recently discussed, for example in *The Art Historian: National Traditions and Institutional Practices,* edited by Michael Zimmermann (Williamstown, 2003), and *Die Kunsthistoriographien in Ostmitteleuropa und der nationale Diskurs,* edited by Robert Born, Alena Janatková, and Adam Labuda (Berlin, 2004).
4. Elkins, in interview with Tamara Bissell, *Umění* 46 (1998): 151. For convenience's sake, I leave aside the rather specific status of Chinese art within other non-European traditions (which Elkins himself notes), and assume that any other tradition could stand here in place of Chinese art.
5. Cecilia Klein, "Objects Are Nice, But ...," *Art Bulletin* 76 no. 3 (1994): 402.
6. *Real Spaces: World Art History and the Rise of Western Modernism* (London, 2003).
7. Such description would escape the often repeated shortcut interpretation of form in relation to meaning, the kind to which ironically Summers himself falls prey in his brief description of the Qin army ("these terracotta soldiers have the presence of life, and were evidently intended as nearly as was practicable to be effigies"; *Real Spaces,* 235). What presence of life? Effigies in which sense? I have discussed these issues and the possibilities of reading the form of soldiers in relation to their function and significance in "Likeness of No One: (Re)Presenting the First Emperor's Army,"

Art Bulletin 77 no. 1 (1995): 115–17. Lothar von Falkenhausen first suggested that the tomb figures (*mingqi*) were intended precisely not to be perceived as lifelike and have presence of life, but rather to proclaim their difference from real people and things (von Falkenhausen, "Ahnenkult und Grabkult im Staat Qin: Der religiose Hintergrund der Terrakotta-Armee," in *Jenseits der grossen Mauer: Der Erste Kaiser von China und seine Terrakotta Armee*, edited by Lothar Ledderose and Adele Schlombs (Dortmund, 1990), 46–47.

8. In some cases, what is examined is the potential of a culture-specific concept to affect the very structure of interpretation, as well demonstrated for example by Kiyohiko Munakata's exposition of *gan-lei* ("symbolic correlation system" or "response of the kinds") for the interpretation of some early Chinese imagery (Kiyohiko Munakata, "Concepts of *Lei* and *Kan-lei* in Early Chinese Art Theory," in *Theories of the Arts in China*, edited by Susan Bush and Christian Murck [Princeton NJ, 1983], 105–31). Another example is John Hay's insightful reconsideration and paraphrase of two key terms of Chinese painting criticism — *qiyun shendong* and *gufa yongbi* (two of Xie He's *liu fa*) through a comprehensive framework of modern Western philosophy; see "Values and History in Chinese Painting, I. Hsieh Ho Revisited," *Res* 6 (Fall 1983): 73–111, and "Values and History in Chinese Painting, II. The Hieratic Evolution of Structure," *Res* 7–8 (Spring 1984): 103–36. But in such cases, in the course of the transfer, the native concepts and categories serve to substantially accommodate a modern interpretation, while remaining embedded in a basically Western art historical framework. On the other hand, some recent attempts to use culturally and linguistically specific concepts and categories, while posing as a "fresh" perspective, should not seduce anyone to expect that such a practice can significantly change the protocols of interpretation or the shape of art history. I am referring to Wu Hung's discussion of monumentality in early Chinese art and his "discovery" of the term *liqi* (ritual objects) in *Monumentality in Early Chinese Art and Architecture* (Stanford CA, 1995), esp. 10–15, 24–28. Robert Bagley, in his harsh review of the book, is nevertheless correct to expose the false pretense of implying that the use of such terms constitutes a new approach with far-reaching implications (Bagley, in *Harvard Journal of Asiatic Studies* 58 no. 1 [1996]: 221–56).
9. *Critical Terms for Art History*, first edition, edited by Robert Nelson and Richard Shiff (Chicago, 1996).
10. Most such terms, however, relate to the appreciation of the beauty or form of manufactured objects and images, but not to other art historical interests and procedures. The examination of indigenous lexica for aesthetic experience has a long tradition and has built a solid ground for the budding field of intercultural aesthetics; see Irene Winter, "Defining 'Aesthetics' for Non-Western Studies: The Case of Ancient Mesopotamia," in *Art History, Aesthetics, Visual Studies*, edited by Michael Ann Holly and Keith Moxey (Williamstown MA, 2002), 3–28; Wilfried van Damme, "Transcultural Aesthetics and the Study of Beauty," online at www.unibo.it/transculturality/files/09%20damme.pdf (accessed 16 September 2005).

11. Robert Nelson, "The Map of Art History," *Art Bulletin* 79 no. 1 (1997): 40.
12. On the displacement inherent in any act of understanding a work of art see Thomas Crow, *The Intelligence of Art* (Chapel Hill NC, 1999), 1–5. Wolfgang Iser, one of the leading figures of literary *Rezeptionaesthetik*, claims in his latest book that any act of understanding has always been an act of translation (*Range of Interpretation* [New York, 2000]).
13. That is the kind of hermeneutic approach generally proposed by Hans Georg Gadamer in his *Truth and Method.*
14. I realize that the notion of understanding a work of art as postponing the final displacement of visual for something else, of extending and complicating the act of translation, and of making such translation recursive from visual form to facts, is a move that is indebted to twentieth-century philosophy; it is a culturally specific modern Western notion. However in my view it is applicable in principle to any visual artifact.
15. www.metmuseum.org. See also *Atlas of World Art*, edited by John Onians (London, 2004).
16. Nelson, "The Map of Art History."
17. The classical formulation of such fundamental differences in Western and Chinese thinking is Marcel Granet, *La pensée chinoise* (Paris, 1934).
18. On the cosmological gulf between China and the West see Frederick Mote, "The Cosmological Gulf between China and the West," in *Transition and Permanence,* edited by David C. Buxbaum (Hong Kong, 1972), 3–21.
19. Craig Clunas, *Art in China* (Oxford, 1997), 9–12. See also one of Cahill's "Five Faults in Chinese Painting Studies," one of them being "harmonizing" (Cahill, *The Barnhart-Cahill-Rogers Correspondence,* 63.)
20. *Time & Space in Chinese Culture,* edited by Chun-chieh Huang and Erik Zürcher (Leiden and New York, 1995), 3; however, with very little comparative perspective and no consideration of current explanatory models in cultural psychology and cognition, the volume — typically — does not deliver such a promise.
21. *Recarving the Dragon: Understanding Chinese Poetics,* edited by Olga Lomová, Studia Orientalia Pragensia 23 (Prague, 2003), 1.
22. Ledderose, *Ten Thousand Things: Module and Mass Production in Chinese Art* (Princeton NJ, 2000). The essentializing overtones were duly noted by the reviewers of this remarkable book; see Jonathan Hay in *Art Bulletin* 86 no. 2 (2004): 381–83. I have argued elsewhere against this essentializing habit and its uses in contemporary art history; see "On Alien Art and Experiencing Art Fully: Gombrich-Kesner Correspondence," *Umění* 42 (1994): 107–15.
23. Richard Nisbett and Takahiko Masuda, "Culture and Point of View," *Proceedings of the National Academy of Sciences USA* 100 no. 19 (2003) 11163–70; Richard Nisbett, Kaiping Peng, Incheol Choi, and Ara Norenzayan, "Culture and Systems of Thoughts: Holistic versus Analytic Cognition," *Psychological Review* 108 no. 2 (2001): 291–310; and see especially Richard Nisbett, *The Geography of Thought: How Asians and Westerners Think Differently, and Why* (New York, 2003), which uses contemporary cognitive research to articulate presumed basic differences in thought and perception between Westerners and East Asians.
24. Nisbett, Richard Nisbett, *The Geography of Thought*, 82–83.

25. Ledderose, *Ten Thousand Things*. Lothar von Falkenhausen in his review of the book rightly points out the difficulty or impossibility of defining cultural specificity of Chinese art in terms of a mediation of artistic creativity through the use of modules (von Falkenhausen, in *Artibus Asiae* 60 no. 2 [2000]: 342–44).
26. John Onians, "Chinese Painting in the Twentieth Century and in the Context of World Art Studies," in *Chinese Painting in the Twentieth Century: Creativity in the Aftermath of Tradition*, edited by Cao Yiqiang and Fan Jingzhong (Hangzhou, 1997), 500–506. The scientific rationalization for such an assertion could be sought in the long tradition of the study of the environmental influence on visual perception, and equally in ecological psychology, both harking back to W.H. Rivers's experimental psychology research in the Torres Straits. See for example J.L. Fischer, "Art Styles as Cultural Cognitive Maps," *American Anthropologist* 63 (1961): 79–93; Michael Robbins, "Material Culture and Cognition," *American Anthropologist* 68 no. 3 (1966): 745–48, and especially Marshall Segall, Donald Campbell and Melville Herskovits, *The Influence of Culture on Visual Perception* (Indianapolis IN, 1966); and for useful overview, Michael Cole, *Cultural Psychology: A Once and Future Discipline* (Cambridge MA and London, 1996), esp. 38–52.
27. Charles Gilbert et al., "Spatial Integration and Cortical Dynamics," *Proceedings of the National Academy of Sciences USA* 93 (January 1996): 615–22; Dale Purves and Timothy Andrews, "The Perception of Transparent Three-Dimensional Objects, *Proceedings of the National Academy of Sciences USA* 94 (June 1997): 6517–22; Antonio Damasio, *Descartes' Error: Emotion, Reason and the Human Brain* (New York, 1994), 108–13. For the role of culture in what he calls the theory of epigenesis by selective stabilization of neurons and synapses, see Jean-Pierre Changeaux, *Neuronal Man: The Biology of Mind* (Princeton NJ, 1997), 241–49; and for a complex overview of synaptic plasticity Peter Huttenlocher, *Neural Plasticity: The Effects of Environment on the Development of the Cerebral Cortex* (Cambridge MA, 2003).
28. *Painting and Experience in Fifteenth-Century Italy* (Oxford, 1972), esp. 29–108.
29. Summers, *Real Spaces*, 41–42. It should be noted (although the proper elaboration is well beyond the scope of this article), that further opportunities seem to open in reconsidering Summers's notions of real spatial (that is, cultural) experiences within the cognitive view of culture, for instance the concepts of cultural models recently discussed by Bradd Shore in *Culture in Mind: Cognition, Culture, and the Problem of Meaning* (New York and Oxford, 1996), esp. Chap. 2.
30. Summers, *Real Spaces*, 53–55.
31. For example with respect to Christian iconography, aspects of attention to images within the framework of ritual and liturgical handling of objects are discussed by Staale Sinding-Larsen, *Iconography and Ritual: A Study of Analytical Perspective* (Oslo, 1984), esp. 95ff.
32. I do not mean to imply that a representationalist account, empowered by recent progress in neuroscience, is no longer relevant or to be discarded. For a typical account along these lines, see Semir Zeki, *Inner Vision: An Exploration of Art and the Brain* (Oxford, 1999).

33. The ancestry of such heterodox accounts of perception includes Merleau-Ponty's phenomenology of perception, as well as J. J. Gibson's ecological paradigm of perception (Gibson, *The Senses Considered as Perceptual System* [Boston, 1966] and Gibson, *The Ecological Approach to Visual Perception* [Boston, 1979]).
34. Alva Noë and Kevin O'Regan, "What It Is Like to See: A Sensorimotor Account of Vision and Visual Consciousness," *Behavioral and Brain Sciences* 24 no. 5 (2001): 883–917; Noë and O'Regan, "On the Brain-Basis of Visual Consciousness: A Sensorimotor Account," in *Vision and Mind: Selected Readings in the Philosophy of Perception,* edited by Alva Noë and Evan Thompson (Cambridge MA, 2002), 567–98, and, most recently, Alva Noë, *Action in Perception* (Cambridge MA, 2004). See also Andy Clarke's "action-oriented" representation model, where perception, cognition, and action are similarly closely integrated. Andy Clark, "Where Brain, Body, and World Collide," *Daedalus* 1999, 257–80; and Clark, "Embodiment and the Philosophy of Mind," in *Current Issues in Philosophy of Mind*, edited by A. O'Hear, *Royal Institute of Philosophy Supplement 43* (Cambridge 1998), 35–52.
35. Shaun Gallagher, *How the Body Shapes the Mind* (Oxford, 2005).
36. Cognitive style can be most generally equated with behavior, or the processes of mediation between stimuli and responses. "The term cognitive style refers to the characteristic ways in which individuals conceptually organize the environment." (Kenneth Goldstein and Sheldon Blackman, *Cognitive Style: Five Approaches and Relevant Research* [New York, 1978], 2 and see the subsequent discussion.) I am using the term "cognitive style" with some reservation, as it is by no means an uncontroversial concept among psychologists and cognitive scientists. For a rather reserved account of cognitive style see Cole, *Cultural Psychology,* 92–96.
37. Linda Schele and Mary Ellen Miller, *The Blood of Kings: Dynasty and Ritual in Maya Art* (London, 1992), esp. 33–40. The exhibition was based on the concept of "Maya art" as a distinct entity, one that represents the entire civilization. The same approach can be found in similar exhibitions. Statements such as "[t]he Maya created one of the great art traditions of the world, one that stands beside the art of the ancient Egyptians or the early Chinese" (p. 40) are necessary to construct and market such an exhibition; but they foster the essentialism with which I am concerned.
38. Some of these problems are discussed in Allan Langdale, "Aspects of the Critical Reception and Intellectual History of Baxandall's Concept of the Period Eye," *Art History* 21 no. 4 (1998): 17–35; for some important observations on the problem of defining "mutual knowledge systems" and establishing links between the specific meanings of objects and artifacts and particular historical properties people may possess, see Whitney Davis's review of *Object and Intellect: Interpretations of Meaning in African Art* (a special issue of *the Art Journal,* 47 no. 2, 1988), in *African Archaeology Review* 1990, 26–27.
39. Taking issue with the way Maya were defined in the exhibition *Blood of Kings,* one specialist typically asks: "What are the deeper aspatial and atemporal generative structures, relations, or meanings that define Maya and give meaning to Maya history within the broader Mesoamerican

cultural area[?]" Don Rice, "Historical Contexts and Interpretive Themes," in *Word and Image in Maya Culture: Explorations in Language, Writing, and Representation,* edited by William Hanks and Don Rice (Salt Lake City UT, 1989), 5.

40. Or essentially what Panofsky called the "principle of disjunction" in *Renaissance and Renascences in Western Art* (Stockholm, 1960), esp. 84–106. As George Kubler usefully reminds us: "[c]ontinuous form does not predicate continuous meaning, nor does continuity of form or of meaning necessarily imply continuity of culture." Kubler, "Period, Style, and Meaning in Ancient American Art," *New Literary History* 1–2 (1970): 143–44.
41. It seems to me that in this issue David Summers's book is curiously silent about the implication of its own principal thesis.
42. For "argument gemeinschaften" see Bätschmann, *Einführung in die kunstgeschichtliche Hermeneutik: die Auslegung von Bildern* (Darmstadt, Germany 1984).
43. In an illuminating case study of such a pattern, Lothar von Falkenhausen described a peculiar twist in recent Chinese archaeology, a process of "regional supremacism" as a new regionalist form of centralism, whereby archaeological remains in a given province are purposefully interpreted as those of a distinct state or ethnic group. He sees such a paradigm as linked to strategies of competitive positioning within the profession in an environment of scarce resources. See von Falkenhausen, "The Regionalist Paradigm in Chinese Archaeology" in *Nationalism, Politics, and the Practice of Archaeology,* edited by Philip Kohl and Clare Fawcett (Cambridge, 1995), 198–217.
44. Such terms are employed by Richard Eglin in *In Defense of Humanism: Values in the Arts and Letters* (Cambridge, 1996); in my view, his assertive use of such concepts with no attempt to link them to contemporary scientific notions of the nature of affective and cognitive processes effectively undermines his purpose of defending the possibility of understanding cultural values.
45. For example I. L. Child and L. Siroto, "Bakwele and American Aesthetic Evaluations Compared," *Ethnology* 4 (1965): 349–60.
46. It is perhaps understandable, but nonetheless regrettable, that the ability to expertly present the new neuroscience knowledge on vision, perception or even consciousness, does not temper the urge of some neuroscientists to construe grand universal theories of aesthetic experience, which range from modestly presented, but not very convincing ones (Semir Zeki, *Inner Vision*) to ridiculously reductive and trivial ones (V.S. Ramachandran and William Hirstein, "The Science of Art: A Neurological Theory of Aesthetic Experience," *Journal of Consciousness Studies* 6 [1999]: 15–51 and see also the largely negative reactions to it in the same volume, pp. 52–75, and in the *Journal of Consciousness Studies* 7 [2000]: 17–42).
47. In her biology-informed anthropology of art, Emily Dissanayake provided a sketch of a psychobiological account of aesthetic empathy. She examines "specific universal predispositions" in human perception/cognition that are "emphatic" in this sense, including spatial thinking and a range of cognitive universals or primitives such as binarism, prototype recognition, closure and boundedess, figure/ground, repetition, analogy, and metaphor. (*Homo Aestheticus: Where Art Comes From and Why* [New York,

1992], esp. 140–93.) Of particular importance are the new findings on the imitative capacity of human minds; see *Perspectives on Imitation: From Cognitive Neuroscience to Social Science,* edited by Susan Hurley and Nick Chater (Cambridge MA, 2005).

48. As one advocate of the much-despised traditional humanism observes: "it is always worthwhile to make the initial assumption that even in foreign countries and in distant ages we have to do with people who are not all that different from ourselves — even through this assumption may occasionally fail to stand a further test." (Ernst Gombrich, "'They Were All Human Beings — So Much Is Plain': Reflection on Cultural Relativism in the Humanities," *Critical Inquiry* 13 no. 4 [1987]: 693.)

3

The Art Seminar

This conversation was held March 13, 2005, at the University College Cork, Ireland. The participants were: Friedrich Teja Bach (Universität Wien), James Elkins (University College Cork/ School of the Art Institute of Chicago), Andrea Giunta (Universidad de Buenos Aires), Ladislav Kesner (then Charles University, Prague), Sandra Klopper (Universiteit van Stellenbosch, South Africa), and David Summers (University of Virginia).

James Elkins: I'd like to begin by speaking, in a general way, about the physical conditions of art history worldwide. The University of Maryland published a document about art history in sub-Saharan Africa; it surveys about ten mainly French-speaking countries. The picture it paints is very different from the experience of art history in much of the world. In several countries there are art historians with no students, virtually no books, and often no slides. From other sources I have been made aware of the fact that in some African universities — in Nigeria, for example — the salaries of the professors are paid so irregularly that they are compelled to charge students for courses, creating a market economy in which students opt for the best combination of utility and cost. And of course it's common experience in many parts of the world that a full-time, permanent lectureship or even a professorship may not pay the bills, making it necessary to have two and even three jobs. It would go without saying that such situations make research impossible — it would, that is, except some researchers, particularly in North America, are not aware how common those situations are.

The question this kind of material poses is whether deficits like these mean there is simply *less* art history being done (so that an infusion of money would decrease the difference betwen such conditions and, say, European ones), or whether it affects the content in some other way.

Sandra Klopper: Perhaps I should say that yesterday, when we were preparing for this panel, Jim said that he found the situation in South Africa, as I present it in my essay, to be depressing. I beg to differ: I don't think our situation is depressing. It simply forces us to be resourceful in ways that make us do things differently. The art history we teach is very different from art history as it is practiced in, say, America and Britain.

The canon of art, as it is taught in first-world countries, presents a problem for South Africa on account of the history of colonialism in Africa. There has been a shift towards validating indigenous art and archaeological material in recent years. This has been happening in South Africa especially since the emergence of democracy in the 1990s, and so, increasingly, we are teaching not European art, but rather concentrating on local and contemporary South African art and popular culture. An enormous shift is taking place, away from a Western history of art.

JE: And yet, as you've said, the textbooks of African art are not themselves produced in South Africa.

SK: Yes, these texts are being produced mainly by American scholars, many of whom first encountered Africa through the Peace Corps or because their parents were missionaries. In South Africa — and the rest of Africa — the pressing need to devote one's energies to teaching students at undergraduate as well as postgraduate level, together with the absence of a large market for academic books dealing with comparatively esoteric subjects like art, mitigates against the production of textbooks. With very few exceptions we therefore rely on texts collated by American scholars for a primarily American audience. These texts often draw on primary research done by scholars based in Africa, some of whom have even been asked to contribute to their production.

But the situation today is very different from what it was when I was an undergraduate student in the 1970s. In those years, many of my lecturers were South Africans who had studied at places like the Courtauld Institute, so they were never exposed to alternative, non-Eurocentric perceptions and values about what constitutes fine art.

JE: When I was assembling this panel, I had difficulty locating art historians who work in Africa; I found a number in North America, but I wanted to avoid inviting too many people from North America and Europe. The University of Maryland study makes an explicit reference to the "brain drain" in sub-Saharan Africa, suggesting that scholars who identify themselves as art historians find that more than simply economic pressures impel them to look for work elsewhere.

SK: Mainly, though, they emigrate because of the lack of adequate resources. Olu Oguibe, a Nigerian art historian, is an example. He is also an artist, and that in itself is common in the African context because art history tends to be taught in a fine-art context.

JE: That also happens, for example, in China. I wonder if the percentage of art historians who are also artists, or who have been artists, is lowest in the United States and western Europe …

SK: Olu speaks about the expatriation of Nigerian art historians; you will find highly qualified, very well-educated Nigerian art historians in many of the larger art history departments across the United States. As far as I know, none ever return to Nigeria.

Andrea Giunta: Such levels of expatriation have not taken place in Latin America, at least not yet. It may be a case where something like the contrary is true: many art historians who do undergraduate or postgraduate-level studies in the United States have then gone back to their countries in order to teach at universities, work at museums or become independent curators. There are temporary migrations, to do residencies as visiting professors, but not an overall "brain drain" (one exception would be Carlos Basualdo, for example, educated in Argentina and working as an independent curator in the United States, fundamentally focused on Latin American art). On the other hand, this wouldn't be very positive for studies of Latin American art in either the United States or Latin America.

What would be ideal would be professors who split their time between the United States and Latin American universities, in order to generate joint projects. It is neither in the United States nor Europe where the highest level of research on Latin American art can be found. It's in Latin America. In spite of the fact that it is true that a professor or researcher in a Latin American university can hardly expect to live on that job alone and is obliged to carry out other related activities (conferences, articles, or curatorial projects), this is a good moment for research. This is not reflected by the same indicators used to measure art history's situation in the United States (the quantity of art history departments, or the number of specialist magazines), but essentially in the increasing number of books being published. This new bibliography does not focus on general histories, constructing a wide-ranging narrative of Latin American art or of each nation's art, and it does not offer a biographical perspective or catalogues raisonné, but rather on the analysis of specific periods and issues. On the other hand, even while the number of art history departments in Latin America remains relatively small, there are networks of exchange that are generated by seminars and symposia that permit researchers to maintain actively in contact. I believe that this network is more visible as seen from the United States (in some art history and Spanish or Romance Studies departments) than it is from Europe.

SK: Ironically, the same is true for Africa because it is in America that the study of African art has really taken off in the last forty to fifty years. In England there is SOAS [the School of African and Oriental Studies at the University of London] and the University of East Anglia, but little else to connect African scholars of African art with Europe.

AG: I would add that generally, art historians in Latin America do not come from a visual arts background. Although some may have initially studied architecture, history or philosophy, a large part of their education is in degree courses in art history or in master's or PhD programs. This formative process has been present for the past fifteen years; previously it was not the case. It corresponds to transformations in the academic field. In this sense, ours is a discipline without a strong previous local tradition.

Ladislav Kesner: Getting back to Jim's question about the physical or material conditions, I am sure that material deficits mean less art history, and they also affect content. On a plane to Dublin, I just read a newspaper article ridiculing a new breed of so-called "turbocharged professors" in my country, who occupy two or three full-time jobs at different universities at once to get more adequate income and essentially spend their time speeding from one place to another; there are such people in art history and the implications are obvious. Material deficits, however relative this designation is, certainly are a very real problem in most places art history is being practiced. That said, I have heard them often invoked as an explanandum for whatever had not been accomplished, or should have been of much better quality.

So I cannot help but to see it also the other way around: poor or insufficient material conditions are also a consequence of art history's aloof isolationism, its inability to demonstrate why it matters and why it should be given more adequate funding. Certainly in my country, the unwillingness of art historians to truly reflect on their audiences, to be held accountable for what they really contribute to society in exchange for public support, and to subscribe to some form of qualitative judgments of their work is endemic.

JE: Let's turn from questions of conditions to questions of content. I propose we divide our conversation into two parts. To begin, let's talk about the books and scholars who compose art history worldwide, and then about the concepts and terms that structure art historical interpretation.

Just to start with an emblematic example: the University of Maryland survey notes that in Dakar, one art historian uses a book called *Aesthetics from Plato to Michaud* for the introductory art survey — it's a book I have been unable to trace.[1] I remember, Sandra, that after a long talk about conceptual issues — those I hope to raise in the second part of our conversation — including mention of Heidegger, Merleau-Ponty, and Husserl, you said, "We no longer use those sources in South African art history: we don't even look at people like T.J. Clark, Thomas Crow, or Michael Baxandall."

SK: Let alone Wölfflin or any of the older theorists.

LK: Baxandall, and specifically his theory of intention, has only recently been received in Czech art history. Sometimes you have to allow time for major conceptual revisions.

JE: In China, Baxandall has only recently been translated, by Cao Yiqiang. That could be seen as an odd choice given the existing translations from English, which include Gombrich (there have been Chinese translations of his books for several decades) and, in 1999 I believe, Wölfflin.[2] That makes for an interesting situation for young Chinese art historians: it is hard to imagine how a history of twentieth-century art historical thinking could be reconstructed from the quite disparate sources that are currently available. Selections like those cannot be taken simply as parts of a larger picture that remains to be completed: they have to tell a story by themselves, and that story is therefore not only partial but essentially different from the stories we might tell.

And this is then different in kind from the situation you described, Sandra, when you remarked that Baxandall simply isn't present any more in South African art history. That is not belatedness; it is more like absence — or really, an amnesia.

SK: I would have been raised on Wölfflin. But perhaps what matters is not the absence of certain discourses around art but the politicization of the discourse. Pierre Bourdieu would be someone we look at extensively, and he would be known to our students; but Baxandall would not. Obviously there are exceptions and these are shifting emphases. But the notion of cultural capital, for example, is current and significant for understanding certain exclusions that are more relevant for us than they would be in a more European environment.

AG: In an art history student's formation in Buenos Aires, Wölfflin, Riegl, Warburg, Baxandall, and also Bourdieu or Williams have a presence. Terms like "belatedness" may turn out to be much more irritating than "genealogy," because it is hardly possible to separate out the disastrous consequences that the narratives of progress have had on the analysis of artistic and cultural processes: when art is considered in terms of advancement or backwardness, it loses its specificity and originality. I certainly don't wish to fall into a naïve use of the term "invention" by proposing a history of the advanced nature or absolute originality of Latin American art, particularly that which is considered avant-garde. But notions such as "backwardness" as articulated from a Eurocentric perspective do not allow for a meaningful visualization of artistic or historiographic processes.

JE: This question of sources leads naturally into discussion of kinds of art history that are practiced and taught. A working distinction can be made between what I call, in a statistical sense, *normal art history* — by which I mean historical writing that is concerned principally with documentation, archival evidence, patronage, conservation, and iconography — and what might be called *theory*. The distinction is a traditionally vexed one on the discipline, but it can be addressed in a very straightforward manner by considering the journals that are classified as art history.[3] A number of them pursue iconographic and other concerns; and others focus more on debates surrounding such issues as historiography, methodology, and politics of the discipline. I bring this in here in order to introduce one of the ways that a conversation might begin on the subject of *kinds* of art history, especially as they can be identified through journals and monographs.

LK: I wonder to what extent this distinction between *normal art history* (or what others would call *positivist* art history, sometimes in derogatory tone) and theory-laden art history or *theory* (again sometimes meant in derogatory sense) mimics the distinction I tried to point out between some local art histories and the international shape of the discipline. I do not want to play the advocate of *theory* here, but quite often the distancing from theory involves ignoring the art traditions outside the traditional Eurocentric scope — as if art history should be protected from both.

Friedrich Teja Bach: Regarding the diversity of art history, I think we should try to see what our expectations are. How unified do we expect art history to be, or how diverse? Only then can we judge whether certain things are significant.

I studied German literature in the 1960s, and my wife taught German literature at Columbia University in 2003.

The two occasions do not have much to do with one another, actually. One main difference was that in 2003, at Columbia, there was no longer talk of literature. They talked about poetics, aesthetic theory, and so on … whereas when I studied German literature in a very philological way. The two contexts were very different, to say the least.

So I would say we should not expect too much homogeneity. On the contrary, the diversity we have been talking about in relation to South Africa would be both expected and normal.

I would also like to say, Jim, that your term *belatedness* creates a certain problem. It suggests a linear development; only in a linear development can one speak of belatedness. That seems to be at the least very problematic.

JE: How, then, would you characterize the fact that Wölfflin was translated into Chinese in 1999? To me belatedness does not imply a linear difference. The time lag poses a specific set of problems, because Chinese students who read Wölfflin in 1999, presumably without the intervening literature and without Riegl, Warburg, and many others, were encountering specific problems of reception. Some of those problems, I would agree, shouldn't be called "belated" because they would in effect be *inventions*. But others would have to be called that, if they led for example to the students adopting style categories.

FTB: Well, but things come up to the surface of history in different manners; some come up and vanish. Some come up again, and their second surfacing would not be a belatedness: they would become actual in a new frame of reference.

And I do think that belatedness means there is up-to-timeness, and everything else is belated.

JE: I would be happy not to use the word belated, but I would not be as happy to draw the conclusion that every occasion is a new one, especially because one of our principal subjects so far has been the diffusion, not the reinvention, of texts and textbooks. I think it is possible to study genealogies of the narrative structures of textbooks, and to find lines of dependence. What significance one might choose to read into those dependences is another matter.

I don't want to imply new is better, old is worse. There is a bibliographically quantifiable diffusion — not a linear development — in texts, which is why it is interesting to consider the editions of authors like Wölfflin or Baxandall.

FTB: In cultural phenomena, belatedness is an actual issue. Popularization largely works with programs that were current forty or fifty years ago. *There*, belatedness is a correct description.

Of course my model would not be textbooks; it would be points where the discipline is working *with* Wölfflin, or *with* Baxandall. A textbook is a level of information for students. I am speaking of moments when the subject rises to the level of an actual discourse, a leading discourse of the discipline. Once something comes up in a discourse, it is in a way new. If Chinese students work with Wölfflin, then theirs would be a different Wölfflin.

JE: That would often be true. But I disagree with your assessment of textbooks: I would say their structure informs the structure of classes at higher levels, and those in turn inform the choices of postgraduate specialization, and ultimately the reasons why monographic studies are made. From my point of view, textbooks can be formative for the discipline, so that it can be quite significant to study when and where they are written and translated.

A concrete example is Burhan Toprak's *Sanat Tarihi*, which tells the history of the Christian West up to Chartres, and then turns to Hindu and Japanese art.[4] The narrative structure there is dependent on Western models (Helen Gardner's book, I think) up to the passage on Chartres. I would think that a textbook like that would necessarily be formative for the shape of the discipline in places where it is read.

To me, it is hard to overestimate the importance of the standard "story of art," which I identify synecdochically with E.H. Gombrich's *Story of Art*. Whole chains of dependence, misunderstanding, abbreviation and expansion, and adaptation come from receptions of the story Gombrich tells so clearly — the very Eurocentric story that has proven so difficult to import into local contexts. Hundreds of textbooks can be marshaled to tell these alternate stories.

AG: If we had had to consider the popularization of texts that had extraordinarily wide circulation in Latin America, perhaps more than Baxandall, Riegl, or Wölfflin, we should consider Ortega y Gasset or Franz Roh and the extraordinary influence they had throughout Latin America during the first half of the twentieth century. The narrative structure of art history in Latin America cannot be separated from Western models, even though it questions them. This also applies to the reading of canonic authors, readings that do not necessarily follow the order delineated by the discipline of art history discipline. These readings are frequently marked by chance or specific interest. Chance intervenes in the form in which one makes contact with certain books. Reading depends on the material conditions related to dissemination: what can be translated, what can be published, and what can be read. Until the 1980s, people in Argentina still read in French, but not in English. And nothing in German.

Almost nothing that was produced in the United States was being translated.

Reading and translation processes are also marked by censorship (if you look at the translations cited by Ana María Guash you realize that while Franco was in power the translations that were read in Spain were done in Latin America, and in Argentina in particular). In this sense, the translation of Wölfflin into Chinese in 1999 brings me to ask myself, not about the question of delay, but about what it is that Wölfflin may have to offer to the analysis of Chinese art that Baxandall or Riegl might not.

The idea that one must have complete knowledge of a discipline in order to make use of its instruments, that one must possess its entire genealogy, is Eurocentric. For an art historian in Latin America — and I suppose in China as well — the genealogy that is of interest has to do with reading cycles and patterns, and with the establishment of a reading canon. Notions such as "backwardness" or voids in reading material can be of importance for those who are concerned with defending a discipline's purity. This, I would dare say, is not a problem for a Latin American, which is more interested in knowing in what way a discipline like art history might serve its own concerns.

SK: We could also talk, as we did yesterday, about the remaining collections of plaster casts after the antique —

JE: They are a kind of art-school corollary of the "essential" writers of art history —

SK: There is a collection of those casts, for example, in the Fine Arts Department at Stellenbosch; despite the fact that we no longer teach the canon of Western art, I was surprised to discover that none of my students had the faintest idea that they were walking every day past a plaster cast representing St. George by an artist they appear not to have heard of.

David Summers: So far, this conversation has been mostly about the diffusion of art history as we know it, and as we know it, art history is obviously not global. I am not surprised if students in Africa do not find Donatello's St. George of great interest, or if they are puzzled or even offended by the expectation that they should. Where do they find art with which they themselves might be culturally identified? Gombrich's *Story of Art* starts off with a section called "Strange Beginnings." The "story" is at least implicitly universal; it begins with Paleolithic art, then there are six or seven examples of "primitive" art. Most of the book is devoted to the story of European art to modernism, with a few pages in the middle on Islam and Asian art, excluding India. This narrative — essentially in the direction of optical naturalism — to my mind is a problem to be solved. It is a terrible face for a would-be global art discipline to present to the world. What is the interest in finding yourself among "strange beginnings," or in finding your artistic tradition exhausted in half a page of prose?

JE: This is what first got me involved in this subject. My own contribution is the book *Stories of Art*, which collects several dozen histories of art written outside the West, including Toprak's that I mentioned, and shows how their different narratives cannot often be taken as art history.[5] To me the lack of viable alternatives demonstrates the pervasiveness and the strength of the standard "story of art" that I find so well exemplified in Gombrich's book. One reason why I think globalism is art history's most pressing issue is that Gombrich's narrative, if I can call it that, and one source of my pessimism on this subject, is that it has proven so hard to either modify the "story of art" in a satisfying manner, avoiding a sense of dependence, or else to produce a newly structured story that can still be persuasive as art history and not as a capricious local invention.

DS: When I began studying art history at Brown University in Providence, the first book I was given to read was Wölfflin's *Principles of Art History.* I was told I would learn how to look at art, that is, "form," by reading it; the course, however, was set up so that we studied modern art first, because it simply is "formal." Then we went back and did the history of art leading up to modernism, including Renaissance and Baroque art.

JE: Where I went to undergraduate, at Cornell University, we were also given Wölfflin as an introductory text. As we read it, we were warned: This is not proper art history; it shows you categories of seeing, but they don't correspond to the discipline as we practice it. I wonder if similar warnings accompany readings of Wölfflin in, say, Chinese universities.

DS: Well, but there was a close formalist connection in those days between art history and art practice. Studio sections, in which we did "formal" exercises, were also part of the introductory course. The rise of contextual art history at first drove a wedge between the history and practice (although art has also become more and more "contextual"). There have been attempts to bridge the gap between form and context — Michael Baxandall or T. J. Clark, for example — but contextual art history pushed hard in its own direction. It seems to me that the situation in which art, considered very broadly, is now practiced and taught as primarily "political" is an anticipatable effort to establish a relation between art that is understood fundamentally contextually and art practice.

JE: I think what you say about that particular reception of Wölfflin is right. And that, again, would seem to me to be a particular reception that would not be available elsewhere: it's not likely, for example, that it could be used as a reason to read Wölfflin today!

DS: Students read Wölfflin now with a high degree of resistance, edging into noncomprehension. This is an old text, which is to a degree about old issues.

JE: I have also noticed a resistance that comes from a certain sophistication about reading. Students recognize Wölfflin through deconstructive texts like Marshall Brown's "The Renaissance Is the Baroque."[6] We're perilously close to saying no one believes the text, and no one thinks it is pertinent to the current discipline: to me that would place it in the realm of historiographic inquiry, rather than methodological interest, and it would make me wonder about times and places where Wölfflin appears to retain methodological pertinence.

Another way to think about art history as a worldwide phenomenon is to take up the question of the relation between art history and neighboring disciplines such as art practice, art criticism, and visual studies. It is important, for example, to pay attention to places where art criticism stands in for art history, where there is no developed art historical practice.

DS: In the United States, certainly, we have many art history undergraduate majors, and the great preponderance of them gravitate toward modernism: that is, they study exactly the kinds of art history that take them close to the critical issues Sandra was discussing. That preference contributes to the blurring of art history and criticism.

JE: The big threat to art history, I think, is visual studies. There is the possibility in many institutions that art history will disappear into visual studies. In most places I know that possess a visual studies or visual culture department (or center, or concentration, or program), the art history department loses students to visual studies.[7] That is in part simply because students would rather study reality television than Rubens. One of the futures for art history might therefore be to dissolve into visual studies.

DS: As I listen to the situation in South Africa, practices there seem to pose a real problem for art history, because it is associated with the "civilizing" aims of a discredited political order.

JE: Yes, Sandra, from your perspective the discipline of art history has, as it were, already dissolved before it has come into existence.

SK: I think we have quite different takes on visual studies in the 1990s, because I think the reason visual studies is triumphing in the African context is because it is abolishing hierarchies; it is, as Nicholas Mirzoeff says, including everything that was excluded in the hierarchies of modernism. That does not necessarily mean visual studies is ahistorical, which is the biggest fear some people have about it. It is thought to be a leveler —

JE: That has been said, yes —

SK: — but I think there is room for a visual studies that is historically nuanced.

JE: That is a charge that is often leveled against visual studies, and it is not always true. There are senses of history in visual studies texts, and there are people who would call themselves visual culture scholars who are interested in the history of their own field, young though it is (perhaps it goes as far back as Burckhardt, if you're thinking optimistically).

But the artists, movements, and central concepts in art history and visual culture follow different lines. One of the reasons I think visual studies is perceived as a threat by some people in art history is an insouciance regarding the genealogies that art history posits for itself, and the notion that it is now time to completely reinvent relevant histories for the new field.

Sometimes Nick Mirzoeff does work this way. He gave an interesting paper last year on images of Babylon and other metaphors that could be used to rethink political images in the present.[8] I thought it was intriguing and provocative, but to some people in art history it would seem overly optimistic about the possibility of forgetting the narratives of art history.

SK: I understand that, and I think there is room for both. In certain contexts, because of lack of resources and because of our very problematic colonial heritage, it offers an out: but we still do a form of cultural studies that is rooted in an attempt to understand the relationship between visual histories and the human endeavor. This allows us to move away from being *burdened* by that colonial heritage. So it's a way of surviving, rather than a way of dying.

LK: I would like to return to the starting point of the seminar, and to your statement, in your review of David's book, that global art history is the most important issue facing the discipline. In my essay I disagree with that, and Andrea has said that in Argentina this would also not be the most important issue. Yesterday we agreed that the topic of this seminar is closely linked to the subject of the social purpose of art history in any particular context. Let's talk some more, then, about why you say that the claim regarding globalism might be mapped into the problem of art history's social purposes.

JE: You were concerned in your essay about the importance of the diminishing public for art history.

LK: Yes, I was noting the gap between what any artworks of any culture — Irish prehistoric monuments, nineteenth-century American painting, Shang Dynasty Chinese bronze, whatever else — may offer cognitively and emotionally, and the very small amount that people in museums and galleries seem to obtain in their mostly superficial encounters with works of art is. I have spent most of my professional career working in or for museums, and my view might be hypercritical or cynical, but the diminishing demand for art and trivialization of art seem to me incomparably more important than the problem of whether art history is sufficiently "global."

JE: I see these issues as completely entwined. Take for example Irish art history. The curriculum that is in place here is based very much on Continental European art. It is biased, also, toward England — there is often material on the Grand Tour, on Palladianism, on Robert Adam, silver, Georgian design, Canova.[9] That comprises a narrative, and also a canon — two of the issues that interest me — and also a terminology and methodology that support such emphases.

Then, and this is where the subjects are entwined, you then have the question of social use, utility, and purpose. Why continue such a curriculum? The assumption would have to be that those artists, periods, and concepts are the appropriate ones for Ireland, for the education of a cultured person in Ireland.

AG: Ladislav, I think we might talk about differences between our two contexts; that might be useful in bringing out this theme. As I understand what you're saying, you have a theoretical frame and a local context, and that is how the discipline works. Maybe I am wrong —

LK: What I tried to briefly underscore in my essay was the distinction between writing in English, addressing the global audience, and a moment, when — writing in your native language — you participate in one of the local art historical environments. Either way you implicitly or explicitly address a different sort of audience, and the writing is subject to different sets of constraints, or demands, and motivated by different purpose. It is certainly not surprising to observe that in most of these local contexts art history (or the local practice of discourses and practices connected to images and objects) is anything but global — for reasons ranging from the lack of resources we touched upon earlier, to more or less overt manipulation of art historical narratives (museum displays included) for the purpose of fostering nationalistic ideologies.

JE: I would think that one of the main difficulties in addressing art history this way is knowing when you can spell out people's motivations. In the case of Irish art history, I don't know any nineteenth-century texts that say, "What Ireland really needs is Continental European art."

Christa-Maria Lerm Hayes [from the audience]: Hugh Lane![10] He bought impressionist paintings around 1910, and said that he did so in order to show them to Irish artists (in a Gallery of Modern Art in Dublin) to help them build up an Irish school of painting.

JE: Oh, yes, right! Thanks for that. Well, anyway the lack of such texts can make it tricky to say exactly what motivations might be. Certainly in the United States it is widely acknowledged that nineteenth-century fascinations with

Europe drove the Eurocentric art historical curriculum. It was even the object of parody in the nineteenth century, for example by Samuel Clemens. There is a literature on the subject, but it is not available as such *while it's being taught.* Then it seems, as Marx would have said, natural.

This varies very widely. When the state promotes an extensive art historical idolatry, as in Romania, then it is immediately perceptible as such and open to critique as soon as the politics permit. But in other cases, and here I include Ireland, it lingers.

I would also be wary of considering this issue as a local one, and contrasting it to global issues: not least because globalism, as a doctrine, can have local motives. Perhaps that's the way it is in South Africa. Globalisms also serve local communities.

FTB: I would like to return to the question about what constitutes the most pressing issue. Ladislav, regarding the specificity of art history, on the one hand, and its ability to enter into dialogue, on the other: I would say they have to go together.

I would rather say the most pressing issue is to ask the question, "Where do they need us, as a discipline?" And of course we are needed where we cannot be replaced. That is the dimension of specificity, and it has to be an open specificity — open to dialogue with other domains, realms, disciplines. That would be a different emphasis than globality, I think. The question is: How far do we have to open the field in order to be open to the dialogue, and where do we lose by opening our specificity too far? That, I think, is the most important question.

JE: How would you specify that specificity?

FTB: It has to do with looking, with seeing, and with a kind of insight they can produce. It is a specificity, an insight, that is different from literature, theory, and so forth. That would be our contribution to the irreplaceable, specific cognitive dimension.

JE: That is compatible with a visual-studies standpoint, even an ahistorical one.

FTB: Sure.

AG: This point you underline, that the principal thing we need to conserve is the specificity, of looking at objects —

FTB: It is not just looking at objects; it is also looking at looking, at ways of looking —

AG: Of course. At the ways of looking. If you look in the index of any book written in Latin America about modern art, you will find the idea that modernism began with the translation of impressionism, twenty-five years later; or the translation of cubism, or the translation of abstraction. (Dada never existed in Latin America — it appeared in the 1960s.) Latin American histories always confirm this chronology, this narrative, of the history of art.

It is useful, therefore, to pay attention to the way we look at the objects, and at the kinds of visuality the objects are constructing. To have all the tools that come from the narrative of the Western history of art, but to work on the differences and contributions made in Latin America: changes that are not independent of Western art history and visuality, but introduce specific characteristics. Sometimes these are large contributions, to Western culture as a whole. Art history could be a useful tool for understanding important differences between Latin American and European visuality.

What does a Latin American art historian expect here? To show that what has taken place in Latin America is not just theory, but different ways of looking at reality, and different ways of considering the context of the real through the image. And to show that if you wish to continue you need images that will add important elements to the narrative.

JE: Let me propose some categories that might apply to the possibilities we have been considering. These are four different ways the narrative that I like to assign to Gombrich's *Story of Art* has been received.

One is emulation or dependence: a country might produce books and scholars interested in *understanding* and *adopting* the standard Western narrative. Books with titles like *Modern Art in Thailand* do that, and they risk being read as dependent, at every point, on Western models.[11] It can be as if the author has taken the standard Western narrative, erased all the proper names of periods and artists, and put local names in their place. This is the principal problem I had with Steven Mansbach's *Modern Art in Eastern Europe*: that it drained the interest from the artists it introduced to its readers by comparing them, initially and with qualifications but always to their detriment, to Western artists who had preceded them.[12] We have not talked about emulation here, but I think it is the most prevalent relation worldwide.

A second is absorption: Andrea, you say in your paper there is no problem with the European narrative because Argentina has long collaborated with modernism, or connected with it —

AG: In Argentina, we don't have a conflict with art history as a Western discipline. Latin America has a very different history than, for example, South Africa; it would be difficult to imagine we don't have a relation to European art. After all, Latin Americans speak Spanish, one of the world's major languages ...

The administrative and educational structures were initially imposed on us, but Western traditions remain extremely important. For us as art historians, the challenge is not to alter the discipline of art history, but to use art history in order to understand culturally specific phenomena. Hence we don't have problems with the limits of disciplines; we can use a variety of disciplines as they are needed.

This does not mean that there is a specific absorption, as might come from James's classifications. A history of modern Latin American art requires specific words for determinate artistic movements. Such specificity deactivates explanations based on emulation, dependence, or absorption. For example, terms like *indigenismo, muralismo, martinfierrismo, universalismo constructivo, antropofagia,* and *neo concretismo* (indigenism, muralism, martinfierrism, constructive universalism, anthropophagia, and neoconcretism) come to my mind. These terms are not on the fringes of European narratives, but they do create disturbance, challenging their limits and established schemes.

JE: A collaborative connection, where it exists, would have to be a precondition for thinking of a local tradition as being absorbed into the Western tradition. If relations of dependence, independence, or (to take up the problematic word) belatedness became preeminent, the anxiety they generate would make it impossible to go on thinking of the absorption of the local into the European.

A third relation is *absence*: when the standard Western narrative is simply excised or was never present. Sandra's description of contemporary South African art history sounds like that: they reject the narrative; they have no use for it.

And the fourth is *reaction*: when the standard Western narrative is rejected, in whole or part, and where it appears as a problem posed to the independence of local history.

I think these are four productively different configurations. Emulation, reaction, and their attendant anxieties would be the whole middle ground, the places where I think most art historical traditions outside the West find themselves. By luck, we have on this panel two more extreme positions, one of relative independence ("absence") and one of relatively reconciled identity ("absorption").

I imagine that what happens in South Africa would seem very strange to students in Buenos Aires. I imagine them being told, "We don't need all that European art: it's an asked-and-answered problem and speaks only to a past we no longer want. Let's go on and do something different."

AG: If I had to position art history in Latin America in the context of global art history according to the categories that James proposes, I wouldn't consider the relation to be one of reconciled identity ("absorption") but rather of reaction. This does not imply the absence of art history as a discipline, but that art history's limits are both used and questioned. It means art history as a discipline is in negotiation with other disciplines.

SK: It's not exactly that we're not anxious. And the same is true of Nigeria, I think. There is still an effort to engage a more traditional conception of art history. But from year to year, there is a dilution in the effort.

LK: Jim, you seem to be concerned about narratives, largely those that circulate among professional communities of art historians and students. I would be more concerned with narratives intended for broader audiences, those who do not read scholarly texts and do not attend conferences. When I was a small boy, one of my first TV experiences was Kenneth Clark's *Civilisation*; you will remember how one-sided or Eurocentric the story is.[13] I don't know what the most general coffee-table books are for audiences here in Ireland, or in England — books that people might buy to get some idea of the history of art. In my country, it's a Czech translation of a Spanish scholar, José Pijoán. The history of art in eleven or so volumes, but again anything non-European art, being allotted absolutely marginal place.

JE: Yes, I know this series — in Spain it's around forty volumes.[14]

LK: It was first translated into Czech in 1972–73, but it keeps being reprinted all the time. It is by far the most widely distributed and popular general source on art in the Czech Republic and surely not only there. This would be the kind of book that the general audience would browse through, to get some general education in the histories and scope of art.

JE: There are other examples as well. In German there is the *Propyläen*, and in Russia a multivolume history that was widely reprinted.[15]

LK: And there is Horst Janson's book —

JE: Yes. I have a particular perspective on these books. I think even the largest of them share a common story: they have demonstrable lineages. The biggest are efflorescences, outbranchings of the core story. The simple narrative of illusionism (to take Gombrich's theme, which is also the exemplary theme) is interrupted, bracketed, divided and subdivided, and rendered effectively invisible: but I think it still persists, which is why to me the entire field of study is in the end the study of a reaction against a single very powerful story.

FTB: Ladislav and Jim, if we talk at this level we should not talk about books at all. We should talk about television series. If we are to talk about how the public is informed, we should forget about books.

LK: But that prompts the question why art history hasn't been more successful in translating the enormous accomplishments of scholarship on so many distinct artistic traditions, its increasing awareness of specific and local practices of art or image-making, into these popular sources and venues of information. Well, to get an answer, people from publishing business, TV stations, editors, etc. would have to join the discussion.

SK: Art historians definitely participate in the promotion of tourism: I would say that's a major function that we don't sufficiently acknowledge. I was involved in an exhibition in Cape Town recently, commemorating the tenth anniversary of democracy in South Africa, and it was a huge international success. Whatever else we thought we were doing, that exhibition played a significant role in the Cape Town tourist industry. The closing date was postponed on two different occasions in response to indications that local and international visitors were keen to see the show. Because of its popularity we were even urged, at one stage, to find a permanent venue for it.[16]

JE: That is not unrelated, given that the kinds of thinking that go into blockbusters and other exhibitions that could be called touristic can often be assigned to art historical narratives. The Art Institute in Chicago, where I work half the year, had an exhibition of Monet's works.[17] Some of us called it the "Money" show, and it certainly had that function: but it had serious art historical content, and at least some of its motivation and coherence — as invisible as that might have been to many viewers — was generated directly from the disciplinary narratives as we have been discussing them. The curator, Charlie Stuckey, had a point to make about late Monet. You are right, Ladislav, the point was not communicated to many people: but a diluted version of it must have been.

AG: This is not a small point: all these books, television programs, and versions of art histories published in what could be called peripheral places, all sharing the same schema. What is this art history, then, and how is it understood throughout the world?

JE: I think all this discussion, no matter how wide it becomes, is on the same subject. I have yet to see a television series on art that cannot be assigned, at whatever remove, to the standard story and its variants. Kenneth Clark is a perfect example: he comes out of an Edwardian education, and that taste and those emphases are perfectly clear. This is not at all to say that Ladislav's concern is solved: just that we are not really changing topics when we talk about television, tourism, coffee-table books, or blockbuster shows.

Just to finish up this portion of our discussion, I would like to mention the relative absence of art historical narratives that do not follow the general lines we have been exploring. There are many eccentric examples, like Toprak's, which don't follow the model. But there is also a broader question: Why have viable alternate narrative forms not appeared in art historical pedagogy? The Chinese scholar Jason Kuo is publishing a book of interviews with Chinese art historians; in it there is vacillation over what counts as *connoisseurship* in modern Chinese scholarship: is it just the name for some Western-inspired protocols of looking, mixed with Chinese interests? Or is connoisseurship the only available name for a truly indigenous, conceptually independent practice that has no institutional name?[18] There are Chinese specialists on both sides of this issue (and those who deny the issue has any purchase or interest).

And more broadly: I don't know any art historians who specialize in Chinese art being hired in Western universities for their ability to deploy Chinese interpretive methods. They are hired for their expertise, and partly for familiarity with Western methods, such as iconography, semiotics, social art history, and so forth.[19]

Why, in other words, do the alternatives continue to remain nearly invisible? There is a depressing parallel to be made here with searches for alternates to Western global capitalism. It's hard to find them, because they are being swamped by the machinery of capitalism.

Questions from the audience?

John Paul McMahon: Concerning colonial heritage: Sandra, when you were talking about the shift to local and indigenous practices, did the tools and modes of analysis change, or did South African art historians retain Western tools?

SK: The whole tradition of iconographic analysis (I removed a lot of stuff here) is still used, and even increasingly so. There is also increasingly a tendency to "indigenize," to localize interpretive tools like these. Quite where this will take us in the long run I don't know. Yet I would not be as pessimistic as Jim seems to be. It is fascinating watching how global practices get localized and indigenized, appropriated and transformed. An obvious example in South Africa is the whole hip-hop phenomenon: it is being localized there, as it is elsewhere in the world. Interpretive modes can also be localized, a point that has been made time and again in the pages of journals like *Third Text*.[20]

Elisabeth Shee Twohig: Galleries haven't been mentioned much; maybe there hasn't been a textbook on the subject yet. I am thinking of how in Sydney there is a gallery that has a section on impressionism, and then one on indigenous art.

SK: Maybe there is no *need* for a textbook. Maybe, Jim, that is not what people do in the peripheries: maybe there simply is no perceived place for a grand narrative of any kind if one is not at the center.

JE: I don't mean to say there should be a physical object of any sort. Galleries imply and embody narratives.[21] The recent intense interest in the new MoMA and its slightly ambiguous, somewhat open-ended narrative — which still retains the essential MoMA story of modernism — is a case in point, perhaps the paradigmatic case.

LK: I am sure there is a demand for a narrative, for some meaningful way to plot the development and conceptualize the variety of arts on the part of general audience, and I even believe that this is one of the things that art-loving people legitimately expect art historians to provide.

Christa-Maria Lerm Hayes: I feel that books both in the center and the peripheries are reacting against the globalism and the money-spinner. When I studied in Germany, we weren't given any textbooks at all. We were discouraged from reading one-volume histories. I am not a pure example, because I profited greatly from the Courtauld survey lecture series, but it was assumed that professors teach to their specialization. One had to learn piece by piece what the jigsaw puzzle of art history was.

Now I teach in Belfast, and I find that for very different reasons there is no survey. It is an art school, and they used to be understaffed; and besides, art students don't like art history anyway. So art history teaching happens in studios, in an ad hoc fashion.

JE: Isn't there a parallel between your description of teaching in Belfast and the situation of art history in some smaller countries, where there can be a sense of independence from the centers? The parallel being that in both cases, in studios and in universities, there is a conceptual dependence on some narrative. What goes on in the studio certainly draws what coherence it has from art history.

John Paul Stonard: Just in terms of trying to get a grip on what is a large playing field: I wonder if you can address the motivation of the question about what could constitute a world history of art. Would you distinguish between an intellectual factors and institutional factors? Teaching has been mentioned as an important factor, and there are issues of expanding audiences by teaching and through museums. But the intellectual part would be the inauguration of new narratives, their invention and dissemination. Is that how you would divide the field, or are they in fact together?

JE: That is a very difficult question, masquerading as an easy one. The two issues you raise are linked; but I think you may be right: a weakness or limitation in the ways I describe the field may be that I can't account for the appearance of new narratives, and yet my understanding of the field turns on them.

Let's move on, then, to our second topic, the concepts that inform art historical writing. In the first instance, we could talk about concepts that have been taken as useful for a world art history, and concepts that have been utilized only or mainly in local contexts. And to begin, there is the project, common also in postcolonial studies, in anthropology, and in linguistics, of mining local contexts for terms that can speak to wider concerns.

Our essays include several such concepts. In my review of David's book, I mention Nancy Munn's use of the Walpiri word *warri-ngirntiri*, as well as the Japanese term *ma* (which has apparently completed an arc of interest and is now waning in Western citations), and several others.[22] But since the exotic is contingent on who speaks, I would also mention the French *tableau*, which my wife Margaret MacNamidhe (who is a specialist on nineteenth-century French painting) has taught me to see as a very complex and virtually untranslatable term — a local term, if such an expression can be applied to the central tradition of Western artmaking in the nineteenth century. Yesterday Wolfram Pichler mentioned the difficulty of putting English *modernism* into German: *Moderne* and *Modernismus* are perhaps inadequate as one-word equivalents.

Teja Bach has suggested for one of our readings an excerpt from a book by Dagobert Frey. There, under the heading "Weg-Motiv," by which Frey means the occurrence of paths and directions in world architecture, I note that the section on India begins with the claim that the "primitive morphological form" of paths in Indian architecture is "the ambulatio (*pradakshana*)."[23] Now *ambulatio*, as I understand it, is a form that first occurs in Roman architecture in the first century BC. *Pradakshana* or *pradakṣiṇa* is the clockwise circulation around the holy site — typically a stupa — that is part of the being-viewed-by-the-god widely known in Western literature as *darśana*.[24] *Pradakṣiṇa* involves honoring but holding oneself apart, seeing and being seen, and it is particular, I would think, to certain times and places that are distinct, in part, from examples of ambulatio such as Pompeii.

An initial question with such terms is how they connect with the terms that ostensibly frame them. In Frey the conjunction of German *Weg*, Latin *ambulatio* (both apparently framing terms, because they are Western), and Sanskrit *pradakṣiṇa* raise this question in an especially clear form. Would it be good to locate as many such terms as possible, to raise art history's sensitivity to local contexts, or would it be, in the end, unnecessary, especially if the Western terms are understood as providing the explanatory ground?

DS: One of the very common forms of space is circumambulation. It is at least a quasi-universal, although it is crucially important that it takes culturally characteristic linguistic and spatial forms. Alexander ran around the tomb of Achilles, people circumambulated the tomb of Augustus, Aztecs practiced circumambulation, and people circumambulate stupas. The ambulatory in a Christian church usually circles a relic.

JE: I would think that if we had a panel of, say, dyed-in-the-wool postcolonial theorists, they might want to say something like, "Well, pradakṣiṇa has to be used when the subject is a stupa, because the indigenous discourse is necessary." There would be skepticism about the idea of an underlying term that would take pradakṣiṇa as a special case.

DS: As you know, I would like to abandon the Eurocentric idea of the "visual" arts altogether and, in general, to replace it with "spatial" arts, the terms of which are much less reductive. Frey was on the right track, but does not go nearly far enough. In my terms, architecture and images are always variants of human social and personal space, so that the third term, in relation to which specific cultural forms and practices — the two are inseparable — may be compared is human corporeality and its significance in the context of any number of possible built environments.

I would not imagine *Real Spaces* working as a textbook that would tell people the "stories" we were talking about earlier. There might be any number of stories — "shapes of time" as George Kubler might call them — which, however, because all are variations on human corporeality, are not mutually untranslatable. Circumambulation is an excellent example of a powerful tendency on the part of people in many traditions to acknowledge centers of value, if in a variety of specific ways. In a course on Indian art, it would be possible to explain what circumambulation means in a certain context. But the idea is to proceed from the possible conditions of shared human spatiality to culturally specific — but not radically different — practices. That is exactly what I would want to do.

JE: Conceptual problems aside, there are also political problems. I imagine that for some readers, those who want to see terms like pradakṣiṇa, the book might be a hard sell. There is a notion that particularity entails skepticism about universals.

DS: I don't think any cultural practice is reduced in belonging to a more general category. Perhaps the political problem arises because Western academics are accustomed to thinking of languages — which are ultimately untranslatable — as the paradigm of reality definition and communication. But then it has to be explained why in linguistically absolutely unrelated traditions very simple real spatial patterns occur in local variants. Pilgrimage is another example. I understand the resistance to the reduction of "our" categories to "yours," but perhaps this is not really a necessary alternative. The history of art has been very nationalistic, and has been deeply implicated in the faith in progress and cultural superiority justifying Western imperialism. It is hard to accept the contingencies of one's origins. I think that's a very general problem ... I often encounter in seminars objections to the implicit relativity of cultural beliefs and practices. But in fact, an important part of the global challenge to which the history of art might also rise is the furthering of the willingness to suspend convictions about the absoluteness of one's own behavior, and to understand the degree to which all behaviors are variations on physically grounded themes.

JE: That's very interesting. It sounds as if your students have diametrically opposed sources of skepticism from mine. On the one hand, suspending belief in the universality of one's own concepts, and on the other suspending disbelief in the possibility of universal or general concepts.

Another problem for an account like Frey's is the connection between a term like pradakṣiṇa and one like *darśan*: in other words the term that's imported brings along its unruly relatives, and the conversation becomes more problematic.

LK: Shouldn't we distinguish more carefully between, on the one hand, culturally specific terms that would be useful or necessary in the study of a particular cultural tradition and, on the other, terms coming from some linguistic or cultural tradition that might be potentially useful in the Western context as well?

In my essay I mention several terms in Chinese art. I would be interested to hear from specialists on Chinese art whether they think expressions such as *fu gu* (the return to the ancient) and *da cheng* (the great stylistic synthesis) might have some potential for use in general meditation on the return to tradition or stylistic emulation —

JE: You mean uses outside of Chinese art?

LK: Yes. So I would ask the people writing Assessments for the book whether they might come up with examples of such terms from various languages and contexts — from Yoruba to Japanese — which could perhaps compose some list of critical or useful terms for art history.

FTB: We should also consider that the willingness to coin terms is not evenly distributed. It is one thing to speak of terms, and another to speak of language. Otherwise we just presuppose that our European willingness to coin terms, or to focus a problem *in terms*, is universal, and that is not the case.

Even this gesture of opening up to terms from other cultures as a step in opening up to other cultures is —

JE: — is itself Eurocentric.

FTB: Yes. That's one thing. A second point regards a distinction David made. If I remember correctly, you said there is a confrontation between undifferentiated space, on the one side, and bounded, centered, or circumambulatory space on the other.

DS: Yes, but my whole book is a qualification of that difference. Qualitatively undifferentiated space is the metric, Cartesian, or Newtonian space underlying modern technology, distribution, and communication. Traditional societies — including traditional Western societies — are more properly uniquely centered and bounded. Nationalism is a late bloom of this kind of centering and bounding.

FTB: I am hesitant to see that as an overall structure. To point briefly to one level of phenomena that is excluded in that structure: Foucault addresses different phenomena in his article on heterotopic spaces. He means social spaces that are pronouncedly fluid, such as cinemas, theaters, and cemeteries. Those are a type of space that goes against the stability of centered spaces: they are heterogeneous to the bounded spaces, internally contradictory, and fluid — they move. This type of space has an important function, and it is left out if you think either of basic undifferentiated space, which we are all afraid of, or of stable, bounded space. I think it would be important to bring heterotopic spaces into the discussion —

DS: I don't think cemeteries, theaters, and cinemas really belong together. The necropolis — a city for the dead — has a long, culturally various history, as do theaters, "places for seeing." It is very useful to consider these histories, and to compare and differentiate the cultural forms of housing and provisions for the dead and for drama. As for cinemas, these are paradigmatically modern, and I think in general that the idea of "heterotopia" was generated by modern utopias, which turned out to be dystopias, sites of uniformity and murderous efficiency. The category in any case is less apt to premodern societies, to the discussion of which urban space, with its confluences of variously centered lives and reactions against them. But I agree that these issues should be carefully studied. What I was after in the chapter on places in *Real Spaces* was basically the fact that the great cultures have been centered, at the same time that they have been isolated from one another. I present these differences as basically arbitrary, although they have deep and long consequences. People who come either to heterotopias, or to urban spaces, are coming to places having been shaped by very different, and very ancient, values.

In the book I wanted to devise a way to set Western culture, including premodern Western culture, against what is often spoken of as "later" culture. I wanted to make what I call *metaoptical* spaces a culture not just of a space that we all fear, but also of a specific kind of projection and control, and a specific relation to nature. I wanted to place Western culture in a problematic but negotiable relation to historical cultures.

FTB: Well, I wouldn't agree with David's response. Heterotopic space bears a weak and a strong meaning. The weaker meaning, speaking informally, is that heterotopic space is a form of urban space. The strong meaning is different: Foucault does not speak of heterotopic spaces as urban spaces. On the contrary, he tries to show that heterotopic spaces are in *opposition* to urban spaces. In a broad sense, then, heterotopic space and urban space are compatible. But if you take the concept seriously, it falls out of your dichotomy of undifferentiated and bounded space. It is something *else*.

JE: Let me take a step back from both your interventions, Teja, and also your response, David. I want to ask if an adjustment or an addition to David's schema might ever comprise an adequate conceptualization of space. I ask that because I wonder if what we are talking about here is conceptualizations of space outside of or before their application to historically defined spaces.

DS: I meant to leave the idea of space itself relatively open, to be defined by the instances, the historical modalities, that I mentioned. It should be pointed out, however, that there is an immediate division of space into real space, including social space (architecture) and personal space (mostly sculpture); and virtual space (painting, in general, "space" seen in two dimensions). All virtual spaces have culturally specific formats, which are real spatial.

An important ingredient of *Real Spaces* was provided by George Kubler's *Shape of Time*. It is a conception of the history of art in which there is not any temporal metric against which everything can be plotted, except for convenience. Kubler's conception is spatiotemporal and is conceived in terms of series, which are not reducible to one another; any work of art is a fusion of such historical strands in one or another circumstance. *The Shape of Time* posits a revisable diachronic structure for every culture, and things can diffuse from one culture to another: but basically the history that one might be concerned with in any given instance is a shape of time — an ongoing shape of time, but in possible relation to other shapes of time. The history of any place can be presented in those terms. The interesting thing about such categories, in my mind, is that they create interrelations: again circumambulation could serve as an example.

JE: Teja, on the question of the adequate conceptualization of space in general, would you say that the addition of Foucault's concept produces a conceptualization of space that could then be used to study *other*, historically specific kinds of space?

FTB: I would metaphorize the question. I am speaking of something like real black holes in the matrix of space: how cultures form, for compensatory or other reasons, such kinds of "black holes" *against* existing spaces. They fulfill an important function in society, and they would be included in a conceptualization — that is the brief answer to your question.

JE: What is concerning me here is the difference between conceptualizations of space that can be adjusted against one another, on the one hand, and on the other spaces that are conceived of as historical *subsets* of those spaces. This is a crucial distinction, I think, because the very concept of space — David's open, undifferentiated, phenomenological space — is something that we are only partly in possession of as a historical concept. We know certain spaces were associated with particular practices in the past, and we are aware of conceptualizations of them — but we also have another intellectual domain, in which we attempt to classify *fundamental* issues of spaces. I don't want to say the "very concepts" of undifferentiated or phenomenologically understood spaces are outside history, because they appear to us as attached to history, but they are related to history in a different way. We take them to be merely *true*, as opposed to kinds of space we would say obtain in various times and places in the past.

DS: I'm not sure I see the problem you are raising. Perhaps it will help to think about the close relation between place-making and local cosmologies … but I am not really concerned with that problem. It would seem to me to be an enormous projection over the art of the world that I would not want to make. I am trying to explain why the whole Islamic world, say, centers on Mecca; why Rome has the status it does; why there is such conflict over Jerusalem; why Cuzco was the navel of the universe. These things are not self-evident, but they have something like the simplicity of presence. When people built Teotihuacán, they buried relics under the major temple platform, and they oriented the site in such a way that they could continue to build as long as they lived in that enormous city. It is the case that cultures in general align their principal buildings in one way or another. That is what I want to take into account when I talk about the qualification of space and time. In a way, it's that simple an issue and the distinctions are that simple. I want to make them into the foundation of a truly comparative art history.

SK: What about diasporic cultures? There is an extremely interesting literature on the ways slave communities engaged with master communities in the use of space, often behaving as Christians in public spaces, but continuing certain ritual practices in private spaces. This had the effect of destabilizing spatial hierarchies and the meanings generated through them despite appearances to the contrary.

DS: I talk about diasporas in the book: the first one, the Babylonian captivity, and how the Jews have continued to contribute to the metaphorical language of destruction and suffering. Or we might consider the Atlantic slave trade and Afrocentrism in the United States: that's a kind of centered thinking, because it implies a kind of return as a solution to problems, and an identification with a center. The question of the adaptation of diaspora communities is exactly the sort of thing I had hoped people would work on using the tools I have provided. Scattering very much lends itself to discussion in terms of centers.

JE: Let me reintroduce the subject from another perspective. It has been observed that no Western architectural treatises use the word *space* before the eighteenth century.[25] Instead the authors talk about objects. That would pose an insuperable obstacle for a certain kind of historical work. There would, I think, be agreement that using space and its cognates to describe Western architecture before the eighteenth century is technically anachronistic: but that would, I imagine, not be generally taken to be a problem. On the other hand, it raises the issue of the historicity of specific concepts of space, and the potential limitations of the uses of the term *space*. The absence of the term makes it necessary to ask what *portions* of our concepts are historically bounded, and what it means when a historian goes outside those bounds and continues to use the terms.

DS: Architecture is the art of social space, and Renaissance architecture is comparable to all other traditions in shaping social space in determinate ways. On the other hand, the intellectual history of space, leading to the way we seem inclined to use the word here, is another history, which postdates Renaissance architecture. I don't see, however, why it is not altogether possible to discuss Renaissance architecture as social space, without encountering the word space in architectural treatise. And it would be of great historical interest when developed Western notions of space, worked out in scientific and technological contexts, begin to be applied to architecture.

Part of the polemic of the book is the rejection of the presumption that art is "visual," which is nothing more than a kind of abstraction from very ancient Western ideas. I have tried to demonstrate that certain categories of space are much more useful. That's why the book is so long.

We spoke of *darśan* before: the idea in that case is that the deity sees you. To understand that you have to read about other things — substitution, icons, invocation, and so forth. It is an excellent, paradigmatic example of an idea that basically can't be addressed in terms of visuality. You have to think differently about the "art" you are confronting in order to describe the practice.

FTB: I would like to come back to the term Sandra introduced, *displacement*. In terms of contemporary ethnographic theory, James Clifford would suggest that the terms of displacement are replacing terms like *exile* and *diaspora*. Those terms are still conceptualized in relation to a center, but displacement has become a general phenomenon and it cannot be captured with the term diaspora. Just in order to save the radicality of the question you posed, Sandra, I think you would have to say displacement is increasingly a general fate, something that affects all of us.

Your question of displacement, properly understood, is a radical one, and it opens the question of centrality and periphery.

DS: I am talking about art history and the formation of cultures, and the evidence that exists for those formations. Your discussion of this, Teja, seems to be a modern projection over these historical processes —

FTB: We are not only talking about history: we are talking, as I said, about cultures, including contemporary cultures. And I would not say displacement is a projection of contemporary cultures.

DS: One of the repeated themes of *Real Spaces* is the contrast between the aggregate premodern world of places and the isomorphism and fungibility entailed by the realization and enactment of modern notions of space. The problem presented by the book's argument is the negotiation of this contradiction. The lives of the vast majority of people are shaped by traditional spaces. If all of that is so, how are traditional places and cultures to be respected and maintained? How are places made, and how might they best be made, in the modern world? "Displacement" seems to me to be a fairly obvious description of that predicament. People may now be authentically and radically displaced in ways that were not possible before. To be sure, the premodern world had its problems, but it was not like that.

SK: Can I take this up a bit further? There is a whole series of pieces that have appeared recently around the issues of asylum and migration. About 150,000,000 people have been displaced in the last several years. That raises interesting issues about cultures and their centers, and about people's relationship to what they understood to be centers, or lack of centers.

DS: I couldn't agree more. But what I would like to insist is that these ideas do have cultural histories. Formulations — "displacement," for example — are shaped for real historical reasons. I would like to contribute to a project in which these specific modalities were not simply erased by being called "displacement." Displacement itself presupposes a certain economic and technological order, and an understood world spatial order, within which this movement is possible, and within which it is for one reason or another considered necessary.

SK: What is coming out of recent literature is a notion of displacement that involves the impossibility of return: not physical return, because that's always possible — but conceptual, because you can never go back to what was there before. There is, if you like, a quality of instability both in terms of the temporal and the spatial.

Christa-Maria Lerm Hayes [from the audience]: I would like to underline what you have said, Sandra. I also note an increasingly positive valuation of hybridity. On notions of space, I wish to give an Irish example, from Belfast, where there are two different cultures who experience space differently. They have clashed and now share a limited appreciation of space, or an appreciation of limited space. You could begin with circumambulation in Irish Celtic cultures: you could adduce the ritual of adding stones to cairns and walking around them three times; there are then the hedge schools [clandestine Catholic schools held outside, in the first half of the nineteenth century] and the dancing at the crossroads [a utopian image made famous by Éamon de Valera, prime minister of Ireland] …

Those kinds of spaces were put in place by various historical necessities, of course. But you may still find today that the Catholic community is open to looking at other cultures, such as South Africa, Israel, Palestine, and other displaced peoples. On the other hand, both communities exhibit a siege mentality. Peace walls [which divide Catholic and Protestant communities in Belfast] are actually welcomed, creating an ever smaller and more restricted sense of space.

DS: There is an important difference between the making of markers by the old Celts (and many other people) and the archaizing reenactment of these forms, which, it should be noted, continue to have to do with identity. And I would be very disappointed if the effect of *Real Spaces* were to create a division between fenced and unfenced cultures, even though, unhappily, defensive walls mark the interrelation of many human groups. An important implication of the book is what my old colleague Richard Rorty calls "contingency."[26] It's a hard thing for people to acknowledge that what they believe most deeply and assuredly is contingent. But, to use another of Rorty's terms, we must all learn to maintain reserve of irony in our beliefs, such that there is room for the beliefs and practices of others. That to me would be the ideal circumstance. We may or may not all be displaced (and some people are displaced more than others), but there is also the possibility of human identification and mutual respect.

LK: I would like to express my reservations about whether in invoking concepts like "displacement," we can move so easily between objects, art history, social movements, political realities, and even ecological forces. I say this even though I fully agree with Teja that we are talking not only about images and art but also implicitly about cultures. But talking about displacement in terms of modern cultural displacement short-circuits the difference between those subjects and the ways displacement could be used to talk about objects and images.

JE: I think I would agree with that. But isn't there a wider issue in all of this? Everything we have been talking about in the last few minutes, beginning with heterotopias, and including circumambulation, diaspora, hybridity, and displacement, involves *adjustments* to conceptualization of space. These ideas may or may not be outside the schemata proposed in David's book. But all of them, potentially, would be acceptable — perhaps as ruptures of preceding categories, or as third terms, or as redefinitions — but they could conceivably all find places.

There are concepts of space that we have historicized fully, and there are others that we haven't fully conceptualized, which we live inside of, which we are in the business here of trying to fix. In my mind the versions of space we are considering are ultimately phenomenological. I think there is a commonly held set of ideas that represent the truths of space for us: it includes the psychological spaces that come out of Ernst Mach, and the "psychophysiological spaces" in Cassirer and Panofsky, and Husserl's and Merleau-Ponty's phenomenological spaces. These would be formulation in which we find truths and starting points, and I want to distinguish them from other formulations that we might say belong in certain times and places in the past.

DS: I have a response to that.

JE: I know you do!

DS: Speaking of historicizing space: the functional category, from ancient Greece to the Renaissance, was place, *topos*. It implied boundedness and denied the possibility of infinity, and to my mind it was a locally cosmological version of the relation between social order and higher order. In general terms, it was comparable to concepts in many other cultures.

In the case of your observation about the word *space* in architectural treatises: these are people who would have thought of themselves as being concerned with a kind of theatrical placemaking. The emergence of the idea of space was a great labor of thought that parallels the emergence of modern science.

JE: But then, for me, there is still the question of what space you begin with, where you stand when you interpret. I think that is at least partially Merleau-Ponty's space, and I find that strange.

I wonder if we might talk for a few minutes about our favored conceptions of space. In relation to phenomenology, for example, a lot of the conceptions we have been considering, including Foucault's, depend on a certain embodiedness, including a social embodiedness. That would comprise one of the strands in our own sense of space. I am asking this because it seems to me we are partly *inside* this sense of space, that we don't have a clear way out of it: and as a consequence, we see what appear to be other possibilities through phenomenological eyes. This would apply to all of us, including me, whether or not we want to begin with the capacious undifferentiated space in *Real Spaces*, or with something like *ambulatio.*

Because we know which passages in Merleau-Ponty or Heidegger seem apposite, we can also see our interest as historically bounded. Even in terms of art history, we can sometimes see how our conceptions of space have only recently become available. Yesterday, Teja, you mentioned the concept of *Raum* — as in *Lebensraum* — and how it enabled a certain kind of thinking about art historical space.

FTB: Yes, I was pointing out the necessity of considering the geopolitical sense of space. It seems necessary to have that in your back yard when you're talking about space, because in the Central European past, Raum had strong geopolitical connotations. Given the term *global*, even aside from one's intentions, it is especially important to think about geopolitical references.

This kind of historicization of your own categories seems important. So does the shift from a more, let's say, ontological position. Heidegger's important emphasis on *Ort* (place) against space in the 1950s and 1960s was not so much a social engagement with space. Thinking in a more political definition marks the second part of the twentieth century apart from the first. And now, we have to ask ourselves about our own position, and what it is we most need to be careful about.

DS: I am not sure that I can recognize my own thinking in phrases like "capacious, undifferentiated space," and I certainly did not mean to leave geopolitical issues aside. On the contrary, much attention is given to the formation of the modern grid of the world. I meant to help geopolitical issues to be negotiated in other terms. It is true that places tended to be regarded as stable entities, but that is one of the reasons they are very dangerous, and therefore one of the reasons we must learn to think about them. People associate centers with collective identity and continuity, but that may create situations in which people not connected to a certain center are not considered human at all. I put Jerusalem in a central place in the chapter on places because it is ambivalent in precisely these terms. Its relationship to monotheism, to the vigorously active world religions that are centered there, has geopolitical consequences. When Hitler was thinking of *Lebensraum*, and of making Munich the capital of the

Movement, and therefore of the world, comparable to Rome and Mecca, he provided the most murderous example of the danger that comes with centrality. This was very atavistic thinking, which was, however, persuasive to millions. We should know how to think about such things.

JE: Teja, I agree with that. Another way of starting the same critique would be to think of modernism, and the way that it disallowed certain kinds of talk about space. Space was immediately apprehensible, "purely optical" in the phrase. A recent book called *After Criticism* proposes an especially radical sense of embodied, political space, and the kind of writing it implies[27] —

FTB: You would have to talk about the "topographic turn" in cultural theory, but that is a phenomenon starting in the 1990s. Here *frame* as a category comes back, because as you said, it is not present in high modernism.

JE: The question here concerns the limits of self-awareness. We can watch ourselves subscribing to a phenomenologically informed concept of space, but since the topic is historical writing, it would seem to me important to continue to see how far out of that we can think, and that would include thinking about kinds of space to which we will not subscribe.

So, to pursue this. Another strategy is to consider concepts of space that are close to us, but to which we can't quite subscribe. An example for me would be Cassirer's and Panofsky's "psychophysiological space." It has been thoroughly historicized, and yet at the same time has elements that may appear indispensable for a working sense of space — for example the claim that objects effectively change size depending on whether they are seen with other objects around them.[28] Or in general terms: an extrageometric dimension of things that arises on account of bodily experience. That would have to be present in any viable "undifferentiated" notion of space in art history.

DS: I'm not sure I understand that, either. Cassirer was first of all a philosopher of science. In *Substance and Function and Einstein's Theory of Relativity* he made the very painful confession that he had to give up the *a priori* notion of Euclidean space.[29] I expect that he gets his concern with phenomenological space and time from that reexamination. He elaborated and expanded psychological and phenomenological space in opposition to what he considered a discredited *physical* definition of space. Even though Euclidean space is discredited it has continued to be very useful for doing things like getting me home to Virginia on schedule.

JE: Although if you were to read texts by people like Peggy Phelan — or for that matter George Lakoff and Mark Johnson, whom Teja mentions in his essay — you'd find a subscription to a radically embodied space not inconsistent with its beginnings in people like Husserl or Cassirer.[30] You are saying that Cassirer is a figure in the history of the conceptualization of spaces, but there are elements of it that contribute to the phenomenologically oriented undifferentiated space that continues to be both useful and true. (As does Euclidean space: but that is another issue.)

There is a crucial difference between all of these semi-conceptualized versions of space, which we are all content to debate, and historically bounded terms such as pradakṣiṇa. I agree with Ladislav that it would be interesting to expand on the uses of such terms in the discussion of art outside their local contexts, but even if one were to do so (and I have tried the experiment), you start from *outside* the concept, putatively from a position of control.[31] Here the issue is different.

What is driving my anxiety here is that this use of a somewhat undefined, phenomenologically oriented space as a starting point may be the worst kind of Eurocentrism, the kind that says: Here is my concept; I know it's embattled, and it engulfs other concepts, but I am going to use it anyway. I think this issue, along with Teja's observation about the Western propensity for coining terms, is a deep problem in our conversation.

FTB: It's certainly true that the Western tradition is particularly obsessed with the term space. No other comparative culture is.

JE: It could be addressed in the ways we have been positing, and perhaps especially by considering "exotic" terms that appear outside our concerns, and letting them illuminate whatever it taken as art history by contrast.

FTB: This would be another question for those writing Assessments.

SK: There are also contemporary scientific terms concerning space …

JE: Ladislav, regarding your idea of using local terms outside their local contexts. I don't think I have convinced anyone with my attempts to do that, and it occurs to me that the difficulty of arguing for a broader application of local terms may illuminate the politics of the discipline in an interesting way.[32]

LK: But Jim, unlike you, I would not be expecting any profound change in the structure of art history, even if non-Western concepts were appropriate for the more widespread use; nor do I suspect that this is inherently an issue of disciplinary politics. Rather I take the fact that this has not generally happened as a sign that the conceptual scaffolding of Western art history and discourse about images indeed is indispensable and that even a skillful adoption of critical terms, desirable as it might be, stands no chance of substantially altering the structure of the discipline.

But I wanted to add a note on space. The lesson of David's remarkable book notwithstanding, I still have some reservations about the general use of the term space for all of art history. Jim, you know that in Chinese painting theory and practice, there is a specific conceptualization of space — for instance Kuo Hsi's "three distances" (high distance, deep distance, level distance).[33] The notion that Chinese paintings (and poems) reveal a distinct Chinese conception or consciousness of space is a staple of much sinological literature. That is well known to all Western art historians who deal with Chinese art, and yet it seems to me that the Chinese concept of space could never be an effective starting point for discussions of space in general. At least I am not aware of any examples in recent scholarship.

JE: Neither am I.

LK: The distance between Kuo Hsi's conception and, say, Albertinian perspective, can be spelled out very easily, but what can you do with it? In other words, while the concept of space might be useful for some more abstract, philosophical reflections, and even intercultural comparisons, I am not sure it has the same explanatory power as other terms in the metalanguage of art history. It does not seem to be as useful analytically or conceptually as terms like style, meaning, function, or intention — at least in standard interpretations and descriptions of works of art.

JE: There is at least one scholar, Wen Fong, who has tried to make the Chinese conceptualization into a schema that could work —

LK: But in the first of his two monographs on Chinese paintings, if I remember correctly, he provides a brief discussion of the structural principles of Chinese landscape painting and treatment of space, but the analysis of space per se never forms a starting point or coherent focus around which the interpretation of a painting evolves.[34]

JE: I have a feeling he gave up on that project, because there's an early article in which he proposes a partly Chinese, but also largely Western, schema for all of Chinese painting.[35]

Then would you say it is mostly a political or institutional problem that these concepts have not taken hold —

LK: I am not saying that; I'm just questioning the prominent position the term space seems to enjoy in this discussion and also the belief that it can form a basis for what you dubbed truly intercultural art history.

DS: In proposing spatial (as opposed to "formal," "spatial," or "linguistic") categories as the basis for an expanded and more inclusive art history, and as one who keeps a watchful eye on the broader world of interpretation, I certainly did not mean to blunder into the "worst kind of Eurocentrism" by saying "here is my concept; I know it's embattled (do I? does it matter?), and it engulfs other concepts (does it?), but I am going to use it anyway." Perhaps any concept considered in itself begins to seem over-general and engulfing, but the question is, does it work? Does it do what we would like a world art history to do? To me, these spatial categories — in concert with other categories, of course — have the high practical value of open-ended flexibility and adaptability, at the same time that they enable new and timely intercultural conversations. Nor am I chastened by reservations over the "Western propensity for coining terms" (although I believe in Occam's razor). One can only be so remorseful about "Western propensities" and continue to talk about the same thing. The history of art, whatever forms it may take, will either be an intellectual discipline or it will not, and, if it continues to be one, it will have a more or less common, if disputed, terminology. And again, the proof of that terminology will be its usefulness.

As for the discussion of space in Chinese painting, this seems to be a defense of some version of connoisseurship. I have only mentioned the notion of virtual space, that is, seeing three dimensions in two, which I think I would be willing to say is a universal condition or possibility of representation. The skills of virtuality seem to me to be highly and characteristically developed in Chinese painting (which is why it is included in Gombrich's *Story of Art*), and it is hard for me to see how it can be described at all without indicating this. Chinese painting has its own culturally specific real/social spatial formats, and if there is an obvious difference between Kuo Hsi and Alberti, I cannot see why the features of each are not of great interest to someone explaining them in context, or why it is not informative to compare them precisely as developments of virtuality.

LK: If we could move away for a moment from the particular problems of space, to the realm of the visual, there are other concepts that might justify a brief reflection on their potential in narratives that would be more sensitive to challenges of world art. There is the gaze — a quite overloaded term, in my mind abused in recent theory, and burdened with the baggage of Lacanian connotations. But the gaze can be augmented by culturally specific concepts of visual practices and skills — such as Craig Clunas's discussion in his book

Pictures and Visuality in Early Modern China of differences between various terms used in classical Chinese texts for engaging with painting (*kan*, *guan*, *du*).[36] There have been other recent attempts to historicize practices of glancing and looking at objects in various traditions.[37] You could, I think, undertake a quite productive study of concepts of looking outside the gaze, a study that would be attentive to particular spatial settings in which objects and images were handled. Some of those might then be mapped back into the European context, perhaps partly replacing overarching concepts such as the gaze.

SK: I do not know about the African literature you mention, but it reminds me of the African idea that there is a figure that is a midpoint between two opposites … for example, in Fang reliquaries there's the idea that figure can be at once the embodiment of babiness and ancientness.

You get a tension between things that are apparently different. Or in Yoruba aesthetics, people talk about "midpoint mimesis": there is a whole idea of balance that is not necessarily about looking, but about doing.[38]

Christa-Maria Lerm Hayes [from the audience]: I wonder, Sandra, if I can draw a line from the balancing which you were mentioning in the African examples, to nonbinary thought in the West, beginning with dialectics, and far Eastern thinking that has never been binary. That could be a place to look if we're in search of international or cross-cultural currents.

I also think of Aby Warburg's project, in which Hopi and Athenian Greek cultures are juxtaposed, and of the ways he organized his library in Hamburg in an ellipse. An ellipse is a geometric understanding of history, and is a shape with two centers. Perhaps that library would be a good place to transport ourselves conceptually!

AG: Another example of a concept used for specific cultures that might be of wider interest is the Peruvian *huaca*, a Quechua word for a sacred thing. It does not denote any specific object: it could be a stone, or an image, but it is not necessarily either —

JE: Yes, a huaca could be a mountain or a mountain range, a mummified ancestor, or a thread —

AG: Yes, even now people working on the syncretic encounter of Precolumbian and European culture study are studying the hypothesis that *color* can also be a huaca.[39] When we look at the syncretism of images, we tend to look for representations, for example in Santería. In such cases, people took Christian images and added supplementary images that denoted African gods or ideas. That practice worked through the syncretism of images. But if people proposed that a *color* could be a huaca, they made something completely outside the control of religious authorities. The color could be used, for a religious purpose, and the colonial powers could not see it.

But is that useful for art history in general? I doubt it: what matters is understanding the local uses.

JE: I also find the huaca fascinating. It is kind of hypnotic, the way it escapes from art historical categories. But it also makes me wonder if something in Western approaches doesn't fetishize elusive concepts. I was entranced by huacas for some time, but then I began to wonder if their occurrences weren't seeming to propose to me something outside of the categories and interpretive reach of art history, and if that itself wasn't the source of my interest. I would hate to think I'd overlook things that seem more easily assimilated, such as varieties of glances and glimpses, or even the Japanese *ma* —

AG: In its context, however, it is necessary to focus on the concept.

JE: True.

FTB: Coming back to Ladislav's comment: I don't think that gaze, as important as it is, is a rival to space. Because if you think about the space, it is hard to imagine anything more fundamental. Whereas if you think about the gaze, you can easily find things that are left out. The gaze and seeing are ways of behavior, and there are other behaviors that do not involve seeing or looking. We have learned in the last few decades that the predominance of the visual is problematic in itself: we have learned to think also of touch, movement, and so forth.

Hence gaze is not as fundamental as space.

LK: Perhaps not gaze per se, but the culture-specific conceptualization of vision is at least equally important as that of space, at least when it comes for laying better grounds for more intercultural art history. They are in fact closely interwoven, because any negotiations of space involve visual-motor activities. Perhaps, Jim, I have misread you in your review of David's book, where you present five models of art history's response to global art history. But it seems to me that you are far too optimistic in assuming that by bringing concepts from outside Western art history it is possible to make fundamental changes in the shape of the discipline. At least I say in my paper that you were too optimistic.

JE: I did not mean to say I'm optimistic that it will make deep changes in the discipline. But I do think that is the way the discipline is going. Work of the kind that interests Andrea, both in her own area of Argentine modernism and in the recent literature on huacas, is a good example of where art history headed. However I do mistrust the assumption, in postcolonial studies in particular, that the more attention you pay to details the more you will be able to passively, automatically erase assumptions about Westernness.

Wolfram Pichler [question from the audience]: I have a question connected with the huaca, non-Western terms, and their possible use in art historical work. I was thinking it would be interesting to think about the ways Hubert Damisch, for example, deals with Chinese painting in his *Traité du trait.*[40] That book had to do with an exhibition at the Louvre on drawing, but its concern is the dialectics of the line and of the stroke in general. (Damisch does not have an essentialist notion of drawing.) One chapter in the book concerns Chinese painting and concepts; the function of the chapter seems to be to gain a new position from which to look at Western images. Even if the central dialectic he works with — stroke and line — do not have to do with Chinese concepts, it seems his idea in the chapter is to make Western images strange.

I think there are similar moves in the earlier work of Norman Bryson: reconceptualizing Western images by using Asian traditions. This seems to be an interesting way to bring together Western and non-Western concepts, without implying dependence or cultural exchange.

JE: I agree, that's the function of that chapter in the *Traité du trait.* I don't agree with it, and I'm not convinced by it, but as a rhetorical strategy I think it works well.[41]

All these examples we have been entertaining, following Ladislav's initial remark, of the potential use of non-Western or local concepts for Western or wider ends — all of them raise for me the same question. Why have they failed? Is it because of disciplinary politics or some other contingent reason? Or is it because of the structure of art history, which can admit new fundamental concepts (as opposed to "exotic" new ones) any more than it can admit new structures of historical narrative?

Whatever the reasons, there is no sign that art history is being fundamentally changed by its encounters with non-Western concepts.

LK: No, it is not.

JE: The new concepts are treated with the kind of care and solicitation you might provide to any delicate, exotic creature that is far from home. The unfamiliar concepts are not provided fundamental interpretive power.

It is also true that if you import *too much*, you can lose your interpretive power for a different reason. Tom Crow wrote an account of Baxandall's *Limewood Sculptors* in his *Intelligence of Art*.[42] There he says in passing that Baxandall's book might have too many terms taken from the fifteenth-century German vocabulary of woodcarving. It's only a brief remark, but it raises a curious problem, and it does so wholly within Western contexts. Another such example, within Chinese studies, is the discussion between Wu Hung and Robert Bagley that I mention in my review. The idea would be that it is possible to pass some border of anachronism into some inappropriate accuracy.

Christa-Maria Lerm Hayes [question from the audience]: Why not begin with the expression *art history*? As John Onians wrote in his first editorial, in the opening issue of *Art History*, it is a bad translation into English of a German term that has meanings that may not be the ones that one wishes to import.

LK: I am trying to imagine if we can get beyond the problems Wolfram describes in regard to Damisch's book. Why can't we reach an informative or original point of view?

JE: One of the reasons why that doesn't work may be that our root-level concepts are underinterrogated. To take the exemplary example of space: perhaps, if every art historian were required to write, in the first footnote of their text, "This is what I believe about Heidegger, and this is what I leave aside," then there might be a basis for an analysis of art history's fundamental concepts. Or, to link this to our first theme, if there were a custom of declaring the reasons for subscribing to certain narratives of art ("This is why I think the sequence from Giotto to Manet is indispensable here, for this context, or this country, or this audience"), then it would be possible to undertake a more concerted analysis of the narratives that seem to structure the discipline. (And I need to add, to counterbalance the skepticism that I know some people feel about the importance of those narratives: that kind of examination would be even more necessary when it appears the narratives are irrelevant or have been overcome.)

This is a good place to stop. I am actually not concerned, Sandra, that South African students may not be learning the Western tradition. It's alarming, but it's okay. I am more concerned about the situation I think is more common worldwide, and that is an ongoing anxiety and negotiation with Western European and North American narratives and concepts of art history.

But clearly, our conceptualization is inadequate. It seems art history is moving blindly into these new occasions, as Damisch and others have done. In my own experience those experiments stand on, and also fall back on, the standard story and its apparently undifferentiated concepts. That's my pessimism.

FTB: David, I would just like to say that in the end none of your categories were contradicted here, by anyone. The problem is that questions arise as soon as one speaks about general terms of a science such as art history, and particularly about the future of that science. So two dimensions came into play: a maximal generalization, and a future direction. In a sense our brief was to speak about the future configuration of the field at a very general level. That is difficult, and in a way perhaps one should not even do that.

DS: I am not worried about the contradiction of my categories. I am, however, perplexed by what might be called the infra-categorical issues raised, which seem to me disenabling. Given the slight movement I have seen in these discussions away from the most conservative art history, mostly toward the incorporation of some terms from one or another culture into the existing conceptual structure, I can see good reason for pessimism regarding the future of the discipline. I do not believe, however, that such pessimism is the only alternative.

Notes

1. Michelle Henderson and Eileen Julien, *Art History in Africa* (University of Maryland: David C. Drikell Center for the Study of the African Diaspora [spiral bound publication], 2003), 11.
2. Translated by Pan Yaochang. The Japanese translation is 1936: *Bijutsu no kiso gainen: Kinsei bijutsu no okeru yoshiki tenkai no mondai,* tr. by Moriya Kenji (Tokyo: Iwanami Shoten, 1936). I thank Jason Kuo for this reference. He adds: "By 1982, it was in its 14th printing. Taiwan reprinted the English translation in 1971; in fact, I was one of the few graduate students who read it then. The Chinese translation — by the same person who had translated Gombric's *Story of Art* — appeared in Taiwan a few years later. I think a mainland Chinese translation appeared even later. So, there was a gap of about 40 years between the Japanese and Chinese receptions of Wölfflin." (Personal communication, September 2005.)
3. See the essay "Is Art History a Global Discipline?" in this volume. The argument is extended in my *Our Beautiful, Dry, and Distant Texts: Art History as Writing* (New York: Routledge, 2000 [1997]), 11–13.
4. This is discussed in the Introduction.
5. Elkins, *Stories of Art* (New York: Routledge, 2002).

6. See Brown, *Turning Points: Essays in the History of Cultural Expressions* (Stanford CA: Stanford University Press, 1997).
7. This is explored in *Visual Studies: A Skeptical Introduction* (New York: Routledge, 2003).
8. Mirzoeff, *Watching Babylon: The War in Iraq and Global Visual Culture* (London: Routledge, 2004).
9. "The State of Irish Art History," *Circa* [Dublin] 106 (2003): 56–59.
10. Robert O'Byrne, *Hugh Lane, 1875–1915* (Dublin: Lilliput Press, 2000).
11. Apinan Poshyananda, *Modern Art in Thailand: Nineteenth and Twentieth Centuries* (Singapore: Oxford University Press, 1992).
12. Review of Mansbach, *Modern Art in Eastern Europe,* in *The Art Bulletin* 82 no. 4 (2000): 781–85. "Response [to Anthony Alofsin's letter regarding the review of Mansbach's *Modern Art in Eastern Europe*]," *Art Bulletin* 84 (2002): 539.
13. The television series; see Clark, *Civilisation: A Personal View* (New York: Harper and Row, 1969).
14. José Pijoán et al., *Summa artis, historia general del arte,* second edition (Bilbao, Madrid [etc.]: Espasa–Calpe, 1944-). The first edition is (Bilbao, Madrid [etc.]: Espasa–Calpe, 1931-); Pijoán wrote vols. 1–16.
15. *Propyläen Kunstgeschichte,* edited by Kurt Bittel et al. (Berlin: Propylaen–Verlag, 1966–75); and *Supplementbände,* edited by Beat Brink et al. (Berlin: Propylaen–Verlag, 1977-). The Russian text is *Universal History of Art.* Akademiia khudozhestv SSSR. Institut teorii i istorii izobrazitel'nykh iskusstv. (Moscow: State Publisher "Art," 1956), translated by Ullrich Kuhirt as *Allgemeine Geschichte der Kunst* (Leipzig: E. A. Seemann, 1965). These and others are discussed in my *Stories of Art.*
16. *Democracy X: Marking the Present, Representing the Past,* held at the Castle in Cape Town from April 2004 to April 2005.
17. Charles Stuckey, *Claude Monet, 1840–1926* (New York: Thames and Hudson, 1996).
18. See my "Afterword," in *Discovering Chinese Painting: Dialogues with Art Historians,* edited by Jason Kuo, second edition (Dubuque IA: Kendall/Hunt Publishing, 2006), 249–56.
19. Discussed in a book only available in Chinese, my *Xi fang mei shu shi xue zhong de Zhongguo shan shui hua* [*Chinese Landscape Painting as Western Art History*], translated from the English by Pan Yaochang and Gu Ling (Hangzhou: Zhongguo mei shu xue yuan chu ban she [National Academy of Art], 1999).
20. K.A. Appiah, *In my Father's House: Africa in the Philosophy of Culture* (Oxford: Oxford University Press, 1992), 137–57; E. Nicodemus, "Bourdieu Out of Europe," *Third Text* 30 (Spring 1995): 3–12.
21. See for example the popular books by Victoria Newhouse, *Towards a New Museum* (New York: Monacelli, 1998), and Newhouse, *Art and the Power of Placement* (New York: Monacelli, 2005).
22. In addition, see *Concepts of Space: Ancient and Modern,* edited by Kapila Vatsyanan (New Delhi: Indira Gandhi Centre for the Arts, 1991).
23. Dagobert Frey, *Grundlegung zu einer vergleichenden Kunstwissenschaft: Raum und Zeit in der Kuunst der afrikanisch-eurasischen Kulturen* (Darmstadt Germany: Wissenschaftliche Buchgesellschaft, 1970 [1949]), especially p. 104.

24. For *darshan*, or *darśana*, see Diana Eck, *Darsan: Seeing the Divine Image in India*, third edition (New York: Columbia University Press, 1998), and the exhibition *Darshan: Blickkontakte mit indischen Göttern: die ländliche und tribale Tradition*, edited by Cornelia Mallebrein (Berlin: Museum für Völkerkunde, 1998).
25. This is part of a critique of space-oriented description of Renaissance art in my *Poetics of Perspective* (Ithaca NY: Cornell University Press, 1994).
26. Rorty, *Contingency, Irony and Solidarity* (New York: Cambridge University Press, 1989).
27. *After Criticism: New Responses to Art and Performance*, edited by Gavin Butt (London: Blackwell, 2005).
28. Discussed in my *Poetics of Perspective*, chapter 5.
29. Cassirer, *Substance and Function and Einstein's Theory of Relativity*, translated by William and Marie Swabey (New York: Dover, 1953 [1923]).
30. Phelan, *Unmarked: The Politics of Performance* (New York: Routledge, 1993); Lakoff and Johnson, *Metaphors We Live By* (Chicago: University of Chicago Press, 1980).
31. Discussions of terms from the Chinese, from *Calligraphers and Painters* by Qādi Ahmad ibn Mir–Munshi, and from the Indian *Atthasalini* and *Viṣṇudharmottara Purāṇa* are in my *Pictures and the Words That Fail Them* (Cambridge: Cambridge University Press, 1998), chapter 6.
32. This strategy also suggested in relation to visual studies in *Visual Studies: A Skeptical Introduction*, 105–6. (The idea there is to use unusual Western sources, such as Vico, instead of the usual ones, such as Benjamin.)
33. In Guo Xi's *Linquan Gaozhi* [*The Lofty Message of Forest and Streams*]. For an English translation see *Early Chinese Texts on Painting*, edited by Susan Bush and Hsio-yen Shih (Cambridge MA: Harvard University Press, 1985): 168–69.
34. Wen Fong, *Images of the Mind: Selections from the Edward L. Ellitoo Family and John B. Elliott Collections of Chinese Calligraphy and Painting* (Princeton NJ: Princeton University Press, 1984).
35. Wen Fong, "Toward a Structural Analysis of Chinese Landscape Painting," *Art Journal* 28 (1969): 388–97.
36. Clunas, *Pictures and Visuality in Early Modern China* (Princeton NJ: Princeton University Press, 1997).
37. For example the contributions in *Visuality Before and Beyond the Renaissance: Seeing as Others Saw*, edited by Robert Nelson (New York: Cambridge University Press, 1996).
38. R.F. Thompson, "Yoruba Artistic Criticism," in *The Traditional Artist in African Societies*, edited by W.L. d'Azevedo (Bloomington: Indiana University Press, 1973): 19–61; J. Fernandez, "The Exposition and Imposition of Order: Artistic Expression in Fang Culture," in ibid., 194–220.
39. Gabriela Siracusano, *El poder de los colores: De lo material a lo simbólico en las prácticas culturales andinas (siglos XVI a XVIII)* (Buenos Aires: Fondo de Cultura Económica, 2005).
40. Damisch, *Traité du trait, Tractatus tractus* (Paris: Éditions des Musées Nationaux, 1995).
41. This is argued in my *Xi fang mei shu shi xue zhong de Zhongguo shan shui hua* [*Chinese Landscape Painting as Western Art History*], unpublished in English.
42. Crow, *The Intelligence of Art* (Chapel Hill: University of North Carolina Press, 1999).

4

Assessments

Ralph Ubl

When we think about introducing terms from traditional Chinese, Japanese, or Indian discourse on art, it is either to enhance our historical and contextual understanding of the art of those cultures, or because we are motivated by theoretical problems within Western art history (as in the work of Damisch or Bryson that Wolfram Pichler mentions). In the first case, most Western art historians not specialized in these fields are just readers of American or English books on Asian art and will probably not contribute any original research of their own. In the second case, the dilettantism is productively acknowledged. We do not read Damisch or Bryson primarily because of their scholarship in Chinese painting but to get a new and, as Wolfram rightly pointed out, "strange" view of Western art. As far as I see "normal" art historical research has not yet met the challenge posed by such strategies of making things strange.

In the Art Seminar, James Elkins encourages us to try a third possibility in searching for non-Western concepts that have the same strength as, for example, the notion of space in our art historical tradition. Reading the transcript and Elkins's review of Summers's *Real Spaces,* I had the impression that it might be quite difficult to find any genuinely non-Western standards of scholarship or art theory that have any chance to compete with our tradition. Speaking of our tradition, I want to emphasize two things: first, that the field of Western art and art theory is so rich, heterogeneous and controversial that I have some difficulties in declaring it as "ours"; second, that although we like to coin concepts (as Teja Bach notes) we are not obliged to focus on monumental terms like "space." Recent art historical literature offers several examples of fascinating and fruitful terminological inventiveness generating highly specific concepts. I think of how French art historians such as Damisch have deconstructed the notion of the picture plane, and created new categories to address the different modalities of surface in painting.[1] So what's the point of longing for a new, monumental category hidden somewhere in non-Western discourse? On the contrary, shouldn't we emphasize that Western art historical thinking has not necessarily to be regarded as monumental? This would be a good condition for dialogue with scholars who are not (or do not want to be) affiliated with "our" tradition.

In the discussion on textbooks Elkins mentions the belated diffusion of Wölfflin and Gombrich in China. As a matter of fact, there is a strong and inevitable dependence on Western standards, which we have to acknowledge whether we like it or not. In China, I met an art historian who introduced himself as an expert on Worringer. As far as I understood him, it seemed to me that he was deeply convinced of Worringer's enduring relevance as a theoretical writer. Actually, a similar misunderstanding occurred in France some thirty years ago. If that earlier misunderstanding was productive, that was due to the fact that Gilles Deleuze had no ambition at all to be regarded as an expert on Worringer but used the latter's writings following his own philosophical ambition.[2] He gave an exciting touch to Worringer's crude and outmoded dichotomies.

Maybe it is useful to compare Deleuze's use of Worringer, or Damisch's and Bryson's use of Chinese aesthetic concepts, with the use of Western art history and theory in Chinese academia. Are we entitled to expect a similarly inventive and redemptive freedom in handling unfamiliar and sometimes odd concepts? As the case may be I think this question contains a good criterion to assess any terminological transfer from another culture or just from a forgotten book. Then belatedness would be indeed an opportunity for creativity, and "our" tradition might be something else than a "textbook."

Maria de Los Ángeles Taberna and Humberto Valdivieso

A Contribution to the Seminar

The Art Seminar has sparked a reflection for us about some ideas and issues in reference to the studies and teaching of art history. Even though these issues are continuously present in our classrooms, it is unusual to see them embodied in exchanges like this one. Wondering how the study of art history can be global is in itself a reflective task that involves all of us. When answers come to us — either in the dialogues promoted by James Elkins or in the individual readings we have done of them, we find more similarities than differences between the singularities of different regions, cultures, or races. That is why we identify directly with Andrea Giunta's exposition. However, there are aspects of art studies in which we agree about the peculiarities of Africa, Asia, Europe, and Oceania.

The first issue we are going to outline will be the material difficulties that need to be overcome in order to effectively study art history. We at the Universidad Católica Andres Bello in Venezuela have enough technological resources both for teaching and for research. Even so, we are aware of the scarcity in resources in Venezuela's public universities, which prevents a balanced awareness the subject. What we all really share is a lack of means for acquiring specialized and updated bibliographies. The high cost of art books and their scarcity in national bookstores is a principal problem for students and educators; it is difficult to find books about non-European art and even Latin American art. The situation is the same for audiovisual materials.

One advantage for us is the possibility of using multimedia technologies and the Internet in classrooms. Virtual access to museums and galleries all over the world decreases, somehow, the costs of art studies and research, but observing images online is merely one element of study and it does not solve the troublesome access to art theory.

As for the condition that teaching and researching present in our universities, we will take into account the thoughts expressed by Andrea Giunta about the Latin American panorama. Venezuela has not gone through a significant expatriation of academics and researchers of art. Usually, those who travel to study abroad return to work in the country. This situation could change due to our political situation, but it is too early to tell.

Our educators and researchers either teach at universities or work in restoration and museology, for both public and private institutions. However, the overall number of professionals in the field is not excessive. The number of publications in history of art has shown some decline in the last years. The majority of these publications come from the Universidad Central de Venezuela and the Universidad de los Andes. The Universidad Católica has published several books about colonial art, pre-Hispanic art, and Jesuit art, among others. Also, private publishing houses devoted to the arts, such as Armitano Editores, have published important catalogs dedicated to Venezuelan artists. Such independent houses have also published the most important history of Venezuelan painting, a book written by Alfredo Boulton. There are also books about colonial art, national art, and contemporary art written by scholars such as Carlos Duarte, Graziano Gasparini, and Carlos

Silva. Exchanges with the rest of Latin American are mainly done by the editorial house Fondo de Cultura Económica of Mexico. Some other publications come from the south of the continent, mainly from Argentina. This reflects how little information we have about art history of the rest of the continent. The Caribbean, Brazil, Canada, and a good part of the United States are absent from the majority of our libraries and bookstores.

As for authors such as Wölfflin, Riegl, Gombrich, Kubler, Francastel, Argan, and Baxandall, among others, they are part of the bibliographies in the majority of the classes of art history being taught in Venezuela. There are, also, Hispanic historians such as José Pijoán, Fernando Checa, and Valeriano Bozal.

Now, looking beyond issues of publication, we find the problem of critical perspective — the approaches with which we analyze the history of the arts in our country, our continent, and the world. It is not a secret, the predominant Eurocentric vision in our studies, and neither is it a mystery that Eurocentrism is permanently altering our historical and theoretical perspectives. It is at this point that we would like to discuss the subject of diversity and homogeneity in the study of art, issues introduced in the Art Seminar by Friedrich Teja Bach and James Elkins.

One of the dilemmas we deal with concerning the study and teaching of Latin American art is its connection with European and African art. Where do these currents converge? Where do they separate? We have on one side our indigenous past, the encounter with European cultures, and later the wars that lead to the long colonial period, which lasted in many South American countries well into the nineteenth century. We must reexamine, then, the interrupted history of aboriginal art in light of the European art that imposed itself through the Continent — for example the remarkable influence of Black slaves who arrived from Africa.

At the Universidad Católica, in the School of Letters where art is taught, we have separated European, Latin American, and Venezuelan arts as different subjects. Even so, there is a continuous dialogue between the instructors who teach the different courses, because it has proven impossible to separate the courses' contents.

As a culture born from the colonization process, our aesthetic terms are included within Western history, but for that very reason we have to pay special attention to the fact, typical of Latin America and the Caribbean, of the *mestizaje* or mixing of races. It is important to look at diversity as a basic element for art studies. On the one hand, it is necessary to understand the historical and aesthetical process of the cultures involved in the configuration of what we call Latin America. On the other hand, we must find out *how* the cultures mixed and what their mixtures produced. The main stream is still the great history of Western art, which has set aside the artistic expressions of other cultures, even though those continue to influence the painting, sculpture, and architecture of South America.

One of the problems in regard to art theory pertains to the research of concepts and chronological patterns for Precolumbian art. The majority of criteria for Precolumbian art comes from anthropology and archaeology. We could cite, for example, a book by Paul Westheim about ancient Mexico, which uses terms such as "horror vacui," "feudal art," and "Baroque ornament" to describe pre-Hispanic civilizations. Similarly, critics have tried to use a homogenous chronology for the whole of the South American indigenous world, even though the features, languages, and artistic expressions of those cultures were completely different. The gaps in histories of Precolumbian artistic traditions are partly a result of these inappropriate impositions. For example, in relation to the Maya culture, periods such as preclassical, classical, and postclassical (that is, Western periods) are used to catalog the Nahuatl people. Yet we cannot stop exchanging ideas and strategies with these other disciplines; we need to realize that Precolumbian art is still a mystery with many questions still unanswered.

The Art Seminar's panel explores the value of incorporating terms from the periphery to the center. That is the opposite of what we have suggested here. One would have to wonder if using a term such as *huaca* for European Art would not foster the same confusion that would result from talking about the Baroque in relation to a Precolumbian façade. Perhaps a strategy such as the one Elkins advocates will repeat mistakes that have already been made in regard to American aboriginal art.

How can we attend to diversity in each culture and also understand the exchanges and transformations that take place throughout Latin America? How can we insert modern Latin American art into narratives of the European avant-garde? The answer will not be found in Gombrich or Wölfflin, even though these authors are still essential for the understanding of the dominant European history. This is not an issue of emulation and dependence in relation to the big centers of power, and neither is it an issue of independence, according to which we might reject whatever is part of our cultural heritage. We can use different approaches and take different points of view without sparking a short circuit. There is no absolute discrepancy between South American concerns and European narratives: the main issue lies in the way we link our development with theirs, bearing in mind the aboriginal origins of our cultures and the contributions we have made to art's history.

A global vision of art studies could give a provisional answer; it might at least clarify this issue — but it is a possibility, not a reality. As we have said, there is no agreement on these issues in relation to Venezuelan and Latin American art. In that sense, there are no global studies of art in Latin America — at least not in Venezuela. It might take a lot longer for such studies to develop here, because we have not yet turned to other regions. The majority of our art programs do not include African, Chinese, Japanese, Hindu, or Canadian art. And even in our own art we include only those that are widely accepted and known by Westerners.

The same even happens with the art of the United States. We teach Jackson Pollock and Andy Warhol, but not Martin Johnson

Heade or Winslow Homer. There is scholarship in Venezuela that focuses on African art in America, and on the art of native peoples, but it cannot be said that there is a comprehensive view of such phenomena.

In spite of these dilemmas, we think it is possible to design a global plan for the study of art history. We need a global point of encounter, a place to meet, or a web where we can exchange ideas about diversity and plurality. In conclusion, our views here in Venezuela must be opened. We must dismantle the centralizing, national view in order to be to able appreciate the singularities of each culture.

—Translated by Norah Olive

Barbara Maria Stafford

Another Kind of Global Thinking

I see my comments as an occasion for proposing that art history completely reinvent itself using, in part, the ongoing discoveries of the neurological sciences to do so. Friedrich Teja Bach astutely asks: "What is the most pressing issue" facing us in the field, and, "Where do they need us as a discipline?" To my mind, answers such as focusing on globalization, on the politicization of the discourse, the trivialization of art, or the different ways of looking at reality — important though they might be — are all symptomatic of a greater problem. Art history's "aloof isolationism," in Ladislav Kesner's phrase, "its inability to demonstrate why it matters," needs to be addressed in connection with radically "other" realms of inquiry currently engaged in wrestling with some of the revolutionary intellectual issues of our times.

Jim Elkins rightly expresses concern for how we might incorporate globalization into our practices, for defining a global art history, and the physical conditions of art history worldwide. But how can these significant concerns be addressed if, as a field, we have not begun to formulate how the social purposes of art might be complexly linked to biological factors and vice versa? How can all sorts of humanistic visual studies be taken seriously when little effort is being made to correlate the structures and operations of the human brain — variable as it is — to the cultural objects that are its most brilliant products?

As things currently stand, it is far from obvious that art history is essential to other disciplines and, in point of fact, that we are not being replaced by them when it comes to attracting students and generating model-inspiring scholarship. Consider, for example, emergent cross-disciplinary "sensuous studies" (investigating the "feeling of what happens" in the multimodal senses from the color of angels to the many kinds of finesse associated with the skin).[3]

Consider, too, the rise of a phenomenologized, haptic media studies (updating Bergson's notion of the primary framing function of the human body by aligning it with developments in information technology).[4]

And then there is the cognitive turn — which I will be concentrating on in the remainder of this brief essay — inflecting everything from architectural theory to modeling in economics, to the new philosophy of mind.

I believe that the problem at hand is not so much that our root-level concepts are "underinterrogated," but that no fundamentally new information is being brought into the field. We spin old concepts, old theories, old methods around and around, growing ever more technically proficient about smaller and smaller matters — or so I think. Most troublingly, and unlike other disciplines such as anthropology, musicology, sociology, and even literary studies (which acknowledges the existence of "cognitive fiction"), we are not incorporating into our ongoing research the perspective-altering insights coming from the brain sciences. This state of affairs is all the more puzzling since neurology offers glimpses into the actual physical workings of such mental operations — basic to the humanities and, especially, to our field — as emotion, perception, attention, spatial and temporal awareness, consciousness, imagination, intuition, the varieties of memory.

Take an exemplary case. Consider David Summers's excellent question: Why has it been so hard either to modify the universalizing "story of art," on one hand, or to create a "newly structured story" that has more than merely local relevance? The rise of contextual art history in the late 1960s and early 1970s turned its back on the important "formalist" researches of Moholy-Nagy, Gyorgy Kepes, J.J. Gibson, among others, in favor of what has now become a primarily political interrogation of artistic practices. This exclusive "reading" of art (the reduction of its performative, spatialized dimensions to a flattened language — critiqued in my books from *Body Criticism* through *Visual Analogy*) had as one of its key consequences the atrophying of any serious inquiry into the role of form, morphology, and structure conditioning what and how we see.

This turn of events could not be more ironic. Take Semir Zeki's and V.S. Ramachandran's seminal books on the modularity of vision (the brain's task of representing the constant, enduring, essential features of objects, surfaces, faces, situations),[5] or the burgeoning research on the neuronal matrix of mental representations (our retention of imprints or engrams of visual and auditory experiences), and mnemonic fusions (reciprocal and irrepressible associations between shapes and memories of our emotional, somatoceptive, and cognitive experiences). Then there is pattern recognition (the common denominator among the multiple instances of an entity), the concerted interest in the filling-in process occurring in optical illusions (showing that perceptions are not necessarily tied to the object-world), and the return of the materialist interpretation of mental reality (the philosophical argument that mental properties, in particular experiential properties, are physical). All of which goes to show that the science of observing, sensing, and categorizing forms is back with a vengeance — everywhere but in art history.

This situation is not only lamentable, but paradoxical, because art history has much to contribute to these "formalist" concerns. If I have succeeded in demonstrating anything then it is that they cannot be dismissed as being simply, or "merely," formal. But to make these intellectual contributions, art history has to abolish, not its passion for genealogy and history, but its internal hierarchies. What has to go is the unnecessarily limiting, exclusive fine-art perspective. The field should be open to every class of image, to every type of imaging from the machinic to the mental, from the autonomous to the deliberate, from the shared to the unique, from the standardized to the variable.

I have cited a few examples of the myriad new publications that are relevant both to old issues and to exciting, unexplored territories and frames of reference. One might, for example, rethink the classical texts of Wölfflin, Riegl, Panofsky, and Kubler in light of them. But I want to conclude in the direction of fresh possibilities. I agree with Summers that we should invoke the embodied term of "spatial" rather than "visual" arts. Not only is the word less reductive, it conjures up relatedness, our boundness, and the boundaries (topos) of all things including ourselves, that must perpetually be bridged. Further, it corresponds more accurately to the spatial properties of our own bodies (bodily schema), the findings about spatial coordination (the performative fact that almost everything a human being does involves the perception of the spatial location of objects), and the coalescence of different stimuli into coherent patterns.

Vision, hearing, touch, and kinesthesis are the spatial senses. Their task is judging the spatial location of an object in relation to sense organs attached to different kinetic components of the body. The rotating eyeball thus embodies not only the nuances of that affective mobility, but reprises the entire art historical problematic of capturing "the shapes of time." That is, as the eye in the body momentarily moves to focus on a moving and changing object, it sets into motion the cognitive process of coordinating and integrating what has been witnessed among the various senses, the attendant motor commands, as well as initiating communicable actions on the larger stage of the external world.

Tracing a cognitive history of space, then, would take us backward in time to the hallucinatory entoptic geometries induced in Magdalenian-era caves and forward to the modern grid, and, now, to Web-based hypermedia. The latter, according to Stephanie Strickland, offer our perceptual system a "new calisthenics," enlarging the window of the present by bringing to consciousness more fine-grained stimuli, microfluctuations, and fractal patterns.

Inflected by brain science, art history could begin the difficult, but exhilarating, work of putting globally distributed visible structures in touch with an ocean of normally invisible anatomical and physiological processes. Bringing really new data to bear on our most pressing questions would invigorate what has become a tired field.[6]

Matthew Rampley

From Big Art Challenge to a Spiritual Vision: What "Global Art History" Might Really Mean

The question as to whether art history is global encompasses three separate issues. First: is art historical research and teaching undertaken globally? Second: might art history manage to establish a set of conceptual and thematic concerns with a global reach, or will it inevitably consist of a set of localized and incommensurable practices? Third: is art history adequate to the task of interpreting the global production of art in all its variants? In responding to these, one is forced to consider some fundamental difficulties that attend the rise of global, postcolonial art discourses. I will explore each of the questions posed above and then conclude with some broader considerations concerning the choices facing postcolonial art historians and critics.

The concern with the global extent of art history is itself the product of a specifically Anglo-American engagement with the aftermath of decolonization and creeping globalization. I had a recent salutary personal reminder of that fact when negotiating the topic of a lecture I was due to give in Riga; I suggested a talk on problems in the art history of non-Western cultures, and was met with a blank response. This was not, I was informed, something that would be of interest to an audience in Latvia. And indeed, why should it be? Latvia does not have the same history of engagement with extra-European cultures as the United States or the larger European states. "Postcolonial" in the Latvian situation denotes "post-Soviet," and has a completely different set of meanings from those circulating in the British or American context. Latvian and other Baltic art historians are primarily concerned with the (re)construction of their own national art histories in a process of cultural self-identification; engagement with the wider global situation could not have the same pressing importance that it does elsewhere.

The answer to the question as to whether art history is practiced globally is that in important respects it is not at all global and that in others it is increasingly becoming so. Crucial, of course, is consideration of the meaning of the term "art history." Taken in its restrictive definition — as an institutionalized discourse on art originating in eighteenth-century Germany and Austria and practiced largely in museums, art galleries, and universities — art history is clearly not practiced globally. There are numerous reasons for this: the material and institutional conditions for the discipline are absent in many countries. Even within Europe, art history in countries such as Britain or Greece, for example, is a relatively recent arrival and in the case of the latter is still a relatively marginal and under-resourced discipline. However, there is a danger that relying mainly on this notion — what James Elkins has referred to as "normal" art history — can result in a reified and limited concept of the discipline.[7]

A more expansive definition of art history, as a reflexive concern with artistic traditions, questions of value, or canons of artistic practice and their genealogies, would lead to an entirely different answer. For wherever art is produced, there is an accompanying reflexive discourse, with an often highly developed and complex conceptual vocabulary. Of course the contentious term here — as difficult as "art history" — is "art." For it is widely recognized that in most cultures autonomous art, as conceived in Renaissance and post-Renaissance Euro-American societies, does not exist. Instead, "art" is inseparable from other social practices, such as sex, religious belief, commerce, agriculture, and so forth. This difference can be overstated, however, for since the work of Pierre Bourdieu and other social critics, it has become apparent that autonomous art has never existed in Euro-American societies either. Autonomous art was thus always a bourgeois ideological projection, based on a disavowal of art's political and social meanings and functions. Moreover, the fact that the terms of reflexive art discourses are often incommensurate with those with which the Euro-American observer may be familiar does not necessarily lead to the conclusion that they are not forms of art history.

It is instructive to consider the case of art history on television, for it is recognized by the discussants as a far more important medium than the book. But when the discussants turn to this topic they mention the familiar touchstone of Kenneth Clark's *Civilisation*. This has long been seen as the epitome of what John A. Walker refers to as the "pundit series": "the TV equivalent of an art historian delivering an illustrated lecture."[8] Such an example does no justice to the breadth and variety of art discourse on European — certainly British — television. Yet more recent examples of art discourse on television show that this model ceased to be relevant some time ago; a striking example can be seen in the appearance of Madonna to present the televised award of the 2001 Turner Prize on Channel 4 in Britain. Madonna failed to follow the usual expectations of such an occasion, and delivered instead a rambling discourse on economics, love and the value of awards, culminating in her famous use of the word "fuck." As Glyn Davis has argued:

> It would, of course, be inappropriate to see this as a radical intervention in art historical discourse. However, the clash of Nicholas Serota and pop icon Madonna produces its own pleasurable frisson; seeing a woman talk about art on television remains a rare sight, and is always to be welcomed; and the language used by Madonna here is strange, unpredictable … The bizarre pre-planned swearing incident — possibly a pastiche of the infamous appearance of the Sex Pistols on the Bill Grundy show in the late 1970s — only adds to the air of awkward staginess.[9]

Another notable art program on British television was *Big Art Challenge*, broadcast on Channel 5 in 2004.[10] It combined game show, reality television, and art criticism; three judges — the art critic Brian Sewell, the founder of the clothing company *Red or Dead* Wayne Hemingway, and the artist Jane Wilson — traveled around Britain looking at art produced by artists and nonartists, attempting to whittle down the large number to a small selection, from which a final winner was to receive a prize of £10,000. This was supplemented with a "People's Prize" awarded by the viewers. What was noteworthy about the program was the way it set up an antagonism between Sewell — the traditionalist art critic — and Hemingway, whose comments were often treated by Sewell as crass, functionalist, and philistine. Though hardly offering penetrating new insights into the artists under consideration, *Big Art Challenge* nevertheless foregrounded the presence of conflicting ideologies of taste, class, and culture, and thereby broke with the liberal bourgeois consensus so often associated with art on television and, in particular, with *Civilisation* and its legacy.

It is important, therefore, to speak of art *histories* in the plural, which are practiced in a variety of institutional settings and which take on numerous, often incommensurate, forms. Rather than focusing on the global reach (or not) of "normal" art history it might therefore be more productive to consider those other kinds of art discourse that have proliferated in a multiplicity of contexts and for a large range of purposes.

While the tradition of art history since Winckelmann is only one of many species of art discourse, there is an increasing global convergence within academic art history on one particular model, and this is linked to the global cultural hegemony of the United States. If art history was dominated by Austrian and German scholars until the 1930s, it is clearly now North American art history and visual studies that provides the dominant model. The enormous accumulation of intellectual and economic capital in North America, and especially the United States, ensures that it has become dominant not only within the Anglophone world but in other areas too. As Sandra Klopper points out, for example, most African art history is produced by scholars from the United States, either by Americans or by Africans who were trained and became professionally established there. This is not necessarily the case globally yet; in regions such as China and India, for example, there remain powerful local discourses that often draw on long traditions of scholarship. The Chinese tradition of connoisseurship and art criticism is well known to Western audiences — even if only in outline — while concepts of artistic style and history have a long-established presence.[11] As Wen Fong has demonstrated, Chinese writing on the arts developed a complex account of historical change and periodicity completely independently of the evolution of Austro-German art history.[12]

A tradition of art discourses has also existed in India; the first art history in a language of the Indian subcontinent — Bengali — was published in 1874, but technical, moral, and philosophical treatises in Sanskrit on architecture, design, and the visual arts were written many centuries earlier.[13] Even here, though, the work of many contemporary leading Indian art historians — such as Tapati Guha-Thakurta or Partha Mitter — is thoroughly informed by the discourses of Anglo-American art history.[14]

An illuminating example of the exercise and effect of American hegemony can be found in the Summer Institute in Art History and Visual Studies organized by the University of Rochester in 1998 and 1999 and funded by the Getty Research Institute. These were directed toward art historians from Central and Eastern Europe, with lectures given by figures such as Norman Bryson, Michael Ann Holly, Stephen Bann, Kaja Silverman, and Kobena Mercer. The intention may have been laudable, but their net effect was promulgation of the message that local traditions of art historical scholarship were to be supplanted by American "new" art history and visual culture. The European participants were passive "recipients" of the addresses of distinguished Anglo-American scholars, and the first results have already become apparent, in the appearance of books by Eastern European authors following the model of Anglo-American Visual Studies.[15] "Anglo-American art history" refers here to the amalgam of Saussurean semiology, Lacanian psychoanalysis, Foucauldian discourse analysis, and Althusserian ideology theory that has become a hallmark of much of the most progressive and influential art historical scholarship generated within the Anglophone world.

My comments are intended neither to dispute the importance or value of Anglo-American art history, nor to defend other species of art discourse *per se*. They merely highlight the spread of a particular species of art history. Whether it will come to supplant all other traditions of scholarship is an open question; shifting geopolitical structures in the twenty-first century may mean that Chinese art discourses come to occupy a similarly dominant role. With regard to China I could not help but be struck by the Eurocentric assumptions of the discussion of the Chinese translation of Wölfflin. It seemed to have occurred to none of the speakers that Chinese scholars and students might treat Wölfflin in the same way that European and American scholars might treat older treatises from China, namely, as a historical artifact.

This leads on to the second and third questions, to do with the possibility and also the desirability of an art history with a global reach. At the root of these questions is a specific inflection of the crisis of ethnographic authority diagnosed and explored by James Clifford.[16] I shall deal with Clifford's own prescriptions later, but it is first worth considering the crisis within the context of art history. Criticisms of the Eurocentric assumptions of art history frequently focus on survey texts such as Ernst Gombrich's *The Story of Art*. Such attacks are widely understood and accepted; in his defense, however, one should recall that it was written for children. There can be few other academic disciplines in which a children's textbook has been treated as a serious academic work. Nevertheless, the collapse of Gombrich's (and others') metanarrative of art has led to a stress on the incommensurability of different artistic traditions, leading to a fracturing of the field.

David Summers's *Real Spaces* is of course an ambitious and complex attempt to reestablish such a global art history on a sounder conceptual basis than Gombrich's book for children. Another work with a similar objective, though within the field of anthropology, is Alfred Gell's *Art and Agency*.[17] Both offer ingenious and novel responses to familiar problems, and present significant possibilities for reframing art historical practice. Gell constructs a matrix for the cross-cultural analysis of art that focuses on the indexical functions of the artwork, which offers important new models for interpreting the relation between the artwork, its recipients, its referents, and its producer. However, the difficulty with Gell's account and with that of Summers is that the price of achieving such a transcultural and global reach is a level of abstraction and generality that bears a distant relation to concrete individual cases. Certainly, neither Summers's analysis of spatiality nor Gell's notion of the art nexus provides an armature that might support a global art history with a single narrative or set of narratives.

Does this mean that in the face of the collapse of the modernist search for totality we have to resign ourselves to a set of heterogeneous discourses emerging out of distinct cultural traditions? I think this is an unnecessarily pessimistic conclusion. As Craig Clunas has argued, the stress on cultural difference erases the numerous parallels *between* cultures.[18] Patterns of patronage in Renaissance Europe were not so different from those in contemporary China, and as James Cahill has argued, the Chinese notion of painting as an intellectual nonprofessional pursuit undertaken by the leisured upper classes was a rhetorical ploy, an ideological projection that deliberately downplayed the commercial basis of the production of pictures. The Chinese painter in the sixteenth century was as much an entrepreneur, working with the vagaries of the market and unpredictable patterns of patronage in the same way that his counterparts at the other end of the Eurasian land mass were doing. There are thus numerous instances when significant and informative comparisons can be made between cultural practices and meaning, and in which the practice of cultural translation is possible.

The discussion concerning the difference between Roman *ambulatio* and early Indian conceptions of *pradakṣiṇa* presents a more difficult issue. As Summers notes, while these two have quite distinct senses, the idea of circumambulation is quasi-universal, appearing in cultures as diverse as archaic Greece, the Aztec Empire, and Christian Europe. It seems that the discussion presents a bald choice, between either a postcolonial stress on the exclusivity of the two concepts or the grand system building of Summers that attempts to discern the wider category of which they are species. Both positions have some justification; following Summers, one might argue that in order to gauge the difference between *ambulatio* and *pradakṣiṇa* one needs to have a shared measure of difference or *tertium comparationis* — what he terms the "possible conditions of shared human spatiality." The idea of circumambulation *per se*, however, is fairly empty and abstract; it is only in its culturally specific forms that it takes on content. I would like to suggest that both Summers's response and that of the imaginary postcolonial critic are making impossible demands on Anglo-American art historical discourse. Summers attempts to remodel it in order to be able to fulfill the dream of a grand narrative, while the postcolonial critic condemns it for its inadequacies in accounting for global art and visual cultures. What both of these alternatives seem unwilling to address is the fact that translation and interpretation always involve *transformation*. Both seem to imagine that the pristine distinctiveness of other cultures can be maintained through the process of interpretation. In the case of Summers this is achieved through constructing a meta-vocabulary that can encompass the most extreme cultural differences. In the case of the postcolonial critic it involves assimilation to the conceptual vocabulary and values of the other culture. Some of the difficulties attending Summers's approach have already been spelled out, and a further problem is that it fails to meet its objective of transcending the limitations of traditional Euro-American art history, for it ultimately still relies on a Western representational apparatus. Substituting "spatial" for "visual" arts may solve certain problems, but Summers's solution is still open to the charge that use of the arts as a single category remains entangled within the legacy of European Enlightenment aesthetics.

It is also worth interrogating the postcolonial response, however, in particular because it is the one with the greater currency at present. It is evident that the insistence on the specificity of *pradakṣiṇa* (and its difference from *ambulatio*) highlights the need for sensitivity to local contexts. One could, of course, include other terms, such as *fu gu* or *da cheng*, mentioned by Ladislav Kesner, or *vāstu-śāstra* (the Sanskrit term for the science of design and architecture) or the various terms for vision among the Baule of the Ivory Coast, ranging from *nian* — which denotes intentional looking, even staring — to *nian klekle* (clandestine looking) to *kanngle* — which denotes an "evil look from the corner of the eye."[19] However, using these and other examples does not overcome the basic fact that they are still being removed from the specific cultural context to which they belong, translated into an alien context and idiom — Anglo-American art history — and set into a network of concepts and comparisons which transform their significance. Thus, the meaning of *pradakṣiṇa* becomes shaped by its *not* being *ambulatio*, by its *not* relying on the Cartesian notion of undifferentiated space of Western modernity and so on — in other words, by a set of oppositions that are the creation and interest of the contemporary Western observer. Likewise, different notions of vision can be compared and explored — by means of the Anglo-American (and specifically post-Foucauldian and Lacanian) concern with the gaze and visuality. Indeed, it is of no small significance that within such cross-cultural comparisons our own self-understanding can also often become impoverished; Summers's neat reduction of Western space to the difference between premodern "differentiated" and modern "undifferentiated" space is an example of just such an impoverishment.

The only way one might mitigate such transformations would be to attempt to become assimilated to the culture of the other, and some have followed this course.[20] James Clifford's response to the crisis of ethnographic authority is to argue for a form of dialogism — using a theoretical framework drawn from Bakhtin — that foregrounds the mutually transformative effect of cross-cultural encounters and mitigates the tendency to cast the ethnographic other as "object." As Clifford notes,

> It becomes necessary to conceive of ethnography not as the experience and interpretation of a circumscribed "other" reality, but rather as a constructive negotiation involving at least two, and usually more, conscious politically significant subjects. Paradigms of experience and interpretation are yielding to paradigms of dialogue and polyphony.[21]

Clifford goes on to cite a number of instances of ethnographic literature that try to circumvent the traditional power relationships within the discipline by thematizing the give and take between the (participant-) observer and the culture in question. This contains a number of possibilities, however. On the one hand it may consist in the complete erasure of the subjectivity of the author. This can be a self-defeating move, however, for, as Elkins has argued, "when the fundamental critical terms are non-Western the work can appear to lose its conceptual, cultural, and disciplinary foundation."[22] In any case, it is a utopian projection, for no matter how much "give and take" there may be, the encounter is still inscribed within the framework of the discipline. In the case of ethnography, the tradition of a poetics of ethnography, involving authorial reflexivity, has now become as orthodox a form of the discipline as the earlier colonial discourses it was intended to critique. There are other implications, too. Specifically, assimilation can lead to a loss of analytical power and end up replicating the practices and discourses of others, rather than interpreting and analyzing them. This is, of course, a minor case of the wider epistemological problem of representation; the difficulty with the emphasis on radical *difference* is that it is paradoxically motivated by a desire for complete mimesis — in other words, a complete immersion in the culture of the other that would overcome its alterity. Famously, Theodor Adorno and Walter Benjamin wrestled with this specific problem, and their work only served to highlight the aporia inherent in mimetic desire. Adorno's exposure of the aporia of the negative dialectic has continued to haunt theoretical reflection on cultural representation.[23]

A useful parallel with the general theory of criticism can also be drawn; one might think of Susan Sontag's famous polemic against interpretation, which was a particularly forceful expression of a long tradition, which held that the act of analysis in some sense degraded the artistic object.[24] Yet this can be set against another tradition of Romantic critical thought, from Friedrich

Schlegel onwards, which emphasized the *necessity* of criticism as a kind of supplement that helped the work achieve what it could not achieve on its own. For Schlegel it was the *externality* of criticism that enabled it to fulfill this function, and he was thus critical of those who wished to "defend" art from the encroachments of analysis. As he put it:

> If some mystical art lovers who think of every criticism as a dissection and every dissection as a destruction of pleasure were to think logically, then "wow!" would be the best criticism of the greatest of the greatest work of art.[25]

This is not to conclude that the intellectual landscape of Anglo-American art history might not or should not be transformed by contact with other discourses and concepts, but as Elkins states, there is little evidence of that happening, or of another discourse that might challenge the dominance of Anglo-American art history. The principal reason for this is that it is the only art discourse that has attempted to account for art globally; others have emerged in relation to the indigenous art practices they describe. Besides, Anglo-American art history tends to take global art very much on its own terms. This is particularly marked in the area I have a particular interest in: twentieth-century and contemporary art.

Since the 1980s the exclusive formulations of the modernist canon have been subjected to sustained attack. Polemics focused first on the artwork of minorities within Europe and America and later, in the wake of exhibitions such as *Magiciens de la Terre* at the Pompidou Center, on the wider global production of contemporary art.[26] This attention is very selective, however. Certain artists have since become the privileged focus of this concern with alterity: Shirin Neshat, Cheri Samba, Shirazeh Houshiary, Mona Hatoum, Simryn Gill. The common denominator uniting their work is that it addresses the same set of cultural, social, political, and aesthetic concerns that interests the American and European commentators examining their work. They have thus become assimilated to the canon of contemporary progressive "advanced" Western art. A typical example might be the volume *Displacement and Difference: Contemporary Arab Visual Culture in the Diaspora* that accompanied an exhibition staged in 1999 at the Brunei Gallery in London.[27] It was an important contribution to the study of a massively underresearched subject. It also brought to public exposure artists whose names are still hardly known beyond their immediate communities: Houria Niati, Thuraya Al-Baqsami, Mai Ghoussoub. What was equally revealing, however, was the choice of work; it was dominated by figurative painting and installation pieces. These were motivated heavily by questions of cultural identity, exploring issues such as gender identities in Middle Eastern societies or broader issues of Arabic cultural identity. Critiques of Orientalism also figured prominently. The pressing question to be asked is: what notion of Arab visual culture was this selection meant to represent? There was a remarkable absence of examples of calligraphy, for example, which is still central to many Arabic cultures. The introduction states: "visual culture [is] an active site for the renegotiation of identities and meanings … visual culture is part of the production of knowledge which is constantly open to new meanings, negotiated through points of identification and difference … meanings are multiple and not pre-determined."[28] Within the terms of contemporary cultural studies and Anglo-American art history these are unexceptionable sentiments, but they seem distant from the concerns of many contemporary Arabic artists, working to illustrate piously the unchanging values of the Qu'ran and Islam, for example. Subsequent events suggest this all too forcefully: secular notions of the fluidity and ambiguity of personal and cultural identity — coupled with the impact of globalized commoditization and usury — are precisely what have been most threatening to many societies.

As is the case with so much postcolonial art history and criticism, the choice of artists in this particular volume is framed by the desire to project onto the visual practices of other cultures the pluralist politics of the critic. Consequently, most of what one might classify as, in this case, Arabic visual culture, is omitted in favor of a Westernized diasporic elite.

It is worth comparing this exhibition with one held in the Tehran Museum of Contemporary Art in October and November 2003, entitled *A Spiritual Vision*. The exhibition, intended to show a "variety of artworks by Iranian contemporary artists whose creations reflect, through various methods, their association with spirituality ... works of art based on spirituality, metaphysical beliefs and the connotations in [*sic*] cosmology."[29] The thrust of the exhibition was to identify a specifically Iranian appropriation of the legacy of European Modernism and, in particular, abstraction, which, for the curators, was a particularly apt vehicle for expression of the Iranian impulse toward the spiritual, the divine, and the mystical. As such, the exhibition built on an earlier display of work by the sculptor Parviz Tanavoli, a leading figure in the *Saqqa-khan-e* movement of the 1960s, which attempted to use the signs of contemporary European and American abstract sculpture to explore traditional Shi'ite and Iranian religious and folk themes.

Thanks to both its location — Tehran — and its conservative content, *A Spiritual Vision* was guaranteed to be ignored by commentators outside of Iran, regardless of the merits of the works on display. It also highlights the challenges facing attempts by postcolonial art historians and critics to extend the reach of art discourse beyond Europe and America to encompass the diverse visual cultures practiced globally: many of them embody values that are the antithesis of those underpinning the desire for pluralism. It is a specific case of a more general problem in liberal democracies: how to accommodate those that do not hold to the idea of liberal democracy. Traditional art history was, rightly, critiqued for projecting a set of Eurocentric values onto the visual cultures of other societies. The paradox is that postcolonial art history is, in the name of pluralism, difference, and polysemousness, open to exactly the same accusation. The challenge, therefore, is how to respond to this. At the very least, if postcolonial art critics are serious in attempting to extend the reach of art history they should be willing to consider not just progressive diasporic art, reiterating the identity politics of the 1980s and 1990s, but also practices that many Western observers might regard as offensive, kitsch, dull, hackneyed, or simply incomprehensible. This might then compel a confrontation with the most important questions of all in this regard: What is the purpose of a globalized postcolonial art history? Who wants it? Who needs it? And to what end? The answers to these questions are not clear, but they are worth asking in any case.

Chika Okeke-Agulu

Art History and Globalization

The fundamental problem this seminar series confronts — the possibility of a global art history — is in some sense a confrontation with an important question facing contemporary society in the age of political and economic globalization. For it is impossible to dissociate this art historical problem from similar debates about the globalization of democracy and free market economy. Thus, in the same way that "democracy," supposedly the most desirable form of sociality invented in Euro-America, is vigorously, even forcibly, exported to the rest of the world, "art history" it seems must follow that same path, being, as it were, a part of the Western imperial, democratic culture. This is in some sense part of Edward Said's argument in *Culture and Imperialism*.[30] In other words, discussions about how global art history is, could or should be, must confront the ideological basis of the notion of the "global," which cannot be extricated from the political, economic, and cultural formations established in the age of colonialism and now supported by Western (post)-capitalist forces.

It is in this sense that Jim Elkins's opening discussion about the state art history in Africa, particularly in Nigeria, reveals certain truths about the connection between art history (and intellectual pursuits in general) and political economy. In the years following Nigeria's political independence in 1960, art history as a discipline was unavailable in many of the new Nigerian universities, and the few students interested in it traveled overseas. After their training, by the mid-1970s, they had returned to Nigeria. For the most part these "pioneer" art historians kept abreast of developments in the field, while establishing art history programs in local universities. But the imposition of IMF and the World Bank's Structural Adjustment and the consequent devaluation of the Nigerian currency in the early 1980s, in addition to widespread official corruption during the military dictatorships, led to economic decline and the impoverishment of universities and the educational system. Consequently, international travel for conferences, and importation of books and journals became virtually impossible, while the distressed local publishers engaged only in production of textbooks. In other words, art historians — like other scholars within the country — neither were able to keep in touch with current debates or developments within the discipline. Nor were there sufficient local structures to sustain a vibrant, even if isolated, internal art historical scholarship. Under these conditions, therefore, the few that were able to travel overseas, usually with the help of foreign scholarships, have never — or at least have not yet — returned, thereby giving rise the situation mentioned by Sandra Klopper. This is part of the current brain drain phenomenon that threatens to emasculate even further the political economies of Nigeria and several other postcolonial, underdeveloped countries in Africa and elsewhere.

Bearing in mind the scenario I have just sketched out, it is less difficult to find answers to questions about production of art history texts and the existence of art historians in places like Nigeria. Certainly there remain many art historians living and working in Nigeria, despite the desperate circumstances in which they work. (There is hardly any independent art history program in Nigeria. Rather, they are usually a part of Departments of Fine Arts, often with only two or three artist–art historians teaching art history. At the University of Nigeria, Nsukka, with one of the oldest art history programs, no more than three students have graduated with a BA in art history in the past thirty years; about the same number have completed the doctoral degree. Elsewhere in Nigeria, the figures are even less.) Only a few who have the opportunity to relocate to the United States or Europe remain in the country, largely isolated and unable to do meaningful research and publication. Further, the relatively small number of art historians and the very modest size of art history programs imply that the "market" for art history is insignificant and therefore hardly able to sustain local production of art history texts. The consequent lack of interest in art history texts on the part of local publishers has therefore given rise to a situation where most books authored by scholars are cheaply produced by vanity presses and, without any formal distribution networks, poorly circulated among the small community of local art historians.

Returning then to the idea of art history and globalism, we must then confront not only the specific circumstance of art historians and art history in the local space but also the possibility or otherwise of a meaningful exchange between the local other and "us." Let us then consider three questions. First: is globalism really art history's pressing issue, as Jim Elkins suggests? Whose art history? Second: should we, in the manner of international development agencies, send scholars along with the latest — or more likely dated — journals and books to sites of impoverished art histories, in order to resuscitate scholarship there? Third: is it even possible for local art histories and their discursive modalities to survive against the hegemonic forces of sociopolitical globalization — along with the attendant knowledge industries including art history?

Globalism is the pressing issue of art history only if we mean Western art history, which, like other knowledge industries, must align itself with the discursive and operative logic of political and economic globalization unleashed by postindustrial Western democracies and free-market economies. In other parts of the world — Nigeria for instance — the evidently more fundamental and pressing need for the discipline is on the order of asserting its relevance in a developing nation with little if any capacity for supporting disciplines whose direct impact on the national economy is questionable. (In 2005 the Nigerian president exhorted graduates of journalism and arts-related disciplines, including art history, to return to the university to pursue more useful academic learning. Though not a policy statement, his pronouncement suggests a view of art history in developing economies as useless intellectual endeavor.) Thus, in addition to proving their relevance within their given societies, the most crucial issue for art history in non-developed economies is far more basic: the production of texts, access to art collections where they exist, institutional support for research, and enabling intellectual environment. Moreover, if globalist art history means accepting the "standard" art history exemplified by Gombrich — in other words if it implies accepting the Euro-American way of thinking about art and art history in the same manner that globalization has often meant the forceful exportation of occidental political and economic paradigms as well as its mores and forms of sociability to other parts of the world, rather than a readiness to learn from other cultures — then it ought to be resisted, or at the very least subjected to vigorous critique in these latter locales.

Any discussion about art history and globalism as an idea will, perforce, confront the question of the processes through which a global art history can be accomplished, and it is this latter question that will reveal the contradictions of this very notion. Already, it is apparent that Euro-American art history accommodates only those art historians from Africa, Latin America, and Asia who have mastered the language of *Western* art history, rather than the possibly new, "unfamiliar" ideas and methodologies they could bring to bear on "our" art history. In other words, it is their familiarity and competence with authors such as Clark, Baxandall, Heidegger, and Merleau-Ponty, together with their understanding of European art historical traditions and theories, that guarantee them access to these institutions, even when in fact their focus is on the work of artists living in Guanghzou or in Ouagadougou. While it might make sense that scholars working in Europe or America ought to master Western art history and its methods, and because to Western art historians Africa or Asia are no more than places to conduct occasional field research while retaining their (intellectual) affiliation to their home institutions — in other words no permanent relocation to these locales — no meaningful exchange or dialogue is possible. Whereas it is natural to gauge the competence of scholars living in Africa by their familiarity with European art historical models and paradigms, the reverse scenario is as strange as it is unimaginable. This tendency to insinuate the importance of European cultural traditions in the very idea of art history as such forecloses any real possibility of refashioning the discipline to reflect other traditions that might indeed suggest alternative notions of art and methodologies of art historical practice. This is the same paradox one sees in mainstream processes of globalization (read Westernization) that resist the formation of multitudinous global culture — what I believe Léopold Senghor meant by his notion of universal civilization[31] — through dialogue between "civilizations," economic and political models and social systems.

We are thus left with two alternatives. The first, pessimistic I must concede, is predicated on the logic of prevailing global economic and political trends: Western models and methodologies of art history will remain the only "viable" option, and the establishment of a meaningful global art history will depend on how efficiently this model is exported to the rest of the globe as well as on the extent to which African, Asian, or Latin American art historians resist or capitulate to a knowledge industry that does not so much acknowledge the possibility of a decentered art history as prepare to exterminate alternative or opposing discourses from the non-Western world. The progress of art history in the age of globalization must therefore be measured by the rate of diffusion of Western paradigms and methodologies, and that is why globalism must be this particular art history's pressing issue. For it must demonstrate its relevance and therefore its contribution to the naturalization of the processes of political and economic globalization. The second alternative, the more optimistic one, will be the rise of a global art history constituted not so much through a diffusion of Western art history as through the formation of several, parallel or contradictory, art historical models and methodologies, each a product of specific cultural and political histories and ideologies. Much less certain than the first, but clearly more accommodating of difference, this future art history will mean a true dialogue across intellectual cultures rather than the expectation that only the ones originating from the West could define the parameters and scope of art history across the globe.

Keith Moxey

Art History after the Global Turn

What are the consequences for the history of art when economic markets are increasingly integrated and cultural interaction has been heightened through technological developments in the field of communications? Should it proceed in a spirit of "business as usual," or should it attempt to accommodate itself to the new circumstances? Is art history a specifically Western discipline, or can it aspire to some sort of universal value? How do its concerns and obsessions appear from a non-Western perspective? How parochial is art history when seen from a global point of view? Can the artistic traditions of non-Western cultures be addressed using interpretive grids adopted in the study of western art? Do these theories and methods inevitably distort our understanding of the non-Western "other?" Can non-Western art history be done without them? The organizers of the Cork Art Seminar, James Elkins in particular, as well as those who took part, are to be thanked for having sought to confront these questions directly.

Art history, like so many Western institutions, was inherited by the non-Western world as part and parcel of the heritage of colonial and neocolonial experience. Like the concept of art itself, art history is inextricably united to the history of the nation state. It was under the banner of nationhood, in the name of the very principle that animated the colonial expansion that allowed European powers to seize most of the known world, that subordinated peoples were able to throw off the yoke of their oppressors. The idea of the nation has proved one of the most dynamic and durable of colonial exports, one whose potential for both positive and negative historical developments never fails to amaze. Just as every self-respecting new nation had to have its own museums, in which artifacts hitherto identified with social and ritual purposes were redefined so as to be elevated to the new status of "art" in order that they might compare and compete with the trappings of Western "civilization," so every nation had to have its own art history. Insofar as former colonies were in a position to erect a university system modeled on that of the colonizing powers, art history was integrated into the curriculum. The insatiable urge to map the world according to universal principles prompted the institutions of the former colonial powers to continue their ambitious attempt to render the world transparent to a single point of view. Ironically enough, the most important agents in the study of non-Western art history have been the Western nations once involved in the colonial adventure.

The focus of the Cork discussions was in large part centered on a recent book by David Summers, *Real Spaces*, that offers a theory and a method by which to study the art of all the world's cultures. In this ambitious and imaginative study, Summers offers a complex argument (to which I must fail to do justice here), in which he argues that all art can be analyzed according to basic principles derived from human "being-in-the-world." Insofar as we are human, "we" are all thought to share the same assumptions regarding space and our place within it. Fully aware of the pitfalls associated with the idea that all humans are somehow the same, Summers believes that "we" cannot help but share these common assumptions because we have no other choice. "We" are condemned to reduce our experience to the same coordinates because of the nature of our bodies and their relation to the circumstances in which they find themselves.

Social space is a condition of human existence — we find ourselves among others — and we do so in culturally specific circumstances. In these terms, social space is second nature in the sense of ingrained habit, but, as I shall argue, there is also a sense in which second nature simply is "nature," since given nature is never encountered in itself, but rather from within a culture.[32]

By fusing nature and "second nature," Summers seeks to avoid the possibility that his system, his account of how "we" understand the world, might be criticized as ideological or representative only of a particular point of view. He thus effectively naturalizes the assumptions that he brings to the enterprise of interpretation. In doing so, his position echoes aspects of that of Richard Rorty, who argues that one's values cannot escape the context of the culture of which they are a part.[33] Rorty, however, seems more prepared to grant the limitations and biases associated with identifying one's views as culturally specific than is Summers. Whereas Rorty sees the impossibility of escaping the values of one's circumstances as responsible for cultural conflict, Summers finds it a basis for reconciliation and harmony.

By insisting that nature is always encountered within a culture, Summers proposes to accommodate and reconcile notions of difference and universality. On this view human bodily experience must correspond to the conceptual framework of his theoretical system. The degree of abstraction on which his concepts operate (planarity, centrality, axiality, etc.) make it impossible to determine whether or not he is right. What matters here is whether an interpretive system based on the alleged universality of human experience is a useful tool to an art history that is increasingly aware of the limitations imposed on its own project by its Western origins and history. Does it make sense to rely on a phenomenological approach to understanding the art of radically different cultures? Does not the cultural aspect of bodily experience outweigh whatever spatial coordinates humans might share based on their bodily structure?

To some extent these are, and must remain, imponderables. For example, are "human rights" best served by arguing that they are an inalienable dimension of human dignity — that the very definition of humanity involves the notion of rights — or is their cause better served by arguing that our own particular, culturally determined values require us to insist that human beings be treated with consideration and respect? The answer will, of course, lie in political circumstance. In certain situations one approach may work better than the other and vice-versa. Summers is leery of approaches to intercultural interpretation that depend on assertions of identity based on cultural specificity. He argues that such assertions are essentialist and lead to conflict and strife. Nevertheless, the pitfalls of a commensurable approach to cultural difference seem as dangerous as those that stress its incommensurability.

It currently seems more important to advocates of artistic traditions that have been and continue to be misunderstood by Western ideas of history and aesthetics that they be able to analyze and deconstruct the peculiar nature of those ideas rather than acknowledge their universal validity. African critics, for example, attempt to determine what values have been and continue to be projected onto the cultural production of their continent in order to determine the reasons for its continuing occlusion from Western consciousness. While the categories proposed by Summers may well result in historical and aesthetic accounts that are less biased than those that have characterized the past, it is the very universality of the ambition that is suspect. What are the specific reasons for Western inattention and disregard? What local characteristics prevent African cultures from being incorporated into the allegedly universal interpretive schemes of the West? The degree to which issues of local identity matter in contemporary African criticism may be gauged from the following statement by Olu Oguibe:

> To reject the exoticization of Africa is to destroy an entire world-view, carefully and painstakingly fabricated over several centuries. This is the imperative for any meaningful appreciation of culture in Africa today, and it would be unrealistic to expect it easily from those who invented the old Africa for their convenience. It dismisses an existing discourse and signifies a reclaiming process that leaves history and the discursive territory to those who have the privileged knowledge and understanding of their societies to formulate their own discourse. This is not to suggest an exclusionist politic, but to reassert what is taken for granted by the West and terminate the ridiculous notion of the "intimate outsider" speaking for the native. It recognizes that there is always an ongoing discourse and the contemplation of life and its sociocultural manifestations is not dependent on self-appointed outsiders.[34]

Oguibe's insistence on the importance of African identity to the understanding of African art might be also be characterized as "essentialist." His is a political rather than a metaphysical essentialism, however. Elsewhere, he is prepared to grant the constructed and malleable status of what is called African while at the same time insisting on its crucial role in interpretation.

In the course of the Cork Seminar, James Elkins reiterates some of the reservations to Summers's text he had already expressed in his review. The most important of these is perhaps his criticism of Summers's conception of space. In the review, Elkins points out that the Western concept of space has a history and that it has a specificity that is incommensurate with notions of space used in other cultures. On this occasion, he argues that in positing a phenomenological space that determines human experience of nature and art as a universal, Summers is imposing a distinctly European notion of space on an art history that is meant to have multicultural implications. Similarly, Elkins and others wondered whether culturally specific terms might not have greater purchase on the significance of different artistic traditions than those coined in the Western tradition. Despite some animated and highly interesting exchanges, the conversation seems to have ended without any degree of unanimity as to whether art history might be global or not.

In his review of Summers's book, Elkins concluded by embracing a paradox: While discerning the greatest potential interest in scholarship that paid attention to both non-Western concepts as well as non-Western methods of analysis, he admitted that this would result in the dissolution of the discipline. Such scholarship would have multiple principles of organization and conflicting terminologies whose mutual incoherence would result in forms of knowledge that would be unrecognizable as art history as the discipline is currently conceived. The fact that art history continues to be identified with Western cultural and economic domination, however, need not necessarily prevent us from discerning the contingency of its narratives. Unlike the Summers proposal, it may not be necessary to treat the assumptions of Western narratives as if nature and culture coincided. While the limits of self-consciousness prevent us from entirely comprehending the full parameters of the ideological circumstances in which we swim, we can at least realize that those circumstances have edges and that they are not universally valid. Like art historians, historians have also become more and more aware of the way in which Western narratives, inescapable though they may be, continue to distort our understanding of the non-Western past. Dipesh Chakrabarty, for example, demonstrates the problems associated with attempting to understand the Indian past through a lens shaped by Hegel and Marx. He argues that these models necessarily relegate Indian history to the margins of world history because neither the world spirit nor the class struggle ever made an appearance there.[35] He suggests that even if Western authors and theories of history have skewed accounts of India's heritage, they cannot be disregarded. If new interventions in historical writing are to give us a better picture of what happened in previous ages, it will only be if such narratives have been absorbed and incorporated in the new. What is called for is a "deconstruction" of the stories that have already been told in the hope that this will allow us to see the necessary "supplements" on which the writing is based. Since writing betrays the time and place of its composition, the values used to create meaning are capable of articulation and contestation:

> The project of provincializing "Europe" therefore cannot be a project of "cultural relativism." It cannot originate from the stance that the reason/science/universals which help define Europe as the modern are simply "culture-specific" and therefore only belong to the European cultures. For the point is not that Enlightenment rationalism is always unreasonable in itself but rather a matter of documenting how — through what historical process — its "reason," which was not always self-evident to everyone, has been made to look "obvious" far beyond the ground where it originated.[36]

It is in a dialogue between the narrative constructed by the dominant tradition of the West and those who have been marginalized as a consequence of that domination that the future of a "global" art history may be perceived. Like any other narrative its thrust will reflect the political circumstances in which it is constructed and its future will be as contingent as anything it may have replaced. Elkins is right when, in his review, he argues that art history cannot remain unchanged as it addresses the cultural production of the non-West. The recognition that art history's fundamental assumptions are culturally determined, that they belong to the dominant tradition of Western thinking, will have to be taken into account. I suggest that it is along the fault lines of cultural difference rather than in a commitment to commensurability that work remains to be done.

Suzana Milevska

Is Balkan Art History Global?

In the title of my text I reformulate the question "Is art history global?" that has been suggested as a starting point of this discussion about the situation in art history today. By so doing I want to point to many difficulties with this question as it is formulated in the title of this volume and to some of its absurd implications in different contexts. If one asks, "Is Balkan art history global?" the question becomes rhetorical, and it is clear from the outset what the answer to it would need to be.

Just to start with the most obvious reason for the negative answer: there are hardly any art historians or art history books from the Balkans that are known anywhere else but in their own region. A second point would be related to the term "Balkan art history": it is known that the Balkans are not a homogenous region; because of many political and military conflicts in the past, the professionals from the countries that form the Balkans do not communicate easily with each other and hardly read each other's art historical texts. Therefore, part of the second reason is that one can hardly claim that there is a Balkan art history as such. The third reason, which is perhaps predictable, is that, being obsessed with their own problems in defining what is regional, national, and international art history, the Balkans did not always follow the same pace as art history in the West. It is difficult to generalize, however, because it can be as difficult a task to compare the situations in art history in Greece, Romania, the countries of ex-Yugoslavia, Albania, and Turkey as to compare the art histories in different continents. The different historic and political background of all these states somehow shaped their intellectual histories as well.

It is to be expected that a similar absurdity will emerge in any attempt to reformulate the question in other parts of the world. The questions, Is Icelandic art global? Is the art history of Armenia global? Is Scandinavian art history global? Is American art history global? will bring new paradoxes. If the answer to each of these separate questions is always negative, how can one then expect that there is any global art history that can aim to compare, synthesize, and analyze all these art histories?

The only rational argument here is that the question is exactly about overcoming any of the borderlines between these different national or regional art histories and thinking the possibility of one art history for all of them. Some of these art histories will not lend themselves to a globalizing definition simply because they belong to small cultural entities, whose members are afraid they might be easily swallowed by a single global discipline. Some of them, as in the case of Balkan art history (and I assume in the case of many other regions), are not even established as such since there are no academic and intellectual forums that would formulate the objectives and extent of such regional art history studies. The issues of different languages and translation, as well as different educational systems, make the initial question even more difficult. When I mention the issue of translation, I do not necessarily think of translation into English. In the Balkans alone, there are about twenty different languages, and in order to have an art history that would comprise the arts of the region one would presume that they should all need to first translate each other's histories.

In order to avoid such paradoxical conclusions one needs to take a step backwards and ask what might make art history global. Several criteria would have to be taken into account in order to define what kind of a global history one might talk about today. If it is easy to agree that the trap of discussing Western versus non-Western art history is not very productive and is limited to certain preconceptions about art history itself, one of my main questions would be: Is there an art history that can be global without the use of such dichotomies?

To confront the question I suggest three topics that can help clarify the problem of thinking about art history in global terms, and illuminate the possibility of finding a single art history that is concerned with world art. I will discuss historicity (the linear historical development of art), translation, and problems of the educational system.

1. Historicity

It is difficult to write and talk about art history today when it seems no one believes that there can be a linear history as such. There are two separate tendencies in the academic world of art history today. On the one hand, art history departments are rapidly vanishing from the curricular maps of Western universities under the pressure of establishing new departments that take on some of the subjects of art history, but disguised in new nonhistorical forms. The subjects of such study are topics and issues rather than historic periods, styles, or national art histories. Visual studies, cultural studies, postcolonial studies, and visual culture, to mention only a few, are growing in new departments that deal with issues similar to those dealt with by art history, but in wider and transdisciplinary perspectives. Art history begins to sound obsolete or even unnecessary.

On the other hand, in order to protect art history as it has been conceived and studied from the outset, as a distinct discipline, the old departments of art history that survive often try to push it in the opposite direction. They become even more conservative and stick to the older way of teaching art history. They retain the division of art into historic periods, styles, and movements, with emphasis given to national and regional developments. These tendencies are particularly evident in so-called "peripheral" cultures and art histories, for example, in art history as it is taught in the Balkans.

The gap between old or traditional art history departments (preserved by professors who were there from the start of the departments, or by the ones who represent the department's second generation) and the newly established forums (staffed mostly by young professionals who have been educated abroad) becomes wider and wider.

The historicity of art history is often questioned as inappropriate, especially when taking into account that new disciplines and theories (and here I want to add gender, gay and lesbian studies, and queer theory), all deal with art history from their own perspective. One of their main aims is to deconstruct art history as we knew it and studied it, in particular because of its inability to embrace cultural, ethnic, and gender differences.

One reason for the recent overshadowing of art history by all these new disciplines and departments is that traditional art history does not allow certain complex cultural questions to enter its methodology. It focuses on art in isolated terms, distinct from the cultural activities that shaped it such as popular culture, media, and cultural politics, and separate from more complex issues such as the patriarchal regimes of representation and state power. For a long period art history has limited itself to a very narrow register of topics.

It does not come as a surprise that there are difficulties with conceptualizing art history in global terms. If art history still relies on the periodization of art styles and movements, and if it concentrates on phenomena that have been expressly developed to interpret Western art, it is difficult to imagine that art history can operate in new contexts with any precision or relevance.

Here I will give one quick example that can illustrate the obstacles one can encounter when applying Western art history in another context: the emergence of modern art in different parts of Europe, in particular in Macedonia. There are many different definitions of the term "modernism" and disagreements about its dating in art history; it is not a fixed term, and that may allow it a certain flexibility, but I find none of its definitions are applicable to the art of Macedonia. The whole early period in which modernist styles differed from one another is missing; no secular easel paining at all was produced in this part of Europe until the 1920s. Art was limited to fresco painting, icons, wood carving, weaving, and embroidery. However, in the middle of the nineteenth century the first photographers started operating in the region. In different parts of the Balkans this gap between the first easel paintings and the first photographs differs, but in Macedonia in particular, easel painting began long after many Western art styles and periods and also long after the first photographs were taken. In this way, one could understand why the introduction of modernism was unlike most places, where photography was available to influence painting.

The signatures of the first known photographer in Macedonia, Hadzi Koste, known as "the fresco painter and photographer," have been found on two frescoes, in the church St. Demetrius in Veles (1855) and in the monastery St. George in the village Čičevo (1860–1868). This is an example of how the medieval medium of fresco painting was practiced in parallel with photography, and how modernism in the Balkans circumvented many of the periods of Western art history.[37] The question here is whether art history as it has been written can deal with this kind of specific historical order without calling it backwardness.

2. Translation

The issue of translation in art history is in a way related to the issue of historicity and backwardness.[38] If Western art history is taken, as it usually is, as a point of reference, then it comes as no surprise that the question of translation produces the effect of lag and backwardness. The sooner the translation of a certain book is published, the more widely it can spread in the academic world. However, it is important to underline here that the translation of art history books from one language to another is, more than any other kind of translation, an issue of cultural translation. The translation of an art historical text is a question not of names, facts, or dates, but of different art concepts, cultural contexts, and geographic settings.

Academics from remote countries that are not a part of the Western scholarly world often complain because they do not have access to the latest books written in English and published by renowned university professors in the West. I find that one of the greatest obstacles to the globalization of art history is the focus on only one direction of translation. I would argue that cultural translation, unlike linguistic translation, is only possible if it goes in reciprocal directions and that art history is not an exception of this rule.

In the roundtable, James Elkins mentions the well-known book by Steven Mansbach.[39] One cannot but agree with Elkins's comment that the frequent comparisons made in the book between Eastern and Western artists often do not add any relevant or contextual information about the Eastern artists. I mention this example only because in my view this limitation in Mansbach's writing on Eastern European art occurs because Mansbach's only source and point of departure would have been the array of Western art history books. Had there been Eastern art history books translated into English, he would have been able to add more local and contextual references. Of course, even if such books had been translated, Mansbach would have probably encountered another problem: the fact that often even in the locally written and published books the most frequent comparisons are (just as happens in his book) between Eastern and Western artists.

(It is worth mentioning in this context that a lot of translation in the Balkans and in Eastern Europe of art historical materials is done by museums. These kinds of textual and visual materials are much more readily accessible to Mansbach and other foreign researchers of local art scenes, but it should not be forgotten that museums often have different interests and policies than art historians, and that foreign researchers need to be aware of museums' particular agendas.)

3. Educational Systems

Both the issue of historicity and the issue of translation are woven into the framework of educational systems. How can one expect that art history can be a global discipline unless the educational systems become global? I will not enter here into a discussion of the ethical problems involved in urging the globalization of the educational system, even though it is also quite urgent. Educational systems are widely discussed in postcolonial theory and even though they are relevant to this discussion on art history, they would require more space than I have here.[40] I will just say that art history is not and cannot be global if globalization is expected to happen only through writing. Writing is an organic part of the educational system.

I will end where I started, with art history departments and their attitude toward historicity, national art histories, and translation. In 1980, I witnessed a dramatic event at the Art History Department in Skopje (then Yugoslavia, today Macedonia). I was a second-year student and I was invited to attend a press conference held by our professors (today most of them are retired). The immediate reason for the conference was a journalist's attack that had been published in a local newspaper by an ex-student of art history from the same department. He had written a severe critique, claiming basically that the professors were lazy, and that they had not produced any relevant articles or books. One of the professors who had been asked to deal with the "hot potato" led the press conference; he brought into the room a great pile of books, magazines, abstracts, and other materials that were to prove that the newspaper article was simply a mean and naïve attempt at revenge for some disagreements between the student and his ex-professors. The number of papers was really amazing, and at first I thought the department was astonishingly productive.

What struck me then, and stays with me even now as I think back to this episode, is that not one single book on display in that pile that was an attempt to summarize Western and Eastern European art in the span of a single volume. Not a single book or essay discussed anything but Macedonian art, regardless of the period (ancient, medieval, or contemporary). All the texts on display were nationally oriented historical overviews of certain medieval monuments, monographs on contemporary artists or on Macedonian art in general, or textbooks that were solely devoted to Western European artists. There was not a single translation of an article or a book by an internationally renowned art historian. (I agree, this kind of translation should be done by professional translators, but professionals could at least be given seats on editorial boards, or be asked to write introductions.) Moreover, there was not a single translation of a book by any of my professors into another language, not even into the neighboring languages — into any of the twenty Balkan languages. This episode took place twenty-five years ago. Many things have changed since then, except the last.

Art history changes. It slowly opens up toward other disciplines and toward nonlinear temporalization. It lends itself to different methodologies that go beyond the comparison between Western and non-Western art. The old joke that you can always recognize if a speaker at a conference has an art history background if you see two projectors starts to fade, and many different instructional methods are being introduced (though not everywhere, of course). This movement within the educational system necessary for any movement towards globalization.

I find projects such as *Is Art History Global?* urgent and necessary mainly because its title shows readiness to question rather than give answers. Perhaps the reason art history is not global now (and I believe it would be naïve to think that it is) is the result of earlier art history, which had all the answers ready at hand before it was even written, and was based on the limited experience of its writers.

To conclude, global art history can only benefit if it translates and incorporates whatever local art historical knowledge is accessible. Perhaps one of the most important aims of global art history is to turn the local art histories into parts of the "glocal" heritage.[41] If questions of historicity and translation become clearer in the light of cultural and postcolonial studies, and if those studies have helped art history to clarify its own objectives, then the educational system should follow, and attempt to create new and more flexible models of teaching that can elevate art history to a global level.

Atta Kwami

Art History in Ghana

There is evidence that art was made 77,000 years ago — a painting, made with red ochre crayons, in a South African cave.[42] If art is global, how can art history not be global?

Art history has the following elements that the roundtable addresses: art making, the training of scholars, patronage, canons, display and exhibition, dissemination, and criticism. The processes whereby senses of identity are constructed by, within, and with artifacts, as the art historian John Picton has shown, provide a useful model for art history: "We must learn to understand how individual people, households, and communities build their identities with one another, and understand the place of artifacts in that process."[43] Yet an absence of documents and texts makes art history difficult in societies where written biographies and contractual documents do not exist. The publication of a photograph from Kumasi in west Africa, "Billboards at the Railway Station," by Karl Hartenstein in his book *Anibue (Civilization)* (1932) raises pertinent questions regarding our approaches to the question of art history as a global phenomenon.[44] Hartenstein was director of the Basel Mission at the time of its centenary anniversary, and produced the book after a tour of the Gold Coast, which was then at the threshold of newly found freedoms of modern living, made possible by the ending of older traditions. His book is seminal in documenting the advent of media trafficking through the agency of modern-day advertising, the West African Publicity Agency.[45] The United Africa Company formed this agency, according to Kwame Akatu, one-time president of the Ghana Association of Advertising Agencies, and author of the authoritative *History of Advertising in Ghana,* in 1927. It placed posters and enamel signs, imported from England, all over the country — on and inside buses, in trains, at railway stations, and on trees.

The question of what is contemporary and modern in Ghanaian art is generally an issue of visual practices with regard to the "just now," involving many traditions that are contemporary with each other. A way of introducing viewers to the contemporary art of Ghana is to explore the country, from its coast up to the northernmost parts. This approach has been applied in dealing with several traditions of making, training, patronage, and display. In this light the models of Modernism (with a capital M) from the citadels of western Europe or the Americas would be untenable in the Ghanaian situation. The emergent global avant-garde creates headless bodies from the spoils of art. Meanwhile, in Africa there are real, disembodied heads.

In the pre–World War II era, in Africa, the global trafficking of images infused the Ghanaian art scene with a contemporary cultural history not dissimilar to that of northern Europe. We had the workings of a local African modernity, sparked by photography, by the end of the nineteenth and the turn of the twentieth centuries. Academic painting and street painting (most importantly in Kumasi, Ghana's second-largest city) are influenced by photography and collage, especially regarding the fusion of image with text. The inception of art school training at Achimota around 1927 also coincides with the first advertising agencies in Ghana.[46]

Kumasi became a great center of commerce in the 1920s and 1930s and continues to be such today. Half a century on, in Kumasi there are over one hundred sign-painting workshop masters with their assistants and apprentices; they are exploring both Kumasi painting and mechanical reproduction, including photography and the opportunities it affords for realistic depiction.[47] It is arguable that the earlier billboards posted at such places as railway stations were a model for the sign painters in Kumasi. The confluence of billboards, collage, photography, and painting is crucial: the first art college of sub-Saharan Africa was relocated to Kumasi in 1952.

The following books were in use during the 1950s at the Kumasi College of Technology, Science and Arts (now called Kwame Nkrumah University of Science and Technology, Kumasi — KNUST): Margaret Trowell's series *Art Teaching in African Schools* (volume 1, *Design*; 2, *Materials*; 3, *Basket Work*; 4, *Picture Making*); *Anatomy for Artists* by Reginald Marsh; and Helen Gardner's *Art Through the Ages* (in an edition published by Bell & Son).[48] Another work, Kojo Fosu's *20th Century Art of Africa* (1986, 1993) was also used. Regarding the pioneering role of Ghanaian art education in West Africa, this was not addressed by Fosu, nor did he address developments in Ghanaian painting. Recent works such as *Seven Stories about Modern Art in Africa*, edited by Clémentine Deliss (1995) and *The Short Century: Independence and Liberation Movements in Africa 1945–1994*, edited by Okwui Enwezor (2001), may have also helped to reverse the trend of Eurocentric histories.[49]

Locally produced Ghanaian resource books are now beginning to appear in the bookshops: Ernest Victor Asihene's posthumously published work, *A Brief History of Art with Special Reference to West Africa* (2004),[50] and Simon Alex Akoto's encyclopedic *Understanding Visual Arts Volume 1: A History and Appreciation of Art for Secondary Schools, Training Colleges and the Universities* (2004).[51] These two books provide interesting information on West African and European developments, from masks to Renaissance, Baroque, rococo, and Neoclassical art.

Indigenous art criticism has always taken place at palaces, shrines, and workshops or household compounds. The arts of canoe decoration, textiles, jewelry, metal work, wood carving, and murals have long been practiced by the Akans and others.[52] The many groups and languages in Ghana all practice indigenous art criticism to interpret everything from architectural forms, including wall paintings, to modernist painting and sculpture, pottery and textiles, wood and metalwork and basketry.

The first written publications by Ghanaian artists are those of Oku Ampofo, a practicing physician (1908–1999); Seth Cudjoe, also a medical officer with the Ministry of Health (1910-); and Kobina Bucknor, a research biologist (1925–1975). All were largely self-taught artists. The first was trained as a painter and writer; the second, as a sculptor; and the last as a painter. Ampofo and Cudjoe rediscovered the power of African art when they were studying abroad, as did Bucknor in New York. Their creations helped to expand the repertoire of modern visual practice. Recent art critics include Nat Armateifio, an architect and former mayor of Accra whose work was published in the late 1970s in *The People's Daily Graphic* (a local newspaper in Accra); and Kojo Fosu, former dean of the College of Art, KNUST, who in 1986 wrote a key work, *Twentieth-Century Art of Africa*.[53]

Asihene (1968–2001), a painter, diplomat, and the first African dean of the College of Art in Kumasi, was an early writer on painting practice. In his "Painting in Ghana," he refers to three kinds of makers. First are those working from "virgin, unsophisticated and unbiased sources"; second, those "copying from … western artists"; and third, those who study their own culture. Asihene is aware of the problems posed by foreign influence and is able to discriminate among different cases.[54] In "Painting in Ghana," he concludes:

> As I sit in my studio in Accra and think of my many brothers across West Africa (most of them in Nigeria), I feel proud that I belong to that large brotherhood of artists bound together

> by common culture and objectives. But then, I grieve and feel ashamed that we have not as yet managed to organize ourselves into the "Great Brotherhood of West African Artists," which should be our pride. I know it is easy to make an emotional statement such as this, but I have the greatest hope that it will come to pass before long.[54]

The discipline of art history has not taken root at the university level, and there is no undergraduate program in art history. A few newspapers such as the *Weekly Spectator*, *The Daily Graphic*, *Graphic Showbiz*, and *The Mirror* carry reports of art events, often in the form of entertainment guides, but no regular columns devoted to art criticism. An exception is John Owoo, formerly of *Graphic Showbiz*, who publishes current art criticism on the website of the Foundation of Contemporary Art. This dearth of criticism may be because the critic is seen as a destabilizing agent in a society where to dare to criticize one's artistic forbears is like showing disrespect to one's father.

For artists like Ato Delaquis or E.K.J. Tetteh, whose ideas are rooted in Ghanaian society, there is very little in print that might help one to appreciate their philosophies as artists or to evaluate their integrity. Yet identifiable positions exist despite the absence of organized criticism. In a predominantly oral culture critical discourse between the artist and the public appears to be embedded in the pictures themselves, which, arguably, are the best manifestations of aesthetic identities. Images are shortcuts to the spoken word where the oral tradition is overwhelming.

The poverty of art historiography in Ghana belies the vibrant modernist and street painting that has emerged over the last half-century. The sight of gaudy portraits, banners with signage, and painted billboards in Kumasi's commercial districts might trick observers into seeing a disparity between sign painting and university-level painting typified by nude studies, landscapes, and still lifes. Yet there may well be a relationship between painting at the university level and the commercial art of the street workshops in Kumasi.

Dan Karlholm

"Does It Work?": A Note on Pragmatic Parts and Global Wholes

Strikingly absent from the Art Seminar's lively colloquium on concepts was the word "global," which is, of course, not even a concept, but an uneasily digested adjective. Global seems to be the latest incarnation of "universal" and the like — a quintessentially Western preoccupation. And what about global art? Show me such a monster, and I'll try to say something about it. Perhaps the minor tone of pessimism throughout this discussion is due to unreasonable expectations concerning part and, in particular, whole.

I will concentrate my response on the first part of the discussion, since I have little to say about the potential use-value of certain concepts for art history, dwelt on in the second part, for the simple reason that the value of these concepts could only be determined in critical practice. David Summers's suggestion to abandon "visual" for "spatial" is, however, of general concern for any notion of what "art" and "art history" is or should become, not least in relation to "visual culture," and I will have to return to it. I very much doubt that the willingness to coin concepts or terms is a particularly Western or even Eurocentric preoccupation. Was it the Danes who forced some fifty terms for snow on the Greenlanders? But the anxiety to meet the standards of a global account (or narrative, or history) is certainly a product of the Western aspiration of conquering the world both literally and symbolically.

My focal point will be relaxingly pragmatic and strategically historiographical, but not in James Elkins's gloomy sense when he not only says that a text that one no longer "believes" is fit for "historiographical inquiry," but also opposes this form of study to any "methodological interest." Disbelief is hardly a precondition for historiographic investigation. On the contrary, if everyone were to believe in Wölfflin, that would be when historiography is most needed. The historiographer does not have to be a gold digger or a waste manager. To me, historiography is a continuous methodological concern. It is a strategy with which to make history and contemporaneity activate each other, making each relevant, so that we do not fall into either amnesia or the confinement of historicism.[56] The translation of Wölfflin into Chinese as late as 1999 should be compared to the equally tardy translations of Riegl and Warburg into English: they energized several contemporary discourses on memory, history, visuality, and theory. The issue is not *when* an authority is read or introduced, but the extent to which, as Friedrich Teja Bach put it, readers "work *with*" the texts, or simply emulate them. I advocate working critically with texts such as Wölfflin's; that is in stark contrast to reverentially following him like some founding father. The distinction, however, between "normal art history" and "theory" is too crude; it only informs the less influential extremes of the spectrum.[57] Where would we place Panofsky's claim, made in 1940, that theory and history are interdependent?[58] There is such a thing as theory, plain and simple, but "normal art history" minus theory does not exist.

The question of what kinds of art history are practiced around the globe is certainly an interesting one. My hope is that we will not be confronted with a global art history in exchange for the many versions, Western, non-Western, Westernized, anti-Western, and so on, that prevail today. I am not sure exactly what the stakes are here. Global art history appears either to be a hypothetical art history, comprising a fair representation of local histories, or else a wholly new species in the textual fauna of art histories. Or is the global art history simply the latest emanation of what used to be called "general" or "total" or "universal" or "world art history" (or simply "art history," without further qualifications), which was never global, despite its intentions, but always local and specific? The "local" history of art, moreover, is never entirely local, since the history of art is, historically speaking, a highly idiosyncratic Western (specifically German) product. This means that every local art history, on Swedish craft or Balinese architecture, is an adaptation to a given format involving more or less explicit definitions of art, development, quality, genre, and authorship. The terms of global and local, on the whole, seem insufficiently dialectic (giving way to neologisms like "glocal," which were not, however, introduced in the seminar), especially when they surface in discussions like the present one as simple contradictions.

Is this a question of "textbooks," those kings of mindless tautologies? Yes and no. I fully agree with Elkins's assessment of their importance: "I would say their structure informs the structure of classes at higher levels, and those in turn inform the choices of postgraduate specialization." His justification is too timid, however: all he says is that they "*can* be formative for the discipline." They most certainly are. You cannot have a discipline without some common historical, empirical, discursive, conceptual and methodological ground — a noncoherent structure with which to measure traditions, innovations, conventional wisdoms, and rethinkings. But textbooks are only one manifestation of the field of knowledge known as art history. Museums and slide libraries, for example, are other formats.

The fact that students do not encounter a survey art history in the country that gave birth to the genre, Germany, is, of course, ironic. But it will not liberate German students from the regime of art history as a world-historical narrative, institution, and archive, where every art-historically classified object is situated in relation to every other.[59] Specialization depends upon generalization, and vice versa. And the general or global art history, glued together by way of a unitary subject of art, is without a doubt the most monographic text conceivable.

I might mention that I have devised an alternative to the survey art history for academic beginners, namely Elkins's own *Stories of Art* — a book he would never, I am sure, use for such purposes, since he seems confident of the general need among students to follow one narrative.[60] I am not so confident of that, and my students confirm the value of being freed from something as authoritarian E.H. Gombrich's *The Story of Art*. As a prelude to introducing Elkins's book to the class, I summarize Gombrich's classic text, with both appreciation and critique, in an hour and a half. The rest of the semester we work with art, visual imagery, history, the canon, the world, and so on, not from the highest point of some Hegelian ladder, but from the local position that we happen to inhabit faced with a database — not only metaphorically speaking — which can be accessed from many different points of view.

I do not share Elkins's pessimism regarding the possibility of modifying the Gombrichian story "in a satisfying manner." Deal with the text, I would say, and give up trying to make it satisfying as such! Satisfying for whom? Us? Them? Everybody? Isn't it exactly such modification, however politically correct, that threatens to drain whatever quality could still be pressed out of this and other old problematic stories? Neither do I sense the need for a "newly structured story that can still be persuasive as art history and not as a capricious local invention." Like the *October* chronicle on twentieth-century art?[61] This sounds like a wholesale condemnation of what the local, for better or for worse, is about. In this phrase, the local just appears insufficiently global — not sufficiently in sync with the dominant Western structure of art history, which is easily recognizable and generally persuasive, and which was invented so long ago that it has become known as an authorless "traditional."

David Summers's memory of reading Wölfflin as a student is amazing, and could perhaps still serve as a source of inspiration. Summers recounts that he read Wölfflin back then as a formal tool, in a manner, that is, comparable to the way Wölfflin himself looked at art. Summers and his fellow students did not treat the text as a textbook; they tried to get behind it, indeed to work *with* its particular view on art. And the art the teachers saw most fit for this purpose was formal modernism (largely beyond the scope of Wölfflin's account). Such a pragmatic, perhaps even quintessentially American, way of approaching texts opens up fresh horizons: what can this reading teach us about what we are interested in? "Does it work," to paraphrase Summers, for us? The question here is not how we really understand the text, but: How do we understand it, and what can we learn from it? Compare this to Elkins's education, where they were given the same text, but told, in addition, that this is not "proper art history," and that it doesn't "correspond to the discipline *as we practice it*" (my emphasis). A more hypocritical pedagogy is hard to conceive of. As we all know, kids do not follow what we say, but what we do.

Today, however, according to Summers, students read Wölfflin "with a high degree of resistance, edging into non-comprehension," which means that the productive situation which must have formed, to some extent, the future author of *Real Spaces* was no longer there. That would be *my* source of pessimism. But there is a remedy, I think, and it is to invite an open historiographic approach to all this, as a way of coming to grips with such a beast as "Wölfflin" (he would occupy a position within art history along with Baroque sculpture or Persian rugs), and to regard him, for example, from the vantage point of visual culture — which would be a particularly rewarding approach to Wölfflin given his interest in the "history of the development of occidental seeing."[62] Fussing about the labels, however, which are always partly misleading, will lead us nowhere. The fact that visual studies also may incorporate studies of artifacts based to a large extent on other senses may only be problematic if these shifting circumstances are not adequately addressed. In many cases, the standard equipment of visual studies (in terms of historical, theoretical, and disciplinary reference points) fails to be of service in the encounter with contemporary art that has little to do with visuality. While art history, on the one hand, always incorporated the study of artifacts that no one wishes to call art, from Neolithic graves to design, it is less often prepared, on the other hand, to respond to nonaesthetic imagery. As a matter of principle, I don't believe in trading this for that, "visual" for "spatial," but in extending the range of possible vantage points.

What threatens art history is not, to my mind, whether it might be engulfed by visual studies. This will never happen, I am sure, not least since visual studies would not want to swallow art history. What it might want is an equivalent position of academic power. The big threat against art history is that it may escape visual studies altogether, but that hasn't happened. On the contrary, there is a give-and-take between these fields. Several distinguished art historians have recently been publishing on visual culture. I actually think that neither camp can survive without the other, although this battle for attention and influence may well be fought under different banners.[63] It is not an issue of active amnesia, arguably, about "the possibility of forgetting the narratives of art history," in Elkins's words, but of working creatively with what is already there (I call that academic postproduction), and of finding new ways of dealing with visual culture or art both at home and abroad. We don't have to agree about very much. Agreeing is — to end on a note of optimism — a kind of death.

Romuald Tchibozo

A Point about the Seminar

The first questions discussed by James Elkins during this seminar, concerning teaching art history in the African subregion, seem to lead to questions about the general situation of the subject in the world. Is it useful nowadays to teach art history? What is the subject's interest? What is its contribution in the development of a country or a locality? If those questions seem to have solutions in Europe, they may not in south-Sahelian (sub-Saharan) Africa.

Most African universities are young and lack resources to develop teaching methods because they depend on the government for funds; and furthermore, concerning Benin, no one teaches art history, due to the lack of material. For instance, during my training course, the professor used slides that he collected himself during his travels; other than that he had nothing. Only when I went to Germany did I feel I could start to learn art history. Ladislav Kesner is correct when he says that a deficiency of resources means less art history. Most students in Benin do not know any other way. Until recently, there was only one professor for the art history course and I am the second one; the University of Benin has only one course in history of art.

The question is to find out how to raise interest for such a course in our context where the creation of art is highly attenuated. I hope the beginning of a solution is to multiply cooperation with other universities around the world; this will help us to participate actively in the creation of books on African art, which is a current concern, as Elkins mentions. This will also help to keep art historians in the field and thereby develop the subject. If human resources are not lacking elsewhere (particularly in Latin America, as Andrea Giunta suggests), that must mean that researchers can be retained. The same interest and motivation must be created in the continent (of Africa) so that professionals can choose to do this work, even if it involves a serious commitment.

Teaching art history is itself a little different in Benin than in Europe, as Sandra Klopper points out. It seems to be normal in Europe, so I hear; but in Benin there is no concentration on African art or contemporary art, and no important theories to study or famous authors to teach the subject. I hope there might be a certain improvement in the teaching of the subject in the coming years, although we must find ways to conceptualize the field, and prepare students in the understanding of different theories, including those derived from antiquity, in order to better understand the salient problems. This agrees with what V.Y. Mudimbé has written:

> The European who grips us could suffocate us. Moreover we in Africa should have not only a rigorous understanding of actual modalities of our integration in the European myth, but also explicit questions that will allow us to be critical of the entire corpus.[64]

At Humboldt University in Berlin, from which I graduated, there is not a professor of African art, and before I arrived, the Institute of History of Art had never had an African student. How can I interpret this? A "belatedness"? Contempt? A simple absence? Or a madness, akin to the way Elkins reproaches Klopper for the absence of Baxandall in South Africa? I think that in Benin such judgments do not exist, and yet there is a problem with teaching that does not take into account the principal people who write on the subject. Finally, it makes sense to teach art history in an area that has a wealth of examples, as Friedrich Teja Bach points out. I disagree with Hans Belting's idea of the end of a kind of art history. In Africa, I think that we are at the beginning of art history.[65]

I don't totally agree with the issue of delays and belatedness mentioned in the roundtable, because even though we may study a classic author — say Wölfflin or Baxandall — art history does not follow such sources. I agree with Friedrich Teja Bach's idea that "if Chinese students work with Wölfflin, then theirs would be a different Wölfflin." Yet books remain very important. They are the beginning of a student's reflections, and they give essential information. However, they cannot be considered as fixed instruments; as Andrea Giunta notes, the texts that are mentioned have a Eurocentric aspect. Nevertheless, it is realistic to ask whether we can say the same thing everywhere. Can we not focus at a particular point, a place or time that will change the priorities of teachers and the documents they use or recommend? Art history differs in different places, and Giunta is right to say that "art history could be a useful tool for understanding important differences between

Latin American and European visuality." That is why I emphasize the theories leading to a certain view of African art in Europe, and principally in Germany.[66] It seems very important to show the difference of vision and appreciation, which from my point of view yields a resolution of the general problem of "global" art history.

The question raised by Elkins concerning the elaboration of alternative rules governing the practice of art history gives me some trouble. Which non-European historian of art can, in one lifetime, elaborate an alternative science to the one that has been established for several centuries? Are Westerners really prepared for such an opening? As David Summers says, "the history of art has been very nationalistic, and has been deeply implicated in the faith in progress and cultural superiority justifying Western imperialism. It is hard to accept the contingencies of one's origins."

John Paul McMahon asked a good question when he wondered if "the tools and modes of analysis change" or if "South African art historians retain Western tools." The great frustration felt by most art historians is not due to their absence from the larger arenas of the diffusion of knowledge, but because of the small audience for their work. In the West, as the panelists note, it is already difficult to translate the English word *modernism* into German; the words *Moderne* and *Modernismus* are neither adequate translations nor synonyms. I am also happy that Bach returned to Klopper's question concerning the word *diaspora,* and that he prefers the word *displacement* because it immediately raises the problem of center and periphery. A Benin proverb says that "the cloth soaks, but whether it has been washed or not, it cannot come out as it had been." From the moment of displacement there are consequences, and no simple return or dispersion (diaspora).

And finally, concerning the association of new non-Western concepts and familiar Western concepts, I cannot imagine how this can be achieved. All other things seem easy by comparison.

Suman Gupta

Territorial Anxieties

In attempting to write a response to the Art Seminar on the theme "Is art history global?" I feel rather like an atheist in a church. I didn't face any difficulty in understanding the details and substance of the arguments, the terminology employed and interrogated is not alien to me, the frame of references is reasonably familiar, and yet the discussion makes me keenly aware of disciplinary claims and territorial allegiances which I cannot and do not adhere to. I have paper qualifications and institutional affiliations in literary studies, research interests in areas that pass as political philosophy and cultural studies, and have been permitted to cultivate academic connections and contacts in various contexts and often with little regard for institutional disciplinary constraints — there is much in the Art Seminar in question that resonates with this background. But I find I cannot engage with the discussion without being made aware of the disciplinary discreteness of the seminar, and therefore being held at a remove in its precincts as a respondent even while being invited into said precincts. I do not mean that anything is actively withheld from my approach in the Art Seminar. On the contrary, I was invited to write this (and am grateful for the kindness) just as I have often been welcomed, though an atheist, in houses of worship of various sorts and have invariably benefited from such entries — but not as one of the faithful.

There is then, admittedly, a certain anxiety on my part in taking the role of respondent here, akin in some ways to the anxiety announced by Althusser (will I make a fool of myself? are they waiting for me to make a fool of myself? have I made a fool of myself already? can I but make a fool of myself?) when reflecting on the spontaneous philosophy of scientists before an audience of scientists.[67] For Althusser that anxiety was both the condition of and the impetus for his carrying on, as it were, to address his audience and having his say — a worthy example. There is good reason to follow that example here: it seems to me that it isn't simply my anxiety that renders me sensitive to the disciplinary discreteness of the Art Seminar, to the territorial and disciplinary claims therein, but that I am *made* so. The claims are vehement and constant, they are borne on me irrespective of my sensitivities, are really announced in overt and tacit and unmistakable ways that cannot be overlooked. Perhaps the impulse that necessitates these claims is itself the product of anxiety — a sort of disciplinary and territorial anxiety on the part of the discussants.

That disciplinary anxiety is the impulse behind the Art Seminar might appear to be an obvious statement. The discussion is about the pressures of globalization, multiculturalism, heritages and differences, geopolitical unevenness in resourcing on art history as an academic discipline. Of course anxiety is at the heart of this discussion. But that isn't quite what I have in mind. The kind of disciplinary and territorial claims that interest me here are, arguably, *prior* to all that: they are constituted within the very announcement of art history as a practice and an object of contemplation, they are the condition of the art historians' (the discussants') identification as such, they provide the structures of discussion that make the Art Seminar possible. The disciplinary discreteness of the conversation, like many of the substantive issues debated in it, can be related to David Summers's *Real Spaces*, which announces its enterprise by a deliberate turning inward:

> What if historians of art, rather than setting out from one or another borrowed principle, were to reconsider the implications of the continuities and patterns demonstrated in generations of art historical practice and research? The history of art might in fact turn out to be deeply significant for the very fields from which it has borrowed, thus to contribute in new ways to broader historical and cultural understanding. The study of what we have come to call art, and its many histories, studied in analogy to nothing else, might tell us more about ourselves than it has yet been allowed to do.[68]

The notion that principles are perpetually *owned* by certain areas of knowledge and can only be *borrowed* by other areas (and have to, in some sense, be *returned*) — and that there's something not quite respectable about this, that it's better to have *proprietorship* ("studied in analogy to nothing else") of one's principles and perhaps *lend* them ("contribute to … broader historical and cultural understanding") — this notion of a commerce of conceptual principles between academic disciplines, and a consequent protectionist zeal, seems to me deeply suspect. Conceptual principles either apply or don't — these are not intellectual property owned by one area or the other — and the contrary assumption probably derives less from the imperatives of research and contemplation than from anxieties which impinge upon these in tangential ways.

This kind of strangely vehement, and excessive, assumption of the discreteness of art history, the *priorness* of art history, to the issues that it engages, is spread across the Art Seminar in different ways. I was interested, for instance, in the way in which the discussants identified themselves or were identified for the purposes of the seminar.[69] Eligibility for participation was determined first and foremost, it appears, by the institutional affiliations of the discussants: all are affiliated in an academic capacity to disciplinary spaces devoted to art history, and therefore presented themselves as representing or were understood to represent the institutional practice of the discipline itself. Given that, the distinctions between them broke down along geopolitical lines, or rather were designed to break down in that fashion: as James Elkins says, "I wanted to avoid inviting too many people from North America and Europe." That discussants speak for and somehow embody the practice of art history as a discipline in certain geopolitical zones at large, rather than express specific reasonable intellectual positions, is indicated in the use of collective pronouns, for example when Sandra Klopper says, "I don't think *our* situation is depressing … The art history *we* teach" (my emphases) she speaks for South African, and sometimes African, art history as a whole; or when Andrea Giunta observes that "*ours* is a discipline without a strong previous local tradition," she speaks for Argentinean, and often Latin American, art history in toto. In his essay, Ladislav Kesner had already identified his geopolitical interests as Czech with a stake in an aspect of "world art" (especially Shang dynasty bronzes), and he fits into the game of the seminar by representing "my country"; Elkins himself throws in the occasional point about Irish art, but ranges more broadly across Nigerian, Chinese, Indian, and other art histories, perhaps as the coordinator's prerogative. This mode of embodying collective, geopolitically distinct institutional positions sets the tone of the discussion: the seminar comprehends voices that are already, so to say, art history itself/themselves, or, putting that another way, these are voices that come with prior claims and prior allegiances in disciplinary and geopolitical terms. Incidentally, following the logic of this spread, it cannot but strike a respondent as odd that a similar privilege wasn't extended to any such representative from, particularly, Asia (Middle Eastern, Far Eastern, or Southern) — that Chinese, Persian and Arabic, Indian art and art histories were left mainly to Elkins, Kesner, and Summers to represent — and that this absence wasn't addressed in the seminar (as the African absence was, and was explained away).

There are other indicative maneuvers, again more a matter of preconditional disciplinary discreteness than conceptual consistency, in the academic discourse of the seminar. The manner in which art history's relation with "neighboring disciplines such as art practice, art criticism, and visual studies" is posited by Elkins and others is worth picking up. This part of the discussion veers uneasily between institutional prerogatives (funding, interests of consumers, contextual political and social functions) and conceptual prerogatives (distinctions and associations in concepts of art history and visual culture, issues of canonicity, ideology). The institutional and the conceptual are, of course (and this is very well demonstrated), intricately interlinked — but not to register any distinction at all seems to forcefully contain the possibility and freedom of conceptual intellection within the perimeters of institutional prerogatives. In the consequent discussion of terminology, terms are tacitly preselected to fit the prior and accepted concerns of art history — the question is, are foreign (for whom?) terms/concepts like *pradakṣiṇa*, *huaca*, etc. (Why dislocate these from entire linguistic systems? How can these be dislocated thus without attention to the broad rationales of translation involved?) useful to us? (Who? Art historians?) When terms aren't so fitted for the disciplinary discreteness of this discursive space they are usually regarded as threatening: Is "space" a peculiarly European preoccupation? Should concepts like "displacement" be allowed into art history since, as Kesner objects, with these "we can move so easily between objects, art history, social movements, political realities, and even ecological forces"? Don't mess too much with art historical discourse, or mess with it only after accepting its given integrity, is the underlying stricture; and it is that discursive boundedness to which Summers ultimately finds himself implacably opposed. Despite his own commitment to doing art history "in analogy to nothing else" he finds himself opposed precisely for infringing the *given* terminology of art history. As he complains at the end, he finds that it is not so much his conceptual approach that is engaged as his perceived betrayal of a given disciplinary discourse of art history: "I am not worried about the contradiction of my categories ... Given the slight movement I have seen away from the most conservative art history ... I can see good reason for pessimism regarding the future of the discipline." This whimper can, of course, be laid at his own door; he had started his own project by binding it to a notion of the disciplinary discreteness and priorness of art history which comes back against him in this discussion.

It would take a great deal more space than I am allowed to conduct a careful analysis of the academic discourse of this seminar discussion. Academic discourse analysis is a well-researched and charted area, and formulations on the use of rhetorical maneuvers, identity claims, textual forms, hedges, etc. to consolidate what

Tony Becher has aptly called "academic tribes and territories" are all at hand for a prolix and revealing exercise of that sort.[70] The gestures in that direction above, cursory as they are, serve to convey the point I began with: that this discussion is conducted within a bound disciplinary space, with a presumed acceptance of the priorness and discreteness of the discipline of art history. Consequently, the discussion appears to constantly gesture outward from this arena — toward broader philosophical concepts; toward the sociology and politics of globalization, postcolonialism, multiculturalism; toward the sociolinguistics of translation; toward cultural forces variously conceived; toward concepts of historiography and the practice of history; toward "social movements, political realities, and even ecological forces" — and is constantly reined in by the disciplinary bounds that are always preasserted and preeminent. This reining in takes the form of academic identity claims (collective disciplinary voices), selection of terminology, constant returns to a range of scholarly reference (Gombrich, Wölfflin, Baxandall, Toprak), deferrals of extradisciplinary connections, assertions of the constraints of institutional practice of art history. Unlike Summers's book, where analogies and borrowings from other areas are (inconsistently when it comes to details) refused, here analogies and connections and straightforwardly relevant extraneous concepts surface constantly in the discussion but are constantly held at bay, turned away from, postponed, or simply uninterrogatively presumed to be sensible and meaningful. There is an indicative little moment when, in connection with the impact of "local" (for whom?) terms in broader application (for whom and where?), Elkins raises the possibility of a "*politics* of the discipline" being at work. Kesner, who takes the remoteness of such "local" terms as evidence of their lack of efficacy (for whom and where?), promptly quells any searching exploration of this politics of the discipline. No one much objects to Kesner's move here. Quite the contrary. It seems to me that the politics of the discipline is the encompassing backdrop to this seminar discussion, so pervasive that it is passed over, like the early Wittgenstein's contemplation of the limits of language, in silence.[71]

I suspect there is some sort of deep disciplinary anxiety that is responsible for these self-imposed constraints; not just the anxieties which are addressed in the contemplation of the global but an anxiety that is, so to say, constituted within the theory and practice of art history itself. I am obviously not equipped to even begin to speculate on the nature of this anxiety. One of the disadvantages of being an atheist in a church is that the sensibilities of faith that attach to that edifice escape me, and equally one of the advantages of this situation is that I do not have to worry about it. But the thing is — and this is the point I am leading up to — that I also suspect that it is impossible to make much progress with a discussion on a theme like "Is art history global?" under these circumstances. I find myself entirely unsurprised that the whole seminar ends on a fraught and stagnant note. This question needs (I am being deliberately imperative here) to be addressed by discussants not *as* but *despite* being art historians. I mean such a question needs to be debated in the spirit of being intellectuals, in Sartre's sense of thinkers who are prepared to meddle where they have no business rather than thinkers who are bound to institutional prerogatives as "technicians of practical knowledge."[72]

The need is in the nature of the question "Is art history global?" If that question suggests that the institutional arrangements for the study of art history have to respond to political, social, or philosophical concepts of wide application and complexity such as globalization, multiculturalism, post colonialism, and postmodernism, then it must be assumed that the question is posed because the existing institutional arrangements and discourses of art history have arguably yet to respond to these, and are as yet not equipped to do so. The need for change then cannot be addressed purely from within; those concepts have to be engaged in all their complexity and breadth and effectiveness to discern why and how they attach to the institutional practice of art history. This entails a willingness to enter into the sociology and the politics and the economics and the linguistics and the technology (and so on) of the global along with and alongside the art historical. Indeed, the problems that require such a wider engagement are written within the enunciation of the question itself. For instance, why is it the "global" that we are concerned with? Is that the same (as appears to be assumed in the discussion) as "world" or "universal"? The current nuances of the "global" (coextensive with "globalization," a very recent word)[73] are quite distinct — and distinctively ideologically loaded — from Vico's "ideal eternal history" or Kant's or Hegel's "universal history," which in turn are ideologically quite different from, say, Spengler's or Toynbee's construction of the West (and its prospects) in the context of "world history."[74] Further, the "global" of "globalization" is vociferously contested political territory, interpreted with different normative emphases from liberal, neoconservative, and socialist positions, and conceptualized in historical terms in myriad ways. Can the question "Is art history global?" be addressed, with evocations of "world art" and "international art," while being innocent of these terminological inflections and their intellectual content? And that's just one level of complexity. Then there's the matter of "culture," and the politics of "diversity," "difference," or "multiculturalism" — and the issue of "Eurocentrism" and "postcolonialism" — all constantly referred and responded to in the discussion as if these are not equally loaded, ambiguous and contested territories too, which have to be delved in some measure in their transdisciplinary dimensions before discerning disciplinary possibilities and responsibilities. Approaching that question must necessarily be an extended and open process. A seminar cannot, of course, set out to reach conclusions but perhaps it can make — and with regard to the Art Seminar in question, could have made — an optimistic beginning by acknowledging this much.

Further, it seems to me, such a debate is likely to be fruitfully progressed not only with a willingness to stray when necessary from disciplinary precincts, but in actively seeking analogues rather than proceeding without analogues. For me, a great many of the issues raised resonated powerfully with debates in (and indeed the anxieties of) the discipline of comparative literature. In particular the recent reemergence of the concept of "world literature" and discussions thereof are likely to be suggestive in considerations of "world art history" and vice versa. The careful charting of the concept of "world literature," from the Eurocentric idealism of Goethe's formulation[75] through the cosmopolitan practice of Erich Auerbach[76] and the universal horizon of A. Owen Aldridge's criticism[77] to its current incorporation (tendentiously) into literary critical practice by Pascale Casanova, Franco Moretti, and David Damrosch,[78] provides a scaffolding that a discussion of "global art history" can build around to some extent — even if it would need to be dismantled later.

This is probably a good place to stop, but there is a tangential matter which I would like to raise. It is linked to the kind of abstract disciplinary territoriality that I have expressed reservations about in relation to Summers's opening remarks in *Real Spaces.* I find myself increasingly suspicious of the manner in which the possessive term "Western" is employed in a large variety of intellectual discourses — as in "Western democracy," "Western liberalism," "Western values," "Western literary canon," "Western philosophy," "Western(ized) society," "Western modernity," and, of course, "Western art" and "Western aesthetics" and "Western art history." The sensitivities that now attach to the idea of "Eurocentrism" appear to be unproblematically deflected by attributing a set of abstract and flowing norms and ideologies to the perpetual possession of an ever-accommodating "West." The deconstruction of the possessive "Western" seems to me an increasingly urgent political and sociological project, especially when that possessive becomes simultaneously the repository of the universal and good, a binary end of the ongoing and (reductively) polarizing neoconservative "clash of civilizations," and a ubiquitous specter manifest amidst and discernible within geopolitical zones which are not regarded as "Western." Again, I do not think that such a deconstructive project can or should be conducted within disciplinary ivory towers; almost any use of the possessive could be targeted from a wide perspective, and the uses of "Western art" in this Art Seminar, and its urtexts, are especially suggestive.

Summers's salutary liberal desire to provincialize Eurocentric art history nevertheless falls into a kind of methodological bind which does little to assuage doubts about the deployment of the possessive "Western." It turns out that his spatial perspective on non-Western arts resorts to antiquity (explained by a methodological decision to stick to the "*first spaces of use*"[79]), whereas the representational perspective remains the almost sole province of the West and moreover the West remains the normative province of modernity ("properly Western"[80]). True that he mentions "other modernities" in passing, but those other modernities seem to have no discernible character or analyzable material basis — none, at any rate, that is given even a cursory mention. In a project of the magnitude of *Real Spaces*, the methodological delimitation of modernity to the possession of the West remains, despite Summers's gestures, a problem. It is a basic problem of being left wondering whether the modernity of Indian representational painting from Abaninadranath Tagore, Rabindranath Tagore, and Jamini Roy to the present, for instance, is contained in or excluded from the West or from modernity; or where, for instance, post-1949 Chinese oil painting, ceramic design, and print-making fit into this schema. The persistence of the problem is amply evident in the Art Seminar, where the fuzziness and simultaneously universalizing and polarizing deployment of the possessive appears in curious ways. In general, it seems that there is "Western art" and then there is "world art" as a separate and distinct outside. Or there is "Western art history" (*the* discipline) and then there is something that isn't there and is sought by the discussants, "global art history," which will allow them to talk about everything else. And oddly enough, modernity tacitly remains the territory of the Western here and now, perpetually the West's intellectual property, while "world art" inevitably harks back to antiquity — Indian temple architecture, Shang bronzes or Tang to Qing dynasty paintings, ceramics and jades, and so on — or some ahistoricized "primitivism" (very politically incorrect term, but that's where I think mention of "indigenous" art and occasionally of "local" aesthetic terminology points patronizingly). The shift away from a "Western history of art" in South Africa that Klopper mentions, or Giunta's observations that "the narrative structure of art history in Latin America cannot be separated from Western models" and that "in Argentina we don't have a conflict with art history as a Western discipline," do little to complicate the normative embrace and geopolitical exclusions of the possessive "Western." And then there is that most revealing intervention from Kesner about the incorporation of "local" non-Western terms into art history:

> I would not be expecting any profound change in the structure of art history, even if non-Western concepts were appropriate for the more widespread use; nor do I suspect that this is inherently an issue of disciplinary politics. Rather I take the fact that this has not generally happened as a sign that the conceptual scaffolding of Western art history and discourse about images indeed is indispensable and that even a skillful adoption of critical terms, desirable as it might be, stands no chance of substantially altering the structure of the discipline.

So, following this, it is not a matter of disciplinary politics that art history (at large) rests upon the conceptual scaffolding of Western discourse about images; presumably this is because Western discourse just is (as a fact) intellectually or normatively right or has some kind of primal and permanent property ownership on the discipline. There is something pristine, untainted-by-an-outside, and resonant with originary and perpetual claims in this deployment of the possessive "Western" in relation to the discipline of art history and the conceptual abstraction "modernity."

I could carry on unpicking uses of the possessive in question in this discussion, but is it necessary? What is missing, of course, is any notion of hybridity, miscegenation, mixture, cross-cultural transferences and translations from and into "Western art history"/"Western art"/"Western aesthetics" or its others (Eastern art, African art) or its other, "world art"/"global art history," in modernity, or for that matter ever. The "Western" can only be belatedly translated elsewhere (why is Wölfflin translated only in 1999 in China and what good would that do is the thing to worry about), and only the Western may (or, for Kesner, may not) accept something from without on its own terms.

Something is not quite right here. But we need more than art history to unravel it, I suspect. This is a rather abrupt point on which to end. But then misgivings of this sort should probably be left lingering, and refused closure.

George Intsiful

Art History in Ghana: A Letter

I mulled over my response for months, and almost missed the deadline, for various reasons including an accreditation visit from the Commonwealth Architectural Association to my department in Kumasi. Now I can make my brief contribution. I enjoyed all the discussions by the various panelists and find that our situation in this part of the world tallies with the views expressed from South Africa. Largely because of the fact that not much of our history has been recorded, and also due to colonial reasons, our department has been modeled after the Architectural Association's school in London. Our curriculum therefore bears a very close semblance to theirs. For the accreditation visit, for example, the yardstick for how well or badly my department is doing was reference to other schools in the Commonwealth. The fact that ours is the only recognized school in the subregion did not stop the team from criticizing our staff-student ratio according to "acceptable" standards.

Over the years, some of us have tried to revise our curriculum to include more works or writings from this part of the world. Unfortunately there have been numerous problems. The few books on architectural history and perhaps art history have been written by expatriates, some of whom were in Ghana or other parts of Africa for six months (or less); but materials from studies they were involved in — largely done by local students and staff — have made these expatriates "experts." Many students are more interested in qualifying as architects than writing art or architectural history. Furthermore, many staff members have tried gallantly to write books and research papers and sometimes it has just not been possible to have them published. Our *University Journal*, for example, has two broad sections for the sciences and the humanities. Since its inception, editors for the humanities section have always come from other disciplines and never from architecture. Thus research papers on architecture sometimes are not even considered, perhaps because they are not easily appreciated or understood by the humanities editor. I have personally had a few papers returned either because suitable referees could not be found or somebody thought they were not interesting enough.

This clearly is the chicken-and-egg case. Is it because architects do not write, or because what they do write has not been understood by the humanities editors? I have tried to put together a book, *Architecture in Ghana*, but have struggled to get funds; money from the Research and Conference Secretariat in the university are shared literally among all the various departments in the university. Perhaps collaborative efforts among art historians from the North and South could help.

I am not citing problems that arise from our meager salaries and inadequate facilities, because I gathered from the panel discussions that they are already well known. Should you have anybody willing to collaborate with me on my book, please link me up with him or her. The material is there and so is the will, in abundance. Resources have always been the problem. I hope my little thought and observation help.

Shigemi Inaga

Is Art History Globalizable?
A Critical Commentary from a Far Eastern Point of View

I missed the chance to attend the roundtable. Reading through the transcription of the meeting, I was at the same time frustrated by the fact that I wasn't there, and also relieved. Indeed my absence not only accounts for the difficulty of realizing a global art history as a professional gathering (the total absence of Asians in the panel, which a Japanese alone can hardly cover) but also suggests an invariant of an aesthetic creed or prejudice about Japan: Japanese aesthetics is characterized by its constant failure in or refusal of representing itself whenever occasion is provided. Hence, my absence could be interpreted as a faithful practice of Japanese aesthetics.

To represent oneself on an international arena is not an easy task for an Asiatic who has a full-time job as a civil servant in his/her own country. March is no less a cruel month than April, as it is the ending of an academic year (in Japan, if not in China and Korea). Administrative obligations prevent our compatriots from attending events taking place in the West. It would be almost impossible for any foreigner to imagine the business of Japanese society unless they were involved in it. For someone who is constantly overcharged and "débordé" in the domestic market of "literary hacks," it is extremely hard to respond to extra requests from abroad. Besides, to gear up for the Western market, one is asked to use a language (English, to begin with) which is practically never in use as a means of communication and writing, so long as one is conducting education and research in the faculty of letters at Japanese universities.

It so happened that when I noticed the silly double booking both for domestic consumption and for export to an international arena, it was simply too late. My lecture in Japan had already been publicly announced. At the very moment when the conversation was recorded at the University College Cork, at the opposite side of the planet, I was giving a public lecture in a Japanese city on the *Hiroshima Murals,* realized by the late Iri and Toshi Maruki 丸木位里·俊 from 1950 up to the 1970s. The series of wall paintings served as a propaganda machine for the world peace movement during the Cold War period and are now in a private museum built in commemoration of the artists. The *Hiroshima Murals* have become internationally famous both in the East and the West and have been much publicized through an album edited by the Pulitzer Prize winner John Dower, a specialist in Japanese modern history and author of the prize-winning *Embracing the Defeat.* Yet, in the academic field of art historical research in Japan, even nowadays such works are rarely mentioned.[81]

It may be of some interest to note that art historical research in Japan mainly emphasizes old masters and inventories of Buddhist relics. Contemporary artworks with highly charged political connotations have been rejected from Japanese academia despite (or rather as the aftermath of) student revolts in the late 1960s, and that exclusion continued into the late 1990s. Those who discuss Maruki's endeavor are categorized either as activists (from "old Marxist" to New Left) or scholars interested in "cultural studies" — which mainstream (male-dominant, positivist and a-politically formalist) art historians still tend to repudiate as an intrusion made against the *status quo* of "normal" art historical research.

The destiny of works done in commemoration of the atomic bombing could have been an appropriate subject for the Twenty-First International Congress of the Art History in Amsterdam in 1996. Indeed the main theme of the congress was "Memory and Oblivion" and there were sections such as "The Art of Commemoration" and

"The Modern Memorial: Victors and Victims of War." However, no Japanese speakers took up war memorials for discussion. Moreover, only four paper proposals were accepted in total from the members of the Japanese Association of Art History, which has more than two thousand five hundred members. And by a strange fate of selection, all four Japanese proposals were put in the poster section, in a clear distinction from proposals made by the scholars and students based in Europe and North America. The Japanese reluctance to speak and the Western unwillingness to give voice to their irrelevant stammer are consistent tendencies in the majority of international humanities meetings (except for psychology and some associations specifically for Japanese studies).

This small anecdote in the guise of an introduction — and to make my apologies for not attending — will suffice to suggest the multilayered difficulties that globalizing art history has to face as a rigorous discipline. In the following analysis, I will subdivide my presentation into three parts, following more or less faithfully the conversation at the University College Cork. First I will discuss institutional problems relative to academic disciplines. Second, space–time frameworks must be questioned, along with geographical boundaries. Third, I will address conceptualizations of key critical terms and their applicability, especially in terms of the political power relationships between center and periphery. Although I am going to provide as many references as possible, it is simply impossible to give exhaustive references, and so I confess from the beginning that the notes remain highly personal and that I am neither capable of covering, nor qualified to cover, all the fields that must be taken into consideration under the rubric of present question.

Western art history and non-Western arts. The most prominent obstacle to the globalization of art historical research is the fact that the International Association for Art History (CIHA) has not been, and is not, even now, worthy of the name. At best, it is an international association, with global attendance, mainly dedicated to the study of Western art history. The so-called Oriental art history may well sporadically and whimsically be included in the research program (for example thanks to the personal initiative of Henri Focillon in 1921, just to mention an example from the founding days).[82] Yet Asia (and the Orient, if you prefer) is a territory reserved for "Orientalists" as far as Western scholarship is concerned. The profound knowledge of the East elaborated by the tradition of Oriental studies (which Edward W. Said criticized as a form of colonial usurpation) is conserved within a closed circle of initiated specialists.[83]

Despite their mastery of difficult Eastern languages and incompatible social customs, most Orientalists in the West have remained more or less at the periphery of the scholarly world, although their modesty, reserve, and devotion to their marginalized professional specialties is occasionally appreciated as a distinguished qualification in the *monde savant*. Even so, they seldom dare to venture out of their protected domain so as to address the ordinary public (with some exceptions, such as René Grousset in France).[84] Proud of their specialization, and in the interest of self-protection, they tend to scornfully criticize laymen's careless access to their academic sanctuary within the ivory tower. And this tendency of self-imposed isolation has been mimicked by "native" Orientalists in the Orient without their suspecting that their own behavior is itself a caricature that inevitably oscillates between the pride of domestic authority in the periphery, and the humiliation of a foreign informant at the center of an academic hierarchy.

Indeed, most of the top-ranking Eastern scholars of the pre–World War II period in the East have been so busy catching up with the Western development of the discipline that they have satisfied themselves with the acquaintance they have made of distinguished Western scholars in their own fields of research. During the prewar period and up until in the late 1970s, each Japanese scholar returning from the Western "center" proudly displayed his (and rarely her) faithfulness to the Western masters in token of his (or her) authority.[85]

In Oriental studies, however, the same attitude inevitably resulted in a double alienation and caused an irritating double bind. While in the West you are expected to behave yourself as an authority and connoisseur of Japanese art history, when you return to your own country, you have to manifest your perfect mastery of the latest Western scholarship. To make things worse, most of the Western scholars and amateurs preferred *ukiyo-e* block prints, whereas this domain of popular imagery in the late Tokugawa period had been scornfully disdained by the Japanese *literati* class and looked down upon by academic scholars indoctrinated in the classical canon of Western art.

To pretend to be universal, one is forced to deny the cultural value of art (one's own art, as it were) that has been highly appreciated by one's own Western teachers. The irony of this double refraction may partly account for the complicated psychological inferiority complex that Japanese scholars of prewar period could not overcome — or rather could not help awkwardly revealing. (A similar uneasiness is felt by African art historians, as witness the harsh criticism to the MoMA *Primitivism in the 20th Century* show.[86])

The other side of the coin manifested itself as a nationalistic statement, which characterized the founding days of modern Japanese art history. *L'Histoire de l'art du Japon*, the first official account of the Empire of the Rising Sun, was compiled at the occasion of *L'Exposition universelle* in Paris in 1900. Previously, a rudimentary guide to Japanese ceramics had been published at the Paris World Fair in 1878 at the heyday of *Japonisme*, so as to satisfy European amateurs' eagerness to identify their Japanese pottery. Yet "arts and crafts" (including pottery) were not sufficient to prove the existence of "Fine Arts" in the Japanese Empire. Something equivalent to the Greek classic period had to be "excavated" from the forgotten relics of Buddhist antiquities.

The first attempts at such an inventory took place in the 1880s and 1890s; the periodization of seventh and eighth centuries. Buddhist temples in Nara and Kyoto from the seventh century was proudly demonstrated in Paris so as to rectify and discredit Western amateurs' "misconception" of Japanese civilization.[87] To have a clear idea of the paradigm shift that *L'Histoire de l'art du Japon* tried to manifest, it would be enough to have a glance at the description on a print craftsman. Hokusai had been regarded by many French amateurs as the peak of the history of Japanese painting as a whole, and he became an object of praise in Louis Gonse's *L'Art japonais* (1883) and Edmond de Goncourt's monographic study *Hokousaï* published in 1896. In *L'Histoire de l'art du Japon* in 1900, however, only thirteen lines were given to his life, placing him among the craftsmen of *ukiyo-e* print manufacture.[88] Thus, the authentic discourse of Japanese art history, with a claim to universality, was reinvented (in Eric Hobsbawm's sense) in Westernizing Japan so as to meet the Western expectation and to satisfy national dignity.

(It would not be useless, in this context, to mention that in contemporaneous India, and especially in Calcutta, attempts were made to establish a "national consciousness" under the Swadeshi nationalist movement by boycotting British products. As Partha Mitter and Tapati Guha-Thakurta have shown, it was in this context that the notion of "essential Indian-ness" was launched mainly by A.K. Coomaraswamy, E.B. Havell, and Sister Nivedita, so as to conceive a new national Indian art history. By refusing to accept any influence from abroad as a beneficial factor in Indian art history, they discredited the value of the Gandhara Buddhist sculptures which had been highly appreciated in earlier Western scholarship because of their affinity with the Greco-Roman canon.[89])

A Japanese author, Okakura Kakuzô (岡倉覚三·天心 1863–1913; better known by his sobriquet Tenshin) was in charge of the editorship of *L'Histoire de l'art du Japon* and also directly involved in the nationalistic formation of Indian art history as an idea through his publication of *The Ideals of the East* (1904), which he completed during his first stay in India. Incidentally the book ends with the slogan: "Victory from within or mighty death without." Being a close friend of Isabella Stuart Gardner, Okakura contributed to the collection and display of the Department of Oriental Art at the Boston Museum of Fine Arts. Clearly, he had it in mind to show the cultural heritage of Oriental civilizations to the Western public so as to obtain universal recognition of the Oriental art history as the indispensable companion to its Occidental counterpart. This intention was also held by Western art historians of the following generation who, like Henri Focillon, tried to establish a universal art history by realizing a synthesis of Eastern and Western scholarship during the cosmopolitan epoch between the two World Wars.[90]

And yet, it must not be overlooked that in his *Book of Tea* (1906), Okakura clearly manifested his unwillingness to present and appreciate Oriental art in a Western fashion. Relying upon Taoist scriptures and Zen Buddhist concepts, Okakura tried to persuade Western readership that the Eastern cult of spiritual aesthetics and immaterial beauty is in sharp opposition to Western physical and material beauty. The emptiness of the tea house, he argues, is hardly compatible with the Western trophy-style display of museum collections, and the practice of the tea ceremony would not be compatible with Western art appreciation, which puts excessive emphasis on the visual at the detriment of the pleasures of the other four senses. Okakura also insisted on the fact that in Asian art history, fine arts could hardly be clearly distinguished from arts and crafts and he (unsuccessfully) coined an alternative term of *kogei* (refined arts 巧藝) so as to cover all the branches of handmade artistic creation.[91] Thus a theoretical resistance to the fallacy inherent in an attempt at globalizing art history was clearly formulated by the pioneer of the Oriental art history at the beginning of the twentieth century.

Art history as academic institution and discipline. This birth trauma, so to speak, was repressed during the process of institutionalizing art history as an academic discipline. And the repressed would inevitably return, revealing innate obstacles to the globalization of the discipline. It was in 1916 that the chair of art history was inaugurated at the Imperial University of Tokyo, with Taki Seiichi (瀧精一 1873–1945) being the first recipient. Several imperial universities in Japan followed suit (including the Keijô University in Seoul from 1926, as Korea had been "annexed" to Japan since 1910, while in the Taihoku Imperial University in Taiwan, inaugurated 1928, the department of art history was not established). There were few chairs in the prewar period. A critical assessment of Meiji Era scholarship made by Kishiro Shûichi (木代修一 1898–) in 1936 counts no more than thirty scholars covering art history, archaeology, and aesthetics, but there is no similar assessment for the following years.[92]

Among legendary scholars of international renown, let me mention just three names. Ômura Sêgai (大村西崖 1868–1927) is known for his studies in Chinese sculpture and painting; his books were translated into Chinese in the prewar period and served as basic references for connoisseurs.[93] The framework of the Oriental art history in Japan was delimited by the generation of Ômura, with its strong antiquarian overtones, and it has not been seriously questioned until recently. It must be also indicated that in the first series of *Selected Relics of Japanese Art (Shinbi taikan)* (『真美大観』 in 20 volumes, 1899–1908) to which Ômura cooperated, the explanation of each plate is given in two languages (a Sanskrit scholar, Takakusu Junjirô 高楠順次郎 1866–1945, a disciple of Max Müller, wrote English commentaries), but in the following volumes of *Selected Relics of Oriental Art (Tôyô Bijutsu Taikan)* (『東洋美術大観』 in 15 volumes, 1908–1918), the explanatory text was written only in Japanese. In the long run, the initial delimitation of the discipline of Oriental art history resulted in its relative isolation from Western scholarship and contributed to the lack of interest among the next generations of Japanese Oriental scholars in modern and contemporary Asian art. (It was only in 1999 that the Fukuoka Asia Museum was inaugurated as the first public institute to deal with modern and contemporary Asian art.)

The most famous Japanese art historian in the West may be Yashiro Yukio (矢代幸雄 1890–1975). A disciple of Bernard Berenson, Yashiro published *Sandro Botticelli* (1925) in English; it remains a major Japanese contribution to the Western art historical scholarship. In this book, Yashiro is known to have introduced retouched photographs framing only the relevant details of works to aid identification. He is also remembered as the first director of the Institute for Art Studies (美術研究所 inaugurated in 1930). Later he published his life work, *Essences of Japanese Art* (『日本美術の特質』1944/65), which discusses national characteristics according to four terms: impressionistic, decorative, symbolic, and sentimental. Based on the author's wide span of knowledge, and bridging the West and the East, the book tries to examine a branch of Asian artistic creation from the perspective of the universal standards of the day. Though apparently old fashioned in its nationalistic approach, this monumental synthesis would be worth being critically scrutinized, so as to measure the possibility of a global art history and to detect the limit of applicability of Western criteria. However, the book remains inaccessible to Western scholarship because it has not been translated.[94] Let me add the name of Shimada Shûjiro (島田修二郎 1907–94), who produced a generation of specialists in Japanese and Chinese art history at Princeton University in the Unites States in the postwar period. His contribution, comparable to that of Wen Fong, must be also judged in terms of globalizing the discipline of Asian art history.[95]

However, none of these names (let alone the multitude of Asian scholars) were mentioned either in Udo Kultermann's readable *Geschichte der Kunstgeschichte* (1981 et seq.) or in Germain Bazin's *Histoire de l'histoire de l'art* (1986), on account of a structural triple blindness. First, any Oriental contribution to Western art historical research is by definition supplementary or auxiliary. Second, the domain of Oriental studies is not included in the "histories of art history," as "history" here implicitly means "Western art history," excluding by definition Orientalist territories. And third, rigorous contributions made by Oriental scholars on Oriental art in Oriental languages are simply nonexistent to those who have no access to the working languages in question (as they are "monopolized" by Orientalists).

Here the problem of working language must be reexamined in relation to the discipline's periodicals. Okakura founded *Kokka*『国華』magazine in 1889, following the model of a *Burlington Magazine* or *Gazette des Beaux-Arts*. Yashiro founded another periodical, *Bijutsu Kenkyû,*『美術研究』in 1932. Both remain basic research periodicals. Though pioneering endeavors in their founding days, these periodicals kept concentrating on the inventory and description of individual artworks and paid little attention to the later development in methodological discussions. In the postwar period *Bijutsushi* (『美術史』 *Journal of Art History*, as it was initially named, founded in 1949) of the Japan Art History Society, was added. It is true that most of these periodicals insert English summaries of their main articles. Yet these publications remain inaccessible to ordinary art history students in the West, and it is a logical consequence that no serious attention is paid to them except for the small circle of Oriental studies specialists. The same would be true of Chinese and Korean periodicals which are piled on the shelves of East Asian research libraries.

To what extent do these Japanese journals care about the globalization of the discipline? It must be said that the persistence of the self-imposed tradition of formal and iconographical analysis means they remain ignorant of theoretical considerations. While Saussurean linguistics and structuralism was already highly fashionable in the 1970s (*Cours de linguistique générale* [1916] was translated into Japanese as early as 1928, provoking academic debate in prewar period; and Michel Foucault's *Les Mots et les choses* [1967] was translated into Japanese in 1974), such critical apparatus was not introduced in academic periodicals of art history until the 1990s, and recent Western studies on the social functions of art and art institutions have been mainly overlooked; they have been seen as simply irrelevant to the kind of art historical research that has been conducted by specialists of Japanese and Oriental art.[96] It was not until the 1990s that gender studies was introduced, mainly thanks to feminist art historians, requiring drastic reform in the conservative Japanese Association of Art History.[97] (Gender studies was the latest Western import; it came from Leeds and North America — and to add here "as always!" would be politically incorrect.)

Two layers of "global art history." When we ask "Is art history global?" we have to divide the question into two levels. First there are the artworks that constitute the corpus of what I will call Global Art History (G.A.H.). Second is the level of the disciplines that contribute to understanding the G.A.H. Quite often the two levels are confused. And worse, Western scholars tend to overlook the fact that the superimposition of these two layers (objects, and agents of research) on geographical and geopolitical contexts makes the resulting permutations extremely complicated. Without entering into the details of institutional history, let me make one statistical remark before analyzing three structural problems embedded in the discipline at present.

Even in the postwar period, the number of chairs of art history in Japan has been relatively limited when compared to those in North American academia. Among ninety-nine national universities (the category of "national university" itself was dissolved in 2004), only eight had a department of art history (and occasionally aesthetics). Several of the main private universities and fine arts colleges (among the total of 989, consisting of 526 private universities and 463 private colleges as of 2003) are equipped with departments of art history. However, in most of the national and municipal universities, an art historical education is subordinate to the curriculum of the faculty of education. Power relationships in the academic market place must be carefully examined in terms of distribution of these educational conditions. In Western institutions, it is Western art history that maintains the dominant position vis-à-vis those sectors "relegated" into peripheral departments with titles such as Asian and African Languages and Cultures, in which the discipline of Oriental art history occupies a very precarious position. In the Japanese case, the following three factors are pertinent in understanding these conditions.

First, the triple juxtaposition of Western, Oriental, and Japanese art histories remains a basic structure of Japanese scholarship. Oriental art history may be subdivided into Indian (that is ancient Buddhist) art history and Chinese art history. In both branches (if not in the Western and Japanese branches of art history) the modern era is excluded by definition, although it is partly recuperated by such non–art historians such as linguists and cultural anthropologists who study "minor" cultures. Because there are very few professorships in the national universities, most institutes cannot afford to have a specialist in both fields — that is, China and India — of Oriental art history. The three branches of Western, Oriental, and Japanese art have little in common, except for the illusory conviction that they belong to the one and same community of art historians.

Second, in several of the leading universities, architectural history is not put with art history in the humanities but is taught in the Department of Architecture in the Faculty of Technology. (The latter is a Japanese reinterpretation of the Prussian model of *Technische Hochschüle*.) Scholars of the pioneering generation, such as Itô Chûta (伊東忠太 1867–1954), founding father of world architectural history in Japan, and Sekino Tadshi (関野貞 1867–1936), an engineer, indefatigable archaeologist, and experienced fieldworker of tumuli and ancient Buddhist architecture in Korea and China, worked together with Ernest F. Fenollosa (1853–1908) and

Okakura in their early investigations. In the following years, because of specialization, art historical research in Japan lost contact with historians of architecture, and it is only in recent years that several joint projects around the university museum have rehabilitated these pioneers from long disregard and academic oblivion.[98]

Third, the affinity between art history and aesthetics differs considerably in the two major imperial institutions in Tokyo and Kyoto; their divergence can be accounted for by their histories. While the graduates from the Department of Art History at Tokyo University show little interest in aesthetics, students at Kyoto University who major in Western art willingly discuss Western aesthetics and philosophy. In Tokyo, aesthetics and art history belong to different departments (one in history, the other in philosophy), which were definitively separated in 1966, while in Kyoto the two disciplines remain together (though the future remains uncertain, due to a recent rush of institutional reforms).

These three factors intersect with each other so as to enhance the specific academic style of each institution.[99] In addition to these initial conditions, the so-called "vertical isolationism" of Japanese academic units is also relevant. Students of Japanese and Oriental art history with an inclination toward antiquarian studies are mainly interested in a positivist approach; they limit themselves to documentation and biographical and iconographical analysis. They show little interest in recent Western methodological discussions. Students of Western art, by contrast, tend to be more directly influenced by the latest Western intellectual trends. They happily and willingly digest theoretical ideas coming from abroad (so long as the theories were fashionable in the West), and yet they usually show little interest in Japanese art. On the other hand, students of modern Japanese art don't feel fully entitled to talk about Western scholarship because of their poor mastery of foreign languages. And thirdly, there is little professional communication between students of ancient and modern Japanese art.

These divergences in professional interest notwithstanding, Japanese academia as a whole has shown extremely high curiosity regarding information that comes from abroad. In the prewar period, many students in aesthetics and philosophy studied in Germany, and after World War II, their destinations became more diverse. The main German classics in art history were translated into Japanese in the prewar period. Wölfflin's *Kunstgeschichtliche Grundbegriffe,* for example, was available in Japanese as early as in 1936 and Riegl's *Stilfragen* in 1942. (It should not be forgotten — though the fact has been repressed for so long — that many prewar Chinese students who had studied in Japan could have had easy access to these Japanese translations. A considerable number of Western books in art history and aesthetics, both modernist and Marxist, were retranslated into Chinese from Japanese during the Chinese Republic period [1913–1949]. Statistical and biographical studies as well as research of readership remain to be done on these prewar period translations into Chinese of Western books.)

To make a long story short, let me note that most of the classics in art history (Wölfflin, Riegl, Dvořák, Antal, Ganter, Wittkower, Hauser, Goldwater, Benesh, Francastel, Pevsner, Friedländer, Badt, Panofsky, Sedlmayr, Gombrich, and others) were available in Japanese by 1970, and were integrated into the costly series of *Bijutsu Meicho Sensho* (*Masterpieces in Art History*, 美術名著選集 from the publisher Iwasaki Bijutsusha 岩崎美術社; naturally the series does not include any non-Western authors!).[100] But it remains unclear if Japanese undergraduate students always found these translations readable. Though reading requirements (such as are common in North America) did not exist in the Japanese university curriculum, students at the top universities were normally eager to read books by the latest celebrities. Erich Auerbach, Eugenio D'Ors, Ortega y Gasset, G.R. Hocke, Carl Jung, and George Steiner, to mention just a few, were on the reading lists of students in the humanities in the late 1960s. Clement Greenberg, Michael Fried, Harold Rosenberg, and Nelson Goodman were favorite names among students of American contemporary art and art criticism. Among British authors, modernists like Roger Fry, Clive Bell, and Herbert Read were well known in Japan. Kenneth Clark's (1903–83) television series on "Civilisation" had an unprecedented success at the end of the 1960s. Japanese viewers of the epoch did not have any skepticism about the program's "Euro-centrism" and they were satisfied with the clear introduction provided by Takashina Shûji (高階秀爾 1932–); for each broadcast he supplied comparative information on contemporary Japanese art and history. Illustrated excerpts of Clark's books were among the most popular English readers in general education classrooms of Japanese universities in the 1970s.

By the late 1970s, the so-called "Three-Divine Apparatus" (Althusserian Marxism, Saussurean linguistics, and Lacanian psychoanalysis) was at the disposal of Japanese students. Jurgis Baltrušaitis, René Huyghe, Hubert Damisch, Louis Marin, Jean-François Lyotard, Jean-Claude Lebensztejn, Pierre Bourdieu, Philippe Junod, and Michel Thévoz (but not, at that point, Daniel Arasse) were among the French authors whose translations were anticipated around 1980 by curious students in art history and aesthetic theory. A new course of "Culture and Representations" was inaugurated in the 1980s at the Komaba campus of Tokyo University, where Jacques Lacan, Roland Barthes, Michel Foucault, and Jean-François Lyotard, among others, had already been invited. The strong intellectual presence of that poststructuralist course at the Komaba campus complemented the more authoritative and conservative academic disciplines of aesthetics and art history at the Hongô campus. Extremely extended reading lists of Western visual cultures were provided mainly by Takayama Hiroshoi (高山宏 1947–) from the mid-1980s; they were enthusiastically consumed by young students.

A critical survey of the entrance examination for the postgraduate in art history in Japan in the last several decades will provide us with an insightful overview of one possible form of "Global Art History." Though far more conservative in methodological approach than the voluntary reading lists of the students in aesthetics, the art history department seems to take it for granted that an exhaustive knowledge of empirical "Global Art History" is a minimum requirement for admission. Candidate students are requested to give detailed descriptions of artists and their works arbitrarily selected from a vast area ranging from Western to Oriental art history and covering the span of art from the Paleolithic period in Asia Minor to Chinese painting and Buddhist iconography. By the same token, it would be of some interest to glance at the *Shinchô Encyclopedia of World Art* (新潮世界美術事典 1985), so as to get an idea of the Japanese vision of "world art." Without explicitly stipulating any editorial criteria governing the inclusion or omission of entries, the encyclopedia presents an imaginary "Global Art History" as it was conceived by the collaboration of more than 500 Japanese specialists. Incorporating more than 16,000 heterogeneous items of Western, Oriental, and Japanese art and artists in a single volume, it successfully gives an illusion that G.A.H. is a closed and complete universe.

And what about the monthly magazines like *Geijutsu Shinchô* (『芸術新潮』 *New Currents in Fine Arts,* to give it a literary translation)? Probably no other monthly in the world covers such a wide variety of topics in art and fashion in such a sophisticated journalistic style. The only problem is that it is written in Japanese and remains inaccessible to those who do not understand it. Here the question arises once again: Is the "Global Art History" we are searching for accessible only to a Japanese readership? This ironic situation reminds me of the imaginary ideal language of Maraui to which Umberto Eco often refers. Every foreign language can be translated into Maraui, he says, because of its incredible flexibility, but the Maraui language itself cannot be translated into any foreign language. By substituting Japanese for Maraui, we might gain a more realistic notion of what Global Art History might be all about.

As a counterpart to this dystopian nightmare of the hidden globalization of world art history, it might be a good idea to revalue the so-called "belatedness" of the Chinese situation. Consider Roland Barthes (1915–1980) as an illustration. Widely translated into Japanese from the end of the 1960s, partly because of the author's personal tie with the *Empire des signes* (1970), Barthes remained practically unknown to Chinese intellectuals before being revealed at the beginning of the twenty-first century. The notion of binary opposition turned out to be in harmony with Chinese dichotomous way of thinking, and Barthes's critiques of structuralist binarisms (especially his introduction of such third terms as *bruissement* or *significant flottant* and his intoxication with the *plaisir du texte*, *subtilité*, or the *saveur* of *l'obtus*) could not have been more fascinating for young Chinese specialists. While Barthes in Japanese (what Kojève called the *snobisme pure*) cannot be anything more than an object of nostalgia within the closed circle of French studies around the turn of the twenty-first century, he has been newly rediscovered and exploited in postmodern China "After Theory" (in Terry Eagleton's phrase).[101]

Category mismatches and conceptual conflicts. Barthes may turn out to be a good metonymic guide or stepping stone in thinking about the global applicability of certain critical concepts. The French term *écriture,* for all its ambiguity, served as a magic wand, enabling Barthes to conceptualize what he believed to have discovered in *l'Empire des signes* — where signs are devoid of the "signified" and the "signifier" floats on the surface of the *sémiosphère,* as if it might define the antipode of French *sémiocratie.* In his famous passage on *tempura,* the French semiotician intentionally traces a parallel between the process of calligraphic performance and the way the Japanese cook who does not cook ("cuisiner qui ne fait pas cuire") prepares an eel (although Barthes must have been confused because eel would not be served at *tempura* counter). Approaching a culture of ideogram and visuality through phonocentric analytical devices was, by definition, an impossible task. *Écriture* seems to designate all that escapes Western theoretical baggage.[102]

Calligraphy, as an exercise of *écriture,* possesses a distinctive social status in the cultural spheres under Chinese influence and is hardly compatible with calligraphy in the Western sense. In the Far Eastern *literati* tradition, calligraphy was not clearly distinguished from painting. In fact Far Eastern painting is not really "painting" but an extension of *écriture* which covers letters and images at the same time (such terms as "letters" and "image" are irrelevant terminology *in stricto senso*, but we have to rely upon them for convenience's sake). "Calligraphy and painting" (書画 *shûhuà* in Chinese and *shoga* in Japanese) is a single classificatory category in the conservation of cultural properties. When the European academic definition of fine arts was introduced in Japan in 1880s, it provoked a harsh controversy. The question of whether calligraphy should be included in or excluded from the category of fine arts was the point at issue. The controversy was literally a "lutte de classement" (as Pierre Bourdieu says), as the disputes over of the classification directly affected the policies of Westernizing museum administration.[103]

The opposition continues today. In the last twenty years, some Japanese art historians specializing in the institutional history of modernist Japanese art proposed that the discipline of art history is a modern invention and a Western import, because — so they said — corresponding theoretical baggage had not previously existed in the Far East (their reasoning was a sort of Occam's razor). Most Chinese specialists in Japan furiously disagree with this interpretation. For them the glorious Chinese tradition was perfectly equipped with an art historical apparatus before the intrusion of Western institutions. To ignore the history of writing on art in the Far East, and to eliminate such writing from the discipline of art history, would entail a hideous distortion of historical reality.

Clearly these Chinese specialists conceive their discipline in continuity with the Eastern tradition, to which Western institutions remain an addendum.

The different social status of calligraphy in the East and the West is at the core of this recent controversy. The issue also reminds us that in many non-Western countries the category of Western fine arts has not yet been legitimized. Many attempts have been made in the modern era to implant Western fine arts as a subject in non-Western countries. Fine arts schools have been founded, exhibitions organized, and public sculptures commissioned. Such investments often caused nationalistic reactions. In some cases, the fine arts initiatives have been seen as attributes or relics of Western cultural imperialism; that has been the case in mainland China as well as in many Islamic countries. Such boycotts of Western products can easily jeopardize G.A.H.

How is it possible to realize a Global Art History, when the very definition of the corpus of fine arts, ostensibly to be included in G.A.H., is in dispute? One very optimistic and "imperial" option would be to declare that one's own criteria are valid throughout the world, and to apply them globally in order to construct a "musée imaginaire" for G.A.H. I will not repeat here the criticism that I made of this possibility at the occasion of *Le Japon des avant-gardes* show at the Centre Georges Pompidou in 1986–87. By systematically eliminating every domain of artistic creation where no equivalent can be found in Western avant-garde, this huge exhibition helped the French public form a firm but tautological conviction: everything recognizable as partaking of the avant-garde in Japan is a Western imitation; and everything original in Japan does not fall into the category of avant-garde. Only the group *Gutai* 具体 attracted the French public's interest because it had influenced the Parisian art scene and had therefore been authenticated *a posteriori*. The logical coherence of the selection in *Le Japon des avant-gardes* perfectly epitomized the grandeur and misery of auto-intoxication. Applying one's own prefabricated category by force, to foreign realities, only testifies to the cultures' mutual incommensurability.[104]

Similar conflicts continue to appear whenever Western authorities force non-Western art to lie in a Procrustean bed, whether the bed is assimilatory (as in *Magiciens de la Terre,* commissioned by Jean-Hubert Martin, which contributed to the invention of "artists" among Tibetan monks and Ghanaian coffin makers) or eliminatory (as in the Kassel Dokumenta, where artists from nonmonotheistic Oriental cultures were once said to be inappropriate).[105]

And yet it must be said that the Asiatic is no more authorized than the Westerner to serve as the ultimate judge of Asian culture. A foreign insight into unknown realities is sometimes capable of realizing unexpected serendipities. And the shock effect of the contact zone is a good example of *das Unheimliche* or Jan Mukařofský's *Ostraniene,* which was to become Brecht's *Verfremdung.* Such a moment can become transfigurative. An electric discharge or a chemical reaction occurs, delivering a rich and salutary message and casting an unexpected light on a hidden political desire for domination — a light that any attempt at a G.A.H must try to snuff out.[106] This brings me to the problem of the universal applicability of certain operational concepts.

Translatability of operational concepts. In the Kantian understanding, time and space are two basic metaconcepts in which the specificities of cultural spheres may be articulated. This paradigm has been called into question in neo-Kantian philosophy. Needless to say, Panofsky's early essay "Perspektive als symbolische Form" is based on his misunderstanding of Ernst Cassirer's notion of "Symbolische Formen"; he argued that Renaissance linear perspective is not universal but culturally bound; and his argument is simply misleading because of its reliance on an apparent divergence of perspectival drawing from the projection on the human retina.[107] Samuel Edgerton's argument on the lack of rationality in premodern Chinese thinking was based on the Chinese incapacity to understand linear perspective, as witness the incomprehensible illustration inserted in a Chinese encyclopedia. And yet we have to make a clear distinction between the potential possibility of rational thinking and its relevance to the society. Besides, "rationality" itself changes meaning in space and time. Mechanics, for example, did not fall into the Chinese traditional category of "rationality."[108]

As James Elkins points out, the fact that the term "space" does not appear in any Renaissance books on architecture testifies to the fact that Kantian "space" is a metaconcept which remained outside the particular concerns of Italian *Quattrocento* artists. No less than "space," such categories as "artist" or "art history" are also retrospective projections of the particular interests posterity has taken in the Renaissance, as Michael Baxandall and Charles Hope, among art historians, and Michel de Certeau in a different context, have already stressed.[109] And yet this does not necessarily prevent us from setting up an inevitably "anachronistic" category of "fine arts" or "art history" and applying them to "our" field of investigation (supposed as "our" territory) so as to single out "pertinent" deeds and events.

When it comes to the concept of time, Walter Benjamin's warning seems indispensable, especially in historiography: discontinuity in history tends to be concealed by the very effort of recapitulating the discredited past. Rehabilitation creates a false continuity thereby eliminating the phases of disruption when the tradition was interrupted. Quite logically, the interruption itself is made invisible by the paradigm (in Thomas Kuhn's sense) that the interruption has created.[110] The same danger is concomitant with any attempt at G.A.H.

As an illustration, let me analyze a Chinese case where an effort to maintain chronological ties apparently subverts Western codes of pictorial representation. Western viewers are often astonished to see many imperial seals covering the surface of precious Chinese paintings. To such an extent that the depicted landscape seems damaged or is almost obscured. For European amateurs this could be nothing but an impermissible violation of the autonomy of the depicted reality. And yet, for Chinese connoisseurs, the superimposition of seals by generations of the royal owners may be a guarantee of the respect the object has been accorded. The partly obliterated landscape supports layers of authenticating chronological inscriptions. Such inscriptions and seals mark an involvement in historicity. Of course, such an explanation is rarely furnished by Chinese experts in the domestic market. It is only on contact with perplexed Westerners that the native informant is obliged to fabricate a justification in defense of his or her own social custom and practice.

As the custom of imperial inscription suggests, it is an open question if the notion of "representation" is applicable to Chinese landscape painting. What is at stake is less the representation of nature, and more the representation of inner nature (I will discuss the irrelevance of the term "representation" below). Consequently, the picture plane itself is not considered something to be seen; amateurs prefer penetrating into the pictorial space as if they were wandering in the depicted landscapes. Marguerite Yourcenar noted this secret when she narrated a story of an Oriental painter who disappeared in his own painting. Yet she intentionally hid her real source (Lafcadio Hearn's retelling of a Japanese legend) and restaged the story into a Chinese fantasy.[111] Ônishi Hiroshi (大西廣 1937–), a former research curator at the Metropolitan Museum, was fully aware of these elisions and misattributions that ordinary Western readers overlook. In the Japanese translation of *Die Legende vom Künstler* by Ernst Kris and Otto Kurz (1934), he added an extended fifty-page essay on Chinese and Japanese legends of artists.[112] Regrettably, Indian, Persian, and Arabic legends are still uncollected. And unfortunately, I dare say, the Japanese version's "globalizing" addendum is not yet retranslated into any Western languages.

One of the frustrations that Orientals frequently feel in considering books such as *Critical Terms for Art History* is the complete disregard of Oriental traditions.[113] In *Critical Terms,*

David Summers's chapter on "Representation" does not mention Chinese practice — an understandable omission, but an omission nonetheless. Oriental experience simply does not fit into the discussion on "representation," as if nothing from Asia were relevant in this context. Probably the only remedy in Western languages is a paper by Imamichi Tomonobu (今道友信 1923–), who argues that there is a "complementary relationship" between Western and Eastern aesthetic theories. Whereas the Western aesthetic tradition shifted from a classical theory of representation (since Plato) to modern expressionism (in Wassily Kandinsky) at the beginning of the twentieth century, Oriental aesthetics shows almost simultaneously a reverse shift from a classical veneration of personal expression (and therefore not a "representation") to a modern creed regarding realistic representations. Though attractive and comprehensible as a hypothesis, this argument relies upon the author's own belief in the applicability of Western binary concepts to Oriental realities, and the compatibility of Western and Eastern concepts. By its very nature Imamichi's argument, sustained by his firm Catholicism, lies beyond objective verification, and lacks a proper philological framework for comparison.[114]

If a student wants to make an intercultural comparison between Western linear perspective and the Chinese notion of "three distances" 三遠 set forth by Kuo Hsi (or Guōxī in Pinyin transcription; 郭熙 ca. 1120–90), for example, he or she might be requested to attend to these elementary philological precautions that Imamichi willingly sacrificed. Indeed, a strict philology would make it simply impossible to propose any cross-cultural comparison: hence the isolation of the Orientalists. It must also be pointed out that similar comparisons between Chinese and Western notions of spatial construction were very popular from the late 1920s through the 1940s in China and Japan. At the height of nationalistic self-consciousness, intellectuals in Asia were busy establishing an Oriental aesthetics in rivalry with the Occidental.[115] The result was a highly schematic contrast between a posited Western superiority in the analytical handling of the material world, and the supposed Eastern superiority in an intuitive approach to holistic spirituality.

It was in this context that Guō Xī's passage from the *Lofty Message of Forest and Streams,* 『林泉高致』 as well as Xiè Hè's (謝赫 479–502) notion of the "rhythmical vibration of vital movement" (気韻生動 *qì yùn shēng dòng*) were singled out as milestones of Chinese thinking and proofs of Oriental superiority (because they came before apparently equivalent formulas in the West). Even the lack of explanatory power of ancient Chinese terms was not regarded as a weak point but appreciated as a profound virtue. One may well discuss and measure the practical value and the limit of efficiency of such Oriental conceptual tools in comparison with the Western terminologies. But it is no less important to keep a watchful eye on the ideological motives that have mobilized these terms as "relevant" counterparts of Western concepts in a given historical context.

The importance of *qì yùn shēng dòng* (and the proposed English translation, "rhythmical vibration of vital movement," already reveals the difficulty and danger of semantic migration) was recognized by Sinologists such as Ise Senichirô (伊勢専一郎 1891–1948), Sono Raizô (園頼三 1891–1973, the translator of Kandinsky's *Über das Geistige in der Kunst*), and Kinbara Seigo (金原省吾 1888–1958; he proudly boasted to have coined the term "Oriental Aesthetics"), as well as the Chinese theoretician Fēng Zĭkăi (豊子愷 1898–1975). Those Oriental aestheticians located the latest development in European aesthetics in Theodor Lipps's (1851–1914) idea of *Einfühlung*. They thought they recognized its affinity with *qì yùn shēng dòng*. It must already be evident that Imamichi is indebted to such precedent scholars, even though he added some necessary sophistication when he proposed his hypothesis to Western aestheticians in the 1960s.

The notion of 間 *ma* that Elkins suggests has also been exploited by several Japanese so as to communicate a subtle but tangible notion which, however, is hardly translatable. *Ma ga nukeru* ("there is a hole in the *ma*") means "to look silly." *Ma ni au* ("to meet the *ma*") means "to arrive at the destination in time" and also "to be appropriate and on the spot," bridging space and time simultaneously. *Ma wo motasu* ("to keep up with the *ma*") means "being on good terms with the circumstances." The famous Postmodernist architect Isozaki Arata (磯崎新 1931–) chose the concept of *ma* as the key term for an exhibition he organized in Paris in 1978, called "Ma Espace-Temps." Carefully avoiding the danger of mystifying an exotic notion, Isozaki tried to recreate the moments where the "gap" emerges, like the *chôra* in the *Timaeus,* between pre- and postlinguistic realities, at a phase prior to the articulation between *chronos* and "space-as-emptiness." Instead of forcing *ma* onto Cartesian coordinate axes, Isozaki reversed the whole process of thinking (hence his refusal to rely on such terms as "in-between-ness" or "pause" which are only retrospective rationalizations) and named each of the subdivided nine sections of the exhibition by borrowing familiar terms from everyday experience in Japanese language, of which the French equivalents are curiously lacking or depreciated.[116]

Augustin Berque's conceptual reflections beginning with his early *Vivre l'espace au Japon* (1981) are suggestive for understanding Isozaki's project. By reevaluating the "step-by-step" (*pas-à-pas*) approach to the living environment, in reference to James J. Gibson's "affordance," Berque clarifies the methodological limits of the Western perspective of geometrical spatial construction. Here we come close to the notion of *pradakṣiṇa* as an ambulatory itinerary in the procession. With each step you take, your relationship with outer reality vacillates. Berque comes to the conclusion that in Japanese spatial construction it is not the individual agents of action but the intermediary space of "mediation" that is valorized so as to guarantee semiotic circulation. By privileging the neologism of the "communization" (that is "to cause things to be held in common") of signs instead of verbal "communication," Berque later elaborated the idea into "médiance."[117]

Curiously enough, similar propositions had been advanced by several Japanese scholars, and their terminologies may be relocated as precedents of Isozaki's and Berque's conceptual hypersophistication. Based on his study of German philosophy, Tsudzumi Tsunejoshi (鼓常良 1887–1981; Tsuzumi Tsuneyoshi in Hepburn transcription) coined the term *Rahmenlosigkeit* 無框性 ("framelessnes") in his *Die Kunst Japans* (1929) so as to characterize the specificities of Japanese artistic style. Compared to the European *Kunstwollen* toward autonomous and individual *Konstruktion*, Japanese aesthetics is collective and lacking in a clear distinction between inside and outside. This framelessness, according to Tsudzumi, may account for many particularities of Japanese art, whether it be the permeability and fusion of different genres in the historical process of literary or artistic development or the free combination and superposition of different layers or elements in artistic and musical creation, which a later generation of theoreticians in the West would call "intertextuality" and "palimpsest."[118] One may easily detect the reason of the success of his German publication if one thinks of the contemporary paradigm shift Cassirer had described in his monumental *Substanzbegriff und Funktionsbegriff* (1910), which Tsudzumi illustrated, as it were, with Japanese art.

Itô Teiji (いとうていじ 1922–), student of Japanese architecture, had also experienced difficulty in explaining some of the common features of Japanese spatial devices to English-speaking audiences. For lack of a better term, he mobilized such terminologies as "intermediate space," "gray zone," or "in-between-ness," all of which both separate and connect several spatial units.[119] On a visit to Japan, Paul Claudel (1868–1955) was amazed to see movable paper walls and gliding doors, which allow free communication between an interior and an outside garden, and which can be adjusted to the motions of sunlight and changes in temperature, or set in harmony with the four seasons. This open-ended flexibility and highly practical adaptability to nature were recognized almost as the antipodes of French rigid rationality. And yet, Claudel found them curiously agreeable.[120]

The "not-yet-separated" phase of space and time, which the *ma* notion designates, was in good tune with phenomenology, both in its reduction of an abstract intellectual framework and in the recovery of a *Lebenswelt.* Indeed the *Lebensraum* can never exist apart from temporality. The sense of "being seen by the forest" which Maurice Merleau-Ponty (1908–61) pointed out in his *L'Oeil et l'esprit* (1964), may be a variant of the mystical experience of "being-viewed-by-the-god" which the sanctuary transmits to itinerant pilgrims.

In this context, let me also refer to Dagobert Frey (1883–1962), because his *Grundlegung zu einer vergleichenden Kunstwissenschaft* (1949) tried to compare and classify different approaches to the sacredness in representative monuments of the main cultural spheres and proposed a typology of human figures in movement by analyzing sculpture and statues. To be more faithful to Frey's initial intention, however, the narrow definition of fine arts would not suffice. The intuitive sense of "being touched" is more fully developed in martial arts, one of whose thinking practitioners is Kenji Tokitsu (時津賢児 1947–), the author of *La voie du karaté, pour une théorie des arts martiaux japonais* (1979). Tokitsu elaborates the notion of *ma* in close relation with *haptinomie* (the principle of touching and combining). Without mystifying the physical experience in the combat, he convincingly demonstrates that control of the in-between-ness of one's own self in front of one's opponent, who is in constant movement, cannot be reduced to a simple mathematical topology of physical power and speed. *Ma wo yomu* ("to read the *ma*") becomes an essential technique in the human relationships.[121]

"Kriegeskunst" may also have a legitimate position in a widened conception of "Kunstwissenschaft." No one can deny the possibility that martial arts might be included in a G.A.H., perhaps in relation to performance art. To realize this possibility must be, after all, extremely "touching." Both, after all, entail "touching."

Elusiveness of an elliptic orbit. To bring my lengthy commentary to an end, two remarks may be necessary. First, the idea of appropriating foreign concepts so as to achieve a renewal of one's own discourse is a common strategy in the West. Both Richard Muther (1860–1909) in his *Geschichte der Malerie im 19. Jahrhundert* (1893–94) and Julius Meier-Graefe (1867–1935) in his *Entwicklungsgeschichte der Moderne Kunst* (1904) inserted chapters on Japanese art between their chapters on Western Realism and Impressionism. Those were not, of course, simple subterfuges to simulate a G.A.H.; both authors were convinced that the intervention of *Japonismus* was indispensable for the development of Impressionism. Thus, in their interpretation, the European tradition was renewed by its impact with the Far East. The same was said of Fauvism and Cubism, of Matisse's Moroccan experience, and the impact of African art on Picasso. In the same vein, Hubert Damisch's (1927–) strategy of relying on Chinese images in his *Traité du trait* (1995) seems to faithfully retrace the same traditional (!) scheme of European dialectics on the level of methodology in critical discourse.

It is not my intention to accuse such an approach of Eurocentrism, self-aggrandizement, or auto-justification. But I am not of the opinion that an appropriation of the Other for the benefit of one's own interest can lead to a G.A.H. Is this a limit of the G.A.H.? Fortunately Damisch's approach as a self-disqualified "analphabetic eye" relieves him of the temptation to usurp the Other. One may easily trace here an affinity with Barthes's self-confessed ignorance of a putatively impenetrable Japan. Referring to the Barthesian notion of *punctum* as opposed to *studium*, Damisch concentrates his attention on the marking of the initial break line (*trait-brisure*), which cannot manifest itself without damaging the very condition of its manifestation. By referring to the initial act of articulation of the universe, which retraces the origin of the oracular scripture incised into the turtle shell in the Yan Dynasty, Damisch voices his expectation of another art history which is resolutely different ("l'attente d'une histoire résolument autre"), a history which emerges through the fissure dissolving the monolithic continuity ("solution de continuité") from the illusory G.A.H.[122]

Second, I have demonstrated that most of these theoretical concepts emerged from the authors' contact with foreign environments and uninitiated audiences. Such notions as *ma*, *Rahmenlosigkeit*, "gray zone," and "intermediary space" would not have been coined or mobilized were it not for the authors' interest in explaining something to strangers who were mainly in a linguistically dominant position. The things needing explanation were so familiar to the "natives" (who occupied the linguistically subordinate position) that they had not paid particular attention to them. The "conceptual scaffolding" of Western scholarship therefore contributed to the invention of such terminologies. Indeed, it has been mainly Western attention that has resulted in the exploitation of "relevant" foreign terminologies (always "relevant" for Western scholarly discussion) for the West's own benefit (which, however, would not necessarily harm those non-Western scholars already "contaminated" by Western scholarship, including the present author).

One must be careful of the distortions that such extraction of terminology from its initial contexts, for the sake of global application, might easily cause. The temptation of an "expanded and more inclusive art history" is the original sin of universalism. Isozaki for example did not want to show the *ma* exhibition in Japan, because he thought it would be tautological to present it there. It might also have aroused Japanese suspicion about the hyperbolic fetishism of the French regarding *things Japanese*. Such French claims of possessing the ultimate degree of judgment ("*la dernière instance*") in aesthetic judgment might have been accused of arrogance by the local culture. In contrast, one must also note that basic terms (in the West) like "expression" or "representation" suddenly lose their semantic stability and methodological reliability once they are confronted with other realities constructed with different grammars and syntaxes, and articulated with wholly different vocabularies and taxonomy.

In a translation from a phonographic Indo-European language to the Chinese language, based on ideograms, the paradigmatic network of vocabularies is almost completely reshuffled, if not entirely destroyed. The devastating confusions which occur in the process of transmission are hardly noticed by ordinary users, who are satisfied with practical communication. Even bilingual speakers tend to forget the gap they constantly cross, because conventional translation paralyzes critical consciousness. But a person who is located in between — a conversant Japanese interlocutor, sandwiched between a Chinese and an English speaker — might well be able to assist at an otherwise impossible border crossing.

Concealed underneath apparently normal communication, two almost incompatible semantic fields are constantly crashing into each other. The network of etymology in European languages can hardly survive when remodeled into the combinations of Chinese ideograms. The two systems cannot be interrelated with one other without an almost complete reconnection of the semantic distribution. In Chinese the relation between "presentation" (表現/表象/表示 in Chinese; 提起/提示 in Japanese) and "*re*presentation" (表現/再現/表象 etc. in Chinese; 表象/再現/上演/代表 in Japanese) is no longer visible; what's worse, the conceptual distinction is often confusing because the terms are hardly differentiated from each other. The conjunction of "expression" (表現/表出) and "impression" (印象) cannot be grasped if the original spelling is not provided in brackets — and this is aside from the confusions that arise among Chinese, Japanese and Korean translations. These inevitable adjustments and qualifications make it extremely difficult to understand philosophic discussions, because binary oppositions in the original are frequently altered and dissolved into new sets of conventional Chinese binary oppositions. (Oriental nationalist scholars who know only Chinese terminology often believe, wrongly, that their own conventional Chinese binary pairs are globally or cross-culturally valid and easily translatable, and they tend to take the lack of translatability as proof of the "cultural invasion by Western imperialism.")

It is easy to talk about "displacement" (as James Clifford does), "heterotopia" (as in Michel Foucault), or "contingency" (Richard Rorty's term), but experiencing them is quite another matter. Linguistically speaking at least, and at least for some Orientals philologically conscious of cross-cultural translation, the utopia of a Global Art History would mean perpetually orbiting along the elusive locus of an ellipse whose two centers are the Western and the Chinese.[123] Without fetishizing elusive concepts from abroad (although at the same time, I have to say that the Baudelairean words "contingent," "ephemeral," and "elusive" summarize the Japanese aesthetics and testify to its *modernité*), let us recognize once and for all that the idea of a Global Art History is itself a highly elusive and elliptic concept (eternally moving in an elliptical orbit), just as the Japanese version of a Global Art History remains elusive and elliptic to Western viewers.

Craig Clunas

The Toolkit and the Textbook

There is such a lot of material in this rich exchange that the thought of "assessing" it is somewhat exhausting, and the invocation of global perspectives — Art History throughout feels like it ought to have capital letters — makes it all the more daunting. I feel competent only to respond from a specific standpoint, that at which I currently work. The Department of Art and Archaeology at London's School of Oriental and African Studies is a bit like the traditional Eurocentric department, still dominant in Britain, but flipped through the looking glass. We *only* "do" Asia and Africa, and it is the sequence of names from Giotto to Cézanne who are the unspoken others of our introductory undergraduate survey courses. We are therefore, if you like, a test bed for the issue discussed here of whether different content *necessarily* equals a different art history, and I would have to say that in our case it most certainly at present does not. The names on our syllabus might be unfamiliar, but nothing else about it would be. It would be quite easy to point at us and repeat Audre Lord's famous tag that "the master's tools will never dismantle the master's house." But equally, it might be said that simply ignoring the fact that the master *has* a toolkit, which he used to build the house in the first place, will most certainly reduce one's chances of dismantling anything, if that is what you end up wanting to do. This is all to say that for our students (who at the MA level and increasingly at the undergraduate level too are of African or Asian heritage), *some* knowledge of the toolkit and its configuration is absolutely necessary. So, I would argue, they get whizzed past Wölfflin and Panofsky (and a lot of more recent stuff) because if they don't and they pick up books entitled things like *Style in the Arts of China* or *Artists and Patrons: Some Social and Economic Aspects of Chinese Painting* or *The Path of Beauty* they will have no way of evaluating why and how they do what they do; they won't even be able to dislike them meaningfully if they want to.

Does this mean that to "do" art history is invariably to do Western art history, as James Elkins argues? It might on one level be true that "Chinese art history" (my own area) *is* "Western," but it seems to me to be a statement that is about as interesting as claiming that the U.S. Marine Corps *is* "Eastern" because explosives are central to its mode of operation. I detect in some of the conversation a tension between the continuing charms of a "West and the Rest" paradigm, and a much more nuanced sense of what the global was, is, and might be, at least as it affects art history. For me, this nuancing is best expressed by the work of Dipesh Chakrabarty, whose *Provincializing Europe* (2000) is lucid on the complicity of Asian elites (he has less to say on Africa) in the creation of the trope of "Europe as modernity." It is for example now well studied how the Japanese word *bijutsu* was a nineteenth-century calque on the German *schöne Kunst* (of course a calque itself) and how it in turn was transmitted to China, the same characters being read there as *meishu*, which any dictionary will tell you means "art." One might therefore argue that the practice of art history in the Chinese language *is* Japanese (much more offensively to some Chinese nationalist sensibility). But we tend not to, because we are still too fascinated by transmissions across an East/West boundary, and not sensitive enough to the actual flows of discourses in the crucial century 1850–1950, when the art history we are debating came into being. The work of John Clark, or of a younger scholar like Aida Yuen Wong, is only now unpicking some of the very complex Chinese–Japanese interchanges of the period, faint echoes of which eventually reached Europe and North America to create much of the way the field of Anglophone Chinese art history is today.

I detect too in the conversation a residual hankering on some parts for the notional perfect textbook, which I think is a local North American issue. Just as Christa-Maria Lerm Hayes reports from her own German experience, the British practice has been to discourage the use of the survey volume — by no means all British art history departments use one systematically, and "Janson" or "Honour and Fleming" have much less resonance here. There's nothing particularly virtuous about this; I think it in fact stems from an ongoing nostalgia for an elite system underpinned by Oxbridge, an imagined situation where a small number of students would "read around the subject." But by now this has been converted into an active mistrust of the single-volume survey, and I think the majority of British practitioners would be with Sandra Klopper in cautioning about the need for a single textbook (even if their students sometimes pined for one). Just to carry on the theme of how local conditions affect the material practices of art history, and not only through shortage of resources, let me invoke the Research Assessment Exercise (RAE), the seven-yearly peer review of published research in all areas of higher education in the UK, on which funding for individual institutions depends in our state system. In this, textbooks and syntheses "don't count" (the normative paradigm being research in the natural sciences), or rather more accurately are perceived by many potential authors not to count, which is the same thing when it comes to inhibiting the writing of them by those of us with UK jobs.

Not that the RAE is some sort of totalitarian apparatus, acting to produce uniformity. Arguably, the effect of the imposition by government of a market paradigm on higher education here has had the effect of producing *exactly* the plurality of art histories which some of the speakers support, if maybe for different reasons. Departments strive (you can see it from their websites) to convey a sense of the distinctiveness of *their* art history from that of their competitors, and this sense of a series of intellectual micro-climates (in content, if not always in approach) has perhaps been more corrosive of the canon than any of the critiques launched at it from inside the discipline. So, when I was at the University of Sussex, nineteenth-century France just didn't happen, it wasn't mentioned in our introductory (the word "survey" was never used) course, which was renamed "Stories of Art" in 1994. But the Ming dynasty did. Students at St. Andrews can learn about the early-twentieth-century Baltic, though not about East Asia. In plenty of places you could go through a degree program without encountering Rembrandt. What many of us are finding now in our teaching is that we are trying to teach students to be critical of something they have never heard of. This may just be a long way of saying that the shape of the discourse of art history is not in the hands of art historians (would it be discourse if it were?).

That brings me to Ladislav Kesner's important points about the relationship of professionals to a wider readership. We should never underestimate the desire for consolation which swirls around discussion of art in the common culture — I would set alongside Gombrich's post-WWII *Story of Art* the almost equally best-selling *Mei ti licheng* (*The Path of Beauty*, 1981) by Li Zehou, consoling a newly rising Chinese middle class that, despite the horrors of the Cultural Revolution, high culture had survived and was of value; that what they thought they knew was in fact true. The main morning news show on BBC radio has just now (September 2005) been running a widely advertised competition to find "The Greatest Painting in Britain" — over 100,000 people have voted online, and out of a hardly startling shortlist of ten picked by experts the winner is J.M.W. Turner's "The Fighting Temeraire Towed to Her Last Berth to be Broken Up" (1838).[124] Is this just part of the "demand for art and the trivialization of art" of which Kesner speaks? Or is it a sign that art history's eschewal of art criticism has marginalized the former as the latter thrives? It's certainly noteworthy that, while a number of practicing artists were asked for their nominations, no one identifiable as an art historian was. And the BBC's relationship to art and art history is certainly very different now from what it was thirty-five years ago when Sir Kenneth Clark, mentioned by a couple of speakers, told me what *Civilisation* was and wasn't when I was a schoolboy. My views then were not solicited. A vote was not taken. But I was equally or even more captivated in my youth by another BBC television series about art, which I think contradicts James Elkins's assertion that no such products have ever challenged the Clarkesque standard narrative; this would be John Berger's *Ways of Seeing* (1972). It was much discussed in its day; the book is still in print and remains on numerous university reading lists here. The Marxist Berger, whose lurid shirts and flares were a compelling visual counterblast to Clark's tweeds for me at sixteen, lambasted the grand narratives, the myth of artistic genius, the work of art as commodity, the male gaze, and so on. And over thirty years later "The Fighting Temeraire" is still The Greatest Painting in Britain (and I *don't* mean that it's not a great painting). Comforting as it might be to art historians' *amour propre* to imagine that something richer or more complex than a consoling succession of masterpieces has never been offered to a wider public, it is the perhaps painful truth that it has been offered, assessed, and ignored.

In a number of recent British and Irish novels, and I'm talking here about serious writing, reviewed with respect in the quality papers, the figure of the art historian is prominent, and in the four examples which I have in mind he (in all cases he) stands for a particular kind of pointless and passionless pedantry, missing the point of Art (with a capital *A*) by knowing too much about it. John Banville's *The Untouchable* (1998) is a thinly disguised version of the life of Anthony Blunt, director of the Courtauld Institute and agent of the USSR, and the same author's *The Sea* (2005) features an art historian beset by a mid-life crisis on a seaside holiday. Adam Thorpe's *The Rules of Perspective* (2005) is set among bickering German museum curators cowering in a basement in 1945 as shells rain down. Zadie Smith's *On Beauty* (2005) centrally features an expatriate British art history professor on the U.S. East Coast who has spent his career taking the enchantment of "genius" out of Rembrandt. In all four cases, it's made obvious to the reader that knowing a lot about the history of art stops you really "getting" it (the "it" in question often being Beauty with a capital *B*, a word art historical professionals shy away from but which links Zadie Smith fortuitously to Li Zehou). I take them collectively (and there may be other examples) to be an instance of the kind of disjunction Ladislav Kesner alludes to between the scholar and the public, a symbolic *ressentiment* against those of us seen as having disenchanted art. I'm conflicted in my response to this — as a former museum curator myself I share some of his sense of frustration at our inability to connect, but I've also seen how discourses of public communication slide into rhetoric about "taxpayer's money," which in turn support only the most banal affirmatory work. I'd be unhappy to align myself with the recently elected pope, reportedly happy to reach a smaller if doctrinally tougher audience, but I don't see it as my job either to provide feel-good narratives.

I have perhaps responded too much in terms of a local British story of the story of art history, but it bears up what David Summers has to say on the important subject of contingency, and perhaps aligns me with the skeptics about a "global art history." A visit now to the art section of a big bookshop in China will immediately show that the exchange market in cultural and economic capital in somewhere like Shanghai today is extremely vibrant in a quite distinctive way. There are signs of a new genre of writing about "value" (*jiazhi*) in art which relates aesthetics and market forces in ways I'm not sure I understand, but which seem to me to be something rather different from *Miller's Antiques Price Guide*.[125]

It is already the case that, just as Andrea Giunta observes for Latin America, the largest quantity of work on Chinese art is now happening in China, and in the Chinese language, a Chinese language fizzing with neologisms. It is therefore interesting that quite a large number of books originally written in English about Chinese art are currently undergoing translation into Chinese, generally work by mid-career scholars active now; soon you won't need English to read this stuff. I think that in a few years there will have come into being in China (as I believe there *already* is in Japan, though this is not touched on in the discussion) an art historical world which will operate quite comfortably without the medium of English. It's the pace of change in China that is truly startling. Conversely, the catastrophic decline in language skills in Britain creates a real risk of an art history here which in terms of research can operate only on that material where the sources are in English; this is a real cause for pessimism which I think far outweighs the issue of whether or not indigenous terms have a place in the discipline.

David Carrier

What Happens When Art History Travels

Like people, languages, political institutions, religions, and scientific theories, works of art migrate from one culture to another. When they do so, they usually are transformed. John King Fairbank's *China: A New History* links "Mao's sinification of Marxism ... with the failure of Taiping Christianity," the nineteenth-century rebellion, one chapter in China's long struggle to assimilate external cultural influences.[126] The early Buddhist missionaries ran into the problem that has faced all purveyors of foreign ideas in China ever since: how to select certain Chinese terms, and invest them with new significance without letting the foreign ideas be subtly modified, in fact Sinified, in the process. Nowadays every American city has Chinese and Indian restaurants whose cuisine has only a vague family resemblance with the indigenous cuisine of these cultures. And America's fast food chains and shops, like our pop music and films, are exported. But in Germany, McDonald's serves beer. In China, traditionally a tea-drinking country, Starbucks sells coffee. Bollywood has recreated Hollywood in very distinctively local terms. And on Indian TV, you can see Hindu rock groups mimicking MTV performances. Thanks to migration, American spoken English is being transformed. The art museum, a creation of eighteenth-century Europe, now is found almost everywhere. Western-style democracy, openly gay culture, and human rights defenders appear in most cultures. And colleges almost everywhere employ pedagogic models originating in England and Germany, and developed in the United States. Some of what a culture creates is of interest even to people with quite different worldviews. Scientific and mathematical discoveries, manufacturing and farming techniques readily transfer from one culture to another. Muslim mathematics, the Chinese invention of paper, and European gun technology, discoveries which contribute to a common stock of knowledge, could be easily borrowed and modified. The Chinese, with their preference for light housing, heavy clothes, and concentrated warmth, used silk for brocade (a heavy textile), while the Romans, with their preference for heavy housing, light clothes, and diffused warmth, used it for gauze (a light textile).

But some of what a culture makes is only of interest to others sharing its worldview. Muslims were interested in European weapons, but not in Christianity. (There were of course Muslims who converted.) Muslims translated Greek philosophy, but were not interested in classical theater. And nowadays Islamists call on Muslim societies to adopt from Western civilization its science, technology, and organization of public services. However they reject the West's ideology and its basis: secular materialism. Renaissance Europeans coveted gold from America, and used foodstuffs like the potato and the turkey, but they were not interested in the Aztec or Mayan religions.

When Western art history migrates, how will it be transformed? Our ways of thinking, rooted in Vasari's history of Tuscan art from 1300 to 1550, have proven to be remarkably supple. Like other Western institutions, art history has been successful because it shows a remarkable capacity for adaptation. There are two large questions facing our discipline.

First, how will it understand art made outside Europe? When we look seriously at art from China, India, and the Islamic world, then it is obvious that new interpretative strategies are needed. Second, how can art history root itself in cultures outside of North America and Europe? The United States has created an elaborate and well-financed educational system, which supports many productive scholars. But even here there are tensions. The normal expectation is that getting tenure requires publishing one book, and promotion to full professor another. But the recent contraction of academic publishing means that this system will have to be modified. So much research is being done. What social goal does this writing satisfy?

I share with James Elkins an interest in questions about these institutions, which deserve more discussion by our fellow academics. In 1991 I published *Principles of Art History Writing,* a book on the methodology of art history. In 2004 China Renmin University Press brought out a Chinese translation. Wondering how readers would understand my account, I added a new preface, asking to what extent can the analysis presented in this book apply also to non-Western art. That question is very hard to answer.

China, I wrote, has a very long history of art that differs dramatically from the story of art in the West. In your country, I said, naturalism developed earlier; the religious traditions were very different from those of European Christian culture; and the importance of calligraphy meant that the relationship between painting and writing were understood very differently. Present-day Western scholars are very sensitive to the dangers of Eurocentrism. We are aware that any adequate theory of art must deal with the art of all cultures. Since the late nineteenth century Chinese painting has been collected in America and there are many distinguished scholars who study your art. But as yet, no one knows how to write a history of world art, a commentary that will do justice to the grand traditions of both Europe and Asia. That is the task of the younger scholars in China and America. If this translation of my book into Chinese contributes in some small way to that goal — so I concluded — then I will be extremely gratified.

The materials assembled by Elkins in this book take me back to these concerns. The problem with transporting Western-style art history to other cultures is not just that it is focused on European art, but that its support system is very expensive, even for wealthy countries. To be an art historian in America you need access to a good library, a digital slide collection, computer services, and of course you need to have enough time away from teaching to do reading and research. Replicating this system in poorer countries is not possible. And so what happens too often is that ambitious scholars move to the United States, the one place where they can get good financial support for their research. And Western scholars also need regular access to significant art collections. Many students in China and India study European art history, but until they travel to the West they will have only a very limited knowledge of these cultures. Westerners interested in Chinese and Indian art have the same problem, but for us international travel is easier. So long as the West is so much richer, it is not possible to have a level playing field. In the Western academic world art from outside Europe remains marginalized. This is inevitable, for it is much easier to write about American or European Modernism than art from other cultures. If you are seriously interested in art in Africa, then you need to be an ambitious traveler. If you want to study Japanese painting, then you need to learn Japanese. Tapati Guha-Thakurta's writing on Indian art, Wu Hung's and Craig Clunas's discussions of the art of China, and Oleg Grabar's publications about Islamic art, make frequent reference to the novel Western interpretative strategies. But there is very little crossover of their concerns into the literature of European art.[127]

Frequently writers discussing art in China, India, or Islam will make reference to European painting and sculpture. But only rarely do scholars discussing Western art allude to art from outside Europe. Insofar as the academic discourse of history is concerned, "Europe" remains the sovereign, theoretical subject of all histories, including the ones we call "Indian," "African," and so forth. Other histories tend to become variations on a master narrative that could be called "the history of Europe." Dipesh Chakrabarty asks the right question: "Why cannot we … return the gaze?"[128]

Kitty Zijlmans

An Intercultural Perspective in Art History: Beyond Othering and Appropriation

Clearly, art history is not global.[129] The possibilities and desirability of a move toward a global perspective are still widely debated and contested. In my opinion, however, art and consequently art history are global issues. Art is produced all over the world, and this global art production is challenging the discipline of art history to rethink its presumptions and revise its concepts and approaches.[130] The Western bias of the conceptual apparatus referred to in the Art Seminar only comes into relief in confrontation with other cultures and traditions. At the University of Leiden, one of the aims of the Department of Art History is to study art history in a global perspective, and that means including perspectives on art other than those of the West. For an art historian who, like myself, is interested in contemporary art, the encounter with, and hence the study of contemporary art from all over the world — including traditional art forms of the present — brings with it a multitude of theoretical and methodological questions and problems.[131] In order to be able to conceive of art history as global and to study art in a global perspective, an intercultural perspective is needed. I agree with David Summers: to study art history in a global perspective does not mean that the result will be one homogeneous global art history. In *Real Spaces: World Art History and the Rise of Western Modernism,* Summers observes: "The 'World Art History' of the subtitle is not a global history (which I think is both undesirable and impossible), but the discipline of art history itself, now faced with the task of providing the means to address as many histories as possible nearly enough in their own terms to permit new intercultural discussions."[132] World art history for me is not an end in itself but an attitude, an awareness of the complexity and interrelationships of art production and reception worldwide. My contribution to the debate will be the exposition of an intercultural perspective for the study of art as a global phenomenon.

1. *Wrong both ways.* Contemporary art from the non-Euramerican world often finds itself in the awkward position of either being neglected completely, or being sandwiched, by the various art institutions, media, and venues of the international

art world, between practices of "othering" on the one hand and of "appropriation" on the other. The first option is not an option when taking seriously the creative practices of any people, no matter where they may live. The two options are related to power structures and the institutionalization of the art world, but at least they make us aware of the fact that the encounter with "other" art is problematic. When it comes to insiders and outsiders, I am the "other" on many occasions. I am Caucasian, female, and North European; I was educated and I currently work at a European university. The subject of my teaching and research is art. (Not to sink into the quagmire of the question "what is art," I take the position that art is what is introduced to me *as* art, by an artist or an art institution. Art is a valuation and is always institutionalized; it always comes to us mediated through some kind of discourse or institution. Following David Summers's observation in the Art Seminar, this also implies the idea of art should be left relatively open, so that it can be defined by the historical modalities and instances at hand.)

The institutionalization of art and the ongoing globalization are intrinsically connected to the history of the European expansion and domination of the world in the past centuries. Although many of us now look back very critically on these practices, they shaped the world as we know it today. Only recently did much art from the non-Euramerican world become visible as *art*, as part of an art discourse, as part of the art system.[133] I would like to ask: is this an act of appropriation? If we consider the international, global art system as being shaped only by the Euramerican art concept, then it is; if we take the art system as a domain that is fueled by practices that vary widely in form and content but have as a common denominator the way people express and give surplus value to their being, it is not. Art is a concept that accommodates a wide variety of practices and interpretations, and it has been co-shaped for centuries by various cultures.[134]

This observation does not, however, solve the problem of how to access non-Western art.[135] The paradox is that, either way we approach it, as "alien" or as "own," we seem to be biased. Alienating means making non-Western art different, and that often means making it unequal or else disregarding it; not paying attention to its differences ignores the characteristics of the art and decontextualizes it. This would imply: wrong both ways. I would like to reverse this implication, and suggest we both include and "other" art at the same time.

2. *From Eurocentrism to art histories.* In his article "The Marco Polo Syndrome," Gerardo Mosquera, adjunct curator at the New Museum of Contemporary Art in New York, critiques attempts to overcome the problem of Eurocentrism and Western domination. For him, "Eurocentrism is the only ethnocentrism universalized through actual world-wide domination by a meta-culture, and based on a traumatic transformation of the world through economic, social and political processes centered in one small part of it."[136] Despite the Western world's self-critique, Mosquera still observes the perpetuation of the distortion that is produced by the West's one-sided (unilateral) perspective and the existing circuits of power. If Third World cultures (Mosquera's expression) want to take part in today's dynamic, they should not isolate themselves into traditions, but instead — so Mosquera argues — make traditions work in the new epoch by vigorously adapting them; Third World cultures should make contemporary art from their own values, sensitivities, and interests. According to Mosquera, the de-Eurocentrism in art is not about returning to purity, but about adopting postcolonial "impurity" in order for cultures outside the West to express themselves. This would result in a syncretistic contemporary culture that connects to local, national, and international contexts. Art for him, and I agree with this, is linked to cultural specificity but possesses a polysemous ambiguity open to diverse readings. He proposes that the West should take an equally pluralistic view of its *own* art and by doing so revise

Western culture. For Mosquera, intercultural involvement implies a critical evaluation of art practices from both sides. Intercultural communication includes not only seeing but listening.[137]

Mosquera's critique points to an implied cultural asymmetry. The West set the standard, and the rest could either adapt, or be traditionalized and exoticized in institutional settings such as ethnological museums. Mosquera critiques the apparent obviousness of this standard as well as its claim of being entirely of Western descent.

I tend to agree with Mosquera that the idea of a purely "Western" art setting the standard is a misrepresentation of something as multifariously complex as the prevailing international art. For centuries art has been fed by a diversity of cultural sources and impulses, and it can never be tracked down to only one point of origin. We cannot, however, unwrite the art history that has been written, nor deny western Europe's importance for the emergence of the modern art concept as we know it today. What we can do, and what has been happening for the past decade, is to reevaluate *how* art history has been written and question *why* it happened in such a way; and we can subsequently reinterpret the past from a multicultural point of view and work toward the writing of art *histories,* of systematic as well as historical studies on the scope of art. As points of departure, two issues are important: first, to take art as a panhuman activity, and second, to take into account art's openness to diverse readings and the generation of meanings.

In regard to art as a panhuman activity: art is a specific form of making the world your own, of acquiring or getting hold of the world (in German *Weltaneignung*), and we do that by creating symbols. The use of symbols is a unique characteristic of humans and art would indeed seem a panhuman phenomenon.[138] To turn to the second point, an artwork never has just one meaning attached to just one context; that would make it historical documentation or merely decoration. A key characteristic of art is that it opens itself to new interpretations time and again. Otherwise, it would be a self-contained ontological object enclosing its one and only meaning, denying both the interpreter's share in the generating of meaning, as well as the role of changing contexts in the interpretation of art. To paraphrase Norman Bryson, artworks have a potential for meaning that is generated by different frames. Context, or as he proposes, "frame," is not naturally given but something that we as researchers make.[139]

3. *Intercultural perspective.* How do my arguments help us to formulate an intercultural perspective? I understand the term "intercultural" as in the Latin meaning of *inter amicos,* "among friends, or *inter culturas,* "among cultures." As a strategy that relates to a diversity of art forms and cultures, an intercultural perspective can profit from a multidisciplinary approach. It addresses art history, philosophy, anthropology, language and culture studies, sociology, even neuroscience. No researcher covers this entire field of academic studies; rather, we participate in it, each starting from our expertise. Consequently, the research starts with the researcher's clarification of the point of view from which she or he operates. Thus "showing your colors" makes clear where you comes from, academically as well as personally, what position you take, and what the aim of your research is. It also makes clear that conclusions drawn from the research are expertise-bound, and thus limited, relative, and not absolute — and therefore dynamic.

Thus, for me, the key issues for the formulation of an intercultural perspective with a strong art historical, art theoretical (in German: *kunstwissenschaftlich*) emphasis center around the following concepts that I will briefly discuss. There is no hierarchy in this listing, nor is it exhaustive:

1. *World Art Studies.* The concept is taken from John Onians, who was the first to use this term to open up the study of art history to a global scope.[140] At Leiden University we have adopted Onians's phrasing, and "World Art Studies" is now used to designate a field of study that covers various,

contingent art *histories* (of the "non-Western" world) and at the same time aims at developing the concepts and approaches to an integrated, that is, multidisciplinary study of art, as a panhuman phenomenon.[141] These two strategies do not exclude each other; rather they keep in balance the dichotomy between inclusion and othering.

2. *Inclusion and othering.* I connect the two by taking seriously what has been presented to me as art—how unfamiliar the works may seem — and thus include it into my research, while at the same time being aware of its "own-ness" or "otherness" (in German: *Andersartigkeit*). Including and othering, then, are two sides of the same coin. "Othering" implies connecting art to its cultural background; one of the entries to a work of art is its cultural background, which can play a larger or smaller role. Hence, "other" artistic practices are incorporated, and by doing so art history will be both revised and extended.
3. *Cultural diversity and syncretism.* We all share culture, but the concept of culture differs greatly, or rather the term "culture" is used in various ways and contexts. It is not just connected to a people, a "tribe," or a nation, but also to the metropolis, specific areas or provinces, to social stratification, specific groups or scenes, and the like. The one word covers a plethora of meanings and attributions, so we have to handle the notion with care. The social and cultural background of an artist only matters, I would say, when the artworks refer to their contexts. That does not make such work a synecdoche. It still matters in what way the works relate to their cultural contexts. The other term I mentioned, *syncretism*, refers to the assumption that in the course of time all cultures (I almost hesitate to use the word) in one way or the other have been influenced and changed by intercultural contacts and exchange, and

therefore are syncretistic. This is an ongoing process and for that reason a dynamic one.

4. *Center/periphery.* The center/periphery model is taken as a flexible one. There is no fixed center, the center is (or in historical research, was) where the action is (was), as seen from the perspective of the art in question. In some cases, the West may well be the periphery. Center/periphery can also apply to the canon. An intercultural perspective rejects the idea of a fixed canon; it is static neither in place nor in time.
5. *Frames and contexts.* Different framings will produce different interpretations. One of art history's most difficult problems is to determine what the relevant context is in which to study an artwork. Art historical research mostly deals with historical topics. The historical past as such is gone; only all sorts of material objects, texts, and data remain. To determine what facts, historical events and aspects are significant largely depends on what the researcher is aiming at to elucidate. This applies to research of the past as well as the present. Aside from being aware of one's own practices of framing, a researcher has to critically evaluate the existing discourse (framings) on the subject, to trace norms and values behind it, and take into account possible cultural differences.[142]
6. *Role of technique and materials.* Art comes as a material and is created by a technique; obvious as they are, these aspects are often overlooked as agents for the production of meaning in both creation and interpretative practices.[143]
7. *Materiality versus immateriality.* In his dissertation entitled "Condensed Reality," the anthropologist Pieter ter Keurs (National Museum of Ethnology in Leiden) emphasizes the importance of the study of material culture, that is to say the materiality of the objects (in his case from two small island groups in Papua New Guinea and Indonesia).

He understands the mere material presence of an object as a cultural fact and introduces the concept of *material complex.* For ter Keurs, a material complex is a "material object with the meanings condensed in it or evaporated from it"; it refers to the object and its socially constructed meanings.[144] The subject's creation or construction of meaning condenses into the material object but in the course of time evaporates from it due to changing contexts and functions. In his view, "the subject is changing in the way it deals with objects and … although the physical object seems to remain the same, the material complex (the material object and the ideas *condensed* in it and *evaporated* from it) is also changing."[145] In my opinion, ter Keurs's ideas about material objects as metaphors — as condensation cores for ideas, concepts, and values in culture — take into account both the material objects as such and the parts played by the subjects (makers and recipients) in the generation of meaning and the changes of meaning over time. He stresses the importance of studying the materiality of the object together with the processes of condensation and evaporation of meaning. This is a useful approach for artworks as well. Where artworks are seen as "concepts," the artwork's materiality is often underestimated.

8. *Art history.* Last but certainly not least, there is the body of approved art historical methods and concepts. In my opinion, every artwork can be subjected to a formal analysis, placed into relationship with other artworks from the past (diachronic) and from the present (synchronic), from its "own" culture as well as others, as long as it is relevant to do so; every art can be appraised for its stylistic quality, eloquence and power of expression, for its technical skill, mastery of the materials, even aesthetics. In order to do so, one needs to be fully informed and aware of one's own point of departure (in my case, art

history) and biases; only then can one contribute to the discourse by sharing knowledge, perception, and insight. An intercultural perspective is a way of learning and of acquiring access to an unfamiliar concept of art. The final question regarding a chosen approach comes down to the basic question Summers poses in the Art Seminar: Does it work?

Hans Dam Christensen
Which Art History?

Is there such a thing as a global art history? At times, the Art Seminar answers the question with a definite "no," even when the possibilities are discussed from several vantage points. Ultimately, the answers depend on which "art history" one speaks of since one can make the overall claim that a global art history exists as long as it is possible to find education and research in the history of art on the various continents of the globe. This is so even when the claim is only possible because research and teaching merge with artistic activity in some places, especially outside to the Western centers, or if a few large geographical areas exist where the history of art is not taught or researched locally. Greenland comes to mind, where Ilisimatusarfik, Greenland's university in Nuuk, and the only one of its kind on the enormous island, does not cover art history, though many scholars who research arctic culture would claim that art has been produced in Greenland since the first Eskimos.

There are several reasons to confirm, or deny, the main question "Is art history global?" A focus on the exclusions as well as the explorations of the many art histories as variations on the same basic epistemological mood would probably ultimately tell us more, but not all, about definitions of "art history." (Here I am paraphrasing David Summers's — Heideggerian? — comment that "all behaviors are variations on physically grounded themes"![146]) Following the late Wittgenstein's well-known game model, it is, however, tempting to note that there need not necessarily be any essential commonality between all that is called "art history." Instead, and from various positions, one could speak of family resemblance.[147] It wouldn't matter, then, whether art criticism and curatorial work are practiced rather than art historical research in any given location. Family resemblance would obtain irrespective of the different institutions' economic foundations or their historical and political conditions. Family resemblance would be irrespective of qualitative, typological, or other differences between the explored artworks. It would also be irrespective of methodological and theoretical conditions, and could be said to exist whether or not it is at all possible to inscribe all these objects in a common metalanguage, as has been attempted in awe-inspiring books, most recently Summers's *Real Spaces: World Art History and the Rise of Western Modernism* (2003) — though I might also mention an earlier example, Wölfflin's pupil Paul Frankl's even more monstrous *Das System der Kunstwissenschaft* (1938).[148] Furthermore, family resemblance could model differences irrespective of the definitions of "Kunstgeschichte," "Kunsthistorie," "Art History," "History of Art," "Taidehistoria," "Historia del arte," "Histoire de l'art," and so forth. Of course, the question whether art history is global only makes sense in relation to specific understandings of "art history." This becomes apparent in the three divisions of the conversation: (1) the material conditions of the discipline, (2) its "classic" texts and figures, and (3) the discussion as to whether its object of inquiry can be inscribed in a metalanguage.

Although the discipline is also called "Kunstwissenschaft," "Kunstvidenskab," and "the science of art," and so forth, the above-mentioned designations and their combinations of "art" and "history" have brought with them the claim that art history *is* its object; that is to say, that the designation of the scientific discipline and the scientific object merge into one. This seems also to be the precondition for the tripartite division of the conversation: apparently, it wants to avoid the merging, and yet the debate's last part, in particular, seems to return to a merging anyway. One reason for this is that the issue concerns both the analysis of artworks and, no less, the possibility of speaking of a common art history regardless of whether it concerns the scientific discipline or the object of study. As exemplified in Summers's book and Ladislav Kesner's essay, the merging happens thanks to a preconceived notion that "the artwork" is the scientific object of the discipline.

But is this not too narrow an understanding of the scientific object? First and foremost, the notion does not frame an object of study that belongs exclusively to art history. Just as the School of Oriental and African Studies at the University of London, mentioned in the conversation, includes African art as its object of study, so the University of Copenhagen — for better or worse — includes Arabic art in the Carsten Niebuhr Department and Japanese art in the Department of Asian Studies. On the other hand, over the years, the Department of Art History at the University of Copenhagen has taught and researched things besides artworks, such as — in a jumble — curatorship, exhibition studies, art pedagogy, aesthetic theory, the historiography of art history, design process, the social history of the artist persona, the history of the art institution, the history of art criticism, cultural economics, and more. Similar instances exist in many other places. Though the discourses and practices of art history privilege the analysis of an artwork, in everyday life, the object of study is considerably more multifaceted than these discourses and practices assert.

This means that even terms as open-ended as "gaze," "visuality," "space," or "form" do not cover art history's broad area of investigation, even when the terms derive from a deep-rooted object-centered tradition. One might argue that artworks relate to one term or another, and perhaps it made more sense to do this in the past, but today the artwork should no longer hold a monopoly on art historical research. In practice, the framework for calling oneself an "art historian" and for practicing "art history" is more flexible. The question, then, of whether a global art history exists is inadequate when restricted to artworks as its starting point. An art historian has usually achieved specialized knowledge through a process of disciplinary socialization, consisting of: (1) knowledge of art and parts of the history of art, one that the majority of interested people can acquire as part of a well-known liberal education, and that often includes a specific (modernist?) idea about aesthetic experience; (2) knowledge of parts of the discipline's history, theory and methods, which requires a certain level of academic schooling and which, together with the first point, covers the area of formal and informal knowledge of traditional art history (supplemented, of course, by knowledge about general rules for academic performance); (3a) formal and informal knowledge of everyday academic activities, which vary from place to place (compare the material work conditions described in the first, short part of the conversation); and (3b) an awareness of the historical sides of life in academia.

This double third point is rarely included in the definition of "art history," yet it is nevertheless a highly significant component. It pleases me, therefore, to find it included in the introduction to the round table and various places throughout, though it eventually pales in relation to the last section and its focus on the (im)possibilities of a common world of concepts for the analysis of artworks. So, in order to assess the seminar conversation, I want to look closer at "the everyday," among other things by means of the partially unanswered question posed by Friedrich Teja Bach: "How unified do we expect art history to be, or how diverse?" The question was touched upon in the conversation, and there will probably be other assessments, too, that touch on this point. The following analysis of the changes of objectives in two curricula for art history at the University of Copenhagen, from 1968 and 2000 respectively, will contribute to the issue with what are mainly unfamiliar texts for most readers.[149] Perhaps my analysis will also set itself apart by focusing on overlooked aspects of scientific practice, sacrilegiously displacing the focus away from the artwork.

Providing a quick inventory of the academic everyday in a typical Western context, one could state that it includes a more or less reflective knowledge of the discipline's research libraries, for example, its image collections and image technologies, relevant museal and archival collections, relevant handbooks, bibliographies, journals, digital databases, and Internet portals. It also includes knowledge of the organization of education, the format of exams, study trips and research, knowledge of the hierarchy of positions and the division of labor, conferences, symposia, guest lectures, and "important" upcoming exhibitions and events, formal research networks and other forms of academic relations, and academic ceremonies such as the defense of a dissertation as well as other academic, public events. I might add participation in informal academic-social networks and awareness of others' informal academic-social networks, informal knowledge of social recruiting, leading educational institutions, actual power relations regarding for example research traditions and theoretical schools (which are, among other things, manifested in various journals), awareness of current VIPs and "classic" texts, typical workplaces, typical art history publishing houses, foundations, bookstores, and more.[150]

This generalized academic everyday life is an often overlooked element in definitions of "core competences," "art history," and the "art historian," and though it may sound strange, it is ultimately more crucial for the way "art history" is defined than the competence of individual art historians. Attending to these elements requires that one acknowledge that an art historian does not just write about art and artists, possess a comprehensive knowledge of artworks, competence in analyzing artworks, or comprehension of particular concepts of history and the aesthetic. Rather, one becomes an art historian when one practices the discipline in particular ways that are both recognized as art history *and* enabled by means of an art historical socialization that includes a certain amount of regional knowledge and disciplinary identity.

Art historical socialization does not require a degree in art history. Scholars outside of the discipline can easily engage in relevant art historical research and become assimilated as art historians, just as art historians can step into and be absorbed by other academic fields. "Assimilation" is perhaps a misleading term for what takes place in practice. Together with an increasing trans- and interdisciplinarity, as well as a redisciplinarity, what is taking place is that other disciplinary traditions begin to have a say and, to a greater or lesser degree, cause fragmentation not only in the single narratives of art history but of all traditional academic disciplines formed in Europe in the eighteenth and nineteenth centuries. The active transformation of disciplines disrupts the authority and continuity of tradition while pointing to the processual and relational identity of a discipline.

Though some art historians, confronted with the newest art history or "foreign" art histories, may hope for a return to the good old days and its education of "real" art historians. Well, this past is mythological. There can be no return to an origin for art history since it has not originated out of nothing; "art history" names, at any moment, a group of already existing discourses that are, moreover, continually transformed due to the social, discursive, and cultural conditions of individuals. Hence, in regard to an origin one may ask: When was it? Does a Danish art historian find an origin in N.L. Høyen (the "father" of the Danish discipline from the beginning of the 1800s)? Or does one find an origin in the art historians from the European *Gründerzeit* of the university discipline in the second half of the 1800s? Or perhaps art historians educated according to the curriculum of 1968 for art history at the University of Copenhagen? Or maybe the quite different curriculum of 2000 for the same institution? Museum art history? University art history? "Normal art history"? "Theory" or "new art history"?

What is more, the theories, methods, and areas of inquiry are also continuously transforming, even when this is not apparent in the academic everyday. Though the citation curve for, say, Panofsky has dipped (as the graph in the Series Preface shows), many art historians still find certain, especially iconographic and formalist methods more "art historical" than other, often newer approaches. This is so despite the fact that these methods, on closer inspection, exist in many and incompatible variations. It is also easy to coincidentally refer to a mutually understood idea of a traditional area of study when one dissociates oneself from new threats. This is, however, a simplification since this area is not a constant either. To many Danish art historians today it seems nearly unthinkable that the discipline should not include contemporary art and (certain types of) photography, even though their inclusion is relatively new in academic life, and perhaps does not even exist in every country's art history. It is equally difficult to imagine that Italian Renaissance art would not continue to be a central part of art historical study. Over time, the idea of the centrality of the Renaissance has been strengthened by the accumulation of literature about the distribution of "masterworks," from photographic reproductions to the use of "masterworks" in, say, advertisements. The Renaissance's place in art history has also been strengthened by study- and research trips to Italy, perhaps facilitated by the Grand Tour of the past, as well as by the values created by the art market and by museum display. Conversely one may ask whether a European art historian around 1900 would have been able to imagine that, just one hundred years later, the art and culture of antiquity would not have the same prominence as before in syllabi, curricula, and teaching. In South Africa the idea of the Italian Renaissance is apparently already being erased. All in all, many places are to an increasing degree focusing on more recent art, design, and non-object-focused areas, such as communication, visual culture, historiography, theory, museology, and curating.

Without speaking of an "origin," one may suggest that there once was a time without "art history" and "art historians," as we know them today. So, if one dares to complete the thought, there may very well be a future without "art historians" because one's art history will not preserve its present form in the long run; it will change into something else. I lean then toward Elkins's concluding category for a future art history, as he articulates it in the review of Summers's book. In other words, the discipline is under continual transformation even if it does not seem as such in our everyday activities. And it is clear that in order for the discipline to survive in the present climate of research politics, at least in Denmark, but probably also elsewhere, it should be continually renewed in relation to significant cultural, political, and social issues rather than rest on dried laurels from the beginning of the 1900s. Instead of having colleagues evaluate the art historian in order to strengthen the discipline and confirm or deny the discipline's dominating theories, one can increasingly expect external research evaluations that weigh more heavily on criteria such as practical utility and applicability, ethical status, and societal relevance. Such a change does not look promising for the discipline of art history, especially since there is a widespread perception that art history already has difficulty in reasoning its necessity and justifying its existence in competition with other university disciplines.[151]

But even without considering such external evaluations, dislocations in the self-perception of the discipline have taken place over the years. This can be established by comparing the 1968 and 2000 curricula for art history at the University of Copenhagen.[152] The curriculum of 1968 begins by stating that the completion of the education requires that the candidate have achieved a "clear and reliable overview of the general history of art in Europe and the near East, considered in connection with the historical circumstances and culture widely understood." The overview requires significant acquaintance with the history of art after the year 1000 and especially with Danish art history, not least an "intimate familiarity with the most important monuments and collections in and outside Copenhagen." After this, the candidate must be familiar with "artistic techniques and have amassed a reasonable overview of aesthetics in general," as well as be "familiar with areas such as urban planning, decorative arts, the history of prints, and such side disciplines as antique mythology, the history of saints, iconography, iconology [in the old sense of the word] and the history of dress." Even "some reading of the masterpieces of poetic literature" is assumed. The text is in many ways a precise description of the expectations of an "art historian." The education aims toward the attainment of "a scientific education that can be useful in museum work, independent research and teaching." Acquiring a sense for museum work is recommended through "volunteer work" at one or more relevant museums. Through this one can gain "familiarity with general museum practice and the art historical assignments that museum employees deal with." But just like knowledge of archives and library collections and the use of bibliographies, this familiarity is only a supplement to the actual knowledge of practice: the skill to research the history of art. The history of art (at least, as far as the "near East"!) is an ontologically based research object, the pivotal point for a core disciplinary competence, as distinct from the individual scholar's competence. The remark about reading the masterpieces of poetic literature, for example, and, parenthetically, the suggestion to take courses along the way on "church history, the history of literature, the history of theater, etc." more than suggest that "culture widely understood" includes a particular notion of education where related artistic forms of expression are more relevant than, say, social historical, ethnic, or gender-related conditions for the production of art.

The more recent curriculum from 2000 begins by stating that the education has as its area of inquiry "the history, aesthetics and science of the visual arts." While the older curriculum almost exclusively focused on the history of art, with the aesthetic field added as a "reasonable overview," here, a significant broadening of the area of investigation has taken place. The education is further broadened by the inclusion of design, museology, non-Western art and cultural studies, photography and video, "just as visual mass media is integrated into the study of the visual culture of modernity." The student must attain "pictorial-, architectural- and space-analytical competence through description of the material on the basis of a critical assimilation of the diverse theoretical complexes and methodological approaches of the discipline." Parallel to this, "the objective of the education is to attain a broad familiarity with the categories of the visual arts and an overview of their historical lines of development from antiquity to the present, placed in relation to the conditions of the social, political, religious, as well as the history of ideas and mentalities." After this, the text mentions that, by means of the introduction to museological issues and contemporary conditions of the politics of art and culture, the objective is "that the student can attain foundational skills in relation to the communicational dimension of the discipline."

In many ways the curriculum of 2000 was probably more progressive in its understanding of the discipline than most contemporary art historical curricula in similar educational foundations. The reason was, in part, that it was developed during joint meetings between students and a somewhat reluctant faculty, one obvious exception being the head of the study board responsible for the rewriting of the curriculum. In connection with a new law for Danish universities, worked out a few years later, the curriculum was to be rewritten again, this time, however, with a new head of the study board (and without joint meetings). The result is that one is presently implementing a curriculum with a more focused, traditional understanding of the discipline. On the other hand, a new graduate-level program in visual culture was initiated in 2002 (with the former head of the study board), compensating somewhat for the current retraditionalization. Because of the joining of institutes in connection with the aforementioned university law, where the Department of Art History now shares an institute with, among others, the Department of Comparative Literature, in a few years the visual culture program will probably join an older and larger program in "modern culture," which has been administered by the study board of Comparative Literature.

The point of my account of the technical circumstances of the education surrounding art history studies at the University of Copenhagen is, first of all, to suggest that in spite of educated attempts, it makes little sense to maintain or build a clarified, scientific metalanguage because it will ultimately simply remain a parenthesis; both the discipline and its area of inquiry are in continuous transformation, even if it does not necessarily seem so in the academic everyday. It then becomes the aim to define art history as processual and relational. Neither the discipline nor its object of study exists in and of itself, but in relation to other disciplines and their objects. It was noted in a different context in the Art Seminar that there are always other disciplines. In other words, definitions of art history and artworks may vary from place to place, even when relative constants seem to exist. Particular discourses (catalogues raisonnés, surveys, artists' biographies) or practices such as that of the art museum maintain a specific understanding of the discipline's tradition and its objects. Though it may be difficult to imagine a late-modern Western society without art museums and their ability to signal political stability, among other things, not only for Western states but apparently also non-Western states,[153] reorganizations of museums have taken place in the past in relation to certain epistemological displacements. Such was the case of the Danish museum system in 1827, which developed from the *Kunstkammer* to newly arranged and divided collections in an art museum, a natural history museum, an ethnological museum, and so forth.[154] And more recently one could refer to the fate of many collections of plaster casts.[155] Might one imagine a future museum that systematically oversees the collecting of the visual culture heritage, one that we today identify foremost, and oversimplified, with the visual arts collected by the art museums?

Lastly, the purpose of the above-mentioned is ultimately to question if it makes sense to pursue the question whether art history is global. This does not mean that it is uninteresting to compare how art history is practiced worldwide. On the contrary, one may become wiser, partly about "naturalizations" in one's own academic socialization, and partly about the historical forms of the discipline, as well as its present and seemingly many definitions. These multiple definitions may artificially prolong the term "art history." Generally, the term has to cover traditional Western European art history ("normal art history"). It must also cover a newer, self-critical (?) art history ("new art history" or "theory"). And it must also cover a "non-Western" art history, drawing attention to Eurocentric as well as, say, Afrocentric and Chinocentric tensions. And the term must also cover the contemporary art scene, which it perhaps makes more sense to explore on the basis of cultural studies, visual studies, or, in certain contexts, computer- and information science, rather than an art history that continues to specialize in form, space, and the gaze. Finally, the term must include — or more likely exclude — visual studies, which can have a very hostile attitude toward art history and which brings into play multiple terms for visuality and culture.

Adducing Wittgenstein's concept of family resemblance, one can claim, then, that a global art history exists. But ultimately, with the above-mentioned displacement in theories, methods, areas of inquiry, and institutional tensions, it will probably not make sense to speak of "art history," whether in the definite or indefinite singular, even if we continue to do so out of habit.

— Translated by Kristine Nielsen

Jorgelina Orfila

Southern Perspectives: About the Globalization of Art History

As the Series Preface states, contemporary writing on the visual arts is not "a wilderness; in fact it is well-posted with signs and directions. Want to find Lacan? Read him through ..." and it proceeds with a series of names. They are strong suggestions, almost impositions for art historians interested in fostering their academic careers. The problem is to know who posted those signs and directions and how they were chosen. Why a psychoanalytical approach? Why Lacan? Should we use Lacan for the study of the Middle Ages, Precolumbian art, and prehistory?

When I came to the U.S. as an Argentine art historian, I had to adapt my use of philosophy and theory to the particular interpretation American scholars had of the authors who inspired me, and abandon the approaches of the authors who for different reasons were among those "not recommended" by American academia. This was not so much a question of reading Lacan (an author famous for his difficult language and complex ideas), but of using his ideas in the way that was delineated by the accepted interpreters. On the other hand, if the Art Seminar had been written seven years ago, the question in the Series Preface would probably have read: "Want to find Foucault?" And if written seven years in the future, the Series Preface might not even mention Lacan. This shift away from the theory of an engaged intellectual like Foucault, interested in the situation of non-Western and Third World countries, toward the writings of an author like Lacan, is very telling in itself and deserves to be analyzed under the light of the latest developments in American history.[156]

The organization and orientation of art history in each country, at any given moment, is not part of a process teleologically oriented toward the advancement of knowledge; rather it depends on political and ideological pressures that are both internal and external to the field. That is why having access to all the books and materials produced by Western art historians will not provide a non-Western scholar the information and orientation necessary to be understood and accepted as *a peer* by his or her First World colleagues. What still surprises me is that when it comes to considering the globalization of the discipline, Western countries' art history tends to be considered as homogeneous despite the different approaches that characterize each country. Such problematic aspects of the West are downplayed, and it is presented as the yardstick against which other countries' art histories are measured.

A quick analysis of the situation in my field of expertise (nineteenth-century French Art) shows that French and American art historians use different theoretical frameworks and methodologies.[157] The same can be said about the "belatedness" in the use of different founders' texts by French scholars. Erwin Panofsky's and Alfred Barr Jr.'s writings were only translated to French in the 1960s. On the other hand, Alois Riegl's work has only recently been rediscovered and translated to English, and it has taken almost a century for art historians to find a way to integrate Aby Warburg's oeuvre in the post-Marxist theoretical framework that we use nowadays. "Western art history" is precisely the result of a particular history of belated acknowledgments and rediscoveries but it has the power to impose itself onto others.

The four categories proposed by James Elkins — a scholar deeply interested in making the voice of non-Western countries heard — to characterize the way different cultures have confronted the Western narrative, not only reflect the central position that this narrative has historically occupied, but implicitly serve also to reaffirm and naturalize this hegemonic position, which reminds me of Mahmut Mutman's comments regarding Orientalism:

> The West establishes not only a hierarchy (such as the evolutionary hierarchies which fix time by distributing it in space) but also a *comparative grid of differences* that is almost invisible but always at work and in which the West effaces its own name

> in order to make it hegemonic; that is, it empties a space (of truth) to be marked as universal. "Difference" is then compared not just against the West, but against a *central* position that the West simply fulfills (science, democracy, progress, reason, etc.). This position or location is not only impossible to deny, but it also might be strangely empowering … for it is not just empty but also always already filled by the West in the very split that it produces … what is historically given to us is an already hegemonized difference.[158]

How or what would be the value of disparaging the Western canon if the Western character of the discipline's methodology, its epistemological strategies, and the institutions derived from them (museums) are not even discussed?

History and art, as we understand it today, are European, mostly nineteenth-century creations essentially linked and determined by the ideologies of nationalism, colonialism, and capitalism. Institutionalized in the latter part of that century, art history is also a product of modernism, and its methodologies and goals have been designed to confirm and even produce the categories it was devised to study.[159] Therefore, the real problem would be to discuss whether it would be possible for art history to turn away from its European origins and expand itself to become the neutral discipline it claims or aspires to be, able to study all the "artistic" manifestations of other world cultures.

This of course has been the goal of the art historians who introduced postcolonial theory and multiculturalism's strategies to the discipline. In my opinion, the interest in visual studies, the substitution of the analysis of space for that of the visual, and the introduction of non-Western terminology have not diluted the essentially Eurocentric orientation of the discipline. It is the universal validity of the "artistic" or the aesthetic as a separate sphere of activity and experience, and as a field for "scientific" study, that has to be reevaluated, together with the use of the word "art" — with its heavily loaded European implications — to refer to the creations of other world cultures.

I think of our discipline as ~~art history~~. I use the erasure as Heidegger did, to emphasize that those terms are not sufficient or adequate to refer to the realities they meant, but only those created by a particular culture; and that the Western epistemological system and its division into specialized fields of knowledge is not organic but historically determined. It is commonly accepted that in the nineteenth century, modern art took the place of religion. But even the perception of religion as an area of life separated from a profane sphere of activity, and the distrust of faith as an epistemologically valid mode of obtaining knowledge opposed to reason, are not universal but characteristics of certain civilizations. Therefore, they must not be imposed on, or presupposed as the inherent teleology in the development of other cultures.

Let me propose an extreme example: even though Buddhists believe in reincarnation, evidence coming from those experiences will not be accepted for the study of Buddhist or Western art. Non-Western countries are only providers of contents — raw materials — but not of the epistemological tools needed to interpret them, a situation that is strangely similar to the economic foundations of colonialism. Hence I do not think that the incorporation of some terms from other cultures taken out of their original contexts would help to change the essentially Eurocentric orientation of art history's methodologies. If art history were to accept this kind of information it would have a limited application and only a local value. But then, why should Western faith in reason and Western epistemology, derived from the Judeo-Christian worldview, be universally accepted?[160] Do other cultures of the world also aspire to be universally understood and have their religious objects exhibited in public displays or are these characteristics of the West alone? I have chosen this extreme example because it exposes one of the most troublesome shortcomings of post-Marxist theory, which by definition cannot incorporate into its theory of knowledge the transcendental dimension of religious belief.[161] This is especially important at a historical moment in which religion reappears as a very strong actor in the political arena.[162]

Together with Slavoj Žižek, Rasheed Araeen has been one of the most vocal critics of postcolonial theory and multiculturalism. He considers that these strategies, after helping to impose the voice of non-Western cultures, were co-opted by the malleable liberal Western cultural system, which incorporates and assimilates criticism without changing its essential foundations. Multiculturalism for Araeen is not "about equality of cultures but (about) how the dominant culture can accommodate those who have no power in such a way that the power of the dominant is preserved."[163]

It is not only, as Elkins remarks, that specialists in non-European fields are not encouraged to deploy their own interpretative methods, and required to know and apply Western methodologies. My experience indicates that non-Western scholars are encouraged to participate in symposia and to provide texts for publishing venues even if they do not work with the "recommended" reading list invoked above, *provided* they work on their own cultures. Their voices are not easily accepted when they study and analyze Western art history and the crucial problems of this discipline. As an Argentine artist once commented, the message from the West is: "the universal is ours, the local is yours." Postcolonial cultural theory in most Western institutions has led to a situation in which the value of what we say is assessed according to the racial and cultural differences we incarnate, and used to redefine postcolonial artists and art historians as a new Other, one that fulfills a predetermined role in the system.[164]

Stephen Melville has noticed that one of the consequences of the Hegelian account of art is that "the emergence of art as a properly historical object is contemporaneous with the possibility of claiming to make art *as* art. The same history that produces the possibility of art history produces the possibility of modernism in art."[165] As "institutional theories of art" are coeval with the emergence of art itself, they allow us to perceive and analyze how Western epistemological tools have shaped the material under study in order to construe the accepted canon. To consider the history of (Western) art history as an essential part of our methodologies is useful not only for the study of European premodern and modern art, but also for the consideration of non-Western cultural manifestations, and would provide a better platform for dialogue among art historians.

In *De près et de loin*, Claude Lévi-Strauss notes the paradox that cultures need a certain degree of isolation but also a dialogue with other cultures in order to improve their cultural capital.[166] My ideal model for a relationship between the First and Third Worlds would be what Heidegger describes in his *Nietzsche* as *strife:* an intimate association in which the opponents never exhaust nor confound themselves, but "raise each other into the self-assertion of their essential natures ... [where] each opponent carries the other beyond itself."[167]

Iain Chambers observes that "the challenge to the epistemology and institutional art discourse must be extracted from the narrative (of modern Western art) and its manner of representing the world." He continues:

> As an announcement of the sublime, art maintains what precedes and exceeds us. This may be to insist on a sense of the sacred that a secularized perspective has banished, it is certainly to stymie the desire to reduce all to the subject-centered objectivity of a little god who believes that the world is ultimately accountable to the subject. This would be to invoke not a Kantian sense of the sublime that threatens the law of reason, but the sublime as the persistent and necessary interrogation of reason and its regime of knowledge ... To rework modernity and its subject-centered understanding of truth, to carry it beyond its occidental owners, might also suggest that the very idea of art and its sense of aesthetics

is an occidental inheritance to be redirected and reworked elsewhere in another modernity.[168]

The challenge for non-Western and Third World art historians today is to abandon the place of the victim and the Other, which the multiculturalist liberal agenda has engineered, and to critically engage in the study of the basic tenets and history of Western art history and epistemology. Globalization will make sense only if it means that art historians from the entire world will have a say in the definition of the epistemological foundations and methodologies that hegemonically define not only the canon but also the theoretical approach and even the structural organization of the discipline.

Charlotte Bydler

A Local Global Art History

Is Sweden a part of the West, as in "Western art history"? I often wonder when I read texts like the Art Seminar. Sweden is, like so many nation-states, a contributor of at most one or two names to general art history textbooks. The artists of this nation-state are, taken as one historical subject, one of the "latecomers" to the smorgasbord of the artistic pantheon. Even if Sweden as a nation-state thus seems to have been excluded from world art history, its contemporary arts infrastructure presently makes the country a much more vital place of production. The ambitious national contemporary arts scene has been extremely pleased to find itself the object of an exoticizing interest in Nordic art since the late 1990s (referred to as "the Nordic miracle" by international freelance curators like Hans-Ulrich Obrist). Swedish artists have not needed to defend their adoption of this "Western" art concept in aesthetic or visual-spatial terms, even though the scant international recognition indicate that the Swedes had difficulties emulating it in a convincing fashion up to the late twentieth century. As David Summers suggests, there are within the idea of "Western" (and "non-Western") always patches of "traditional," and we may add "local," "national," "regional," "international," and perhaps even "global" communities and concepts.

Within the frame of the Art Seminar discussion, the global issue is divided in two sections — one part on the available production of books and scholars, and a second part on concepts and terms. This makes good sense, except in one respect: what happened to the problematization of *themes* (*motifs, topoi*) in artistic production and historiography — themes that are related to specific archives of examples in more or less widely disseminated texts? A thematic section would have focused attention on interpretations of forms and concepts, beyond simply registering their existence and morphological variation. Such a section could furthermore have included the question of the *urgency of thematizing global art historical writing*. Why here, why now? I will first consider the language-concept issue, then turn to the need for a global art history, and end on the local nature of this interest in the global.

First, no tendency to take an increased interest in local or vernacular art terms can be seen in contemporary art historiography in Sweden, where the English language rules supreme alongside references to a canon of Euro–U.S. artists.[169] This speaks clearly about the channels for visibility on the international (global) contemporary art scene, and the terms for access to these. Art historians and artists have turned to a common *lingua franca* rather than to terminological authenticity. Use of local terminology is an issue in other subcultures within the art field, which means that it turns up in references to local contexts around particular artworks. Whether linguistic categories would determine or (dis)enable the artistic-aesthetic perception (as in the Sapir–Whorf hypothesis) is a notoriously slippery issue. If various social groupings among speakers of a given language use its words differently, do they still perceive the world similarly? And how could we determine this in an academically satisfying way? Terminology seems to be best left to interpretation, on an *ad hoc* basis.

Language use aside then, is art history a global discipline as judged by its archive of examples? And is this question the most pressing one facing the discipline today? I have a pragmatic view of "the global issue" as regards writing art history. Like the "Japan issue" or the "the feminist issue," the "global issue" is a problem *to* someone, for specific reasons. Ladislav Kesner does not have the same experience of the global issue as Elkins, or me (I aspire to participate in the contemporary arts field from a Swedish perspective). Within contemporary arts — really, the most internationalized stratum of the contemporary arts scene, that which supports an increasing number of biennial and triennial exhibitions — the boundaries between "Western" and "non-Western" art scenes are severely blurred. The most frequently cited artists and curators travel extensively and there is a real difficulty in saying whether concepts and other contributions to the current contemporary arts agenda bear a recognizable cultural, or even national, identity.[170]

While wealthier states with global agendas tend to pay for blockbuster exhibitions and art history publications, the artists have both wider and more local points of reference. Artistic traditions and their history of reception in Thailand, Nigeria, and Sweden, for example, turn out to be increasingly interesting to contemporary arts professionals. I certainly do not think that the professional community within contemporary arts (freelance or museum curators, critics, and art historians) really masters this field, but it is as close to "global art history" as we get. Within this globalizing contemporary art world, the issue of a global art history is certainly pressing. Professionals are expected and called upon to commission exhibitions, comment, and criticize art from basically any part of the world.

The baseline regarding the availability of translations and publishers (and also exhibitions) seems to be audiences in the U.S., Britain, and other primarily English-speaking publics. The Argentine and South African situations (and less so the Czech perspective) come in a little obliquely, and do not reveal pressing anxiety over the question "Is art history global?" Perhaps because in these locations, local agendas have been established for so long that the idea of defending a global overview and readership (and perhaps also ownership of the art concept) seems absurd from the outset. Besides, what is this "Western" art concept? It is most likely not even an institutional art concept, just one invoked among peers, so that its porous philosophical status and extremely flexible genealogy, full of breaks and parallel inventions, does not form a problem. Perhaps, as Andrea Giunta and Sandra Klopper suggest, these locations were already firmly established within "Western" art history, and have contributed so richly to the "Western" art concept and other words for artistic practices and movements that they do not need to question the art concept to get into the exhibitions, catalogs, and curatorial ranks.

As I understand Klopper's and Friedrich Teja Bach's observations within the context of the Art Seminar, the question of *displacement* can be useful here. The *displaced* is then the theoretical subject of art historiography, a perspective on things rather than an empirical artist or art historian. The notion of displacement destabilizes spatial hierarchies of senders and receivers, and turns the issue of historical causality into one of more negotiable genealogy and interpretative communities. It is a warning that concepts and movements with "proper names" in art history may be impossible to distinguish from common goods in the art world.

What is needed is knowledge of art history as it is applied in influential and networked economic machines. Klopper mentioned tourism, and I would like to add art museums more specifically. Museum collections have a cultural and economic value that is rather immune to relativization by academia. Museum staff is usually recruited from the ranks of classical scholars and object specialists, not students of new media or visual studies. The spatialization of art history, or the revision of art concepts, are unlikely to be taken up in art museums. Curators typically seek to promote and enhance the collection's value and to make it relevant to present-day society. These specialists have practical use for intimate knowledge about artists of the textbook pantheon, if not of the actual textbooks. Such curators believe in the validity and value of their knowledge, and cannot be expected to overthrow the value of collections in their exhibition practice.[171] Museum collections are a conservative force to be reckoned with in art history because they directly affect art historical research. As the South African post-apartheid example demonstrates, when museum collections changed, the make-up of art history changed.

Indeed, why should art history in South Africa need Wölfflin, but not Bourdieu? This question belongs to wider claims of explanatory force within the discipline. I am reluctant to embrace a global methodology for art history if it is not a part of a larger puzzle, so that it can be amended by contact with local interpretations, archives of artists, and textual sources. So if world art history is a pressing issue, we still need to ask *for whom*. Students, readers, and other publics of art history compose pressure groups: they all inform the job market for scholars.

The discipline will go wherever there is need for it. But can we even dream of a history of artistic practices where the U.S.–European variety is inserted as one among many others? Hardly, as things are now. There is a canon of references that "must" go into a book, with due critical self-reflexivity, before more peripheral work is cited. First there are the archives of artists safeguarded by prestigious museums; then the archives of authorities from Plato to Wölfflin, guarded by libraries and our peers among art historians who have invested their professional careers in the traditional canon (including its critique). The only thing to be hoped for is adherence to academic ideals: do not totally forget more peripheral sources, and try to avoid reinventing the wheel due to ignorance of sources in local languages. What the Art Seminar discusses is, basically, a local U.S.–European art history that has been globalized. This is the one that is most widely disseminated, but let us not forget that it is also a local story and that a world survey looks different from a Swedish perspective.

Allow me a brief detour to illustrate a fundamental problem in art history. Reading Marx's account of the universal logic of capital, Dipesh Chakrabarty made a distinction between *History 1* and *History 2*. In both, history's connections demonstrate a universal logic only in retrospect. History 1 tells about what we now perceive as events that produced the logic of capital. But there are other relationships that do not necessarily contribute to the reproduction of the logic of capital.[172] This is what Chakrabarty called History 2. It includes pieces within the logic of capital that are "not yet" subsumed under the logic of capital, and which may not become so. As Chakrabarty notes, "not yet" is the place of the Third World. Also in the general, universal, art history, there are latecomers who have "not yet" adopted the aesthetic practices of the globalized art world. Chakrabarty makes a point of the outside (History 2) that exists inside the History 1 of capitalism, always ready to reveal that it is not a correct representation of reality. Likewise, things outside the European art paradigm exist inside its history, where they are made to appear as historic steps on the way to a globalized international art world that they have "not yet" reached. These "deviances" threaten the construction of art history and its claim to universal legitimacy and truth.

Since the art history under discussion here is founded on reference works and on the values of European avant-gardism with its "global" supplements, it is a local (History 2) affair. It is local not only because it only admits European artists, art historians, and concepts but also because its funding is available on a national basis. As it is administered, global art history sees to the needs and influence of the institutions of certain core countries — Western ones.

Visual or spatial arts: either way it is phrased, I find it difficult to cling to the idea that there is an art concept that is sufficiently unified to be traced without an interpretive intervention from an art historian. This means that speaking about "world art history"

— and specifically the claim that art history and the art concept have a "Western" identity — is rather unconvincing.

Frank Vigneron

Damned If You Do; Damned If You Don't

One has to admire the obstinacy of David Summers in wanting to create concepts that could account for everything in the open-ended domain that has come to be called art. Notions like "place," "images," or "planarity" are reminiscent of the Deleuzian "precepts," and I believe they are entirely relevant because they answer to specific demands.[173] According to Deleuze, each new concept of philosophy — or of art history as far as we are concerned — is the answer to a problem that needs to be solved; for instance, the Platonist theory of form came to be created as Socrates and Plato tried to address the issue of choosing the right candidate for leading an improved Athenian democracy to the discovery and definition of unchanging concepts, like courage or justice. Summers's concepts may not be entirely new; like the "fold" Deleuze saw in the philosophy of Leibniz, they are mostly a reworking of older concepts that needed to be adapted to a new situation. It is obviously a remarkable project and, precisely because the author does not claim to have written a global history of art, it is a wonderful attempt to answer the problem of globalization and its new cultural requirements. I think the requirements Summers sets himself can be stated this way: to formulate concepts that can be used in any circumstances, for the art history of any cultural domain in relation with any other; and to avoid historicity. This statement obviously does not do justice to the richness of *Real Spaces*, but I think it is a fair assessment of its mission.

The first question that springs to mind, however, is precisely about that tentative escape from historicity. If the idea were to establish some universal concepts, as in the structuralism dreamt of by Claude Lévi-Strauss, this attempt would resemble the kind of research that was the pride of French academia in the

1960s, something that would be toppled by Michel Foucault and his notion of archaeology of knowledge.[174] If, according to phenomenology, every artwork is an act of freedom, chronology may not lead us to an understanding of what the result of that act is. For Merleau-Ponty in *Eye and Mind*, the artist paints as if painting had never existed, speaks as if no one had ever spoken before.[175] Since creation is an act of freedom, the work does not stem from the circumstances of the life of the artist. But at the same time, if the life of the artist had been different, he or she would have produced a different artwork. We see here the kind of notion Martin Heidegger would have liked, a sort of circle out of which one cannot escape: just as art is made by the artists, and the artists are artists because they are making art, Merleau-Ponty wrote that the circumstances of our lives make us who we are but that we are also creating the circumstances of our lives as we go. There is no actual starting point to that situation and the answer lies in something like a constant feedback. This naturally limits the sort of freedom Merleau-Ponty talks about; as in Heidegger, freedom can only be exerted in a limited way and in the full knowledge of our limitations. For both Merleau-Ponty and Heidegger, Being always projects itself into the future, so "to be unfinished" is the essence of Being. Since nothing can ever be finished, a teleological idea of historicity is impossible and this leads to the concept that everything is always made as if it were for the first time. Thus there are very strong philosophical justifications to this reworking of historicity into something that would reject the idea of time unfolding in a single line.

Apart from the fact that, no matter how we see it, this phenomenological view of an artistic act made for the first time still puts us back on the track of unfolding time, the fundamental problem is that the form of the book does not lend itself very well to something like a world art history without historicity, something so varied and complex that it could be dubbed "deterritorialized fluxes," an entirely Deleuzian concept. A world art history without chronology could work better with hypertext, — that is, without linear writing — because the form of such a book might create more problems than solutions. I will come back to that idea of hypertext later, but the problem is so complex that I cannot hope to formulate a solution in here: solving the problem of a hypertextual narrative would entail escaping a vicious circle and creating an ahistoric world art history that is in the form of a metanarrative that would also avoid being linear. Avoiding linearity might very well be the latest utopia of our word-ridden world, but for the moment, we have to conclude that there is another insurmountable methodological problem to such an endeavor: how can we make the art of specific peoples in "real places" understandable to the layman without explaining how geographical and social forces have shaped specific art forms over time? It seems nearly impossible, for pedagogical reasons, to escape some kind of historicity.

This effort does require an encyclopedic or superhuman knowledge of the history of every society and cultural domain, and it relies therefore a little too much on secondary literature (I'm sure the author does not speak every language on earth). James Elkins mentioned the problem of where the scholarship should come from, and whether it is appropriate to use Western interpretive strategies to study Chinese painting for instance.[176] But I believe this issue is not limited to the problems raised by the exclusive use of Western metanarratives; it comes down to the use of a single language and how it unwittingly impoverishes the debate. For all its profound interest in embodied experience, *Real Spaces* is a book: a paradoxical object (and quite a ponderous one) that relies on language to convey meaning. To truly be a world art history, it should also avoid the many traps of cultural imperialism: it should lend itself to other languages. In a recent issue of *Artforum*, Daniel Birnbaum interviewed the artist Rirkrit Tiravanija. "Asked if his nomadic way of life should be seen as an attempt to create many centers," Birnbaum reports, "he replied that, on the contrary, he's much more interested in the multiplication of peripheries. 'Because then you will understand,' the artist offered gnomically, 'that the center lies on the outside.'"[177] The problem, in a world where we need more peripheries and no center, is that a world art history is necessarily centralizing, if only for questions of language.

I should present my own situation briefly to show why I find this issue so interesting. I am French, born in Hong Kong of French parents who remained only three years on the territory. My being born in Hong Kong is therefore purely accidental and I had no really deep connection to the place when I first arrived. (Living here for fifteen years and marrying a local girl, I have obviously changed that.) I came back to Hong Kong out of curiosity in 1990 to teach French and have remained here ever since, completing in the meantime a D.E.A. in comparative literature and a Ph.D. in Chinese art history, but both in French universities, traveling back and forth between France and Hong Kong. Teaching French made me realize how the language we find in textbooks is different from the actual French spoken in the area where I grew up (the north of France, where the local form of French has been recently renamed "Picard" because some linguists reject terms like "dialect" and "patois"). While I was still teaching French, I realized that the Hong Kong Chinese, whose everyday language is Cantonese, had developed a system to actually write their own language, creating in the process a number of new characters and a very imaginative way of mixing their own vernacular with the more official looking or sounding *putonghua*. Seeing also how issues of cultural identity have reinforced the attachment of the people of Hong Kong to their place and language, it became very obvious to me that there was something truly enriching in keeping one's own local culture constantly in the background. The more localized the interest, the more globalized it eventually becomes because it circumvents issues of national culture, and frontiers tend to disappear in the process.

Within this fascinating debate about language and cultural identity, my employer, the Chinese University of Hong Kong, had decided to take a position that would not simply erase the problem. Since its creation in 1963, the university has implemented a policy of bilingualism, using Chinese and English. Even though the reasons for such a position have their roots in the colonial past of Hong Kong, bilingualism has recently become one of the most important tools for an increased internationalization of the students body and staff, a decision which should create the conditions for more and more non–Hong Kong residents to apply. To choose English as the medium of teaching is therefore entirely acceptable, and in fact, increasingly encouraged. The term bilingual might not be entirely appropriate though since the term "Chinese" as it is used in Hong Kong covers in reality two very different languages, namely *putonghua* (the official language of the People's Republic of China) and Cantonese.[178] I should make clear that Cantonese cannot be understood by a person from Beijing for instance, and there are as many differences between the two languages as there are between French and Italian, or Italian and Spanish. The concept of bilingualism somehow hides the problem of which type of Chinese to use for the classroom and this, much more than the use of English which has become a very common language on the mainland, has created unexpected hurdles for international and mainland students. That situation has not yet been entirely resolved, but it is not felt as too much of a problem since it has led many students from the mainland to get a crash course in Cantonese; after a year or so, many of them end up understanding the local language and speaking it decently.[179]

One more thing is relevant here: being French and having grown up in France also puts me in a position of outsider when it comes to academia. I wrote my thesis in French; French sinology is developing in a number of interesting directions, but when we compare the sheer number of theses and research papers done in English in the same domains, we have to realize that there is, as one says, no contest. I am therefore increasingly forced to write in English. There would be no real problem there (English is as good a *lingua franca* as any other — a better one than any other in fact: since there is no need to enforce its practicality, it has already become, in its many forms of "broken English," the international tongue) if my thinking had not been shaped by the considerations on language and local culture I have already explained. However unpractical multiplying the languages of academics may be, I cannot help seeing the use of a single idiom as cultural pauperization, and the fact that international academia (if there is such a thing) does rely almost exclusively on English for communication is only one more proof of its being incapable of being heard by the majority of people (yes, I have read Bourdieu). Keeping all this in mind, you will forgive the tone of this article on the idea of world art history which will often sound utopian and a tad militant.

If, as James Elkins notes, space is "a problematic starting point for an art historical analysis that means to bridge Western and non-Western cultures," there are other concepts in *Real Spaces* that will create gaps between the original text and a translation, gaps which can only be bridged with structures that might not look like solid paths. Elkins mentions the pressing problem of non-Western languages and their utilization in studies of non-Western cultures. What seems to me regrettable is the one-way street such studies always seem to take: the starting point is a study of art historical objects in the context of the language of that same culture, but the resulting study always end up being written in one and the same language, namely English. Obviously, there are incalculable advantages in having a *lingua franca*, but it would be extremely naïve to believe that any given language can convey any concept with absolute efficiency and reliability: no translation is entirely transparent. As long as world art history is exclusively written in English, it submits to a kind of imperialist historicism. Ideally, a true world art history would be written in as many languages as there are actors in the domains of art history and art production. What would be truly interesting is to see how such a book would be translated in other languages. How many languages is another, maybe simply financial, problem; if Tintin has been translated into Catalan or the Luxemburg tongue, would there be an editor adventurous enough to invest money and time in such a publication? And yet, is it really a "world art history" if it is formulated in only one language?

One captivating project would be the translation into different languages of key concepts, like the ones created by Summers. Elkins mentioned the absence of an equivalent for the "Chinese *liqi*," which would already make clear the fact that some concepts can be understood through explanation and illustration but not translated with a single word. But the problem goes deeper. In the Chinese realm, we will see that other concepts coming from Western languages have been successfully transposed into modern Chinese, but that, because they refer to ideas that are originally profoundly different, they do not create strict correspondence of concepts in the receiver's mind. It is obvious that one English signifier cannot "materialize" the same signified when translated into another language. It might be interesting to give a specific example.

James Elkins made a list of various terms from other languages (*warri-ngirniti*, *tableau*, *Weg*, *ambulatio*, etc.) and the question was whether they could be used in English art history to describe situations and concepts that did not exist, or did not exist in exactly the same way, in Western art. On the other side of the translation problem, it was also mentioned that the English term *modernism* could not transposed untouched into German — but translation offers problems that are far more complex precisely because they are about very small differences. Differences so slight in fact that they usually pass unnoticed and would seem unimportant if they were not about conveying very rich notions. Let's take the term "metaphor" for instance, a central concept for Summers. It presents us with very interesting problems of translation in the Chinese language. An English–Chinese dictionary would give us two possible translations: *biyu* (比喻) or *yinyu* (隱喻). The first expression is made up of a term that can be translated as a verb, "to compare" *bi* (比) and the character *yu* (喻); the second one is made up of the verb "to hide" *yin* (隱) and the character *yu* (喻). It is that last character that interests me here. The word *yu* (喻) is also part of the translation of the word "allegory," which is *fengyu* (諷喻) in modern Chinese (the character *feng* 諷 meaning "to be allusive," "speak indirectly"). *Yu* has been translated as "metaphor" for a very long time but has presented historians of literature with extremely complex problems to solve. Unfortunately, this term can be stretched in translation to encompass other meanings. As Stephen Owen notes, "Yü … is the term often translated as 'allegory': this term is as close as Chinese comes to the notion of an 'intended message,' prior to and independent of the text and transmitted through it."[180] This rather dramatic twist in the plot of how to translate "metaphor" into Chinese, this sudden reference to "allegory" when one is aware of the intense debate that has been going on about the nature of the "Chinese allegory," becomes even more twisted when it becomes impossible to avoid other words and other complex concepts of literary theory.[181] Owens used the term "metaphor" in another chapter of the same book, to comment on the Chinese literary concepts of comparison (*bi* 比) and what he calls "affective image" (*xing* 興), which Haun Saṣsy prefers to translate as either "stimulus" or "allusion." There would be no point continuing since this debate about the nature of metaphor and allegory in Chinese literature is one of the battlegrounds upon which specialists are the most keen to demonstrate that there can be no equation between the Western and the Chinese traditions.

If it were not enough to understand that these terms are far from transparent on the Chinese side, it might be interesting to briefly see how the term "metaphor" has been tackled in a more specifically Western tradition. Obviously, the field that is the most concerned with these questions would be hermeneutics and, if one would like to favor a more contemporary approach to that problem, it would be best to turn to the work of Paul Ricoeur.[182] In relation to the problems of art, Ricoeur is interested in the concept of symbol (an interest which is already problematic, when it comes to translation, since it harks back to Platonism), and he therefore attempts to give to the understanding of that concept a more rigorous, scientific method. Relying on hermeneutics, linguistics, and semantics, he tried to show that symbols have the same functionality as words, their meanings depending on context: with a symbol, any given expression, while signifying one thing, signifies at the same time *another* thing without ceasing to signify the first. This capacity for polysemy is what Ricoeur calls the allegorical function of language. Ricoeur's hermeneutics is thus about the diversity of meanings of any given discourse or artwork. To support his argument and widen its domain of application, he then refers to Freud, who also saw in the narrative of dreams a multiplicity of meanings, and then to linguistics to clarify the fact that hermeneutics is completely different. Linguistics is a self-sufficient universe of interdependent signs, while hermeneutics is entirely open to any kind of sign, to any kind of language, and any kind of lived experience. The power of the symbol is in its double meaning and symbolism is found in nonlinguistic reality. Symbolism thus marks the opening of language toward something other than itself.

Ricoeur then turns to Saussure to elaborate on the notion of sign. Saussure wrote that signs have two kinds of relationships: a syntagmatic relation (a relation between existing signs within a sentence, characterized by presence) and an associative relation (a relation between different signs which are similar and could be substituted with one another, characterized by absence). Then, he refers to structural linguistics with Roman Jakobson, who calls the syntagmatic relation a "concatenation relation" and the associative relation a "selection relation." Ricoeur finally assimilates the syntagmatic or concatenation relation with metaphor and the associate or selection relation with metonymy. In relation to what constitutes metonymy and metaphor, and to return to the Chinese semantic field, Ying-hsiung Chou has situated the concepts *bi* 比 and *xing* 興 within a Jakobsonian analysis: *bi* 比 is a metaphoric operation in which one term substitutes for another, while *xing* 興 is a "contiguous association," it is treated as a metonymic operation (the idea being that the connections between a *xing* 興 sentence and what follows are absent: one term is not substituting for another, it is simply juxtaposed thus creating a whole series of culturally defined resonances).[183] The word "metaphor" cannot be translated into any other language without creating in the process a long series of connections with other related concepts, like *bi* 比 and *xing* 興 in Chinese. Whereas "metaphor" shows the way to various things in English, its Chinese translation will show the way to other things and it is these connections that generate a richness of meaning which is extremely difficult to convey for the attentive translator.

These differences might be felt as rather too subtle for most readers (the "inattentive readers" most people have become in a world where books are more common than cockroaches), and it is true that we are seldom called upon to think about these connections when reading anything. But they should be revived to get access to a richer understanding of any text, and translation might even be the ideal tool to do so, both for the readers and for the translator. I would definitely disagree with David Summers that languages are "ultimately untranslatable," but it is true that translation can only be made of constant interpretations and frequent approximations. By approximation I mean something like Chen Xiaomei's notion of "misreading," that is "an act of dialogue between text and interpretation, between past and present, and perhaps most importantly in the study of cross-cultural literary relations, between individual readers and their various social and historical formations."[184] But if translation is like a funnel, transforming, shaping, and misinterpreting things always in the same direction — into English — it is bound to be limiting. Ideally, and if art history is truly a way to disseminate a rich but practical understanding of all types of art to all types of individuals into all types of culture, translation should be like a food processor with the lid open, multiplying concepts and their approximations in every possible direction: deterritorialization on an epic scale. I am obviously not thinking about academics here; the "targeted audience" for such an endeavor would be, first and foremost, the artists themselves, the producers of art in all its forms.

To take the question of translation at a very practical level with a specific example, it would be very interesting to put theoretical texts on painting, a very rich corpus of texts in several cultural domains, through the process of translation. One would have, in the first place, to submit to the demands of international research by putting these texts in English. As a second step, it would be fruitful, for instance, to try to put texts written in English, French, or German into modern Chinese. Starting from there, there would be no limits to the translations: from Italian to Yoruba, from Chinese to Bengali, from German to Ourdou (and why not also from English to French). In fact, translation would not only be useful for people from other cultural backgrounds, it would also be a way to force any speaker to think about the concepts they are using in a way that would resurrect meaning. Concepts tend to become like tools in a phenomenological sense; the more we use them, the more we tend to put their meaning in a mental background that can become so comfortable it erodes the original meaning of the concept. (The image that comes to mind is Merleau-Ponty's walking stick for the blind: after a while, it becomes an extension of the arm and is no longer a stick.) As in Heidegger's "The Origin of the Work of Art," where our perception of the painting of shoes painted by van Gogh makes us aware of the "thingness" of a real thing, translating a concept may be seen as a creative process. It forces us to think about the concept's meaning or meanings and their ramifications in specific contexts.

Translation could therefore become a major tool of art history in a practical context, and by that I mean not only the writing of art history and the analysis of the concepts of art making and art reception against various cultural backgrounds, but also the manipulation of concepts by artists throughout the newly created peripheries mentioned by Tiravanija. It would not be a matter of transferring Western analytical tools in the understanding of the artistic traditions of the rest of the world, but of understanding one's own art tradition through the prism of other languages and, therefore, other ways of thinking. Elkins mentioned the fact that there are no art historians specializing in Chinese art being hired in Western universities "for their ability to deploy Chinese interpretive methods. They are hired for their expertise, and partly for familiarity with Western methods, such as iconography, semiotics, social art history, and so forth." I might add that there are fewer and fewer specialists of Chinese painting in China who can afford to deploy Chinese interpretive methods. That new generation of Chinese art historians in mainland China and Taiwan are truly caught between hammer and anvil. They have to satisfy their old mentors and a vast majority of Chinese amateurs, painters, and art lovers, who expect them to use such concepts as *zhuo* 拙, *qiyun shengdong* 氣韻生動, or *pingdan* 平淡 (concepts which have been in use for so many centuries and are so well adapted to the discourse on Chinese painting there is absolutely no point getting rid of them); but they also have to satisfy the criteria of a more internationalized readership who expect them to have read Pierre Bourdieu and Jean-Luc Nancy.

The clearest example of the type of hybrid objects this situation may produce is *Three Thousand Years of Chinese Painting*,[185] part of a series titled "The Culture and Civilization of China." In this work, written by academics for a nonprofessional audience, the chapter on Yuan dynasty painting was written by James Cahill, the one about the origins of Chinese painting by Wu Hung and the one about Ming dynasty painting by Yang Xin 楊新, deputy director of the Palace Museum in Beijing, whose prose cannot but feel considerably less inventive to a Western audience who can only have access to the English translation. Cahill and Wu Hung's chapters apply the rules of Western connoisseurship and academic research, while Yang Xin is more interested in a taxonomic version of art history, which follows perfectly the traditional *literati* way of doing such an exercise. The sensation however does not stem from a lack of inventiveness on the part of Yang Xin, but is probably a result of the fact that the concepts used in his chapter had to be bent and oversimplified to work in an English text that did not allow for long footnotes. The laudable ambition of this series was to "illustrate the cultural riches of China, to explain China to both interested general readers and specialists, to present the best recent scholarship, and to make original and previously inaccessible resources available for the first time," but they still decided to publish it only in English and Chinese — an effect of globalization and market economy I suppose. I remember that the sixty volumes produced by the People's Art Press of Shanghai in the 1980s had been subject to partial translations in such languages as French, German, Spanish, or Russian.[186] As a matter of fact, this problem of oversimplification created by the demand for translation does not need to be the rule and it is possible, using footnotes, examples, and illustrations, to convey the sense of such concepts in a meaningful and enriching way. When it comes to teaching Chinese painting and calligraphy in studio courses however, the debate about the possibility of translation and the use of foreign language can generate a lot of resistance.

This brings me back to the debate about the internationalization of the Chinese University of Hong Kong. Its fine arts department is an excellent example of the type of transformations taking place in everything related to the expression "Chinese art" today. It was founded at the same time as the university in 1963 and is therefore the oldest tertiary institution teaching Chinese art on the territory. From its beginnings, the department never tried to choose between studio art and art history (which is very much a part of the *literati* tradition of art practices) and, very soon, its most famous department head, Lü Shoukun 呂壽琨 (1919–1975), oriented the learning and practice of art toward a mixture of Chinese and Western art (obviously, I am using the words Western and Chinese provisionally here; they distort what was happening to an absurd degree). It has therefore been thirty years since the beginning of a process of hybridizing that is still evolving and taking new shapes. The concept of hybridity emerges often in discourses about the Chinese artists who, for political, economical, or other reasons, have decided to live and produce artworks in foreign cultures. Many mainland-born artists nowadays live in North America or Europe and explore ways to produce meaning using elements from their own native culture and the culture they live in. In Hong Kong, hybridity is taking particularly interesting shapes because of the unique historical position of the territory: it has always been geographically attached to the centers of Chinese "high" culture, but it was, on an epistemological level, sufficiently separated from these centers to create the conditions of an autonomous and original cultural identity. It is in that context that the department added a small measure of hybridity in hiring a Frenchman whose task was to teach Western art history with a comparative approach.

A major concern of the studio art professors in our department was whether it was wise to teach the practice of Chinese painting using English as the medium of instruction. Someone like me, coming from a university system where every concept of Chinese art had to be mediated through another language, could only state that it was possible. But then, I realized I was not doing any kind of art that could be called "Chinese painting" and that I could not be sure that the concepts I had been taught in an art historical context in France were particularly useful in a classroom situation with Chinese students in Hong Kong. The only argument I could give, in fact, was the one I have just made: it is interesting to teach art history in English because the problems of translation reveal epistemological discrepancies which can shed new light on the understanding of one's own artistic tradition. Instead of the transparent notions they are when used by a Chinese native speaker, they would become in English somehow more opaque, revealing shades that would have remained hidden otherwise, just like scientists have to dye cells to reveal their interior structures under the microscope. Similarly, teaching in English also justified a comparative approach to the teaching of art history, even though I am painfully aware that it might not be practical in a class of Chinese painting practice — it is like learning to master a language using only formative grammar: nearly impossible for normal, everyday communication. That is also why Summers's book is particularly useful to me, as a comparatist: it offers useful tools to put researchers on the right track, but then it goes back to being far too general. I believe that comparisons made by one scholar should be restricted to smaller topics, and a more comprehensive project should be collegial.

The problems of generalizations can be illustrated quite easily. For instance, according to Wen Fong (quoting Norman Bryson in *Vision and Painting*), Chinese paintings always show the process of making the artwork, whereas Western paintings always hide and cover ("it is an *erasive* medium").[187] All that is obviously true and inherent in the choice of medium; one cannot hide a brushstroke once it is made whereas one can cover anything made with oil paint. Both Wen Fong and Bryson rightly emphasize the all-important role of the brush ink in the making of Chinese painting, which often seems to be the only thing that matters to art theorists like Dong Qichang 董其昌 (1556–1636). It is surprising, then, to see that Chinese artists still want to hide their own selves inside the process of making the artwork by revealing the brush strokes (with the avowed goal to make the workings of Nature itself apparent). On the contrary, Western artists will often insist on expressing themselves while covering the canvas, either hiding the brushstrokes or making them so obvious that they become a constitutive part of the viewing experience, thus still achieving the ancient requirement of *mimesis*. (One thinks of the Impressionist artists who tried to achieve the imitation of nature by "breaking up" the colors and the light into brushstrokes, their goal still being to emulate Nature seen through the human eye.)

The question then is whether the choice of an "erasive" medium to define even one aspect of Western art is really the best one. Even taken as a purely technical definition, this relegates to the backwaters of Western art such media as watercolor or ink painting (there is such a thing in Western art too) whose technical requirements are sometimes very similar to that of Chinese inkbrush painting. Second, hiding and revealing seem to characterize one thing from a technical point of view and a completely different thing on a more spiritual or theoretical level: the hiding would then be about the canvas and the oil paint in the West, but about the artist's self in China; whereas the revealing is about the artist's self in the West, but about the brushstrokes and the process of making in China. Even though a definition like Wen Fong's, one that involves just a few words (the proverbial nutshell), is useful in laying down a sort of working ground, it is very important to unravel what it implies in order to establish a much more detailed, albeit more complex, conceptual definition that can take in as many aspects of both painting traditions as possible. In the end however, since the artists are always more imaginative than the art historians or art critics, there will always be artworks that will not let themselves be fitted into any theory, in particular the "grand narratives" of art history that are aimed at generalizing the nature of Western or Chinese. It might be safer, and hopefully more instructive, to restrict the comparative debate to very specific issues: while the grand narratives are quite exciting and also necessary to establish a foundation, a number of short essays on narrower problems might also lead to interesting answers on the reasons why Western and Chinese art look and feel so different.

Such an endeavor has not yet been undertaken, at least not on a scale that would make it interesting, and this creates a problem when it comes to establishing a practical framework for researchers and a starting point for students. In our department, there is no "one-volume freshman world art survey" (but this might change soon as I will put *Real Spaces* on every "required readings" list), each professor preferring to give a different bibliography at the beginning of each course. The term "textbook" is also seen with a lot of distrust by most of my colleagues, and would have made most of my former university professors in France faint with horror. As far as the courses on contemporary art are concerned in this department, the only available surveys of twentieth-century art (like *Art Since 1900*[188]) for instance, the works and choices of Chinese artists remain in complete obscurity. (In fact, if they are written in the English language, these surveys will be too often heavily tilted toward English-speaking world art, leaving aside many interesting European artists.) The surveys rely on notions of "good art" or "high art" that are not really acceptable in serious art history today. Even though I understand perfectly that it is hard to refrain from laughing when we consider the artworks of Chinese artists during the 1960s for example, one cannot understand the art of contemporary Chinese artists today without knowing about the Yan'an 延安 talks of Mao Zedong and what they produced — what is usually referred to as Chinese socialist realism. Even those books dealing with other parts of the world use the "first world" art all too often as their standard for comparisons. Visual culture might still be an unstable field, "subject to intensive debates," but it should not be ignored and should be integrated as a major analytical tool in the teaching of a comparative art history.

I understand that Summers does not really expect his work to become an internationally acceptable art history, and this fact seems well enough illustrated by the title of the book. To see that

"The Rise of Western Modernism" is the subject of the last chapter of the book is more than a good indication that its reading somehow culminates in his theory of a world of forces. All the same, the claim of being a world art history puts the book in a position where it will be expected to at least partly fulfill that position. In spite of its desire for objectivity, and its very structuralist rejection of historicity, such a world art history can only be written for "us," that is those who grew up in a civilization of the book. But even the book form is culturally determined and, unless we accept another step toward cultural pauperization, we should remember that there are other forms of transmission for knowledge and analytical tools. I am reminded of a scene in Werner Herzog's 1972 movie, *Aguirre, der Zorn Göttes*, in which a Yanomami tribesman was given a Bible by a conquistador, with the (translated) comment that it was the "word of God." The man put the book to his ear and, hearing nothing, threw the book to the ground and was subsequently killed for being sacrilegious. I suppose throwing *Real Spaces* to the ground would also be sacrilegious, and I do not intend to do so. But the "voice of the ages," knowledge on paper, is not for everyone on the face of the earth. And, in that light, writing a world art history that would be for the whole world is an impossible task because it requires writing, and writing in an academic jargon understood by quite a small fraction of mankind. I hope that state of affairs will continue, because if "universals" can be used in every situation, it might mean the death of cultural diversity. (Summers is not naïve, and I am perfectly aware that creating all-purpose universals was not his intention.)

In this world thirsty for more "centers," or more "peripheries" depending on which side of the divide you situate yourself, the desire for a world art history makes sense insofar as it can find its place without falling into the usual pitfall of academic and linguistic imperialism. It can be a precious pedagogical tool for a certain type of initiated art historian, especially those dealing with comparison, but to fulfill the role of initiator in what has come to be known as the globalized world, it would be preferable to use a form other than the book. As I have already explained, hypertext would be an interesting option, if it were not even worse than the book as a solution for opening up that project to other, very different, cultures like the oral cultures of South America or Africa: a book can always be transported anywhere, while a website with hypertext does necessitate at the very least a computer, and optimally a connection to the Internet. Similarly, that hypertextual tool would have to be adapted to many languages, and therefore, many kinds of episteme (I still like to believe that, in spite of globalization, human beings are not thinking alike everywhere).

Such an endeavor is idealistic; it would have to be collegial and would necessarily be never-ending and, therefore, not practical: no one would be able to access it in its entirety. It would be like Borges's library of Babel: out of reach but everywhere. That does not mean it is not desirable, and it would be like the gigantic map in another of Borges's short stories, a situation that Jean Baudrillard exploited in a famous text.[189] A "hypertextual multilingual world art history" would be a map of art so accurate it would also cover its entire domain, but hopefully this time, not smother and destroy the ground it covers. It would obviously be more like art than science, if we believe that such distinctions can be made on the ground of objectivity. An exhaustive history of all art(s) translated in every possible language, a *grand oeuvre* that would be like peace on earth, desirable and unreachable, always meeting with a multitude of delays like a work by Marcel Duchamp.

David Summers has put himself in an impossible situation, and I must admire him for that. He has answered a pressing demand in writing this book, knowing very well he would be criticized from all parts for having done so. It is admirable and necessary in education systems that are more and more centered on the demand for creativity and on cross-cultural approaches, but also, however it wants to fight it, disturbingly "imperialist" and insufficient. Between Summers's book and the project I evoked earlier, we are still left with an alternative, but something that would amount to being caught between a rock and a hard place: it is either *Real Spaces* with its edifice of concepts, useful and somewhat reductive, or a prowling hypertextual edifice, useless and decidedly utopian. Molar or molecular as Deleuze would put it. In any case, the simplifying one or the complexifying one, and I use both terms with the utmost respect, we are left with tools for conducting art history that are not very practical for the layman, the nonacademic, nonartist who would like to be led by the hand in his or her first approach to the art of the world. If one could say "damned if you do; damned if you don't" about *Real Spaces*, one would certainly have to say the same about the alternative I just proposed. Whether you choose the molar or the molecular method might simply be a matter of personal choice (you know: freedom, that thing Merleau-Ponty said existed only insofar as it is conditioned).

And, in the end, I also exercised that presence or lack of freedom: I wrote this article in English.

Carol Archer

Macao: An Art Historical Discipline Waiting to Happen?

For such a small place Macao has an extraordinarily active arts community. There are a large number of art institutions and artists' associations, many of which receive government support.[190] It would seem reasonable to assume that there would be a corresponding wealth of art history courses on offer in Macao's high schools and tertiary education institutions. But few high schools in Macao teach art, let alone its history.[191] And it is not possible to major in art history at any of Macao's handful of universities.[192] Indeed, someone interested in studying art history would be hard pressed to locate a single art history course. The situation is better, however, for the aspiring Macao artist, art teacher, or designer. Diploma programs in visual arts education and design are available at the School of Art at the Macao Polytechnic Institute. There are several introductory art history courses on the books at that institution, and doubtless some art history would be integrated into the predominantly practice-focused classes. Nevertheless, it is fair to say that at this point in time, an integrated program in art history remains everywhere unavailable in Macao.

As Friedrich Teja Bach pointed out in the Art Seminar, the public learns about art history in a range of ways. In Macao, the art museum plays an important role. Exhibitions at the Macao Art Museum tend to promote three parallel art histories. First, local Macao art history is represented by a permanent display of pictures from the late Qing dynasty. Detailed paintings and drawings of ports, local people and village life, mostly by non-Chinese artists such as George Chinnery, Marciano Baptista, and Auguste Bordet, underline understandings of Macao as a place where East meets West. Also prominent in the museum's calendar are regular exhibitions of contemporary Macao art and a Design Biennale that showcases the work of artists from Macao, the PRC, Taiwan, and Hong Kong. Second, Chinese art is a staple of the exhibition program, with exhibitions centering on various periods, schools, or artists. And third, art from Europe, and especially Portugal, is frequently on display. The emphasis in these latter exhibitions tends to be on modernist and contemporary works.

This tripartite manner of presenting art history invites interpretation in terms of a changing sense of local identity in the wake of Macao's return to China in 1999. A second line of inquiry would locate this manner of presenting art history in relation to tourism, a major industry in Macao. In the Art Seminar, Sandra Klopper related an exhibition in Cape Town to the promotion of tourism. The balance the museum strikes between exhibitions that present the great narrative of Chinese art history and those that present the particular "East meets West" story that sets Macao apart from other Chinese tourist destinations invites further study.

None of these narratives of art history, taken separately, depart significantly from the kind of art history that James Elkins has described as "normal." But little effort is made to integrate the three strands into a seamless whole. Perhaps this approach might be understood, as Klopper suggests with regard to the African situation, as a consequence of Macao's self-perception as a place at the periphery of the dominant narratives of Western and Chinese art history. And if the exhibition practices at the museum do not present art history as a single "grand narrative," the frequent exhibition of objects that would be categorized as craft or applied art indicates an implicit disinterest in the media hierarchies that pertain within many conservative Western art-historical contexts.

Apart from the seminars and courses held at the museum, how else might the Macao public learn about art history? Students of one Macao university may not be able to take formal courses in art history, but it would be difficult for them to avoid seeing a huge new sculpture of Poseidon and his servile handmaidens as they walk past the Greek Mythology Casino each day. Many of the busloads of tourists who visit the casino have their pictures taken in front of Poseidon or the gigantic Zeus sculpture that presides over the hotel's high-ceilinged lobby. Other recent additions to the Macao cultural landscape include monumental ancient Egyptian-style statues and a mini-Venice precinct complete with canals.

The relative dearth of formal art historical education and scholarship in Macao makes pressing the need to present convincing arguments about why art history matters. At the same time it offers an opportunity to argue for an art history that would be relevant to the contemporary Macao context — one that might avoid perhaps the "aloof isolationism" that Ladislav Kesner suggests is characteristic of the discipline in some quarters. What kind of art history might that be? I have suggested that the museum presents art history as a multistranded affair and accords comparable status to craft, design, and other forms of art. Outside the gallery context, Western cultural capital is increasingly deployed by Macao's burgeoning casino and tourist industries. Perhaps the kind of art history appropriate to Macao bears a resemblance to the visual studies that Sandra Klopper claims is triumphing in the African context "because it is abolishing hierarchies."[193] In other words, what is called for is a discipline which, taking proper account of the historical and cultural specificity of its objects, is able to analyze art that ranges from casino sculpture to media culture to painting.

Heie Treier

Ideologies of Style (An International Experiment)

In her book *The Social Production of Art,* Janet Wolff says: "The ideological nature of art is mediated by the aesthetic level in two ways: through the material and social conditions of the production of works of art, and through the existing aesthetic codes and conversations in which they are constructed."[194]

Styles may carry, under certain conditions, ideological implications. They do not coincide in different cultures, depending as they do on the context of local history, politics, religion, language, geography, climate etc. At the beginning of 2004, I asked my colleagues in various countries to reply to two unconventional questions pertaining to the cultural milieu of their respective countries and to accepted social customs and clichés which are considered quite natural in that particular region, but which are unfamiliar to the outsider. I drew on the example of Abstract Expressionism as the model for constructing a certain "American style."[195] My questions to my colleagues were:

1. What style has assumed the position of a national style in your native culture? Who constructed it?
2. How is the concept of avant-garde defined in your native culture? Who constructed it?

With respect to the concept of style, I assumed that there is a certain, prevalent common understanding of its meaning and empirical frame of reference, mainly because whole generations have been brought up to view the history of style as paramount to the history of art. I also wished to focus on the meaning of "national" and its claimed relation to the avant-garde. Has the relationship between these two been seen as hostile?

The respondents who communicated with me by e-mail were Kaija Kaitavuori and Jari-Pekka Vanhala (Finland), Monika Wucher (Germany), Irena Buzhinska (Latvia), Lolita Jablonskiene (Lithuania), and Karin Hallas-Murula (here in Estonia). I conducted verbal interviews with the following art critics: Olesya Turkina (Russia), Izabela Kowalczyk (Poland), Udo Kultermann, Dorothee Bauerle-Willert (Germany), Thomas McEvilley, Donald Kuspit (U.S.), Matthew Rampley (England), and Simon Rees (Australia and New Zealand). I also referred to texts by the following art critics: Dace Lamberga (Latvia), Raminta Jurenaite (Lithuania), Boris Groys (Russia), Sten Karling, Johannes Semper (Estonia), and Jean-Louis Cohen (France). The respondents belong to large and small cultures, in the West and in the East. English is the native tongue of only a few.

I did not expect the respondents to have ready-made replies, and I did not expect them to represent their own cultures as an integrated whole. The results are not statistically valid around the world. Rather, I was interested in two things. First, at the collective (community) level, how are aesthetic terms constructed in the context of one's national culture? How are the meaning and ideology of styles, which are taken for granted within the culture, constructed? Second, at the individual level: How do counterparts from different countries construe the same aesthetic terms?

I tried to keep this opinion poll on a somewhat informal and light-hearted level because my goal was not to be politically provocative or incorrect. National attributes are an increasingly touchy subject and have not infrequently become a veritable taboo.[196] I therefore tried to treat the concept of "national" in a neutral way. This survey was prompted by the desire to discover how seemingly universal international art terms have been defined in different cultural contexts.

While the responses are given in full as an appendix to my thesis, some conclusions can be drawn here.[197] One hypothesis of the experiment focused on the mechanism behind the rise of national styles as a somewhat heroic phenomenon in art. Can one see here a direct association with the economic or political development of a state (that is, a democratic, nontotalitarian polity)? Will the aesthetic code that dominates the period of a political system's ascendancy acquire, in the long run, a special significance related in historical memory to the sensation of victory? This is how Thomas McEvilley interpreted it in the case of the U.S., and he explained it as one of the root causes for constructing abstract expressionism as an "American style" emerging immediately after World War II. Evidently the same interpretation also pertains to France. Louis Cohen pointed out that victory fostered cultural chauvinism, and that the French tended to see classicism as their national tradition.

In the case of Estonia, where I live, I see the same logic in the heroics of functionalist architecture of the 1920s and 1930s — namely, during the period of Soviet occupation, radical architects mythologized functionalism as embodying our political emancipation. As Izabela Kowalczyk underlined in the case of Poland, "national" was depicted by the historical paintings of Jan Matejka in the late nineteenth century, constructing the historical victories of Poland. By contrast, Udo Kultermann responded to all questions with non-answers. Dorothee Bauerle-Willert emphasized the lack of national unity of Germany. Her answer differed dramatically from the one sent by Monika Wucher, which stressed a consistently influential tradition in German art that addresses national characteristics.

In many cases, the national style has been constructed by depicting the natural environment and landscape of one's own country — such a tendency seemingly unifies, in the first instance, the young and small national cultures during the epoch when the state is making its entrance into the political arena of the world. Nature and landscape were important in the art of the turn of the twentieth century in Finland (Kaitavuori and Vanhala), Australia (Rees) and Latvia (Buzhinska), as they were important in constructing the official "Estonian style" of the 1930s (Hallas-Murula). Matthew Rampley also underlined the different psychological background of large and small cultures. While the U.S. was still young in the nineteenth century, artists sought their identity through landscape painting, as pointed out by McEvilley.

Simon Rees made a sharp distinction, based on the example of Australia, between the national-conservative and international-avant-garde tendencies. However, in Lithuanian culture the modernist movement of Expressionism has, for instance, acquired a central role in defining national culture (Jablonskiene, Jurenaite).

According to Rees, the stars of Australian art history are the artists who come from Australia and who have been accepted into the canon of international modernism. Absent from the official contemporary history of Lithuanian art are, as reported by Lolita Jablonskiene, both George Maciunas and Jonas Mekas, two important figures in the New York avant-garde scene.[198] The history of art in Estonia also lacks reference the architect Louis Kahn, even though he was born in Estonia and spent his formative years here.[199] The Cold War has constructed the self-perception and art historical writing of the cultures that found themselves east of the Berlin wall.

The fact that the avant-garde is international and therefore unrelated to national cultures was emphasized by Donald Kuspit and many others. This is the canonical treatment of the Western avant-garde. In the case of Russia, both Olesya Turkina and Boris Groys highlighted the national aspect of the Russian avant-garde. The case of Latvia is utterly ambivalent. As suggested by Irena Buzhinska, one is at a loss about how to place Gustav Klucis — he was a staunch internationalist and an inveterate communist and did not associate himself with Latvia. Hence, when living in Russia, Klucis behaved in keeping with the canon of the Western avant-garde, whereas the logic of Russian avant-garde itself had national aspects. By contrast, in the Finnish (Kaitavuori, Vanhala) and British (Rampley) context, the avant-garde has gone unformulated for some obscure reasons yet to be identified.

The most interesting outcome of this survey is not that the universalist model of treating art often turns out to be a myth but that both the inherent logic and the ambivalence of different cases become apparent in great detail. Every respondent is right within his or her perspective, but that does not preclude intense and lengthy debates.[200]

Atreyee Gupta and Sugata Ray

Responding from the Margins

Over the last twenty years, scholars writing in, and on, the non-West have all too often lamented the "inequality of ignorance" that marks the production and dissemination of knowledge in the West.[201] One is tempted to revisit Dipesh Chakrabarty's now oft-cited critique:

> That Europe works as a silent referent in historical knowledge becomes obvious in a very ordinary way. ... Third-world historians feel a need to refer to works in European history; historians of Europe do not feel any need to reciprocate. ... "They" produce their work in relative ignorance of non-Western histories, and this does not seem to affect the quality of their work. This is a gesture, however, that "we" cannot return. We cannot even afford an equality or symmetry of ignorance at this level without taking the risk of appearing "old-fashioned" or "outdated."[202]

It is therefore with great hope that one greets projects such as David Summers's *Real Spaces* and James Elkins's grievance that Western universities never employ art historians working on the non-West using non-Western interpretive models, but, on the contrary, consider the ability to explain the non-West through Western paradigms as "good" scholarship.[203] The non-West thus becomes a mere shadow, a replication of the Western master-narrative. As an alternative and a corrective measure, Elkins proposes the use of non-Western methodologies within the Western academy to write "a *genuinely* multicultural world art history." The Art Seminar is a definite step toward this *genuine* "multicultural world art history."

But with hope comes trepidation and a postcolonial unease with the burden of genuineness, authenticity, and purity that is here demanded of the non-West. "Genuine" world art history, a project by and for the West, is a meticulous "mining" (in Elkins's word) of representative concepts and ideas from indigenous knowledge pools, in order to negotiate, in Summers's words, "differences between the *modern* West and *other* cultures ... between the modern West and its own foundational institutions as well as its own historical consequences."[204] While "a simple return to the premodern is not an option," Summers's *Real Spaces* betrays its obsession with originality, purity, authenticity, and authorship.[205] This obsession allows Summers to discuss spatiality in premodern non-Western contexts, for example in Elephanta, Ming portraits, and Hokusai, but not in the 1970s reinvention of narrative space in India (the Baroda School) or in the 1920s reassertion of inkbrush painting in China.

The non-Western modern, the Creole, the hybrid, and the *mestiza* do not find any space in Summers's *Real Spaces*. His attempt to "put the world in a book" (as Elkins says) unfortunately remains lopsided — perhaps the contemporary non-West is *not yet* a part of this "world"?[206] The "modern world picture" (*Weltbild*), after all, is not a disinterested or "objective" picture of the world, but, as Martin Heidegger puts it, "the world conceived and grasped as a picture."[207] It is the modern subject who observes, manipulates, and orchestrates his "picture" of the world. As Heidegger reminds us, "[w]herever we have the world picture, an essential decision takes place regarding what is, in its entirety."[208]

It is then not surprising that while world art history invites the West to celebrate multiculturalism through an unabashed embracing and appropriation of the non-West (thus tainting and enriching the traditional Western narrative exemplified by Gardner, Stokstad, and Janson),[209] "we," the non-West, are asked to perform "our" pure Chineseness or Indianness "based on their ['our'] interpretive methodologies from the culture they ['we'] study."[210] A case in point is Elkins's critique of postcolonial scholars, for example Gayatri Chakravorty Spivak and Geeta Kapur, as "concerned with multiculturalism but unwilling to forgo certain Western interpretive models."[211] The fact that Spivak draws her methodologies from Derridean poststructuralism and Kapur from Lyotard is sufficient to mark them (for Elkins) as fundamentally dependent on "Western interpretive models." Kapur and Spivak's potent critiques of Euro-American imperialism are lost in Elkins's quest for a "multicultural" world art history. Similarly, Elkins considers current scholarship on Chinese painting too "Western" because it pays more attention to "[Chinese] politics, [Chinese] identity, and [Chinese] patronage" rather than to Confucianist methodologies — and is therefore inadequate for "a genuinely multicultural world art history."[212]

"Western interpretive models" (informed through the Enlightenment, history, and rationality) are colonial bequests that have violently shaped the postcolonial. As Thomas B. Macaulay, the head of the Indian Law Commission, infamously proposed in his 1835 *Minutes on Indian Education*: "We must at present do our best to form a class who may be interpreters between us and the millions whom we govern; a class of persons, Indian in blood and colour, but English in taste, in opinions, in morals, and in intellect."[213] The British education system that was imposed in the nineteenth-century colony was but a manifestation of this imperial desire. One is here reminded of the tragic figure of the Malagasy in Frantz Fanon's *Black Skin, White Masks* (1967): "the Malagasy alone no longer exists ... the Malagasy exists *with the European.* The arrival of the white man in Madagascar shattered not only its horizons but its psychological mechanisms."[214] How then can "world art history" ask the non-West to feign amnesia and return to a past "untarnished" by the West? For whose benefit?

Despite its best intentions, then, this project is dependent on a territorialized binary: the (multicultural) "West," contained within a geopolitical space called Euro-America, and its Other, a (monocultural) "non-West," that is, the rest-of-the-world. A corollary to this binary is the idea that the Enlightenment (with history and rationality as its handmaidens) is a privilege of the "West" (as a geopolitical space), while the authentic "non-West" (again a territorial space) *lacks* history. Thus, history-writing as practiced in the contemporary non-West is seen as merely derivative. The non-West's prerogative remains premodern models exemplified by the sixth-century *Viṣṇudharmottara Purāṇa* or Qādi Ahmad ibn Mir-Munshi's sixteenth-century *Calligraphers and Painters*. But of course, Western art history, according to Elkins, "is a history, and theirs [the non-West's] are not."[215] The contemporary non-West is here trapped in a peculiar bind where any attempt to write history is marked by the ultimate sin of the provincial — that of derivativeness. But then, nothing else qualifies as history.

The "West's" inability to accept as authentic what the "non-West" has in various ways done with *original* Euro-American discourses speaks eloquently of a privileging of the *original* in "Western" traditions. The result is a Euro-American claim to an exclusive sovereignty over products of its own discourses. Postcolonial scholarship has contested the validity of such Eurocentric claims, arguing for an "Enlightenment from below."[216] Rather than a "wholesale rejection of the Enlightenment,"[217] scholars such as Rey Chow, Gayatri Chakravorty Spivak, and Dipesh Chakrabarty have attempted to use the project of Enlightenment against itself — to take the logic of Enlightenment to its radical extreme — and mobilize the "West" against itself. Spivak very succinctly terms this radical possibility as an "enabling violation" brought through the colonial encounter — "the enablement *must* be used even as the violence is renegotiated."[218]

It is through Spivak's "Enlightenment from below" and the figure of Fanon's Malagasy that we address this roundtable. The risk of being labeled too "Western" or "dyed-in-the-wool postcolonial" (as in the Art Seminar) is something we perhaps cannot avoid — for, after all, our perspectives are inevitably framed through our Western-educated, Indian middle-class upbringing, and an experience of the discipline through a rigorously postcolonial art history department (at M.S. University, Vadodara) in India. However, we neither speak for the non-West nor ventriloquize for Indian art history — such "mastery" is beyond the prerogative of a response from the margins. And, for the sake of brevity, we take the liberty of focusing on only two of the many issues raised in this roundtable: "books and scholars who compose art history worldwide" and "concepts and terms that structure art historical interpretation."

1. *"[B]ooks and scholars who compose art history worldwide."* Even a cursory reading of the roundtable transcript gives an impression that (Western) art history textbooks are central in defining the global contours of the discipline. Thus the *lack* of a Chinese translation of Alois Riegl and the very recent ("belated") translation of Heinrich Wölfflin (in 1999) explains a certain *delay* in the "development" of the discipline in the non-West.[219] Despite Friedrich Teja Bach's insistence that Western textbooks (for example Wölfflin) are reinscribed with newer and different meanings by non-Western readers and Sandra Klopper's observation that "there is no *need* for a textbook … if one is not at the center," Elkins insists that the "structure [of textbooks] informs the structure of classes at higher levels, and those in turn inform the choices of postgraduate specialization," so that "textbooks can be formative for the discipline." Rather than an unproductive discussion on whether art history in the non-West is belated (or not), Bach makes the more useful suggestion that we engage with the discourses of the discipline as they are formulated at particular historic points. "It would be points where the discipline is working *with* [or against] Wölfflin or *with* [or against] Baxandall."

Using India as an example, we will briefly attempt to delineate the discursive framework of the discipline as it was shaped — now a hundred-odd years ago — in the margins. The purpose of this exercise is to demonstrate that the genealogy of the discipline (at least in India) is formulated not through the lack or availability of Western textbooks but, as Bach suggests, through specific historic and political moments where the methodological tools of Western art history were consciously *used* even as its narratives were contested.[220] The strong anticolonial strand in Indian art history (and possibly in all ex-colonies) is rather insensitively ignored in Elkins's concern with when and where Wölfflin was translated.

Going beyond the binaries of (exotic) indigenous texts and models of dependency to understand non-Western art histories, we propose that it is within the discursive frameworks of modern disciplinarity that one finds its anti-Western strand.[221] Raja Rajendralal Mitra's *The Antiquities of Orissa* (1875) is such an example of a conscious rejection of the imperial master-narrative while retaining the language of the masters.[222] While Mitra's scientific drawings and mode of writing drew from earlier British accounts of Indian architecture, his analysis essayed a significant departure from his colonial predecessors. For example, while the overabundance of decoration in Orissan architecture was seen as "decadent" by the colonial antiquarian James Fergusson, for Mitra "it became a marker of 'grandeur,'" "the very soul of an architectural monument; it was what determined "India's place in the history of art."[223] Although Mitra was certainly not the first of what Max Mueller described as a native "scholar and critic in our [Western] sense of the word," it was probably the first time that (Western) history had been *used* to contradict the Empire's history-writing in India.[224] Not surprisingly, the Empire's wrath resulted in Mitra's removal from office.

Rajendralal Mitra, however, was an archaeologist, not an art historian. But then, the peculiar genealogy of art history in India can only be traced through the disciplines of archaeology, Indology (including linguistics, aesthetics, and literary studies), ancient history (including paleography and numismatics), museology, and art history. This history of art history in India is yet to be written, but clearly the murmurs of anticolonialism that are found in Mitra's text reached a tumult in the early decades of the twentieth century, when the nationalist project of "imagining" India called upon art history, archaeology, and museology to produce an ancient "history" for the new nation-state. The Department of Ancient History and Culture was established in 1918 at Calcutta University under the guidance of Asutosh Mukherjee for this very purpose.

The publication of R.D. Bhandarkar's *Vaiṣṇavism, Śaivism and Minor Religious System* (1913)[225] and T.A. Gopinatha Rao's multi-volume *Elements of Hindu Iconography* (1914)[226] were important steps in the establishment of art history in India — for, unlike the prejudices of earlier European studies on Indian religions, these were first attempts to systematically catalog and analyze the peculiarities of the multiarmed, multiheaded, "strange" gods of India. And by the 1920s, Stella Kramrisch, a Jewish *émigré* from Vienna, and Ananda K. Coomaraswamy, a Sri Lankan geologist from London, further destabilized the art history conjured up by the Empire.[227] One could then trace a more nuanced genealogy of the discipline in India through precisely these moments of anticolonialism.

However, ours is not a nativist or atavistic attempt to produce an "Indian" art history. Coomaraswamy and Kramrisch's transnational interpolation in writing a persuasive anticolonial art history forecloses any possibility of a relativist argument or of reading art history in India as the product of a purely local (and hence more authentic) mode of knowledge-making. Further, like all "stories of art," the Indian anticolonial (nationalist) story is too fraught with omissions and deliberate erasures. It remains an upper-class/upper-caste (and mostly male) story, and in this regard, its problem is not unlike the omissions in the Eurocentric "story of art."[228] But by no means was this beginning a "capricious local invention," as Elkins says. And it was certainly persuasive as art history.

2. *"[C]oncepts and terms that structure art historical interpretation."* Although Summers's call "to abandon the Eurocentric idea of the 'visual arts'" is well taken, the move to "proceed from possible conditions of shared human spatiality to culturally specific — but not radically different — practices" seems at its best problematic and at its worst perilous. His thesis is based on an assumption that not only are there "conditions of shared human spatiality" across the globe, but it is possible to have an *equal* dialogue between the West and its ex-colonies, disacknowledging or disregarding the implicit politics of power that have created modern speech and still render it legible.[229] But, this is merely the problematic part.

What is perilous is Summers's insistence that "[t]raditional societies — including traditional Western societies — are more properly uniquely centered and bounded," and "the lives of the vast majority of people are shaped by traditional spaces." Moreover, in the Indian context, Summers asserts that it is through concepts such as *pradakṣiṇa* (circumambulation of a holy site) and *darśana* (beholding the divine) that we can better understand this experience of "traditional spaces" by "the vast majority of people." Further, *pradakṣiṇa* and *darśana* are but local manifestations of a more universal phenomenon — a variation of a universal way of experiencing space in "traditional societies."

Perhaps, *pradakṣiṇa* is the governing principle through which a "vast majority" of Indians experience sacred spaces — but then, it only remains an experience of the privileged "majority." After all, no member of today's Scheduled Castes could perform *pradakṣiṇa* or have *darśana* of the divine at any Brahmanical temple in premodern India.[230] Where does this experience of space (as opposed to upper-class/upper-caste experiences) figure in this notion of a "centered and bounded" traditional society? How does one even begin to think about *any* marginal experience if the central point of reference still remains the "majority"? At the risk of sounding dated, we argue that the category of experience can only be explained through the contextual, the historical, and the sociopolitical, and not through a diffused universalism.

"Pilgrimage," as Summers points out, "is another [such] example." In India, the Dalits (untouchables), systematically excluded from actively participating in early-twentieth-century nation-building, now partake in ritualized pilgrimages which allow them to construct their own vision of a more inclusive nation-state.[231] This "pilgrimage" hovers somewhere between the religious and the political and is critical for Dalit community formation. But surely all pilgrimages are not the same. The *radical* disavowal of an exclusively upper-caste India through Dalit pilgrimages is annulled if one applies the conceptual universalism that Summers proposes. The political potency of differences, local interventions, and resistances are subsumed within this overarching tendency to universalize; by the same move, any interventionist attempt, even that made by Summers himself, loses its own radicalism and replicates the very discourse that it sets out to challenge.

Another issue with regard to concepts and terminology raised in the roundtable is the possibility of assembling a compendium of "terms from various languages and contexts — from Yoruba to Japanese — which could perhaps comprise some list of critical or useful terms for art history," as Kesner puts it. Elkins suggests that this compendium could "raise art history's sensitivity to local contexts" while simultaneously providing "the potential use of non-Western or local concepts for Western or wider ends." But, as he himself also points out, such encounters between non-Western concepts and Western art history have failed to transform the epistemological frameworks of the discipline in any way.

That may be inevitable, for while *darśana* might be useful to understand the specificities of an "Indian" experience of the divine, it is certainly not a universal category which informs the experience of devotees in disparate cultures — from Nigeria to Japan. For that matter, one cannot even talk about one "Indian" experience of the divine. For example, the *darśana* practiced at the sixth-century Śaiva cave at Elephanta is certainly not the *jharokā-i darśan* (balcony of audience) at the Mughal court, or the *darśanic* gaze of the millions of devotees of Bollywood today.[232] Thus, while one greatly appreciates the Western quest for non-Western "useful terms," a laundry list is perhaps not enough to "raise art history's sensitivity to local contexts" — there remains a need to historicize these terms within their temporal-contextual usages. A disacknowledgment of the fluidity in meanings and practices not only effaces heterogeneities, contingencies, and alterations in (non-Western) cultural practices but also reinscribes an imagined purity/authenticity.[233] This essentialism effectively reproduces, *yet again*, a homogenous, timeless non-West.

The modern West's desire for its Other — the exotic, the pre-modern, the irrational — has repeatedly marked its understanding of the non-West. With the celebratory multiculturalism that Western globalization entails, the West today *again* desires cultural differences that only a "pure" non-West can offer. Anything different is seen as merely derivative and today's "native" post-colonial intellectuals are therefore "told that we are *too* Western."[234] Like Karim, in Hanif Khureshi's *The Buddha of Suburbia* (1990), we too are chastised for not performing our Indianness better.[235] And, courting the risk of sounding tedious, we end our diatribe, *yet again*, resisting the West's desire for its "pure Other."[236] As Jimmie Durham, the Cherokee artist-activist, puts it:

> [But] don't worry, I will not advocate. I'll not ask you to give up your God nor your Refrigerator, nor to switch allegiance. In turn I ask that you ask no stupid questions like, "Do you want to [or, why don't you] go back to your old ways?"[237]

Thomas DaCosta Kaufmann
Is Art History Global?

Is art history global? Art, however it be defined, has been created on all of the inhabited continents, and can thus claim to have a global history. Art and its history are also discussed in one form or another throughout the world. But the question of whether art history is global, in other senses, including those discussed in the Art Seminar, is much harder to answer. This discussion may even have inadvertently pointed to some impediments for the construction of a truly global art history. In the end, these impediments may have to do with the difficulties that art historians have in dealing with the Enlightenment heritage of art history and its legacy, which may be reclaimed for this task.

James Elkins is no doubt correct in attempting to shape discussion by emphasizing the physical conditions, as he calls them, for art history, and then its content. For what art history is may obviously be determined by where it is done. And as the initial conversation suggests, conditions vary widely, since institutions and resources are so disparate in different parts of the world. As a result there may be no uniform social practice that can be defined as art history. Consequently, it seems necessary to seek for other criteria to determine common aspects of the field: Elkins proposes some of them, specifically books and scholars, concepts and terms.

However, it is doubtful if any one selection of books and scholars including those mentioned could possibly define a field as varied as is art history. The particular selection of scholars and books is in any case debatable. If the text by Michael Baxandall regarded as exemplary is *Painting and Experience in Fifteenth-Century Italy*, it seems pertinent to know that Baxandall himself referred to this opusculum as a "pot-boiler" without a trace of irony, and more than a little shred of accuracy. (He regarded his magnum opus as *The Limewood Sculptors of Renaissance Germany*.) If the book meant is *Patterns of Intention*, to which one participant refers, this book has hardly enjoyed universally favorable reception, even in England, where Martin Kemp (now Regius Professor of the History of Art at Oxford) gave it a devastating, but fair, review in the *Burlington Magazine*. On the other hand, Ernst Gombrich's perennial best-seller, *The Story of Art*, supposedly stands for normative art history, yet comes in for critique for its supposedly Eurocentric and partial tale of art. Yet although this book has sold hugely, and has been published in many languages, it is now approaching sixty years old, and can hardly stand for the present state of the field. Much less may it be taken as paradigmatic, or as some sort of textbook, neither of which it intended nor probably is widely considered to be. As Gombrich himself once indicated, *The Story of Art* was in fact written at the behest of the Phaidon publisher Bela Horovitz as a kind of complement to his world history for children, with a specific sort of ideal reader in mind — Horovitz's intelligent then-teenage daughter (now the London publisher Elli Miller). At least the participants seem to agree that Wölfflin has not retained its importance. Even so, the work of contemporary authors mentioned, however admired, can hardly be regarded as of comparable importance.

It is also questionable if terms or concepts supply better definitions. Fields are not determined by their jargons, even if they create them. Moreover, as the discussion of space suggests, agreement about concepts may be hard to find.

This does not mean that some kind of general description or definition is impossible to make. Although he did not believe in the existence of disciplines, Gombrich may have pointed to a way in which such discourses evolve, by emphasizing the role of problems. (One of his dicta was there are no disciplines, only problems.) Whether or not one agrees with Gombrich on this point, it is instructive to consider how problems call forth interpretations of phenomena, objects, or issues. Around them originate traditions of discussion, though traditions of course die, and new ones are started all the time. In this way debates about some problems (e.g., the origins of Gothic architecture) have determined the course of scholarly discussion, and of teaching. Traditions of discussion of certain issues or themes characterize "schools" of art history, such as that in Vienna. From such discussions of problems concepts emerge, and are developed: for example, in the Vienna

School the concept of "style" which has engaged professors from Riegl to Rosenauer arose (as is shown by Riegl's *Stilfragen* and *Spätrömische Kunstindustrie*) out of a concern with the classification and evaluation of objects. This suggests that concepts may arise from the practice of art history.

James Elkins also mentions art historical practices such as patronage, conservation, and iconography. But he distinguishes these concerns from theory, which is also a component of art history. While it is not absolutely clear, the course the discussion takes and characterizations of art history made by other participants allow for the inference that concepts come not from practice, but from theory. While in some cases this may be so (as in some examples of Kunstwissenschaft), it is nevertheless noteworthy what is left out of such an account. For instance, issues of dating and attribution, to a culture, place, or individual, are absent from Elkins's list of practices. Perhaps they are considered settled, or passé. (Other thinkers of a similar stamp seem to think so: "style" was missing from the first edition of *Critical Terms for Art History*, and may have remained so, if this lacuna had not been called to the editors' attention.) Yet dating, attribution, and "style" (whatever it might mean) remain fundamental to art historical pursuits wherever they are followed. There is no theory that has any relevance that lacks substance. Moreover, as the Vienna School suggests, art historical practice may generate a considerable theoretical literature.

The failure to mention dating, attribution, and style (or to have Wölfflin, perhaps, stand for them) points to some problematic aspects of some contemporary critique of art history: theory is separated from practice. Moreover, the concept of theory itself is restricted to a very limited group of theorists, many of whom have little to do with art history. Tellingly, the names of philosophers mentioned as paradigmatic are Husserl, Merleau-Ponty, and Heidegger: while these thinkers are fashionable in certain quarters, and, especially in the instance of Heidegger, have been formative for certain types of postmodernist theory, they are by no means representative even of the range of possible contemporary theories. In any case, the emphasis on philosophy (Cassirer is also mentioned) in such a context accompanies a devaluation of empirical practice, or even the particular visual qualities of art history, as at least Friedrich Teja Bach tries to suggest in the seminar. There are other clues to this prejudice: while Elkins more neutrally calls the practices he mentions normative; other participants, notably David Summers, speak of "traditional" and "conservative" art history, which implicitly bear negative connotations. But if art history does not deal with objects and with the visual, what distinguishes it? (The same could be said about visual culture or visual studies, which there is not space to consider.)

These views not only affect how global art history may be framed, but also bring up the consideration of the history of the discipline in relation to Enlightenment discourse. For instance, while other Enlightenment notions are under attack (for example Bourdieu, who is also mentioned favorably in the seminar, had Kant in his sights in his book *Distinction*), the distinction between theory and practice, in which empirical scholarship is disparaged in favor of what now called Theory, is one prejudice that the discussants seem to share with the *philosophes*. This differentiation repeats the philosophes' distinction between "philosophy" or criticism and erudition, the latter being at best necessary, but inferior. But as I have argued elsewhere about the historiography of art before Winckelmann, the contrast between philosophy or critique and erudition makes a distinction that is ultimately untenable, even if it is also one that has continued to dominate many views of the history of eighteenth-century scholarship.

There is a certain irony here, for other Enlightenment ideals, such as cosmopolitanism and *Bildung*, seem to be rejected, and a kind of cultural chauvinism expressed. This last is evinced in Andrea Giunta's claim that "it is neither in the United States nor Europe where the highest level of research on Latin American art can be found." This claim ignores much fundamental work in what is a burgeoning field that deals with all periods. (In the United States David Stewart, Mary Miller, Cecelia Klein for the Precolumbian era; Tom Cummins, and Valerie Fraser [in England] for the viceregal period; and Leonard Folgarit [in the U.S.] and Dawn Ades [in England] for the modern, are just a few among a host of scholars who might be mentioned in contradiction.) Similarly, the idea of a kind of universal or cosmopolitan *Bildung*, by which one would learn about more than one's own particular time and place, gives way to an emphasis on the local and contemporary. This sort of concentration of the present and the local is mentioned in regard to South Africa, but it is no less prevalent in the United States, in Australia, and increasingly in Europe, than in South Africa or South America. In any case it is surprising to hear this accepted as understandable, that someone in Africa (or America) can understandably not identify culturally with say Donatello. This takes for granted the vexed issue of cultural identity, more a shibboleth than a fact. It would seem that the flip side of Eurocentrism is provincialism.

The participants take for granted that the normative aspects of the field are Eurocentric. Undoubtedly some of the Eurocentric prejudices of the early modern era (the "tyranny of Greece over Germany") were built into some of the foundational works of the discipline (Winckelmann), with consequences for its continuing history and present practices, and it may be that some areas of the world are privileged at the expense of others. Yet this is not the whole story, neither of the origins of art history, nor of the continuing course of a discourse that originated in the Enlightenment. Like many of the social sciences and natural sciences (geology, botany) to which it has sometimes been compared, the modern discourse and discipline of art history originated in the eighteenth century. Changes in perspective in these fields do not mean that some of their fundamental procedures have been nullified, any more than changes in perspective in art history necessarily undermine its methods.

In any event, the charge of Eurocentrism masks a more complicated story, for there are other possibilities inherent in art history. Early historians of art, architecture, and music (Monier, Bourdelot, Printz, Fischer von Erlach, Valentini) outlined views of art and culture that had a broader, comprehensive aspect. They envisaged a universal history of art that would encompass the world in all times and places. Later art historians from Kugler to the present have similarly tried to trace out such a universal history of art. While such writings may now seem limited, even suspect, they offer at least the possibility for constructing a larger story. Moreover, especially in the example of someone like Leibniz, who as we now know (through Horst Bredekamp) was intensely interested in the visual, many Enlightenment figures (including Montesquieu) eschewed "Eurocentric" views. The *Bildung* and view of culture and its history that thinkers like Herder (in *Auch eine Philosophie zur Geschichte der Bildung der Menschheit*) envisioned certainly did not privilege the culture of any one area.

Non-Western concepts, and even views of art, might invigorate the field, as several participants suggest. Still, it remains a challenge to see how any of them offers such a universal perspective. Traditional views of art in China do not seem to allow for this possibility, for example. It is also mistaken to think that there is any contemporary example of such a possibility, outside a Western tradition.[238]

Elkins, however, does seem to be right in suggesting that globalism is, if not the most pressing issue for art history, at least one of them. There might be various ways of seeing how art and its history are comparable throughout the globe, or link by exchange and cultural transfer, or have certain common features. But that would involve emphasizing art, history, and the practices by which they are studied. And perhaps reclaiming some of the forgotten aspects of the cosmopolitan goals of the Enlightenment, and of other aspects of Western thinking, which may (Kwame Anthony Appiah) deserve renewed attention.

Sandy Ng

Is Globalization Killing Art History?

I must admit that this fascinating conversation between scholars from different cultures has provoked a certain level of anxiety, because it appears that the field of art history is disintegrating. It would be wise to admit that canonical texts will continue to center on Western cultures even though we are becoming increasingly connected as human beings. We also have to recognize that there is no single grand narrative that tells unbiased stories of each culture. Global art history merges art from different cultures, but ultimately it is still dominated by a Euro-American perspective.

To overcome the pitfalls of our present system of art education, I strongly believe in offering thematic courses that are largely cross-cultural. I am currently teaching two such courses; one on color and the other on the human body. It is a challenge to cover a variety of issues but students can read different kinds of texts, and they are able to investigate issues that concern their interests and personal aspirations.

The majority of my students here in Hong Kong are local residents with some visiting students from Europe, America, and Australia. A large number of students are more interested in Western art than Chinese art because the language of instruction at the University of Hong Kong is English, and it is difficult for students to translate primary Chinese texts into English for their writing assignments. The university library has good resources mainly in Chinese and English. I think students find it challenging to interpret texts that are written in different languages, demonstrating that linguistic ability is one of the main barriers of teaching and studying art history.

Visual studies is becoming more popular because it is entwined in popular culture. Blockbuster exhibitions, coffee-table books, and TV series based largely on Western art and culture further the status of visual studies even as they foreground non-Western art as the exotic "other." It is therefore important to teach courses, publish, and curate exhibitions that are cross-cultural, so we can at least focus on comparative studies that will bring in art from cultures outside of Europe and America.

I am afraid that using non-Western terms such as the Chinese term *fu gu* ("the return to the ancient") will only foreground the unfamiliar nature of non-Western art and our relative lack of knowledge of these other cultures. After all, one must have a certain level of understanding of Chinese to use the term *fu gu*, and we must define such terms in their own contexts before translating them for global use.

I do not think we should be pessimistic about the future of art history. Perhaps it does not matter that Western art is not part of the art history curriculum in South Africa, and that students in China only started reading Wölfflin's works several years ago. Modernity is both chaotic and ever-changing so art history must evolve to better reflect new situations.

Mariusz Bryl

Translate/Transcend

1. The question "Is art history a global discipline?" is undoubtedly risky, particularly because it has been formulated during the era of globalization. If globalization is considered inevitable and obvious in its nature and consequences, the answer can only be affirmative. It may however not be so self-evident, as in the case of the notorious slogan the "flow of images": recently, in the *Journal of Visual Culture* (August 2003), Norman Bryson aptly proposed the "dearth of images" as an organizing principle of today's visual sphere. Perhaps we should hope, then, that our debate about the "inevitable" globalization of art history (Elkins: "My notion is that ... art history is becoming a global enterprise") will be a critical response to "global" art history rather than a symptom like Bryson's

sense of visual culture studies. Maybe globalization does not pave the way to global disciplines but, on the contrary, by explicitly making all differences visual, to the ultimate fragmentation and delegitimation of disciplinary claims of uniform self-identity. At any rate, the question "Is art history global?" comes from Anglo-American art history, which is a symptom in itself. At the present moment, "global" art history can be articulated only in English. Therefore, my position is that of a language outsider, yet speaking from the discipline's center, if we take into account the history of academic art history in Poland, which is already a century long.

2. In superficial terms, if we assume that "globalization" means the institutional expansion of the discipline, the future is obvious: departments of art history will continue to be created. I was surprised when a scholar (at the Getty Research Institute) was astonished by the small (!) number of countries in which academic art history exists. An impressive list made by Elkins seems to imply exactly the opposite: the effects of globalization are indeed dazzling. For the sake of illustration, I need an example: a colleague in my department, a specialist in Chinese and Japanese art, told me that about a dozen years ago his colleagues from Taiwan were surprised to hear that he defined himself as an art historian. "What is this art history?" they had asked, much bewildered. And today — *voila*! In 1999 Wölfflin was accepted as a university textbook in China! Yet this is really not a good occasion to speak of "belatedness." The English-speaking "globalists" ought to realize their own "belatedness" as well: Warburg was translated into English around 1999, after almost 100 years! What a success! What speed! If I am not mistaken, still waiting — to take into consideration only the "fathers of art history" — is Max Dvořák, one of the two German art historians whom Kleinbauer stigmatized as "untranslatable" into English (*Modern Perspectives,* 1970). The other was Warburg. By the way: my home department was founded at the beginning of the twentieth century by a Polish art historian educated in the first Vienna School, a disciple

of Dvořák. And one more thing: in Poland there are only ten academic centers of art history, which may suggest that as regards this discipline Poland is still a "developing country." Nonsense! What counts in art history, as in the humanities in general, is not quantity but quality!

3. Of all the views expressed in the debate the closest to my own is that of Kesner, particularly when, referring to hermeneutics (Gadamer, Iser) he speaks for a model of scholarship as translation. Indeed, if we define art history as a discipline which attempts to understand other people through works of art (visual artifacts), it turns out to be continuous translation. There is simply no other way to understand the Other, be it an Egyptian from the period of the Old Kingdom, a fifteenth-century Florentine, a contemporary Australian Aborigine or, for that matter, Lucien Freud. In each case there is a need to translate (in Polish, this verb means also "to explain," "to elucidate") concepts, ideas, functions, forms, ways of seeing, and ways of using visual artifacts, into terms intelligible to the scholar and to his or her audience. Translation keeps contact with the Other always by approximation, and never fully — but on the other hand it stems from an optimistic belief in intelligibility, in the possibility of communication with the Other. (By the same token attending to translation implies a better understanding of one's own self.) As a Western academic discipline, art history must continuously engage two problems: the imperative of elucidation and the occurrence of subjectivity. In this context, to quote Kesner's brilliant formula, there is much space for "art history as a patchwork of specifically defined local traditions or 'period eyes.'" The dominant paradigm of our discipline, which I believe to be historico-relativist, works exactly in this way, translating what is "theirs" into what is "ours" by means of intersubjectively communicable and verifiable language (discourse).

4. Hence, Summers's dilemma can be formulated in the following manner: how, within this historico-relativist paradigm, unquestioned by the author of *Real Spaces* (and by none of those

who have taken part in the debate), can we do justice to the newly acknowledged universal dimension of art? With all due respect to the erudition and brilliance of Summers (which make his book truly fascinating) the task that he embarked on is impossible. The category of "real spaces," which would lead to truly comparatist ("global") art history, is burdened with an unmediated opposition between the specific and changeable ("specific ways" in which "social spaces and artifacts are formed") and the universal and permanent (all art has "a certain universality"). Under this burden it actually breaks down whenever it is confronted with the reality of individual artifacts. The author's attempt to distinguish among various spaces is also of no avail. On the contrary, even though the term "real spaces" becomes analytically operational, it loses all its comparatist power. The ultimate result, contrary to Summers's obvious intention, must be some new contextualism synthesizing all the available, more or less traditional, ways of pursuing contextual research. His referring to Heidegger, absolutely appropriate as regards the universality of art, does not change anything. A genuine "Heideggerian turn" would have to be ontological, which is impossible within the historico-relativistic paradigm. That paradigm would have to be overcome, and for this neither Summers himself, nor any other participant in the debate, is actually ready. The most straightforward in this respect is Elkins, both when he graciously, for the sake of argument, assumes art has a universal aspect ("The question, for a world of art history modeled on Summers's, is whether that universality [given, for the sake of argument, that it exists]"), and when he distances himself from Heidegger's philosophy because of its pathos ("it opens the door to pathos") and generalizing ("*Ur*-conditions … often too general to have much grip on the specifics of artworks"). Among the English-language scholars who explore the theoretical foundation of art history in a dialogue with Heidegger, the most interesting so far has been Stephen Melville, but his research is difficult to instrumentalize for the needs of global art history.

5. In any case, at least the direction (Heidegger) which Summers has taken, trying to do justice to "a certain universality of art," is appropriate. However, from the viewpoint of comparative art history, any reductionist steps (for example, the reduction to geographical conditions; see the ridiculous *Atlas of World Art* edited by John Onians) or quantitative methods (for instance, neurophysiological study of the brain and human perception apparatus) are total failures. While the former (Onians) lead to errors and absurdity,[239] the latter, regardless of the precision of its procedures and instruments, ultimately does nothing but confirm that we humans belong to one species and share the experience of perception by using such terms as order, rhythm, symmetry, and the contrast of figure and ground. What a discovery! Those terms have always been present in aesthetic reflection (it was Arnheim who, in his mature phase, starting with *The Power of the Center*, did the most to make them functional for the semantic study of visual structures). In short, and once again: what matters is quality, not quantity. Not humans, but human beings (*Dasein*). Summers understands this very well: his "real spaces" are at least of a qualitative-anthropological kind, just as are Belting's network of terms "*Bild-Medium-Körper-Ort*" (in the book *Bild-Anthropologie*). In each author's work, however, the terms are imposed on all (both outer and inner) human images, which subverts the boundaries of any, even a "global," art history.

6. Thus, anthropology. But what kind of anthropology? Ultimately, any answer to the question about the universal aspect of art depends on our idea of human being. The search for "rudiments" can take two directions: downward (when we "go down" to physiology, instincts, conditioned reflexes, and geographical determinations) and upward. Only the latter direction matches our condition as *Dasein*, both thrown into the world as it is and transcending it toward the ultimate conditioning, *Grund*. As it turns out, we are moving back to Heidegger, though perhaps not George Steiner's version of him (Steiner is mentioned in passing in the debate); the polemical fervor of *Real Presences* opens not just

a door to pathos, but a whole city gate. Nor will Etlin's "defense of humanism" be of much use. Kesner is right when he doubts the operative value of Etlin's generalizing categories for art history. What should be done, then, to avoid pathos and generalizing? The way has been shown by the literary scholar, Karlheinz Stierle, in a polemic with Gadamer and Jauss (*Äesthetische Rationalität*): the medium of the work of art should itself be subject to theorizing.[240] (My appeal to the reader: please, forget Greenberg with his modernist teleology and pseudo-formalism which have done so much damage to thinking about art in terms of its medium.)

7. If the possibility of transcending, being toward the unconditioned, defines us as human beings, and if in art our essential disposition finds its confirmation, it is only thanks to the medium of the work of art, not as a material vehicle, but as the ultimate instance that conditions all that makes itself visible in and as a work.[241] With reference to art, then, we should not speak about "a certain universality," but "the universality" as a constitutive, defining moment. The only way to introduce the universality of art in the practice of art history is by taking account of the medium as that which is ultimately conditioning and which matches our essential effort to reach the unconditioned. For the lack of a better word, we may call it the *absolute,* understood, however, nonsubstantially, in the spirit of Heidegger's critique of the Western metaphysics. An ontological turn of this kind (again, we must remember that this is ontology as understood by Heidegger) would mean a radical change of the paradigm from the historico-relativist to the existential-hermeneutical, as Michael Broetje argues.

8. My message is the following: let us retain both mutually exclusive paradigms within art history, respecting their identities. In fact, both guarantee the "globalism" of our discipline, even if the term is understood here somewhat differently than it is in the Art Seminar. The historico-relativist paradigm (art history as the practice of "translation" resulting in a "patchwork" of various traditions, cultures, and ways of seeing) has a brilliant

global future, if one believes in the global victory of the Western understanding of scholarship and such disciplines as art history. We should not be afraid of being absorbed in visual studies. The best defense against such danger is the perspective of Horst Bredekamp's *historische Bildwissenschaft* which is presently the most advanced version of the historico-relativist paradigm, combining high theoretical level with political commitment: the ability to analyze images critically is supposed to protect us against their uncontrolled power. Unfortunately, one can hear in this the echo of Marxist, virtually iconoclastic distrust in the irrational aspect of images (as Karl Werckmeister has argued). A minor controversy whether one should deal with objects or subjects may be left to the theorists of visual studies (Mieke Bal vs. Nicholas Mirzoeff, in the *Journal of Visual Culture*).

If, however, we search for the universal, let us follow our existential experience of transcending ourselves, particularly when we, as subjects, experience works of art. Transcendence must not be rejected, for it always returns — often in a grotesque, New Age form — and we must not be ashamed of it. Either we make an effort to understand ourselves as transcending *Dasein*, endowed with spiritual life and conscience, or we will not understand ourselves at all. It is not accidental that one of the deepest readings of Heidegger's essay, "*Der Ursprung des Kunstwerkes*," is Wojciech Suchocki's book *W miejscu sumienia* (*In Place of Conscience*): conscience, the "real space" of art.[242]

Ekaterina Degot

In a Globalist Era, Which Art is Not Global Enough? The Good Old International One

The idea of "global art history" seems to be an oxymoron: it contains a contradiction between the spheric and the linear, between revolution on its own axis and a movement forward. Won't slogans of the "global" bring the "end of history" back into style?

"Globalism" seems to have come into demand in art history in reaction to the recent curatorial discourse of international biennials. These biennials will probably be remembered as something that was as central to the twenty-first century as the world industrial exhibition was to the 1800s—biennales involve the elevation of multiculturalism, replacing the exhibitions' faith in linear progress. In the same way that the world exhibitions' eclectic architecture aided the emergence of classical art history as a narrative of styles, so global biennals are supposed to stimulate the emergence of a new art history, which, probably, will not be a *history* in the first place.

We are all looking for the language and theory of *inclusiveness*, which would be opposed to modernist aesthetics of exclusion with its claim of "less is more" and its severe reductionism. (The term "art of exclusion," by the way, comes from Vittorio Pica, the founder of the Venice Biennale, which began as an international exhibition in the spirit of the nineteenth century and is now attempting to move into postcolonial multiculturalism.) Today, both the nineteenth and twentieth centuries seem to belong to one and the same epoch, one that began with the broadening of art's thematic spectrum in realism and ended with the reduction of its expressive means in modernism, "narrowing its area of competence in order to determine effects exclusive to itself," as Clement Greenberg put it.

But to achieve this, we would first and foremost need to get rid of the imperative of originality. The real integration, the real globalism (although we still have to decide if we need one) would imply the equality not just of artists, who would have the right to exhibit and to be praised; it would imply the equality of art works, with no "outstanding" and "mediocre," no "new" and "old." It would have to challenge the bourgeois notion of "quality" and the fetishism of the art work altogether, envisioning a possibility of artist without professionalism, the artist without art production. And we are far from that.

In fact, it is just in the domain of non-European "world art" that notions of "innovation" and "epigonism" are being eradicated, the obvious reason being the fact that not many Euroamerican experts feel competent to tell if an Australian Aborigine's art work is original or derivative. As soon as we return to the sphere of the international traditions of so-called realist, or mimetic, painting, there is always someone to be charged with backwardness and banality. Under the present conditions of euphoria, when it seems any exhibited item gains the status of an art work, to produce something that might *not* pass the exam, one definitely has to turn to realist painting, in the manner of the nineteenth century. This kind of art can be found in all countries on all continents with no exception, but it is least integrated into international exhibitions or the discourses of art history — unless, of course, it is "authentic" nineteenth-century French painting. Otherwise such painting is simply considered kitsch, even if for many countries it was actually the language of modernism. It just does not have enough ethnic specificity. This is definitely the case of Soviet figurative painting, including late Malevich, which would be easier to integrate into international museums if it were based on ethnic, rather than political and economic, differences (the absence of private market). But it is "differently different" and cannot pass through the all-too-fine sieve of multiculturalism.

So what is less global than everything else? The answer is clear: the *international* (this term being an old Eurocentric version of the current "world art" trend), and even *internationalist*, but that is another story.

Russian art is quite familiar with these issues, because secular European painting only established itself in Russia at the end of the eighteenth century. Russian artists of the 1800s and early 1900s, including the famous ones such as Ilya Repin, often began their careers as icon painters. In this sense, they are not so different from those contemporary African popular artists who gave up making masks and started painting in the "European style" exclusively for the domestic market (which was also very much the case of Russian realists), because the foreign market wasn't really interested in such "derivative" works.

When this copying of European models turns out to be "all wrong," however, it can bring rather fascinating results, especially if one considers how Russian avant-garde artists including Malevich followed this path — which makes me think the next Malevich might come from this "Westernized" and "unauthentic" African continent. Feeling excluded from the European art market and European art history, Russian avant-garde artists of the early 1900s were very much concerned with the search for an alternative language of inclusion that could challenge the hegemonism of Western modernism (especially cubism). In 1913, Ilya Zdanevich and Mikhail Larionov published their "Yes Manifesto," in which they answered all the contradictory journalists' questions with an invariable "yes," creating a disturbing confusion. Their next project, the same year, was called "everythingism": an artist was supposed to embrace all styles, all cultures, anything. For Kandinsky, the term for a symphonic "everything" that was to resonate in his paintings was "Moskva" (Moscow).

Another attempt to capture inclusiveness in one word brought the famous and often misunderstood term "non-objective" art. It is usually interpreted as the Russian word for abstraction, but Russian artists usually avoided the latter term. "Non-objective" art work is actually an art work which would not be an object at all, which would erase the whole boundary between the subject (the artist) and an isolated artifact, which would question the imbalance of subject–object relationship in an extremely radical way, and seek to transcend the inequality of "good" and "bad" art works (the abolition of academic criteria was helpful to that).

The claim to produce professional art works of quality and in quantity seemed strange and unfair to many Russians, and especially Soviet artists who understood this pressure as a market-driven infringement upon their freedom. As early as 1919, the future constructivist Varvara Stepanova wrote, ironically but proudly: "But where is our artwork? All we see are experiments and follies." In 1924, Alexander Rodchenko, having seen the Parisian galleries and what they had done to former avant-gardists such as Fernand Leger (who now catered for the market), wrote that he would prefer, at least from time to time, "to lie around in the sun, doing nothing, basically.... And then, suddenly, to start making photos, movies, God knows what else ... to be a child, to forget everything ... to fix padlocks, to read Pinkerton." Today, of course, it is easy to imagine not only photos and movies but fixing padlocks and reading Pinkerton as "special projects" for some biennial, especially if one could find a way to integrate these gestures into the market.

To finish, I'll give my answer to another question that came up at the Art Seminar, namely whether a local art historical tradition can produce terms that it might make sense to spread to other territories. My choice would be the modest but in fact exceptionally subversive term "easel art," normative in Soviet art history, but nonexistent in any other language. The French *peinture de chevalet*, the English *easel painting*, or the German *Tafelbild* quite descriptively refer to a painting standing on an easel, invented in the Renaissance. In its Soviet sense, sculpture, graphic art, and even photography, jewelry, and furniture can be described as "easel" art, which means having (under capitalist conditions) the same "frame of separateness," the same sense of isolation, the same portable character. According to the State Academy's *Dictionary of Artistic Terms* (1923–29), it is art, emancipated from the wall, made for the private market, and clearly oriented toward imminent sale.

I think that today, Soviet critics of bourgeois art wouldn't stop with terms like "easel installations," "easel video," or "easel performance." They would probably think of "easel Chinese scrolls," "authentic easel African dance," and, in general, "the global easel art."

Leonard Bell

Is Art Global? Reflections from Another Place

The Art Seminar threw out and addressed a welter of issues, problems, and questions relating to the teaching and writing of the visual arts, their histories in various parts of the world, how art history has been conceptualized, and the need to reconceptualize the discipline given the exigencies of this new era of the "global." For James Elkins, globalism is the most pressing issue facing the discipline. For Ladislav Kesner it isn't: there are more serious concerns and problems. "What is to be done?" was the implied question sustaining the conversation, though in the case of South Africa, it would seem, what is to be done has already been done.

Art history as discourse and practice has been variously defined, conceptualized, and put into operation since its inception. There has never in fact been a single art history. Are there, though, any working or workable models for a new art history? An art history in which voices, aside from Euro-American ones, would be heard, listened to, and thus inform in substantial and sociopolitically beneficial ways the practice of art history, not just in their localities or origin, but also in Europe and North America? Can the future of the discipline be planned for, or does the very notion of planning betoken imposition of historiographies from above, rather than their emergence from below? Here is a paraphrased line from the Mexican film, *Amores Perros* (2000): "When man plans, God laughs."[243] Almost invariably preplanned cities have an unreal quality, the feel of three-dimensional blueprints dropped in from a utopian elsewhere. And almost inevitably too, attempts "to put the world into a book" founder on the messiness, the contradictions, and imponderables of that world, its resistance to neat and tidy, harmoniously ordered formulations and categorizations. Caryl Phillips's observations in his *A New World Order* (2002) may be apt: "Our identities are fluid. Belonging is a contested state. Home is a place riddled with vexing questions … As the laborious certainties of the old order continue to fade, and the volume of global conversation increases, ambiguity embraces us."[244]

The things worldwide that come, or could come, within the ambit of art history make up an ocean of material, a vast and unruly space, in which any singularity of conception or ideology would drown. It is a matter, then, of learning or working out how to navigate that ocean. Rather than attempting to prescribe a route in advance, it might be more productive to set out into what is still little-known territory, with fewer preconceptions about what can or needs to be done. It might be better to adopt more exploratory and fluid approaches, working methods characterized by the mobility necessary for ocean travel, and an openness to the possibilities of coexistence of multiple voices, and contradictions, even collisions, among those voices. After all, paradigm shifts, creative innovations, and productive transformations have frequently come out of the sometimes anarchic energies and imaginations generated by the displacements, meetings, and mixings of the hitherto different and unlike.

Productive and mutually advantageous interactions cannot, of course, be ordained in advance. They happen, or don't happen, on the ground, in the street, according to a diverse range of factors — historical, sociopolitical, geographical, economic, cultural. Pessimism and fear that new and different initiatives will inevitably be swamped by supposedly overarching or omniscient global forces are not likely to help, though doubt, uncertainty, and self-criticality may. Paul Auster's aphorism may provide an apposite ending: "The question is who is who and whether or not we are who we think we are."[245]

Notes

1. Hubert Damisch, *Fenêtre jaune cadmium ou les dessous de la peinture* (Paris, 1984); Wolfram Pichler and Ralph Ubl, "Enden und Falten: Geschichte der Malerei als Oberfläche," *Neue Rundschau* 114 no. 4 (2002): 50–71.

2. Joseph Vogl, "Anorganismus: Worringer und Deleuze," in *Wilhelm Worringers Kunstgeschichte,* edited by Hannes Böhringer and Beate Söntgen (Munich, 2002), 181–90.
3. Steven Connor, *The Book of Skin* (Ithaca NY: Cornell University Press, 2004), 257.
4. Mark B. N. Hansen, *New Philosophy for New Media* (Cambridge MA: MIT Press, 2004), xxii.
5. Zeki, *Inner Vision: An Exploration of Art and the Brain* (Oxford: Oxford University Press, 2004), 9–10.
6. For further reference see Christiaan D. Van der Velde, *The Mind: Its Nature and Origin* (Amherst: Prometheus Books, 2004), 81; Richard L. Gregory, "Pattern Recognition," in *The Oxford Companion to the Mind,* second edition (Oxford: Oxford University Press, 2004), 698–702; Donald Hoffman, *Visual Intelligence: How We Create What We See* (Berkeley and Los Angeles: University of California Press, 1998); Paul F. Snowdon, "[Galen] Strawson's Agnostic Materialism," *Philosophical and Phenomenological Research* 58 (June 1998): 455.
7. James Elkins, *Our Beautiful, Dry, and Distant Texts: Art History as Writing* (University Park: Penn State Press, 1997).
8. John A. Walker, "Clark's 'Civilisation' in Retrospect," *Art Monthly* (December/January, 1988/1989): 16.
9. Glyn Davis, "Art on British Television: From Clark to Collings and Beyond," unpublished paper delivered to the symposium *Art History in National Contexts: Structures and Institutions of Scholarship* (Edinburgh, October, 2004).
10. www.five.tv/home/frameset/?content=10086819&, accessed February 2006.
11. On Chinese art discourses see *Theories of the Arts in China,* edited by Susan Bush and Christian Murck (Princeton NJ: Princeton University Press, 1981), and Jianping Gao, *The Expressive Act in Chinese Art* (Stockholm: Almqvist & Wiksell, 1996).
12. Wen Fong, "Archaism as a 'Primitive Style,'" in *Artists and Traditions: Uses of the Past in Chinese Culture,* edited by Christian Murck (Princeton NJ: Princeton University Press, 1978).
13. The first art historical treatise written by an Indian was Ram Raz, *Essay on the Architecture of the Hindus* (London: Royal Asiatic Society, 1834). The first overview of the art history of India in Bengali was Shyama Charan Srimani, *Suksha Shilper Utpatti o Arya Jatir Shilpa Chaturi* (*Fine Arts of India, with a Short Sketch of the Origins of Art*) (Calcutta: Roy Press, 1874). The best-known Sanskrit treatise was *Architecture of Mānasāra,* translated by Prasanna Kumar Acharya (London and Bombay: Oxford University Press, 1933). The treatise is usually referred to by the title "Mānasāra" but the full title is: *Mānasāra-vāstu-śāstra.* "Mānasāra" denotes "the essence of measurement" or "the system of proportion," while "vāstu-śāstra" can be translated as "the science of architecture, design and sculpture." Within the treatise "Mānasāra" refers to systems of measurement, but also appears as a personal name and as a term for a class of sage-artists concerned with the science of proportion. For a commentary on the text see Prasanna Kumar Acharya, *Indian Architecture According to Mānasāra-Śilpaśāstra* (London and Bombay: Oxford University Press, 1928).

14. See Tapati Guha-Thakurta, *The Making of a New "Indian" Art* (Cambridge: Cambridge University Press, 1992) and *Monuments, Objects, Histories: Institutions of Art in Colonial and Postcolonial India* (Delhi: Permanent Black, 2004); Partha Mitter, *Much Maligned Monsters: A History of European Reactions to Indian Art* (Oxford: Clarendon Press, 1977).
15. See, for example, Margaret Dikovitskaya, *Visual Culture: The Study of the Visual after the Cultural Turn* (Cambridge MA: MIT Press, 2005).
16. James Clifford, "On Ethnographic Authority," in Clifford, *The Predicament of Culture* (Cambridge MA: Harvard University Press, 1988): 21–54.
17. Alfred Gell, *Art and Agency* (Oxford: Clarendon Press, 1998).
18. Craig Clunas, *Pictures and Visuality in Early Modern China* (London: Reaktion Books, 1997).
19. See Susan Vogel, *Baule: African Art, Western Eyes* (New Haven CT: Yale University Press, 1997), 82.
20. See Wu Hung, *Monumentality in Early Chinese Art and Architecture* (Stanford CA: Stanford University Press, 1996).
21. Clifford, "On Ethnographic Authority," 41.
22. James Elkins, "Review of David Summers, *Real Spaces: World Art History and the Rise of Western Modernism*," *Art Bulletin* 86 no. 2 (June 2004): 378.
23. See, for example, Michael Taussig, *Mimesis and Alterity: A Particular Study of the Senses* (New York: Routledge, 1993).
24. Susan Sontag, "Against Interpretation," in Sontag, *Against Interpretation and other Essays* (London: Vintage, 1994), 3–14.
25. Friedrich Schlegel, "Critical Fragments," § 57 in Schlegel, *Philosophical Fragments*, translated by P. Firchow (Minneapolis: University of Minnesota Press, 1991), 7.
26. Jean-Hubert Martin, *Magiciens de la Terre* (Paris: Center National d'Art et de la Culture Georges Pompidou, 1989). An important early anthology of texts on minority culture was *Out There: Marginalization and Contemporary Cultures,* edited by Russell Ferguson (Cambridge MA: MIT Press, 1990). This was since matched by *Over Here: International Perspectives on Art and Culture,* edited by Gerardo Mosquera and Jean Fisher (Cambridge MA: MIT Press, 2004).
27. *Displacement and Difference: Contemporary Arab Visual Culture in the Diaspora,* edited by Fran Lloyd (London: Saffron Books, 2001).
28. *Displacement and Difference*, 11.
29. Exhibition description on the Museum website: www.tehranmoca.com/exhibition/Aspritual_Vision/moreinfo.htm, accessed February 2006.
30. Edward Said, *Culture and Imperialism* (London: Vintage Press, 1993).
31. Léopold Sédar Senghor, *Négritude et civilisation de l'universel* (Paris: Seuil, 1977).
32. David Summers, *Real Spaces: World Art History and the Rise of Western Modernism* (New York: Phaidon, 2003).
33. Richard Rorty, "Postmodernist Bourgeois Liberalism," and "On Ethnocentrism: A Reply to Clifford Geertz," in *Objectivity Relativism and Truth: Philosophical Papers*, vol. 1 (New York: Cambridge University Press, 1991), 197–202 and 203–10.
34. Olu Oguibe, "In the 'Heart of Darkness,'" in *Reading the Contemporary: African Art from Theory to the Marketplace,* edited by Olu Oguibe and Okwui Enwezor (Cambridge MA: MIT Press, 1999), 320–327, 326.

35. Dipesh Chakrabarty, "Postcoloniality and the Artifice of History: Who speaks for the 'Indian' Pasts?" *Representations* 37 (1992): 1–26. See also his *Provincializing Europe: Postcolonial Thought and Historical Difference* (Princeton NJ: Princeton University Press, 2000).
36. Chakrabarty, "Postcoloniality and the Artifice of History," 20–21.
37. Photographs of both signatures were reproduced in the magazine *Kinopis* [Skopje] 16 (1996): 122.
38. Maria Todorova formulated the Balkans as determined by the issues of backwardness, "sense of lag and lack": Maria Todorova, "The Trap of Backwardness: Modernity, Temporality, and the Study of Eastern European Nationalism," *Slavic Review* 64 no. 1 (Spring 2005): 140–64, especially p. 145. In her article, Todorova focused on the issue of backwardness as a dominant trope in east European historiography, especially within the discourse of nationalism until the end of the twentieth century.
39. Steven Mansbach, *Modern Art in Eastern Europe: From the Baltic to the Balkans, ca. 1890–1939* (Cambridge MA: University Press, 1999).
40. Here I refer to some recent critical observations on globalization as an ethically problematic cultural and political phenomenon such as this in Arjun Appadurai's writing: "The globalization of culture is not the same as its homogenisation, but globalization involves the use of a variety of instruments of homogenisation that are absorbed into local political and cultural economies." Appadurai, *Modernity at Large: Cultural Dimensions of Globalization* (Minneapolis: University of Minnesota Press, 2000), 42.
41. For a short but provocative discussion on the popularity of the concept of "glocal" see Bruno Latour, "On the Difficulty of Being Glocal," *Domus*, March 2004, available at www.ensmp.fr/~latour/presse/presse_art/GB-02 Domus 02-04.html, accessed February 2006.
42. James Meek, "World's First Artwork Found in Africa," in *The Guardian*, London, 11 January 2002.
43. John Picton, "On Artifact and Identity at the Niger-Benue Confluence," *African Arts* 24 no. 3 (1991): 35.
44. Karl Hartenstein, *Anibue (Civilization), Die "Neue Zeit" auf der Goldkueste und unsere Missionsaufgabe* (Stuttgart and Basel: Basel Evang. Missionsverlag G.m.b.H., 1932), 14–24.
45. See Kwame Akatu, *A Short History of Advertising in Ghana* (unpublished 3-page document, Accra, *ca.* 1980).
46. See Kwami, "Kumasi Painting: 1952–2005" (unpublished Ph.D. thesis, The Open University, Milton Keynes, 2005). See also my paper "Walking Down Hotel de Kingsway — A research Note by Atta Kwami," in *Landscape and Art* (London, UK); *The Journal of the Landscape and Arts* 26 (2002): 4–5; "The Invention of a Tradition," in *Kumasi Junction*, edited by Atta Kwami et al., exhibition catalog (Llandudno, Wales: Oriel Mostyn Gallery, Printed by University Press Kumasi, 2002), 6–7; my paper, "Signs of the Times: The Work of Sign Painters in Kumasi City," read during the International Conference on Global Icons, 20–22 May 2004, Berlin.
47. The canon of Ghanaian art is generally decorative realism. This development is also visible on grave monuments and other forms of commemorative portraiture found mostly in central and southern Ghana, and particularly in Kumasi. Painting has generated its own momentum, giving art making an impetus unequalled in other cities in Ghana. The biting satire of social

commentary in street painting is apparent in many pictures alluding to current affairs. Some street paintings moralize abortion, AIDS, and images of Gulf War "heroes." The media of screen-printing, photography, film or video, as well as computer art, are now new vehicles for dealing with aspects of identity.

48. Trowell's books are (London: Longmans, 1951–52); Marsh's *Anatomy for Artists* is (New York: American Artists Group, 1945); it is a fairly uncommon book. [- J.E.]
49. *Seven Stories about Modern Art* is the catalog of an exhibition at the Whitechapel Art Gallery (Paris and New York: Flammarion, 1995); *The Short Century* is the catalog of an exhibition organized by the Museum Villa Stuck, Munich (Munich and New York: Prestel, 2001). [- J.E.]
50. Ernest Victor Asihene, *A Brief History of Art with Special Reference to West Africa* (Accra, Ghana: Woeli Publishing Services, 2004).
51. Simon Alex Akoto, *Understanding Visual Arts Volume 1: A History and Appreciation of Art for Secondary Schools, Training Colleges and the Universities* (Kumasi: Akoto Classic Publications, 2004).
52. Akan is the largest linguistic group making up the Asante, Brong, Akwapim, Fanti, Akwamu, Kwahu, Guan, Akim, and Agona. Originally, Adansi and Denkyira were a distinctive part of the Akan group, but they were later subjugated by the Asante. Other major groups are the Ewe, Ga, Dagomba, and the Frafra of northeastern Ghana, who compose a cluster of four culturally, linguistically, and historically related groups — the Gurensi, Tallensi, Nabdam, and Kussasi — the Walla, Mamprusi, Gonja, Dargati, Nzema, and many others. The anthropologist Jon Kirby estimates the overall number at fifty different ethnic groupings, though they share a common past, culture, and set of aspirations, being related by close blood ties. Recent archaeological evidence supports the view that the people of Ghana, particularly the Akan, have been autochthons for thousands of years, dating back to "Old Stone-Age times." Peter and Ama Shinnie, *Early Asante* (Calgary: University of Calgary Press, 1998).
53. (Accra, Ghana: Gaskiya Corporation, Zaria and Artists Alliance, 1986, 1993).
54. Ernest Victor Asihene, "Painting in Ghana," in *Cultural Heritage*, souvenir catalog (Accra: Arts Council of Ghana / Mobil Oil Ghana Limited, 1968), 16–18.
55. Ernest Victor Asihene, *A Brief History of Art with Special Reference to West Africa* (Accra, Ghana: Woeli Publishing Services, 2004), 83.
56. My view on historiography is developed in Dan Karlholm, *Handböckernas konsthistoria: Om skapandet av "allmän konsthistoria" i Tyskland under 1800-talet* (Stockholm & Stehag: Symposion, 1996), and, in particular, *Art of Illusion: The Representation of Art History in Nineteenth-Century Germany and Beyond* (Bern: Peter Lang, 2004).
57. In addition to Ladislav Kesner's remark on Elkins's distinction, that "often the distancing from theory involves ignoring the art traditions outside the traditional Eurocentric scope," I would say that often the embrace of theory implies relying exclusively on French philosophers.
58. Erwin Panofsky, "Introduction: The History of Art as a Humanistic Discipline," in *Meaning in the Visual Arts* (1955) (Middlesex: Penguin Books, 1987), 30, 46.

59. See Karlholm, "The Virtual Museum of General Art History," *Art History*, vol. 24, no 4 (September 2001), and Donald Preziosi, *Brain of the Earth's Body: Art, Museums, and the Phantasms of Modernity* (The 2001 Slade Lectures in the Fine Arts, Oxford University) (Minneapolis: University of Minnesota Press), 92–115.
60. James Elkins, *Stories of Art* (New York: Routledge, 2002), 57.
61. Hal Foster, Rosalind Krauss, Yve-Alain Bois, and Benjamin Buchloh, *Art since 1900: Modernism, Antimodernism, Postmodernism* (London: Thames & Hudson, 2004).
62. Heinrich Wölfflin, *Principles of Art History: The Problem of the Development of Style in Later Art*, translated by M.D. Hottinger (New York: Dover, 1950), 12.
63. See my attempt to discuss the present state of research within visual culture studies: Karlholm, "Visuella kulturstudier: Betraktelse över ett expanderande forskningsfält," *Konsthistorisk tidskrift/Journal of Art History*, 72 no. 3 (2003), 186–205.
64. V. Y. Mudimbé, *l'Odeur du père, essai sur les limites de la science et de la vie en Afrique Noire, Présence Africaine* (Paris, 1982).
65. Hans Belting, *Das Ende des Kunstgeschichte, eine Revision nach Zehn Jahren* (Munich: C.H. Beck, 2002).
66. Romuald Tchibozo, *l'Art et l'arbitraire: une étude de la réception de l'art africain contemporain en Occident: le cas Allemand de 1950 à nos jours* (Berlin: Humboldt Universität zu Berlin, 2003).
67. Louis Althusser, "Philosophy and the Spontaneous Philosophy of the Scientists (1967)," translated by Warren Montag, in *Philosophy and the Spontaneous Philosophy of the Scientists*, edited by Gregory Elliott (London: Verso, 1990). Althusser expresses this rather differently, of course: "With philosophers you know what to expect: at some point they will fall flat on their faces" (p. 76).
68. David Summers, *Real Spaces: World Art History and the Rise of Western Modernism* (London: Phaidon, 2003), 15–16.
69. The methodological tactic employed here is inspired by that branch of sociolinguistics which focuses on "academic discourse" analysis. The claims of identity in academic discourse is a reasonably well-researched area: see, for instance, Roz Ivanič, *Writing and Identity: The Discoursal Construction of Identity in Academic Writing* (Amsterdam: John Benjamins, 1997); Ken Hyland, "Options of Identity in Academic Writing," *ELT Journal* 56 no. 4 (October 2002): 35–43; Ken Hyland, "Self-Citation and Self Reference: Credibility and Promotion in Academic Publication," *Journal of the American Society for Information Science and Technology* 54 no. 3 (2003): 240–51.
70. Useful overviews of the area from different perspectives are available in *Writing and Revising the Disciplines,* edited by Jonathan Monroe (Ithaca NY: Cornell University Press, 2002); Ken Hyland, *Disciplinary Discourses: Social Interactions in Academic Writing* (Harlow UK: Pearson, 2000); Paul A. Prior, *Writing/Disciplinarity: A Sociohistoric Account of Literate Activity in the Academy* (Mahwah NJ: Lawrence Erlbaum, 1998); David Russell, *Writing in the Academic Disciplines 1870–1990: A Curricular History* (Carbondale: Southern Illinois University Press, 1991). The sociolinguistic area of those sources could be thought of as a focused subset of larger educationist or anthropological or sociological or psychosocial approaches

to the academy. The reference to Tony Becher's title-phrase captures this, I think, most effectively, since his book (recently updated) remains a comprehensive account of this area: in the recent edition, with Paul R. Trowler, *Academic Tribes and Territories: Intellectual Enquiry and the Culture of Disciplines* (Buckingham: The Society for Research into Higher Education and Open University Press, 2001/1989). The anthropological turn of this title was inspired by Clifford Geertz's work in the area, some of which appears in "The Way We Think Now: Toward an Ethnography of Modern Thought," in *Local Knowledge* (New York: Basic, 1983). Social stratifications in the academy are most influentially examined in sociological terms in Pierre Bourdieu, *Homo Academicus*, translated by Peter Collier (Cambridge: Polity, 1988). Also an interesting contribution to this area, wedding literary criticism with social history and psychosocial concepts, is Marjorie Graber, *Academic Instincts* (Princeton NJ: Princeton University Press, 2001).

71. Ludwig Wittgenstein, *Tractatus Logico-Philosophicus*, translated by D.F. Pears and B.F. McGuiness (London: Routledge and Kegan Paul, 1961), proposition 7: "What we cannot speak of we must pass over in silence."
72. Jean-Paul Sartre, *Plaidoyer pour les intellectuels* (Paris: Gallimard, 1972).
73. The word "global" enters academic vocabulary with some of its current nuances mainly through Marshall McLuhan's coining of "global village," first in *The Gutenberg Galaxy: The Making of Typographic Man* (Toronto: University of Toronto Press, 1962). "Globalization" — as a replacement for "internationalization" — seems to appear from the mid to late 1970s, in two significant areas. First, it seems to be associated with discussions of the need to extend American sociology to the Third World, as in Paul Lamy, "The Globalization of American Sociology: Excellence or Imperialism?," *American Sociologist* 11 no. 2 (May 1976): 104–113; Fredrick H. Goreau, "The Multinational Version of Social Sciences," *International Social Science Journal* 35 no. 2 (May 1983): 379–90; Walter Parker, "Globalizing the Social Studies Curriculum," *Educational Leadership* 42 no. 2 (October 1984): 92. Second, it has to do with extending corporate capitalism, as in Raymond F. Hopkins, "Global Management Networks: The Internationalization of Domestic Bureaucracies," *International Social Science Journal* 30 no. 1 (February 1978): 31–46; and particularly the influential article Theodore Levitt, "The Globalization of Markets," *Harvard Business Review* 61 no. 3 (May–June 1983): 92–102.
74. Vico, *The First New Science*, translated by Leon Pampa (Cambridge: Cambridge University Press, 2002), Bk II Ch. VII; Kant, "Idea for a Universal History with a Cosmopolitan Purpose," in *Political Writings*, translated by H.B. Nisbet (Cambridge: Cambridge University Press, 1991/1970), 41–53; Hegel, *The Philosophy of History*, translated by J. Sibree (New York: Dover, 1956); Oswald Spengler, *Decline of the West* (London: Allen & Unwin, 1932); Arnold Toynbee, *A Study of History*, abridged in two parts by D.C. Somerville (London: Oxford University Press, 1946).

75. On this see Stefan Hoesel-Uhlig, "Changing Fields: The Directions of Goethe's *Weltliteratur*," in *Debating World Literature*, edited by Christopher Prendergast (London: Verso, 2004), 26–53; Hendrik Birus, "The Goethean Concept of World Literature and Comparative Literature," in *Comparative Literature and Comparative Cultural Studies*, edited by Steven Tötösy de Zepetnek (West Lafayette IN: Purdue University Press, 2003), 11–22.
76. Erich Auerbach, "Philology and *Weltliteratur*," translated by M. and E.W. Said, *Centennial Review* 12 no. 1 (Winter 1969).
77. A. Owen Aldridge, *The Reemergence of World Literature* (Newark: University of Delaware Press, 1986).
78. Pascale Casanova, *The World Republic of Letters*, translated by M.B. DeBevoise (Cambridge MA: Harvard University Press, 2004/1999); Franco Moretti, "Conjectures on World Literature," *New Left Review* Jan.–Feb. 2000, 54–68, and later, "More Conjectures," *New Left Review* March–April 2003, 73–81; and David Damrosch, *What Is World Literature?* (Princeton NJ: Princeton University Press, 2003). Casanova produces a theory of international literature based on competition between different national literatures, with each fighting for control over "literary time." In political terms this appears to be analogous to the ideas of realists in "anarchic" international politics, such as Kenneth Waltz or Robert Gilpin. Damrosch emphasizes the circulation of literature in formulating world literature; all texts cross and are received beyond their culture of origin. His analysis reflects on the relationship of circulation to national literatures, on the centrality of translation in dispersing texts beyond cultures of origin, and on the conditions of reading that attach to such texts. Franco Moretti's provocative essay "Conjectures on World Literature" assumes a world-systems perspective of literature. Moretti contemplates the scholarly pursuit of world literature as occurring at a metatheoretical level of "distant reading" — where the conventions of close reading and attention to particular literary texts is dispensed with in favor of discerning patterns and regularities/irregularities in scholarship which has read, interpreted, and assimilated literary texts in different languages and traditions already.
79. Summers, *Real Spaces*, 56.
80. Summers, *Real Spaces*, 549.
81. John W. Dower and John Junkermann, *The Hiroshima Mural* (Tokyo: Kôdansha International Ltd., 1985); 小沢節子 Kozawa Setsuko, 『「原爆の図」描かれた<記憶>、語られた<絵画>』*Genbaku no Zu: Egakareta kioku* [*The Hiroshima Mural: The Depicted Memory*] (Tokyo: 岩波書店 Iwanami Shoten, 2002); and 稲賀繁美 Shigemi Inaga, 「戦争画とへ平和画のあいだ」 "Sensôga to Heiwaga no aida" [Between War Painting and Peace Painting], 『あいだ』 *Aida* 113 and 114 (2005).
82. Henri Focillon, "L'estampe japonaise et la peinture en Occident," *Actes du Congrès international d'histoire de l'art à Paris en 1921* (Paris, 1923). See also Sadao Fujihara, "L'Extrême-Orient d'Henri Focillon," *La vie des Formes, Henri Focillon et les art* (exhibition catalog, Musée des Beaux-Arts de Lyon, 2004), 241–48.
83. Edward W. Said, *Orientalism* (New York: Vintage Books, 1978). The Japanese translation by 今沢紀子 Imasawa Noriko was published from 平凡社 Heibonsha in 1986, with an important commentary by 杉田英明 Sugita Hideaki.

84. René Grousset, *Bilan de l'histoire* (Paris: Plon, 1949).
85. See Sukehiro Hirakawa, *Japan's Love-Hate Relationship with the West* (Kent: Global Oriental, 2005); gives a nationalistic but masterful overview of the problem.
86. *Primitivism in 20th Century Art,* exhibition catalog, edited by William Rubin (New York: Museum of Modern Art, 1988). The Japanese translation, with an important critical commentary by 吉田憲司 Yoshida Kenji, is: (Kyoto: 淡交社 Tankôsha, 1995). See further James Clifford, *Predicament of Culture* (Cambridge, MA: Harvard University Press, 1988).
87. Shigemi Inaga, "Cognition Gap in the Recognition of Masters and Masterpieces in the Formative Years of Japanese Art History," in *Japanese Hermeneutics*, edited by Michael Marra (Honolulu: Hawai'i University Press, 2003), 115–126. Recent studies have revealed that 蜷川式胤 (1835–1882) Ninagawa Noritane's『観古図説』*Kanko Zusetsu* (or *Kwanko Dzu-setsu* [(1877]) contributed to the drastic change of the Western view of Japanese ceramics in the late 1880s. See Imai Yûko, "Changes in French Tastes for Japanese Ceramics," *Japan Review, International Research Center for Japanese Studies* 16 (2004): 101–27.
88. Shigemi Inaga, "The Making of Hokusai's Reputation in the Context of Japonisme," *Japan Review, International Research Center for Japanese Studies* 15 (2003): 77–100. The persistence of the Western and "international" view of the Japanese art history may be epitomized by Henri Focillon's oddly "anachronistic" *Hokousaï* (1916/25), and its divergence from the Japanese "domestic," aristocratic and academic conception may be testified to by Akiyama Teurukazu's *La Peinture japonaise* in Skira edition (1961) which remains a classic.
89. Partha Mitter, *Art and Nationalism in Colonial India 1850–1922* (Cambridge University Press, 1994), Tapati Guha-Thakurta, *The Making of New Indian Art* (Cambridge University Press, 1992); *Monuments, Objects, Histories: Institutions of Art in Colonial and Postcolonial India* (Delhi: Permanent Black, 2004).
90. Shigemi Inaga, "Un destin de pensée," in *Approches critiques de la pensée japonaise XXe siècle*, edited by Livia Monnet (Montréal: Presses Universitaires de Montréal, 2003), 329–48.
91. Shigemi Inaga, "The Making of Museums and Collections in Modern Japan with Special Reference to the Construction of 'Asian Art' and "Japanese Art'," International Symposium, "Interpreting Asian Cultures in Museum," at the British Museum, March 2000 (unpublished; Japanese translation as 「近代の国家コレクションと民間コレクションの形成」『記号学研究』 *Studia semiotica* 21, 2001, pp. 75–101). Okakura's conception of "arts and crafts" may well be compared with A.K. Coomaraswamy's *Mediaeval Sinhalese Art* (1908) in the light of the medievalism of William Morris.
92. 木代修一 Kishiro Shûichi, 「美術史」 "Bijutsushi [Art History]," in 『明治以降における歴史学の発展』 *Meiji ikô ni okeru Rekishigaku no Hatten* [*Development of History as a Science since Meiji Era*], edited by 歴史教育研究會 Rekishi Kyôiku Kenkyû Kai [Committee for the Historical Education Studies] (Tokyo: 四海書房 Shikai Shobô, 1933), 247–323. 『日本における美術史学の成立と展開』 [*The*

Establishment and Development of The Discipline of Art History in Japan] (東京国立文化財研究所、2001; exclusively in Japanese), despite its huge volume (504 pages), limits its investigations to the early stage of the discipline and shows the impossibility of any exhaustive overview.

93. 吉田千鶴子 Yoshida Chizuko, 「大村西崖の美術批評」 "Ômura Seigai no bijutsu hihyou," [Art Criticism by Ômura Seigai], 『東京芸術大学美術学部紀要』 *Tokyo Geijutsu Daigaku Bijtsugakubu Kiyô* [*Bulletin of the Faculty of Fine Art, Tokyo National University of Fine Arts and Music*] 26 (1994): 1–35.
94. See『矢代幸雄資料展』*Archive of Yashiro Yukio* (Kamakura and Hayama: 神奈川県立近代美術館 The Museum of Modern Art, 2005). 藤原貞朗 Fujihara Sadao, 「美術史学と国際主義 1920年代の美術史家の国際的成功とその意味」 "Internationalism and the Study of Art History: The International Relationship of the Art Historians in the 1920s and its Significance" (in Japanese), *Art Forum* 21 no. 9 (2004): 90–95; 高階秀爾 Takashina Shûji, 「解説」 "Commentary," to 矢代幸雄 YASHIRO Yukio,『世界に於ける日本美術の位置』*Sekai ni okeru Nipponbijutsu no Ichi* [*The Position of Japanese Art in the World*], 1956 (Tokyo: Kôdansha, 1988), 200–210.
95. John Rosenfield, "Japanese Art Studies in America since 1945," in *The Postwar Development of Japanese Studies in the Unites States*, edited by Helen Hardacre (Leiden-Boston-Köln: Brill, 1998), 161–194. Numerous regrettable errors in the spelling of French intellectuals (Jean Lacan, instead of Jacques Lacan, to begin with) mentioned in this important paper suggest not only the author's forced pretense of raising "Japanese Art Studies in America" to the height of leading theoretical scholarship in the humanities but also its baselessness in the respectable but marginalized discipline. See also Mimi Hall Yiengpruksawan, "Japanese Art History 2001: The State and States of Research," *Art Bulletin* 83 (2001), and the reaction it provoked; and Wen C. Fong, "Why Chinese Painting Is History," *Art Bulletin* (June 2003).
96. On the latest development of the research in the social history of art conducted in Japan around 1985–95, see the following critical overview: Shigemi Inaga, "De l'artisan à l'artiste au seuil de la modernité japonaise," *Sociologie de l'art* 8 (1995): 47–61.
97. 『美術とジェンダー』*Bijutsu to Jendâ* [*Art and Gender*], edited by 鈴木登幾子 Suzuki Tokiko, 千野香織 Chino Kaori and 馬渕明子 Mabuchi Akiko (Tokyo: Brücke, 1997); and *The Present, and the Discipline of Art History in Japan* [1997] *An International Symposium* (Tokyo: Tokyo National Research Institute of Cultural Properties/Heibonsha, 1999). See also my critical review and overview of the symposium, 「<今日本の美術史学を考える>を聴いて」『あいだ』 *Aida Extra* 25 (January 1998): 2–15. Concerning the debate in which my review is involved, see Ayako Kano, "Women? Japan? Art?: Chino Kaori and the Feminist Art History Debates," *Review of Japanese Culture and Society*, Center for Inter-Cultural Studies and Education, Josai University, vol. 15 (Dec. 2003): 25–38. In this report Kano mistranslates my key passages and comes to an incorrect conclusion. See also *Art and Gender 2, Intersecting Visions*, edited by T. Suzuki, A. Mabuchi, Ikeda Shinobu, and Kim Hyeshin (Tokyo: Brücke, 2005).

98. Exhibition, 『建築家　伊東忠太の世界展』 *Kenchikuka Itô Chûta no Sekai Ten* [*Itô Chûta, An Architect's World*], Tokyo, Watarium Museum; Ôsaka, Kirin Plaza Ôsaka, 2003. See 『伊東忠太を知っていますか』 *Itô Chûta wo shitteimasuka* [*Do you know Itô Chûta?*], edited by 鈴木博之 Suzuki Hiroyuki (Matsudo: 王国社　Ôkokusha, 2003); and 『関野貞　アジア踏査』 *Sekino Tadashi Ajia Tousa* [*SekinoTadashi, Asian Expeditions*] (Tokyo: 東京大学·東京大学博物館 The University Museum and The University of Tokyo, 2005). No English explanation is provided in these important publications.
99. Shigemi Inaga, "The Invention of a Discipline and Its Social Background: Art History in Westernizing Japan — A Critical (Re-)view," unpublished paper initially written in 1998 as a contribution to the failed project of a book tentatively entitled *Art and Its History*, which remains unpublished as of 2006.
100. The full list of the 岩崎美術社 Iwasaki Bijutsusha series can be consulted at www.oi-bijutsukan.com/iwasaki-books.html. Naturally the publisher does not monopolize the publication of Western art history and many other translations have been published by other editors. Among the prominent editors in recent years, let me mention in particular 平凡社 Heibonsha Limited, Publishers (www.heibonsha.co.jp/); ありな書房 Arina Shobô (www.jade.dti.ne.jp/~arina/); スカイドア Skydoor (www.skydoor.co.jp/); 彩流社 Sairyuusha Corporation Ltd. (www.sairyuusha.co.jp/); and Brücke (which has no website as of April 2006).

For an overview of the intellectual atmosphere in Japan in the last 25 years, see 「現代思想の 109 人」 "Gendai Shisô no 109 nin" [109 Prominent Figures of Contemporary Thought], numéro special hors série of 『現代思想』 the *Revue de la pensée d'aujourdh'hui* 6–7 (1978).「ブックガイド 現代思想の２２冊」 "Book Guide: 22 Books of Contemporary Thought," Special issue of 『現代思想』 the *Revue de la pensée d'aujourdh'hui* 14 no. 1 (1986); 『美学の方法』 *Methodes of Aesthetics*, edited by 今道友信 Imamichi Tomonobu, vol. 3 of 『講座美学』 *Aesthetics* (Tokyo: University of Tokyo Press, 1984); 『西洋美学のエッセンス』 *Essence of Western Aesthetics*, edited by 今道友信 Imamichi Tomonobu (Tokyo: ぺりかん社 Pelican, 1987), and 「現代思想を読む２３０冊」 "Gendai Shisô wo yomu 230 satsu" [230 Books: A Reading List of Contemporary Thought], special issue of 『現代思想』 the *Revue de la pensée d'aujourdh'hui* 29 no. 15 (2001). These references are exclusively given in Japanese.
101. For the proceedings of a recent international symposium on Roland Barthes, held in Japan, with an important Chinese contribution by 董強 Dong Qiang, "Alors Barthes? Barthes et la Chine, un rendez-vous manqué," see *Roland Barthes, Résonance des sens*, University of Tokyo, Center for Philosophy, *Bulletin* 2 (2004).
102. 稲賀繁美 Shigemi Inaga, 「黄金の三角地帯を目指して」 [In search of The Golden Triangle: from *Roland Barthes, Résonance des sens*], 『あいだ』 *Aida* 97 (January 20, 2004) 32–35 which provides a critical assessment of the above-mentioned symposium.
103. 小川裕充 Ogawa Hiromitsu, 「書画と美術：'今日本の美術史学を振り返る' に寄せて」 [Calligraphy and Painting versus Art: On the International Symposium "Today, Looking Back on Japanese Art History Studies,"] 『美術史論叢』 *Bijutushi Ronsô* 14 (1997–98): 157–66. On

this controversy, also see my "The Invention of a Discipline," and further *Histoire de l'écriture: de l'idéogramme au multimédia,* edited by Anne-Marie Christin (Paris: Flammarion, 2001), which claims to establish a global theory of *écriture,* including Arabic and Far Eastern practices.

104. Shigemi Inaga, "L'impossible avant-garde au Japon," in *Connaissance et Réciprocité,* edited by Alain le Pichon (Lovain-la-neuve: Ciaco éditeur, 1988), 197–207. This was retranslated into English by Margaret MacDonald as "The Impossible Avant-Garde in Japan: Does the Avant-Garde Exist in the Third World?: A Borderline Case of Misunderstanding in Aesthetic Intercultural Exchange," *Yearbook of Comparative and General Literature* 41 (1993): 67–75.
105. Jean-Hubert Martin, "Who Is Afraid of Redskins, the Yellow Peril and Black Power?," in *Memory and Oblivion, Proceedings of the XXIXth International Congress of the History of Art,* edited by Wessel Reinink and Jeroen Stumple (Dordrecht, the Netherlands: Kluwer Academic Publishers, 1999), 961–64.
106. Here, as I understand it, is the best potential of John Clark's unprecedented endeavor, published as *Asian Modern Art* (Honolulu: Hawai'i University Press, 1991). See also Clark, *Japanese Exchanges in Art* (Sydney: Power Publications, 2001)
107. Erwin Panofsky, "Die Perspektive als "Symobolische Form"," *Vorträge des Bibliothek Warburg,* 1924–25 (Leipzig-Berlin, 1927): 258–330. Japanese translation by 木田元 Kida Gen et al. as 『<象徴形式>としての遠近法』 (Tokyo: 哲学書房 Tetsugaku Shobô, 1993). It is true that the retina is concave, but the projection of vanishing lines on a flat paper set vertically in relation to the eye does not show any divergence from the mechanical tracing of the linear perspective. Precisely the same form is traced on the retina. In this sense Panofsky was mistaken to recognize a "psycho-physiological" construction in linear perspective. As for Sam Edgerton's account of Chinese rationality, see "The Renaissance Artist as Quantifier," in *The Perception of Pictures,* edited by Margaret A. Hagen (New York: Academic Press Inc., 1980).
108. On linear perspective in a transcultural context, see Shigemi Inaga, "La réinterpretation de la perspective linéaire au Japon (1740–1830) et son retour en France (1860–1910)," *Actes de la recherches en science sociale* 79 (1983): 29–46.
109. Michael Baxandall, *Painting and Experience in Fifteenth Century Italy* (Oxford: Oxford University Press, 1972; Japanese translation by 篠塚二三男 Shinozuka Fumio et al., as 『ルネサンス絵画の社会史』 from 平凡社 Heibonsha in 1989); Michel de Certeau, *L'Écriture de l'histoire* (Paris: Gallimard, 1975; Japanese translation by 佐藤和生 Satô Kazuo as 『歴史のエクリチュール』 from 法政大学出版局 Hosei University Press, in 1996).
110. See Walter Benjamin, *Passage* (Japanese translation by 今村仁司 Imamura Hitoshi, 三島憲一 Mishima Ken'ichi et al. as 『パッサージュ論』 from 岩波書店 Iwanami Shoten, 1993–95, in 5 vols.), 9a, 5; also Pierre Bourdieu, *Les règles de l'art* (Paris: Éditions du Seil, 1998; Japanese translation by 石井洋二郎 Ishii Yôjirô, as 『芸術の規則』 from 藤原書店 Fujiwara Shoten in 1995–96, in 2 vols.), 507, n. 38.

111. Marguerite Yourcenar, *Les Nouelles orientales*, reprinted in *Oeuvres romanesques* (Paris: Gallimard, 1982), 1143–53; Shigemi Inaga, "The Painter Who Disappeared in the Novel, Images of an Oriental Artist in European Literature," in *Text and Visuality, Word and Image Interactions III*, edited by Leo Hoek and Peter de Voogd (Amsterdam: Rodopi, 1994), 117–27. For a more penetrating challenge to the Western visual theory of representation, see Shigebumi Tsuji, "The Holy in the Dust: A Japanese View of Christendom's Cult of the Non-Representational," in *Seeing the Invisible in Late Antiquity and the Early Middle Ages*, edited by Giselle de Nie et al. (Utrecht, the Netherlands: Brepols, 2005), 185–209.
112. Ernst Kris and Otto Kurz, *Die Legende vom Künstler, Ein geschichtlicher Versuch* (1934); Japanese translation by 大西廣 Ônishi Hiroshi et al., 『芸術家伝説』 (Tokyo: ぺりかん社 Pelikan sha, 1989).
113. *Critical Terms for Art History*, first edition, edited by Robert S. Nelson and Richard Shiff (Chicago: University of Chicago Press, 1996; Japanese translation by 加藤哲弘 Katô Tetsuhiro, 鈴木廣之 Suzuki Hiroyuki et al. as 『美術史を語る言葉』 from Tokyo: ブリュッケ Brücke, 2002).
114. Imamichi Tomonobu, "L'expression et son fondement logique," *Revues internationales de philosophie* 52 (1961). The English translation is in *Modern Japanese Aesthetics: A Reader*, edited by Michael Marra (Honolulu: University Hawai'i Press, 1999), 220–28. The problem of compatibility in cross-cultural comparative studies in aesthetics was examined by the same author in his "Compatibilité et contrariété," presented in le Collège international de philosophie à Teheran in 1977.
115. Shigemi Inaga, "Images changeantes de l'art japonais: Depuis la vue impressionniste du Japon à la controverse de l'esthétique orientale (1860–1940)," *JTLA : Journal of the Faculty of Letters* [The University of Tokyo, Aesthetics] 29 (2006: forthcoming). Korean translation: "Japanese Art in Transition: How the West Perceived the Essence of Oriental Aesthetics," 『美術史論壇』 *Art History Forum* 18 (2004): 171–97.
116. 磯崎新 Isozaki Arata, 『建築における日本的なるもの』 *Kenchiku nio-keru Nihonteki namono* [*Japanese-ness in Architecture*] (Tokyo: 講談社 Kôdansha, 2003), 83–105. An English translation is forthcoming from the MIT Press. Despite the fact that the *Ma-espace-temps* exhibition was later held in Japan, Isozaki here refuses to recognize it. On Isozaki's reflection on *chôra*, see www.anycorp.com/, accessed February 2006.
117. Augustin Berque, *Vivre l'espace au Japon* (Paris: Presses Universitaires de France, 1981). See also his "La logique du lieu dépasse-t-elle la modernité" in *Approches critiques de la pensée japonaise XXe siècle*.
118. Tsudzumi Tsunejoshi, "Die Rahmenlosigkeit des japanischen Kunststils," *Zeitschrift für Aesthetik und allgemeine Kunstwissenschaft* Band 22, Heft 1 (1928); and Tsudzumi, *Die Kunst Japans* (Leipzig: Insel-Verlag, 1929); Japanese adaptation by the author: 鼓常良『日本藝術様式の研究』 (Tokyo: 章華堂 Shôkadô, 1933).
119. Itô Teiji, *The Garden of Japan* (Tokyo: Kôdansha International, 1984); adapted into Japanese by the author as いとう ていじ『日本デザイン論』 *Nippon Design Ron* (Tokyo: 鹿島出版会 Kashima Shuppan-kai, 1988).
120. Claudel, "Ça et là," *Connaissance de l'est* (Paris: Mercure de France, 1907/1913), 114–16.

121. Kenji Tokitsu, *La voie du karaté- pour une théorie des arts martiaux japonais* (Paris: Seul, 1978*); Les katas: arts martiaux & transformations sociales au Japon* (Paris: DèsIris, 2002).
122. Hubert Damisch, *Traité du trait* (Paris: Réunion des Musées nationaux, 1995) 19–38, 182–88. Though Damisch does not mention the fact (which is favorable for his working hypothesis), the Chinese character 創 *chuang*, designating the opening, means at the same time "creation" and "wound." See Shigemi Inaga, "La blessure créatrice entre poterie et la sculpture, ou Yagi Kazuo entre la tradition japonaise et l'avant-garde occidentale" (paper read at the international symposium, "La Rencontre du Japon et de l'Europe: Images d'une Découverte," Strasbourg, Université Marc Bloch, 8 Dec. 2005; forthcoming).
123. On the elliptic structure of Aby Warburg's project see 田中純 Tanaka Jun, 『アビ・ヴァールブルク　記憶の迷宮』 *Aby Warburg: Da Labyrinth des Gedächtnisses* (in Japanese) (Tokyo: 青土社 Seidosha, 2001), 237–44. For an overview of recent Japanese scholarship in visual studies, see *Art History Forum* (in Korean), special issue on "Depiction and Description," edited by Shigemi Inaga, no. 20 (2005), published by the Korean Center for Art Studies, which ambitiously aims at realizing G.A.H.
124. See www.bbc.co.uk/radio4/today/vote/greatestpainting/winner.shtml, accessed February 2006.
125. Searching *meishu* ("art") and *jiazhi* ("value") together on Google in Chinese produces 1,230,000 hits. There is a history to this, embodied in something like the 1922 essay "The Value of Literati Painting" by Chen Hengke (1876–1923), discussed in Aida-Yuen Wong, "A New Life for Literati Painting in the Early Twentieth Century: Eastern Art and Modernity, a Transcultural Narrative," *Artibus Asiae* 60 no. 2 (2000): 297–326.
126. (Cambridge MA and London: Harvard University Press, 1991), 75, 325. See also Pamela Kyle Crowley, "The Historiography of Modern China," *Companion to Historiography,* edited by Michael Bentley (New York: Routledge, 1997), ch. 24.
127. See S.A.M. Adshead, *China in World History* (New York: St. Martin's Press, 1995), 37. Jacques Waardenburg, "Reflections on the West," *Islamic Thought in the Twentieth Century,* edited by Suha Taji- Farouki and Basheer M. Nafi (London and New York: I.B. Bauris, 2004), 272.
128. Chakrabarty, "Postcoloniality and the Artifice of History: Who Speaks for 'Indian' Pasts?," in *A Subaltern Studies Reader, 1986–1995*, edited by Ranajit Guba (Minneapolis: University of Minnesota Press, 1997), 263.
129. I thank Wilfried van Damme for discussing this text with me, and for his critical remarks and helpful suggestions.
130. See for example Gerald R. McMaster, *The New Tribe: Critical Perspectives and Practices in Aboriginal Contemporary Art* (University of Amsterdam, 1999). In his dissertation, McMaster, an aboriginal Canadian artist and theorist, introduces "the new artist," who is not the subject of the gaze but who speaks and who "recognizes the unlimited potential of art to express — poignantly and critically, personally or universally, locally or pan-tribally — issues, situations, and perspectives that are extra-tribal." McMaster, *The New Tribe,* 235.

131. Kitty Zijlmans, "East West Home's Best: Cultural Identity in the Present Nomadic Age/East West Home's Best. Masalah Identitas Budaya dalam Era Nomad, Kini," *GRID, A Collaborative Project Between the Artists Tiong Ang, Fendry Ekel, Mella Jaarsma, Remy Jungerman*, edited by Tiong Ang et al. (Yogyakarta, Indonesia: Cemeti Art House, 2003): 81–88; and Kitty Zijlmans, "Kunstgeschiedenis en het discours over mondialisering," *Marokko: Kunst en Design 2005*, edited by Charlotte Huygens et al. (Rotterdam: Wereldmuseum, 2005), text in Dutch on pp. 21–25, and in Arabic beginning on p. 80. John Clark's book *Modern Asian Art* (Honolulu: University of Hawai'i Press, 1998) gives a thorough insight into the complexity of modernism (modern*isms*) in Asia, and the way in which modern and traditional art practices in the various regions are related. See also François Jullien, *La valeur allusive des catégories originales de l'interprétation poétique dans la tradition chinoise: contribution à une réflexion sur l'altérité interculturelle* (Paris: École Française d'Éxtrême-Orient, 1985).
132. David Summers, *Real Spaces: World Art History and the Rise of Western Modernism* (London: Phaidon, 2003), 12.
133. In his theory of society as a complex of social systems which distinguish themselves on the basis of their specific types of communication, and hence their function, as he puts it, *of* society (economy, law, politics, religion, education, science, media, art), the German sociologist Niklas Luhmann refers to art as a self-generating, autopoietic social system. Communication systems (such as art) do not stop at national borders or at the rim of a continent. From this point of view, art — the occurrence of an autonomous art system — is the effect of an internal evolution within art, and hence, in my opinion, a global issue. See for Luhmann's theory: Niklas Luhmann, *Social Systems*, translated by John Bednarz Jr. with Dirk Baecker (Stanford CA: Stanford University Press, 1995) [German ed.: Luhmann, *Soziale Systeme: Grundriss einer allgemeinen Theorie* (Frankfurt: Suhrkamp, 1984)]; Luhmann, *Art as a Social System*, translated by Eva M. Knodt (Stanford CA: Stanford University Press, 2000) [German ed.: Niklas Luhmann, *Die Kunst der Gesellschaft* (Frankfurt: Suhrkamp, 1995)].
134. In the opinion of Rasheed Araeen, the absence of artists from all over the world from modern culture is due to their exclusion from the history of mainstream art. He strongly pleads for a new concept of art historiography beyond its dominant European narratives. See *The Third Text Reader: On Art, Culture, and Theory*, edited by Rasheed Araeen, Sean Cubitt, Ziauddin Sardar (London and New York: Continuum, 2002).
135. I am aware of the Western-based and hence biased point of view in using the term "non-Western." For the sake of argument, I use the term nonetheless.
136. Gerardo Mosquera, "The Marco Polo Syndrome: Some Problems around Art and Eurocentrism" (1992/93), *Theory in Contemporary Art since 1985*, edited by Zoya Kocur and Simon Leung (London: Blackwell, 2005), 218–25 (here 219).
137. Mosquera, "The Marco Polo Syndrome," 221–23.
138. Franz-W. Kaiser, *Kunst ⇔ Wirklichkeit: Untersuching von Arten der Weltaneignung.* (dissertation, University of Leiden, forthcoming 2006).
139. Norman Bryson, "Art in Context," in *The Point of Theory: Practices of Cultural Analysis*, edited by Mieke Bal and Inge E. Boer (Amsterdam: Amsterdam University Press, 1994), 66–78.

140. In 1992, following the gift of the Robert and Lisa Sainsbury Collection of art from all over the world to the University of East Anglia, John Onians founded the School of World Art Studies and Museology. It was the first program in art history aimed at studying art worldwide. See Onians, "World Art Studies and the Need for a New Natural History of Art," *Art Bulletin* 78 no. 2 (1996): 206–9; and *Atlas of World Art*, edited by John Onians (London: Laurence King Publishing, 2004). At the University of Leiden a similar programme is being developed. See my "Pushing Back Frontiers: Towards a History of Art in a Global Perspective," *International Journal of Anthropology* 18 no. 4 (2003): 201–10; and my "Die Welt im Blickfeld: Unterwegs zu einer global orientierten Kunstgeschichte," in *Kunstgeschichte und "Weltgegenwartskunst": Konzepte–Methoden–Perpektiven,* edited by Claus Volkenandt (Berlin: Reimer Verlag, 2004), 243–59; and further *World Art Studies: Exploring Concepts and Approaches*, edited by Kitty Zijlmans and Wilfried van Damme (forthcoming, 2006).
141. Ellen Dissanayake, *Homo Aestheticus: Where Art Comes From and Why* (New York: Free Press, 1992); Wilfried van Damme, *Beauty in Context. Towards an Anthropological Approach to Aesthetics* (Leiden/New York/Köln: E.J. Brill, 1996).
142. Mineke Schipper, *Beyond the Boundaries: African Literature and Literary Theory* (London/New York: Cassell, 1989).
143. Helen Westgeest, "Identity and Materiality — Cultural Studies in Artistic Practice," in *The Reflexive Zone: Research into Theory in Practice*, edited by Anke Coumans and Helen Westgeest (Utrecht, the Netherlands: HKU, 2004), 188–201.
144. Pieter ter Keurs, *Condensed Reality: A Study of Material Culture, with Case Studies from Siasso (Papua New Guinea) and Enggano (Indonesia)* (dissertation, University of Leiden, 2005), 75.
145. Ter Keurs, *Condensed Reality*, 182.
146. The "Heideggerian" aspect is discussed in James Elkins's review of Summers's book in *Art Bulletin* 86 no. 2 (2004): 373–80, reprinted as a Starting Points essay in this book.
147. Ludwig Wittgenstein, *Philosophische Untersuchungen* [1953] (Frankfurt am Main: Suhrkamp, 2001).
148. Paul Frankl, *Das System der Kunstwissenschaft* (Brünn: Rohrer, 1938).
149. The analysis and the reflections on the "ontology" of the discipline is taken from a more elaborated version in Hans Dam Christensen, "Hvad er kunsthistorie? Betragtninger over kulturforskningens nutid og fremtid," in *Det kunsthistoriske studieapparat. Hånd- og debatbog fra den videnskabelige hverdag*, edited by Dam Christensen and Louise C. Larsen (Copenhagen: Multivers, 2004), 263–86.
150. Dan Karlholm, "Vetenskapens vardag," in *8 kapitel om konsthistoriens historia i Sverige*, edited by Britt-Inger Johansson and Hans Pettersson (Stockholm: Raster Förlag, 2000), 93–118, discusses several of these aspects.
151. See *The New Production of Knowledge. The Dynamics of Science and Research in Contemporary Societies*, edited by Michael Gibbons et al. (London: Sage Publications, 1994) for an analysis of the changes in knowledge production. See also the "sequential" *Re-thinking Science: Knowledge and the Public in an Age of Uncertainty*, edited by Gibbons et al. (Cambridge: Polity Press, 2001).

152. "XIII. Kunsthistorie," in *Studiehåndbog for det filosofiske fakultet* (Copenhagen: Københavns Universitet, 1968), and *Studieordning for Grundfagsstudium i Kunsthistorie 2000-ordningen* (Copenhagen: Institut for kunsthistorie, 2000).
153. Carol Duncan, "Art Museums and the Ritual of Citizenship," in *Exhibiting Cultures: The Poetics and Politics of Museum Display*, edited by Ivan Karp and Stephen D. Levine (Washington: Smithsonian Institutions Press, 1991).
154. Villads Villadsen, *Statens Museum for Kunst 1827–1952* (Copenhagen: Gyldendal, 1998).
155. See for example http://www.gipsen.dk, accessed February 2006.
156. I am fully aware of how Lacanian theories have helped in the critique and reassessment of modernist art history. But psychoanalysis is wholly determined by its modern European origins and its use in this context reinforces and naturalizes its pretended universal value. And this at the moment when psychoanalysts are speaking of ethno-psychoanalysis, that is, that psychoanalytical practice has to be adapted to the cultural background of patients as the value of language and even mental diseases vary enormously from one culture to the other.
157. This is an oversimplification because American scholars' approach varies immensely from one school to the other. It is also interesting to note that there are French books that analyze the phenomenon of "French theory" in the U.S. On the other hand, French intellectuals have been deeply influenced by the philosophy of Heidegger whose work is almost taboo in America academia.
158. Mahmut Mutman, "Under the Sign of Orientalism: The West versus Islam," *Cultural Critique* (Winter 1992–1993): 174–75.
159. See especially Donald Preziosi, *Rethinking Art History: Meditations on a Coy Science* (New Haven CT: Yale University Press, 1989); Larry Shiner, *The Invention of Art* (Chicago: University of Chicago Press, 2001); Jörn Rüsen, *Western Historical Thinking: An Intercultural Debate* (New York, 2002); and *Art History and Its Institutions: Foundation of a Discipline*, edited by Elizabeth Mansfield (London, 2002).
160. Edward Said commented in *Covering Islam* that "it is always the West, and not Christianity, that seems pitted against Islam ... the assumption is that whereas 'the West' is greater than and has surpassed the stage of Christianity, its principal religion, the world of Islam — its varied societies, histories, and languages notwithstanding — is still mired in religion, primitivity and backwardness."
161. It is interesting to note that few of the most influential theoreticians have thought of the problem of religion and belief. Nevertheless, this part of their work has not been picked up by American scholars. See among others Jacques Derrida and Gianni Vattimo, *Religion* (Stanford CA: Stanford University Press, 1998).
162. Slavoj Žižek once commented that after its political failure, the left had contented itself with the domination of the cultural sphere leaving to the right the control of the political. It is tempting to find a parallel with the situation I commented on above.
163. Rasheed Araeen, "A New Beginning: Beyond Postcolonial Cultural Theory and Identity Politics," *Third Text* (Spring 2000): 16.

164. It is precisely this analysis that indicates the value of James Elkins's project. I would like to thank him not only for inviting me to express my opinion but also for his constant interest and openness to consider these issues. As well, I would also like to express my recognition to Faya Causey, Philip Conisbee, and to June Hargrove and Sally Promey, who, although not necessarily sharing my ideas, have supported me in my efforts to develop them.
165. Stephen Melville, "The Temptation of New Perspectives," in *The Art of Art History: A Critical Anthology*, edited by Donald Preziosi (Oxford: Oxford University Press, 1998), 404. I would like to thank James Elkins for calling to my attention Melville's work.
166. Claude Lévi-Strauss, *De près et de loin* (Paris, 1990), 206–7.
167. Heidegger, Martin, *Nietzsche- Volume 1: The Will to Power as Art* (New York, 1991), 174.
168. Iain Chambers, "Art after Humanism: A Comment in the Margins," *Third Text* (Spring 2000–2001): 84.
169. See, for example, *Samtidskonst för lärare och andra konstintresserade*, edited by Karin Malmquist and Matilda Olof-Ors (Stockholm: Moderna Museet & Lärarförbundet, 2004); Mårten Castenfors, *Sveriges konst 1900-talet, part III, 1970–2000* (Stockholm: Sveriges Allmänna Konstförening, 2001); and Sören Engblom, *Art in Sweden: Leaving the Empty Cube: Contemporary Swedish Art*, translated by Hugh Rodwell (Stockholm: Svenska Institutet, 2000/2002).
170. See Charlotte Bydler, *The Global Art World Inc.: On the Globalization of Contemporary Art* (Uppsala, Sweden: Acta Universitatis Upsaliensis, diss., Figura Nova Series 32, 2004).
171. In an entertaining article, Joseph and Lisbeth Koerner have even compared museum collections' relation to the art market with a gold reserve. Joseph and Lisbeth Koerner, "Value," in *Critical Terms for Art History*, edited by Robert S. Nelson and Richard Shiff (Chicago: University of Chicago Press, 1996).
172. Commodity and money, for example, existed before capital and must be subsumed under it — with violence (by the State) if it be necessary. Dipesh Chakrabarty, "Universalism and Belonging in the Logic of Capital," *Public Culture* 12 no. 3 (2000): 653–78.
173. The Deleuzian precept fits perfectly in his theory of flux of desire and the forces they generate. These forces are the only object of painting, for Deleuze and Guattari, and they are acting on the body thus creating sensation. Sensation in turn is composed of precepts and affects which can be fixed in time through the making of an artwork, the artist being the only person who manages to make these sensations survive his/her own death. Deleuze has in mind painters like Francis Bacon or writers like Marcel Proust. See Gilles Deleuze and Felix Guattari, *Qu'est-ce que la Philosophie?* (Paris: Les Editions de Minuit), especially chapter 7, "Percept, affect et concept," 154–88.
174. The difference between the structuralism of Lévi-Strauss and that of Michel Foucault, even though he never accepted that label, is usually referred to as poststructuralist. There is still no completely convincing definition of what the difference is between structuralism and poststructuralism, and many of their representatives even refused to be labeled as either one or the

other. It is however widely accepted today that the main distinction comes from their conception of history. Whereas the structuralists were looking for structure that would be valid at any time in the history of mankind, the poststructuralists did not believe that structures could remain unchanged for an indefinite amount of time. Michel Foucault, for instance, was one of the first to reintroduce historicity into structuralism and established that different ways of relating to the world and creating knowledge, what he called "episteme," appeared and changed over long periods. See François Dosse, *History of Structuralism* (Minneapolis: University of Minnesota Press, 1997).

175. Maurice Merleau-Ponty, *L'Oeil et l'Esprit* (Paris: Gallimard, 1964).
176. He wrote that "the Subaltern historians are comfortable with Marx, Hegel, Heidegger, Jakobson, Habermas, Foucault, Barthes, and Derrida," putting them all together under the appropriate label of "Western". I cannot help pointing out that their given Western persona tends to hide the fact that they were writing in German, French, or Russian. There is no room for that in these lines (and a personal violent reaction against the dumb and meaningless label of "East meets West" that is still glued to most clichés about Hong Kong has made me particularly sensitive to that problem), but the whole concept of Western should not be used so casually. I am, however, sure James Elkins is perfectly aware of that problem and I am using it myself in these lines because it is not really the place to address that complicated issue. Let's keep it simple for a short while.
177. Daniel Birnbaum, "The Land," *Artforum* (Summer 2005): 346.
178. "Languages" and not dialects — the word *dialect* applies to dominated forms of communication. Cantonese may not be the official language of any state, but it is the tongue shared by a very large number of Chinese who have used it as a dominant form of communication for a very long time. It is also the medium of a culture that has taken very specific traits, albeit quite recently, that is the culture of the Pearl River Delta.
179. In a recent (February 2005) clarification on what language to use when there are non–Chinese speakers in the classroom, the pro vice-chancellor of the university had this to say: "The actual language of instruction can be changed from that indicated in the undergraduate teaching timetable if agreed by the teacher and all students registered for the course (by secret ballot) after the last day for adding courses." This is, to my knowledge, a very rare type of democratic decision making in a tertiary institution and a remarkable example of multiculturalism that should be picked up by more and more universities in the world.
180. Stephen Owen, *Readings in Chinese Literary Thought* (Cambridge MA: Harvard University Press, 1992), 167.
181. See, among others, Haun Sassy, *The Problem of a Chinese Aesthetic* (Stanford CA: Stanford University Press, 1993) and Pauline Yu, *The Reading of Imagery in the Chinese Poetic Tradition* (Princeton NJ: Princeton University Press, 1987).
182. Paul Ricoeur, "The Problem of Double Meaning as Hermeneutic Problem and as Semantic Problem," in *Art and Its Significance: An Anthology of Aesthetic Theory*, edited by Stephen David Ross (Albany: State University of New York Press, 1994), 384–96.

183. Ying-hsiung Chou, "The Linguistic and Mythical Structure of *Hsing* as a Combinational Model," in *Chinese-Western Comparative Literature: Theory and Strategy,* edited by John J. Deeney (Hong Kong: The Chinese University Press, 1980), 60–61.
184. Chen Xiaomei, *Occidentalism* (New York: Oxford University Press, 1995), 84.
185. Yang Xin et al., *Three Thousand Years of Chinese Painting* (New Haven CT: Yale University Press; Beijing: Foreign Languages Press, 1997).
186. *Zhongguo Meishu Quanji* 中國美術全集, 60 volumes, Shanghai Renmin Meishu Chubanshe 上海人民美術出版社.
187. Norman Bryson, *Vision and Painting: The Logic of the Gaze* (New Haven CT: Yale University Press, 1983), 89–92, as quoted in Wen C. Fong, *Between Two Cultures, Late Nineteenth- and Twentieth-Century Chinese Paintings from the Robert H. Ellsworth Collection in the Metropolitan Museum of Art* (New York: Metropolitan Museum of Art; New Haven CT: Yale University Press, 2001), 6.
188. Hal Foster et al., *Art since 1900: Modernism, Antimodernism, Postmodernism* (New York: Thames and Hudson, 2004).
189. Jean Baudrillard, "The Precession of Simulacra," *Simulacra and Simulation* (Ann Arbor: University of Michigan Press, 1994), 1–42.
190. Antonio Conceição Júnior's article titled "Contemporary Art in Macao" provides a summary of Macao's main art institutions and artists' associations and their history, as well as introducing some prominent local artists (www.arscives.com/antonio/contemporaryart.macau.htm). Not included in that article are the Old Ladies' House Art Space, and two additional associations that support artists and promote the arts in Macao — Macau Art Net (www.macauart.net) and Creative Macau (www.creativemacau.org.mo).
191. In the absence of a uniform Macao-wide educational system, and hence the syllabus documents that would point to an overall picture, I am basing my comments here on discussions with teachers and lecturers. I have been told that art is generally not taught at all in high schools, although, in a few exceptional high schools, classes in practical art, rather than art history, may be offered.
192. The main tertiary education institutions in Macau are the University of Macau, the Inter-University of Macau, Macao University of Science and Technology, Macao Polytechnic Institute, and the Institute of Tourism.
193. I'm quoting a remark by Sandra Klopper in the Art Seminar, p. 129 of this book.
194. Janet Wolff, *The Social Production of Art* (London & Basingstoke: MacMillan Press, 1982), 66.
195. See Erika Doss, *Benton, Pollock, and the Politics of Modernism: From Regionalism to Abstract Expressionism* (Chicago, London, 1991); Anette Cox, *Art-as-politics: The Abstract Expressionist Avant-Garde and Society*, 2nd ed. (London: UMI Research Press, 1982).
196. In Estonian too, the word "national" easily evokes notions of "nationalist" and thus sounds pejorative. A historical investigation into the depreciatory use of the word in Estonian art would first of all have to study the Stalinist rhetoric of nationalism, and be aware of the persecutions it accounted for.

197. Heie Treier, *Kohalik modernsus kunstis: Eesti varamodernistliku kunsti teoreetiline ja ajalooline kontseptualiseerimine ning Karl Pärsimägi paradigmaleidmise perioodil* [*Local Modernity in Art: The theoretical and historical conceptualisation of early Estonian modernist art and Karl Pärsimägi in the period of finding the paradigm*] (Doktoritöö, Eesti Kunstiakadeemia Kunstiteaduse Instituut [PhD thesis, Estonian Academy of Arts, typescript]. Tallinn, Estonia, 2004).
198. Things change — Jonas Mekas represented Lithuania in the Venice Biennale in 2005.
199. Kahn's style has reportedly been influenced by the mediaeval architecture of Kuressaare, his hometown. For Udo Kultermann, Kahn comes from Estonia. "The very suggestion by Kultermann, that we might treat Kahn in the context of Estonia is telling. The fact that we cannot consider people from Estonia as 'Estonians,' testifies to one core category of constructing the Estonian national identity — the purely [imaginary] ethnical origin. The problem is the same with the 'nationally suitable' ideologies — the example of Klucis regarding the Latvians is particularly interesting." (Dr. Katrin Kivimaa in her review to my thesis, October 2004).
200. The essay was published in the *Journal for Northeast Issues* in Hamburg, Germany. Heie Treier, "An International Experiment," *Journal for Northeast Issues. Art and Related Disciplines* 4 (2005): 20–21. Edited by Projektgruppe Hamburg.
201. The phrase "inequality of ignorance" has been formulated by Dipesh Chakrabarty, *Provincializing Europe: Postcolonial Thought and Historical Difference* (Princeton NJ: Princeton University Press, 2000), 28; see, for example, Aijaz Ahmad, *In Theory: Classes, Nations, Literatures* (London and New York: Verso, 1992); Rey Chow, *Writing Diaspora: Tactics of Intervention in Contemporary Cultural Studies* (Bloomington: Indiana University Press, 1993); and Rustom Bharucha, *The Politics of Cultural Practice: Thinking through Theatre in an Age of Globalization* (London: Athlone, 2000) for similar concerns in different contexts.
202. Chakrabarty, *Provincializing Europe*, 28.
203. Elkins, review of David Summers, *Real Spaces*, reprinted in this volume as a Starting Points essay.
204. The act of studying objects and cultures from across the globe as equal participants in the production of "world art" may indeed be a new and radical idea in the West. On the contrary, art history undergraduate courses in India, for example at the M.S. University, Vadodara, have always not only covered Indian art from protohistory to the contemporary but also included the histories of Euro-America, China, Japan, South-East Asia, and Australia among others. Further, alongside art history, undergraduate students take compulsory courses in both Indian and Western aesthetic theories. The quotation is Summers, *Real Spaces*, 25. Emphasis not in original.
205. Summers, *Real Spaces*, 25.
206. While Summers acknowledges that "other [non-Western] modernities" are not constituted through just "the spread of Western modernity, rather they are, in all cases, interactions and adaptations," his concern remains the modernity that "is more properly Western ... as part of a broader

Western culture." Is the non-West, so delightfully woven into the earlier parts of the text, then merely a device to "demonstrate familiar works and patterns of meaning [the Western modern] in different terms [through the non-West]"? Summers, *Real Spaces*, 549.

For example, the Rothko Chapel (1970) is here not only understood through Western architecture but also, the Ka'ba in Mecca, Sumerian and Hindu temples, and a Buddhist *stūpa*! Summers's 664-page *magnum opus* of world art culminates with, not surprisingly, homage to the Abstract Expressionist "master" Mark Rothko in whose works Summers sees a "historical or cultural construction, a use of historical forms at a remove from historical traditions, forms maintained in relation to forms of other traditions, the common term being human real spatiality." Summers, *Real Spaces*, 651.

One cannot but remember James Clifford's caustic comments on the "celebrated" exhibition *"Primitivism" in 20th Century Art: Affinity of the Tribal and the Modern* (1984–85): "The allegory has a hero, whose virtuoso work, an exhibit caption tells us, contains more affinities with the tribal than that of any other pioneer modernist. These affinities "measure the depth of Picasso's grasp of the informing principles of tribal sculpture, and reflect his profound identity of spirit with the tribal peoples." Modernism is thus presented as a search for "informing principles" that transcend culture, politics, and history. Beneath this generous umbrella the tribal is modern and the modern more richly, more diversely human." James Clifford, *The Predicament of Culture: Twentieth-Century Ethnography, Literature, and Art* (Cambridge MA: Harvard University Press, 1988), 191.

Or, Edward Said's critique of Europe's "desperate attempt[s] at a new inclusiveness" — a twentieth-century reaction to the vulnerability of the idea called "Europe": "When you can no longer assume that Britannia will rule the waves forever, you have to reconceive reality as something that can be held together by you the artist, in history rather than in geography. Spatiality becomes, ironically, the characteristic of an aesthetic rather than of political domination, as more and more regions — from India to Africa to the Caribbean — challenge the classical empires and their cultures." Edward Said, *Culture and Imperialism* (New York: Knopf, 1993), 189–90.

207. Martin Heidegger, "The Age of the World Picture," in *The Question Concerning Technology and Other Essays*, translated by William Lovitt (New York: Harper & Row, 1977), 115–54, at p. 129.
208. Heidegger, "Age of the World Picture," 130.
209. For examples of traditional Western narratives, see Helen Gardner, Fred S. Kleiner, and Christin J. Mamiya, *Gardner's Art through the Ages*, 12th ed. (Belmont CA: Thomson & Wadsworth, 2005); H.W. Janson, *Janson's History of Art*, 6th ed. (Upper Saddle River NJ: Prentice-Hall, 2004); and Marilyn Stokstad, *Art History*, 2nd ed. (Upper Saddle River NJ: Prentice-Hall, 2005).
210. See Elkins's review of David Summers, reprinted as a Starting Points essay in this book.
211. In the review, Elkins critiques Gayatri Chakravorty Spivak's *Critique of Postcolonial Reason: Towards a History of the Vanishing Present* (Cambridge MA: Harvard University Press, 1999) as "principally" derived from "Derridean poststructuralism and psychoanalysis" while Kapur's "sense of

modernity and its aftermath in *When Was Modernism? Essays on Contemporary Cultural Practices in India* (New Delhi: Tulika, 2000) draws on Jean-Francois Lyotard's discussion of the sublime and on Hal Foster's sense of the 'anti-aesthetic.'"

212. Kapur, *When Was Modernism?*, 378. Our critique is by no means a diatribe against Elkins. Rather, it is an attempt to respond to a recent tendency within the Western academy to criticize the "Westernness" of scholars working in, or on, the non-West. An arbitrary example of this tendency is David Carrier's recent review of Tapati Guha-Thakurta's *Monuments, Objects, Histories: Institutions of Art in Colonial and Postcolonial India* (New Delhi: Permanent Black, 2004). Carrier writes: Guha-Thakurta's "way of thinking about art institutions, historiography, and political power owes nothing, so far as I can see, to any specifically Indian tradition... Perhaps a development of an indigenous Indian art history will lead some scholars to reject secularizing Western styles of interpretation." David Carrier, Review of Tapati Guha-Thakurta, *Monuments, Objects, Histories* in *caa.reviews* (3/14/2005) See www.caareviews.org/detail.lasso?rev=Guha-Thakurta. Date accessed: 01/10/2006. The assumption here is that a quintessential "indigenous Indian art history" should essentially be nonsecular (religious and/or nationalist). Any departure from this norm, then, becomes merely the "perspective of a frequent visitor to the West, a cosmopolitan feminist professor." Thus, Guha-Thakurta's critiques of mid-twentieth-century nationalist art histories and the rise of religious fundamentalism in India marks her, in the eyes of Carrier, as a "defender of our [Western] ways of thinking" — and therefore not Indian enough.
213. T.B. Macaulay, "Education Minute," (1835) in H. Woodrow, *Macaulay's Minutes on Education in India* (Calcutta: C.B. Lewis, 1862), 104–16.
214. Frantz Fanon, *Black Skin, White Masks*, translated by Charles L. Markmann (New York: Grove Press, 1967), 97.
215. Elkins, *Stories of Art* (New York: Routledge, 2002), 115.
216. Spivak, "Righting Wrongs," *The South Atlantic Quarterly* 103 no. 2/3 (Spring/Summer 2004): 523–81, at p. 565, n 3. Along with Spivak's attempts to problematize the notion of human rights as exclusively a "Western" discourse; see, for example, Chakrabarty, *Provincializing Europe*; John Clark, *Modern Asian Art* (Honolulu: University of Hawai'i Press, 1993); Chow, *Writing Diaspora*; and Bharucha, *The Politics of Cultural Practice.*
217. Spivak, "Righting Wrongs," 565, n 3.
218. Spivak, "Righting Wrongs," 524. Emphasis not in original.
219. Despite Friedrich Teja Bach's explicit comment on the problematic of the term *belatedness* to mark art history in the non-West, Elkins insists that "the principal subject has been the diffusion, not the re-invention of texts and textbooks. I think it is possible to study the genealogies of the narrative structures of textbooks, and to find lines of dependence."

    E. H. Gombrich's *The Story of Art*, 16th ed. (London: Phaidon Press, 1995), the classic metanarrative of (Western) art, is cited by Elkins as the urtext of the discipline spawning innumerable "dependence, misunderstanding, abbreviation and expansion, and adaptation" both in the West and the non-West. Paradoxically, *other* stories, which have not fallen into the trap of (Western) narrativity, cannot be read, according to Elkins, as "art history."

For a critique of Elkins's very limited notion of art history, see Parul Dave-Mukherji, "The Other/s' Stories of Art in the Age of Multiculturalism," *American Council for Southern Asian Art Newsletter* 64 (Fall/Winter 2005): 10–13.

220. The situation in India seems to be very similar to the genealogy of the discipline in Latin America as described by Andrea Giunta during the Art Seminar roundtable.
221. In context to Indian art history, for a more detailed discussion, see Partha Mitter, *Much Maligned Monsters: A History of European Reactions to Indian Art* (Oxford: Clarendon Press, 1977); Guha-Thakurta *Monuments, Objects, Histories*; and Pramod Chandra, *On the Study of Indian Art* (Cambridge MA: Harvard University Press, 1983).
222. Rajendralal Mitra, *The Antiquities of Orissa* (Calcutta: Bengal Secretariat Press, 1875).
223. Guha-Thakurta, *Monuments, Objects, Histories*, 105.
224. Max Mueller (1876), cited in *Sahitya Sadhak Charitmala,* edited by Brajendranath Bandyopadhyay (Calcutta: Bangiya Sahitya Parishad, 1943). As cited in Guha-Thakurta, *Monuments, Objects, Histories*, 96. For Mitra's career and the controversies regarding his scholarship, see Guha-Thakurta *Monuments, Objects, Histories.*
225. Bhandarkar, *Viṣṇovism, Śaivism and Minor Religious System* (Strasbourg: K. J. Trubner, 1913).
226. Gopinatha Rao, *Elements of Hindu Iconography* (Madras: Law Printing House, 1914).
227. While British archaeologists and antiquarians had unanimously marked India through a *lack*, the nationalist counter-discourse sought to challenge this. According to colonial discourses, Indian philosophy was essentially degenerate and the Hindu mind "feeble" — the notion of *māyā* (illusion) led to irrationality. Ananda Coomaraswamy, in *The Dance of Śiva: Fourteen Indian Essays* (New York: Sunwise Turn, 1918), reversed this rhetoric by proposing that *māyā* was not illusion but *śakti* (creative energy). In defense of the nonmimetic nature of religious art in India, he suggested that artists were not concerned with naturalistic representations but aimed to re-present the transcendental body. This theory of transubstantiation was further elaborated by Stella Kramrisch in *Indian Sculpture* (New York: Oxford University Press, 1933). The anticolonialism in both Coomaraswamy and Kramrisch's writings has been discussed by many scholars, for example, Chandra, *On the Study of Indian Art.*
228. For a critique of the nationalist project of art history writing in India, see, for example, Guha-Thakurta, *Monuments, Objects, Histories*; Annapurna Garimella, "Engendering Indian Art," in *Representing the Body: Gender Issues in Indian Art,* edited by Vidya Dehejia (New Delhi: Kali for Women, 1997), 22–41; Sonit Bafna, "On the Idea of the Mandala as a Governing Device in Indian Architectural Tradition," *The Journal of the Society of Architectural Historians* 59 no. 1 (March 2000): 26–49; and Padma Kaimal, "Shiva Nataraja: Shifting Meanings of an Icon," *The Art Bulletin* 81 no. 3 (September 1999): 390–419.
229. Dave-Mukherji poses a similar critique of Elkins's *Stories of Art.* She writes: "Is it possible to place the two unequal halves [the West and the non-West] within the dialogic space of encounter while avoiding a lapse into cultural relativism? If we assume with Elkins that the dialogic encounter is only

possible if and when the two halves meet as equal partners, our basic premises of understanding the modern are at stake. As amply demonstrated by Timothy Mitchell, modernity and modern forms of representation would have been unthinkable without its close relationship with Orientalism and the construction of a colonial order." Dave-Mukherji, "The Other/s' Stories of Art," 12.

230. Article 341 and 342 of the Indian Constitution specifically recognizes certain low castes and tribes that have traditionally been economically and socially disadvantaged and therefore entitled to protection and specified benefits under the Constitution. These marginal groups, the Scheduled Castes and Scheduled Tribes, were until very recently excluded from worship in most Brahmanical temples and in some cases still remain illegally excluded.

231. Gary M. Tartakov, "A Geography of Dalit Pilgrimage" (paper presented at *34th Annual Conference on South Asia*, Madison, WI, 10/07/2005).

232. For Mughal use of *darśana* as a political strategy, see Catherine B. Asher, *The New Cambridge History of India 1:4 Architecture of Mughal India* (Cambridge: Cambridge University Press, 1992). For the *darśanic* gaze of Hindi film-viewers, see Madhava M. Prasad, *Ideology of the Hindi Film: A Historical Construction* (Oxford: Oxford University Press, 2000); Philip Lutgendorf, "Ramayan: The Video," *The Drama Review* 34 no. 2 (1990): 127–76.

233. In fact, there can be differences in cultural practices at any given moment. For example, while it is generally assumed that the *pradakṣiṇa* of sacred monuments in premodern India was always clockwise, the iconographic program of the sixth-century Viṣṇu temple at Deogarh (Uttar Pradesh) suggests that devotees performed a counterclockwise *pradakṣiṇa*. For a more detailed discussion, see Susan L. Huntington, *The Art of Ancient India: Buddhist, Hindu, Jain* (New York and Tokyo: Weatherhill, 1985). This suggests that the practice of *pradakṣiṇa* in premodern India varied according to ritualistic requirements, localized traditions, or for reasons that are no longer apparent.

234. Spivak, *The Postcolonial Critic: Interviews, Strategies, Dialogues*, edited by Sarah Harasym (New York: Routledge, 1990), 8.

235. Karim, the south London–accented protagonist of Hanif Khureshi's *The Buddha of Suburbia* (London: Faber & Faber, 1990), had to smear himself with brown polish and practice his Indian accent to play the role of Mowgli (of Rudyard Kipling's *The Jungle Book*) for his London audiences. The analogy between Karim and the postcolonial scholar is drawn from Leela Gandhi, *Postcolonial Theory: A Critical Introduction* (New Delhi: Oxford University Press, 1998), 127.

236. Spivak, *The Postcolonial Critic*, 8.

237. Jimmie Durham, "Belief in Europe," in *Unpacking Europe: Towards a Critical Reading*, edited by Salah Hassan and Iftikhar Dadi (Rotterdam: NAi Publishers, 2002), 290–93, at p. 291.

238. For instance, a scholar such as Wen Fong, whom Elkins singles out elsewhere as somehow Confucian in his approach to art, certainly scoffs at this idea himself: he was trained by Kurt Weitzmann (among others at Princeton), and if one reads his earlier theoretical pieces carefully, he was fully informed by and cites such Viennese scholars as Riegl and Hans Sedlmayr.

239. See Wolfgang Kemp, "Die Idee der Weltkunst in East Anglia," *Merkur* (2005): 1.
240. Karlheinz Stierle, *Ästhetische Rationalität: Kunstwerk und Werkbegriff* (Munich: Fink, 1997).
241. See Michael Brötje, *Der Spiegel der Kunst: Zur Grundlegung der existential-hermeneutischen Kunstwissenschaft* (Stuttgart: Urachhaus, 1990).
242. Wojciech Suchocki, *W miejscu sumienia* (1996).
243. *Amores Perros* [Love's a Bitch], directed by Alejandro Gonsalez Inarritu, Mexico, 2000.
244. Caryl Phillips, *A New World Order: Selected Essays* (London: Random House, 2002).
245. Paul Auster, *The Red Notebook: True Stories* (New York: New Directions Books, 2002).

5

Afterword

Globalizing Art History

Shelly Errington

The question posed by the seminar and book's title itself is global, sprawling and boundless, not just for its scope but for its ambiguity.[1] Does it ask if art history is globally practiced, or that its theory is relevant for all times and climes on this planet? Is art history the name for the writings of people with a certain training in universities done in different material and institutional circumstances, whether in Ghana or Denmark; or is it a set of emplotments and rhetorical moves developed in the nineteenth century (periodizing, classifying, and so on); or is it a grand Eurocentric narrative currently being asked to show global relevance for all past and future arts? Are all these elements interconnected, so that the definition of any implicates the definition of all? Or should we count as "art history" only the high theory and deep analysis of respected and university-trained art historians, ignoring the art-writing and art-history speak by dealers, curators, and educational sites of public culture?

Then too, for art history, one must have art. Is that category as unproblematic as some art historians, even some assessors of the Art Seminar, think? But so many things count as art these days, one wonders whether a single word, and, especially, the hierarchies and narratives implied by the concept since the end of the eighteenth century — should be applied to them all and incorporated into a global art history narrative.

On top of that, there's the use of the word "global" rather than, say, "worldwide" in the title. It makes the topic seem fraught with political and timely significance, evoking as it does globalization, the hegemony of Europe and the United States, colonialism and imperialistic capitalism, a grand narrative purporting to reveal the shape of history itself, time–space continuum collapses (that's Walter Benjamin and David Harvey I'm alluding to, the mechanical/digital replication of pictures and the Internet), the spread by fiat of a certain economic organization of the production and circulation of goods, enforced not by the IMF and the World Bank but by the "disciplining" of art historians ... but I am going off the deep end, a result of immersing myself for several weeks with the myriad writings — impassioned, thoughtful, comprehensive, contentious, and quite different — offered by the seminar participants and the assessors.

As the writer of an Afterword, I am in the enviable position of reflecting upon these issues and learning from these authors. As a cultural anthropologist, I am committed to being secular and ethnographic. By "secular," I mean that I do not necessarily share the enabling assumptions of the discipline of art history. As an analogy, historians and anthropologists only began making some sense of "religion" when they ceased to judge whether other religions were based on the True God, or not. By "ethnographic," I mean the effort to look at "art history" as an alien would, outside the enabling assumptions its practitioners generally must make in order to be counted as members in good standing of the community. I hope, therefore, that the deeply thoughtful and committed practitioners of art history reading this will bear with me as I think through these issues as a secular alien might.

Three Issues

To provoke conversation at the Art Seminar, James Elkins lays out in his initial essay the most straightforward version of the question this seminar addressed: Can [Western] art history, he asks, "become a discipline that keeps a recognizable shape wherever it is practiced[?] [Are its] methods, concepts and purposes suitable for art outside of Europe and North America? … if not, are there alternatives that are compatible with existing modes of art history?" He mentions "formal analysis, periodization, and iconography" as among the basics of Western art history.

This formulation raises three issues for me: narrative (*which* art history narrative?); art (what counts as art?); and tautology (if it is global, is art history tautologous in its definitions of what counts as art history and as art?).

First, narrative. "Western art history" as a narrative and an approach has changed a great deal over a period of a little more than two centuries: from the formal analysis of particular works of the late nineteenth century, to the social art history of individual works and schools of the late twentieth century, to the highly abstract and theoretical interrogation of the basic premises of the discipline of the late twentieth and early twenty-first century. All are legitimately called part of "the discipline of art history." Which of these defines the "recognizable shape" and practice of "the" discipline that can/should/has been made global?

Second, what counts as art. I also wonder what was meant by "art outside of Europe and North America." Does James Elkins mean Chinese art? Perhaps, because several art historians of Chinese art were invited. Does he mean easel art and sculpture — what I call "art by intention"[2] — made outside of Europe and North America, in places as far away as Ghana, Argentina, and Macao? Perhaps, since respondents were invited from those places. Yet it is unclear what the problem would be in using art historical methods — however defined — to analyze Thai paintings, or the paintings made in, say, Australia or Hong Kong, by artists consciously influenced by Western art, or working in Western-derived media (e.g., oil or acrylic on canvas or paper).

An issue does arise in my mind, however, when it comes to what I call "art by appropriation," artifacts that have been designated "art" by museums, markets, or scholars, but whose premises and ability to signify meaning have little or nothing to do with the kinds of artifacts that "the" discipline of art history was invented to analyze. I am thinking here of ritual objects found at archaeological sites and what is sometimes called "tribal art" or "art of Africa, Oceania, and the Americas." Because the conviction is widespread among art historians that art is made by all cultures, I would think that those sorts of artifacts would be among what counts as "art" and would have to be included in the subject-matter of a global art history.

And speaking of what should count as "art," I would like to add a third type of art, which I want to call "art by elevation." At this point in history, artifacts formerly considered "crafts" are being elevated by museums, galleries, and the market to the status of "art," and reputable art historians as well as art historically trained critics do artwriting about them.

And what of "visual culture"? Does Elkins want to know whether "art history" and its methods will accommodate all of these "arts," as well as Chinese scrolls, as well as easel art from all over the world?

Third, the matter of tautology, or its close cousin, the self-fulfilling prophecy. Craig Clunas tells us that art and archaeology at SOAS is "a test bed for the issue discussed here of whether different content *necessarily* equals a different art history, and I would have to say that in our case it most certainly at present does not. The names on our syllabus might be unfamiliar, but nothing else about it would be." If "globalizing" a recognizable form of art history means simply adding more and more content to the category "art," the supposed universality of art becomes a self-fulfilling prophecy, not a discovery.

I'm reminded of the language notebook of a priest I met in 1968 in coastal Papua New Guinea, where Austronesian languages, whose verbs are not conjugated, are spoken. On page after page after page in his home-made language-learning notebook the priest had written, in tidy groups of six identical words, three to a column, all the "verbs" of the local language. I found it hilarious, although I was tactful enough not to say so. His notebook was obviously modeled after conjugations of the Latin verbs he had learned. Is the paradigm of verbal conjugation globalizable? The answer is obviously "yes."

Some of the world's most extraordinary artifacts — finely crafted, ritually dense, aesthetically pleasing — *can* be "conjugated" within the narrative of Normal Art History, but it may not be the most profound way to understand them. I'm not (figuratively) challenging Chomsky's universals of language and mind here (or for that matter challenging the universality of art): I'm saying that if you are learning an Austronesian language, it is more helpful get a grip on the basic idea of focus, roots, and aspect than to begin with verbs, adjectives and adverbs, declensions and conjugations — categories of speech that are useful if you are learning German, but not helpful for, say, Tagalog. Tagalog is a different world.

I will take these three issues in order.

Art History: the Narrative

"What is 'art history'?" asks the alien from the planet of cultural anthropology. After some fieldwork in texts and conversation, she finds out: Art history is a narrative. Like all narratives worth investigating, it has a material existence: practitioners, critics, and factions; support systems, direct and at a distance, in the forms of institutions, markets, libraries, collections, and collectors. These material conditions must be investigated ethnographically for a complete understanding of how the narrative exists in the world, but let's begin with the narrative.

Art history is inevitably linear because it is a form of history (I'm talking about the form of narrative called "history," not to not be confused with events occurring within the medium of duration). That is not a bad thing. Of course, imagining the past as events unfolding along a line of time is not the only way to construe the past. Some people (in anthropology, the classic examples come from African lineage systems) keep track of the past through genealogies. Other societies might give the past a shape using *topoi* (literally), locations that act as memory nodes and prompt narratives about events that occurred there — one thinks of the Ilongot of the Philippines, and also of the Bosavi of Papua New Guinea, who map their worlds and the past through memories of significant events at particular places; or the Australian Aborigines, who imagine the above-ground past as "tracks" that the ancestors traversed before they went into holes in the ground. Javanese stories, it has been argued, do not imagine "history" (an open-ended line of events) at all but rather a dynamic equilibrium that can be pushed off balance and then put back in order again.[3]

Although linear narrative is not the only way to construe the past, it is the way that Europeans orient themselves in the medium of duration. Linear "time," in its modern form itself a nineteenth-century construct for organizing the narratives of *history* or *histories*, will be persuasive to those educated in the West. And that is not a bad thing, either. All art historians make use of — situate their explications — within time, even if they deal with only one piece of work.

Many art history textbooks go beyond merely linear time to posit that history shows progress in some sense. They make use of large master narratives invented in Europe in the nineteenth century, which posited stages of evolution with or without an engine to move societies or items from one stage to another, through which it was assumed all societies or items would pass. These stories culminate in Europe as the highest form of civilization, having the most advanced technology, economy and political form. Of course, that was the standard way to write not just art history but history itself until the late twentieth century.

It is perpetually criticized. I first understood the issues as an undergraduate when I read Ernest Gellner's *Thought and Change* (1964), which devastated the notion, I thought. But this dragon so deeply organizes Euro-American thought that it keeps coming back and must perpetually be re-slain — the latest but probably not the last widely read exposé of the progressivist assumptions in European historical narratives is Chakarabarty's *Provincializing Europe* (2000).[4]

In any case, the idea that linear time (which I believe is a neutral and harmless, and in some cases helpful, notion) is going somewhere (which is a very pernicious illusion) is still embedded in many narratives about the past in popular culture. It's all over Disneyland and Disney World, not surprisingly, because it was popularized in world's fairs, on which Disneyland is based. And about twenty years ago in Chicago I saw an exhibit at the Museum of Science and Industry (itself a world's fair leftover) on "money": it began with shell money of the Pacific Islands, moved through coins (the Romans and whatnot), paper money, and ended up with ATM cards. Aside from the fact that shell money in the Pacific was not really used like money — still, even if it were, it has nothing to do with coins or ATM cards. It was not an "early stage," because it has no historical connection to the rest of the story. This kind of thinking was extremely pervasive a century ago, and until the very late twentieth century a diluted version of it continued to be used in "educational" magazines and in public museum and TV displays such as "Stone Age Tribes meet the Modern World" or "Vanishing Primitive Man."

You may laugh. We moderns, you may say, especially we post-moderns, know better than that. And we do. But it wasn't always so funny, connected as it was with the shaping of the past and the construction of knowledge in colonial empires, and currently in neoliberal ones. Its traces continue to shape the discourse on art. Maria de Los Ángeles Taberna and Humberto Valdivieso, for instance, mention its application to the Maya. If it were simply names, one could discount its importance; but those names imply repressed epistemologies as well as emplotments. Here's an example: Maori art was exhibited at the Metropolitan Museum in New York in the early 1980s. In the exhibit I saw some wood — hair combs as I recall — that were carved with curvilinear decorations, and others of the same sort that were carved with more geometric shapes. The museum label explained that, although their temporal sequence is not scientifically known, it is assumed that the geometrical ones were earlier, the curvilinear ones, later. Is that the passage from Greek Archaic art into Classical Greek art, or what? I presume so: in the exhibit, Maori art was periodized into pre-Classical, Classical, and Modern, and as I recall it, the contemporary began in the early nineteenth century when the British began to take over New Zealand. (After the takeover, Maori art was in decline, of course, because that was the preferred narrative about tribal arts until very late in the twentieth century.) So, you may laugh when you see this narrative at Disneyland, but which art historian can doubt that this notion has been deeply influential in speculative periodizations of art whose chronology is unknown?

A few years ago I surveyed the narratives in multiple editions of several textbooks of the *History of Art* throughout the twentieth century (Gardner, Pijoán, Gombrich, Janson, Honour, and Fleming) to understand where they placed "primitive art," which I was writing on at the time, and whose institutional and scholarly standing changed throughout the century.[5] I found nothing that will surprise, but several things of interest to the ethnographer trying to understand the narrative form *art history*.

First, the most striking feature is the essentialist linear unfolding of the story through a homogeneous medium of time: these texts are never, to my recollection, about cross-influences, mutual constructions, the invention or emergence of categories of art or craft or their statuses, or the material conditions of artists' or other people's encounters with art or arts, or about the trained sensibilities and assumptions that audiences brought to viewing or using works of art — no "ways of seeing" or "period eye" interrupt the forward march through time. And of course there is the periodization, which seems to be very important in the conceptualization of time, which is imagined as basically linear within periods but episodic between them — there is a jump linking periods. Another equally significant feature is the bland and unremarked belief that we can identify what counts as art in any place or time, and that, using the tools of art history, we can understand it adequately. The enabling assumption is that those items that are authorized as art always were art and always will be, that great painters and paintings influence other great painters and paintings (and if they don't, they are a dead end we can forget), and that some are better than others.

Another point hard to miss by one who reads even superficially in art history is that the center and the weight of the discipline's attention is the Greeks and the Renaissance, and that the great achievement of the West is the transition to virtual space, to optical illusionism (to use David Summers's language).[6]

Do these textbooks represent professional art history? At one level, of course not, and some Art Seminar participants believed the seminar should ignore textbooks; others in the seminar believed textbooks are important because they shape public perception of art. Are most people, after all, who go to a blockbuster show and like the way Impressionism looks, going to learn more about it by picking up T.J. Clark? That's doubtful. They will have been forced to read a textbook in college, or they will have looked at a TV program in which someone, preferably with an English accent (or Australian, in a pinch), introduces you to some grand narrative. (This issue was discussed in the roundtable — if we are dealing with grand narratives, we should study TV as well as textbooks, it was said; but it is my impression that they are roughly equivalent in structure and sensibility. That said, it seems that the popularity of sweeping TV narratives may be especially pervasive in the United States, judging from the reports from even European places like Denmark and Ireland, never mind those outside Europe and North America.)

In 2002 James Elkins published a book in which he surveyed the shapes of time and rhetorical strategies of a number of art history textbooks in Europe and elsewhere.[7] These strategies, it turns out, inform or form those of what he calls "normal art history," also called "conservative," "conventional," or "positivist" art history. According to Elkins, this normal art history (henceforth NAH) has a number of well-known rhetorical moves (such as periodization, categorization, and others) and its content "is concerned principally with documentation, archival evidence, patronage, conservation, and iconography." The bulk of the profession (whose bulk itself is in Europe and the United States) studies art (Western art, overwhelmingly painting, sculpture, and architecture) and the "canon" of artists. And he claims that the "plots" of art history, regardless of content, are rather few.

For all I know, maybe NAH is not to be despised. For all I know, NAH may do the basic work of attribution, periodization, influences, and so forth, which may be the necessary preliminary steps before an art historian can write more deeply and insightfully about an artwork or period. Perhaps it is no accident that Baxandall, Crow, Clark, Nochlin, and other prominent art historians whose writings are of wide interest work on Western art, which has long been periodized and categorized by NAH.

What I have against NAH it is that these plots, categories, and rhetorical moves are as predictable as they are pervasive. I seldom read this kind of art history because I find it boring, particularly when applied to art I am certain *could* be strange and unfamiliar. When I pick up an art history book about the arts of the Oogaboogi or about the ancient civilization of Karunggangan and find that the table of contents is divided into Painting, Sculpture, Architecture, and Decorative Arts, not to mention Early Classic and Late Classic, I sigh and put it down. Barbara

Stafford suggests "that no fundamentally new information is being brought into the field. We spin old concepts, old theories, old methods around and around." If so, it is probably NAH she is talking about. If these crypto-Platonic categories were *true*, it would be one thing. But even if art-making (in some sense) is universal, painting and sculpture are not.

In my view, the rhetorical moves of normal art history are worth acknowledging, as is the link between the grand master narrative and imperialism — even if no readers of this tome practice or espouse either one — partly because the enabling assumptions of both are more pervasive, and more repressed, than one might initially imagine — and therefore relevant to whether art history can be/should be/is globalizable in any but a trivial and tautologous sense.

In short, there is nothing wrong with linear time, or with situating artworks in time or in a "period" of history, and there may be nothing wrong with NAH when it is applied to its appropriate objects — particularly if NAH is a precondition for other kinds of art history, and if it is applied to the categories of art for which it was invented.

A few assessors and participants, however, seemed to imply that the narrative(s) of art history themselves are inevitably Eurocentric and falsely universalistic. In any case, "normal art history" is extremely pervasive and is historically if perhaps not necessarily (I don't know this, but Elkins seems to suspect it is) based ultimately on the grand Eurocentric narrative of the unfolding of the world's art that elicited from assessors the gamut from off-hand acknowledgments to passionate attacks.

The Eurocentrism and Imperialism of the Master Narrative

As a nation-state with a centralized and homogeneous elementary-school curriculum, the French as a colonial power apparently used the same textbooks throughout the colonies. Thus little Berber, Senegalese, Malagasy, or Tahitian children were obliged to learn and recite French history, beginning with "*Nôs ancêtres, les Gaulois* ..."[8] Not until the mid-twentieth century, when colonies in Africa and Asia threw off their colonial rulers and became nation-states themselves, did the former colonies begin writing their own (nationalist) histories. In other words, it was not only art history's master narrative that was Eurocentric around 1960: the writing of *history* itself was Eurocentric. Accounts about the past produced in the colonies, whether those accounts were oral or written, were dismissed as "myth," rather than taken seriously as alternative ways of conceptualizing the shape of the past.[9]

Is the grand textbook version of art history, the Eurocentric and implicitly progressivist one, globalizable? This seminar's conversation began with the material practices of the teaching of art history, and quickly moved to the issue of textbooks used (or not used) in Latin America, Africa, Eastern Europe, or Denmark. We discovered that, in some places, there is no tradition of using textbooks structured as grand narratives, and some assessors speculated that that is because those countries had not been imperial powers. In other areas, the material conditions do not support the use of European textbooks — there may be issues of translation, or the poverty of the students, or the lack of introductory courses. But, most important, students are not interested in that narrative. And why should they be? Having a South African college student read Janson would be like obliging her to learn and recite a narrative beginning "*I nostri antenati, i fiorentini* ..."

Consequently, many of the participants and assessors do not use textbooks in their teaching. Instead, they write and teach about individual artists, or the emergence of national traditions of art, or about visual culture or about single pieces of art. They can ignore the grand Eurocentric narrative, and they have found productive and intellectually fruitful ways of dealing with their choice.

If the master narrative can be ignored or played with or read against, why does this topic inspire such firmly expressed and even outraged opinions? What was the link between a Eurocentric, periodized, art historical master narrative that places the Greeks and the Renaissance as the peak of human artistic endeavor, and the colonial enterprise — and why does such a master narrative still plague us? I will summarize in a few paragraphs what we all know in order to set up the discussion of some less obvious points.

What Eric Hobsbawm called "the long nineteenth century" (1789–1914) was the period when both art history and the nation-state were invented in Europe, as well as the period when European colonial expansion was accomplished. The intertwined history of these three developments could be written as a single book, although to my knowledge it has not been done explicitly. (We have plenty of scholarship on pieces of it.)

Emerging European nation-states depended on their colonies not just economically but imaginatively, coming to define themselves artistically, photographically, architecturally, and in innumerable other ways in contrast to their colonies in a set of binaries all too familiar — the civilized versus the savage, the agent of history versus the passive recipients of history, the emblems of progress versus the emblems of backwardness and decadence.

An element in Europe's self-assumed superitority to its colonies lay in its privileged relationship to the Greeks and Romans, whose culture and art were evoked at every turn.

Art historians know, far better than I, the place of the Renaissance canon in the development of their discipline. In fact, it would be amusing to talk about the art historical long nineteenth century, book-ended not by the French Revolution and World War I but with Winckelmann's *History of the Art of Antiquity* (1764) and the Armory Show (1913) — why not? Close to the beginning of this era, high art's proper categories were named — the *belles artes* of painting, sculpture, and architecture; artifacts were sorted into categories ranging from high (useless and suitable only for contemplation, thus ends in themselves) to low (useful crafts); and the basis for categorization shifted away from a variety of *technes* — which previously had made these arts incomparable — to the eye of the beholder who had taste, who could compare.[10] During this period, "the antique ideal then stood unquestionably as the highest model of art" and, of course, of ideal human beauty.[11] During the long nineteenth century, European education emphasized the Classics, with Greek and Latin the languages *de rigueur.* Greek and Roman models and Classic architecture figured prominently in the teaching of art in academies. (And of course imperial powers, from the British Empire to the Third Reich, liked to invent ceremonies and parades featuring officials dressed up in Roman cloaks and helmets.) The dichotomy between civilized and savage, with the civilized imagined as a Greco-Roman ideal of art, beauty, architecture, and imperial power, had to be narrativized in a way that was self-justifying for Europeans at home, particularly in the second half of the long nineteenth century — for consumption by an emerging and increasingly urban "public" that was becoming literate, gaining the vote, and which consumed newspapers and photographs, as well as for the self-regard of colonial administrators and their growing bureaucracies abroad.

A category and image of beauty, as any semiotician knows, immediately produces its anti-image. The living image of anti-beauty was found empirically in the regions to be colonized, and she was brought to Europe as an exhibit. Thus the superiority of the Greek ideal was demonstrated in its anti-Venus: the dark, short, wide African body of Sara Baartman, brought to Europe in 1810 only twenty years after the Dutch moved into South Africa, and put on display as the "Hottentot Venus."[12] Without the ideal of Venus, there would have been no anti-Venus, no "Hottentot Venus" as a visual emblem reminding the Europeans of the "ugliness" and "strangeness" of the peoples they were on the cusp of colonizing.[13]

At first glance it would seem that European art — especially framed paintings, iconically representational, on a flat surface using marks that through visual conventions were readable as virtual space — was the standard against which all other art was judged during the long nineteenth century. But it was deeper than that: what else *was* art in European eyes — what else other than optically naturalistic easel painting and sculpture, and the architecture produced in Europe, or, if produced in the colonies and other out-of-the-way places, the same thing made there but conforming to European schemata?

In the nineteenth century, not very much. In the twentieth century, more and more. In the twenty-first century, we are heading toward including everything handmade — ancient and modern. All this has implications for a globalizing art history.

A Satellite View (The Details Are Too Far Away, But You Can See the Continents) of "Art" in the Nineteenth and Twentieth Centuries

Many objects poured into European and North American seats of commerce and government during the nineteenth century, especially in the second half, as a result of imperial conquests combined with the new public, state-sponsored places to house artifacts.[14] A few found homes in fine arts museums, but many more in natural history museums and world's fairs, all of which served not only as repositories but also as classifiers and frames for narratives about the artifacts. Most did not conform in any way to the Renaissance canon, hence did not make the cut as high art, but were categorized as antiquities, curios, decorative and utilitarian arts, or material culture.

Where there is art, as semioticians know, a category of anti-art or primitive art must be generated. Those two poles can then generate the range of everything between them — easy, as a hierarchy from beautiful and useless to ugly and utilitarian was already in place.[15] It's my understanding that at some point in art history writing, the very early Renaissance painters were considered "primitive" because they had not yet fully rationalized perspective as a visual organization of the picture plane. In the second half of the nineteenth century, Japanese art filled the conceptual category of "primitive art" — *primitive* because of its incompletely rationalized perspective (as I learned by reading William Rubin), *art* because it influenced the Impressionists.[16]

How did art history and the training of art and artists in a Western mode and with or in relation to Western categories develop in the nineteenth century, in the Meiji Restoration in Japan, say, or in the colonies of Africa and Asia, or in Latin America? Each area is historically unique, and participants and assessors (some of whom hint at these developments) can fill in these stories for themselves.

However complex the mutual constructions of artistic modernity might have in fact been in the contact zones between European and non-European in the nineteenth century, from the point of view of nineteenth-century European public narratives, the influence of European art was one-way: Europeans possessed Art, whereas others only aspired to it. Also not in doubt is that the narrative of art that situates optical naturalism as the peak of human artistic achievement worked well in the self-justifying story of the civilizing mission of Europe that needed to be told.

To return to Europe, the hierarchies of artifacts ranging from high art to primitive art, decorative art, and nonart (crafts, utilitarian objects) were reified, literally, by their institutionalization and framing in temples and sites of culture — high and low — museums and world's fairs. As a result, at the dawn of the twentieth century, Europeans and Euro-Americans already had set in place a body of received knowledge concerning hierarchies and classes of objects, as well as powerful narratives about how to judge, rate, and think about them.

Thus it was a radical move when *l'art nègre* was "discovered" in Paris and exhibited with modern art at the Armory Show, events that kicked off the art history project of the twentieth century, which as I read it, was to discover, appreciate, institutionalize, valorize, and authorize all sorts of artifacts as "art," worthy of the name — a complex tale. Newly cosmopolitan in the 1920s, American art historians looked beyond merely national and

European arts to other civilizations and cultures, including the "primitive" and American folk art, among many others. The first edition of Gardner was 1926 — a good beginning for that project, because her warm appreciation of non-Western art-making prompted her to include it in her grand narrative. Art historians who follow the social histories of the arts' "discoveries" and the rises and falls of the market, or who specialize in some non-easel art from outside Europe, or from Europe before the Renaissance or after around 1900 (why not 1913?), will be acquainted with some of the struggles that curators and dealers and art historians went through to validate exotic artifacts and bring them into the great narrative of the unfolding of universal art.

My guess is that these struggles during the first half of the twentieth century to valorize "arts" from all over the world, so important a feature of the market, collecting, and museum and gallery exhibits in the metropoles, were markedly less intense in the colonies and other places peripheral to the metropoles. My guess is that in many places subject to or highly influenced by European colonial rule, the Renaissance canon and optically naturalistic art continued as the most valued standard. In the first half of the twentieth century, local artists from the colonies, some of them tribal, were trained to paint and draw "realistically" and use high art media. Other artists of the colonies and peripheries, especially those of the Europeanized elites, traveled to the metropoles and studied art and went back to the colonies and created regional schools and styles, based on European art's media, conventions, and standards. From the point of view of the metropoles, these styles and artists were presumably considered at best of mainly local interest — perhaps worthy in their way, but a dead end in the great unfolding universal story of art. At worst, they were probably considered poor imitations or dismissed as skillful but derivative.

The works and styles of artists from the colonies and peripheries, created in the nineteenth and first half of the twentieth century, began changing in status at mid-century, when the colonies became independent nation-states. Those new nation-states began not only writing their own histories[17] but creating their own national museums of fine art and adopting flags, monuments to the revolution, airlines, and other accoutrements of a proper nation-state. Currently, during the very late twentieth century and the early twenty-first century, art historians, including the participants and assessors of this seminar, are rereading such events. They do not see their national traditions as merely the passive recipients of Western art, nor do they believe that European art developed of its own accord, unchanged and uninfluenced by movements and artifacts and styles from outside Europe and North America — although that is the story that continued to be told until the late twentieth century, and, so far as I can tell, often continues to be told now.[18]

Back to the metropoles during the twentieth century, however: optical naturalism, while far from abandoned by conventional and popular arts, was rejected by the avant-garde, while at the same time all sorts of artifacts, of many shapes and media and from many lands, attained acceptance as forms of art — some minor, some not mainstream, but nonetheless with the material supports that would turn them into the subject matter to which NAH can be plausibly applied: collectors, museum shows, provenances, periods, and even the appearance of individual genius touched with transcendence. By the end of the century, formerly utilitarian folk objects could be exhibited in major museums (as in the Abby Aldrich Rockefeller collection of American folk art), the Metropolitan had its wing of Primitive Art (now called AOA Art), and Outsider Art had its galleries and collectors and glossy coffee-table catalogs. By the early twenty-first century, it seems that everything handmade has turned into art.

When I say "everything has turned into art," I distinguish three types of art: by intention, by appropriation, and by elevation. Also, I am not suggesting that the hierarchies have changed radically. Some art is more equal than others, and it always will be. Nonetheless, everything is becoming art (or at least a collectible).

Everything Is Becoming Art (Or At Least a Collectible), and There Is More and More of It

For art history we must have art. A conviction pervades the discipline of art history that all humans everywhere have produced art. For some art historians, this category is unproblematic. The conviction no doubt springs from several sources. One is the humanistic tradition that we honor other humans' artifacts by calling them "art." The related Hegel-influenced corollary is that all humans are touched by the divine and capable of transcendence. Add to that, in the late twentieth and early twenty-first century, political correctness and multicultural leanings, plus the market forces of a highly commercialized art world, and it becomes not-politically-correct to dispute it.

In my view, the issue hinges not on the *word* art but on the narratives and institutions that support it and the categories and characteristics that the word names in the minds of practitioners.

The process that turns non-art objects into art has been going on for some time. The trajectory begins with art-appreciation language and art-writing, sales in a gallery or on the Internet, and eventually placement in a museum. Here is how it works:

1. Western artifacts formerly classified as collectibles, antiquities, folk, or decorative arts are exhibited in a museum, hung and lit so as to make us see them newly and appreciatively, and art-writing is produced by serious art critics in glossy museum catalogs claiming these artifacts are worthy of the name of art. This sort of thing happens all the time, but to me a particularly striking example of it was in 1990, when the DeYoung museum in San Francisco exhibited Amish quilts owned by a private collector in a show paid and curated by people he chose, with an expensive ($100)

catalog written by Robert Hughes, and with celebratory museum labels taken from quotes in the catalog.

You may think this is a good thing: the museum gets a heavily subsidized temporary exhibit, the collector's collection is increased in value, the art historian is paid handsomely, a beautiful book that makes money for the museum store is produced, the public comes to understand how much we should appreciate these stellar and underrated artifacts. Or, you may think it is a bad thing: the collusion among museum, art historian, collector, curator, and market may not conform to your idea of how artifacts with transcendent qualities enter the story of art. But whether you think it a good thing or a bad thing, you cannot evade knowing that it happens. A lot.

2. More art is being made in places that did not formerly produce it. All over the world during the twentieth century and before, colonized and indigenous people were taught to make marks on quadrilateral flat surfaces that can circulate (i.e., not frescoes) and could iconically represent some three-dimensional things outside the flat surface. These artifacts, often made for the market, were formerly known and dismissed as "souvenir art," "tourist art," or "airport art." Nelson Graburn's collection *Ethnic and Tourist Arts* initiated a trend in anthropology to take made-for-the-market artifacts as topics for serious study. (It also coined or at least popularized the term "Fourth World," as a way to refer to marginalized minorities within the nation-state, whether the nation-state were itself "First," "Second," or "Third" World.)[19]

   Since then, and probably bolstered by the trend in anthropology to study commodities and commoditization, many worthwhile studies have been published on the production and marketing of high arts from the Third and Fourth World — arts that refer to the native, the local, and the indigenous, even if they enter global markets. In my circles, some of the best known are Walter Spies in the 1930s teaching the Balinese to use pen and ink and wash and to depict village scenes; the teaching of Dorothy Dunn in the 1930s and the "Santa Fe School" of Southwest Native American painting; and most recently, the spectacular entrance into the art world's eyes in 1989 at the Asia Society in New York of Australian Aboriginal art, in which designs formerly done on bark or bodies or sand or *churringas* are done in acrylic paints on canvas.[20] In the realm of sculpture, think of Shona sculpture from Zimbabwe ("Spirits in Stone") or the new masks of the Northwest Coast of North America. These artifacts indisputably *are* art: they are art by intention and were produced in the media of high European art, and they are having great success.

You may think this is a good thing: artists of whatever creed and nationality make art and a living, as do dealers and NAHistorians, and the public comes to appreciate the vast variety and beauty of different art traditions. You may think it is a bad thing: these artifacts may not seem "authentic" to you; or you may bemoan the erosion and decline of older forms of *technē*; or they may seem too minor for your attention, too derivative or regional or ethnic. But whether you think it a good thing or a bad thing, you cannot evade knowing it is a real thing.

3. People around the world create an amazing array of new kinds of objects, neither "traditional" nor derivative of Western forms and sensibilities, but using new *technes*, new iconography, and for new purposes. These objects are being photographed, analyzed, appreciated, and written up in catalogs, and NAH is being done on them. A book that can be seen as emblematic of this process is *Africa Explores* by Susan Vogel,[21] in which some of the striking

items are coffins in the shape of airplanes, cocoa-pods, and hens, among others.

You may think this is a good thing: it shows the eclectic and generous appreciation by art historians of the universal human creative art-making spirit. You may think this is a bad thing: this is "visual culture" and it is diluting the methods of art history, and, also, it isn't really Raphael. But you cannot deny that it is a real thing, that lots of new kinds of objects are being considered by art historians; they are being collected and analyzed and photographed and glossy catalogs are being produced.

4. The *technēs* formerly used to make utilitarian objects are being used to create high-end art pieces, even if they are not easel arts. In the United States, most "crafts" museums I visit display and sell very high-end, sometimes monumental, art pieces that have nothing to do with usefulness. Why are these things classed as "craft"? Because they are made in materials that are traditional craft materials, like fabrics or straw. No one wants to be a craftsman these days; they want to be artists, making unique things that are signed by the artist and collected by the wealthy, written about by scholars, photographed for glossy catalogs, and eventually, perhaps, enter art history textbooks.

In the Third and Fourth Worlds, parallel movements are occurring, for partly different reasons. I am currently working around Lake Pátzcuaro (state of Morelia, Mexico) to understand some of the effects of globalization on the production and marketing of folk art (*artesanías*). Utilitarian objects, formerly made locally and by hand, are either being made more mechanically (for example, copper pots are being made in molds rather than hammered) or are being replaced by factory-made items, some from China and beyond. Craftsmen who make hammered copper now make high-end bowls and vessels that count as sculpture, and they export to European galleries. Potters may make vases and bowls, skillfully painted with one-of-a-kind scenes, that sell in galleries in Puerto Vallarta, San Diego, and beyond. Makers of other sorts of crafts are caught up in the Purépecha cultural revival, and make very labor-intensive one-of-a-kind artifacts that sell for hundreds or thousands of dollars. Objects like these may be based on the techniques and materials of crafts, but they are art because they are useless — good only for contemplation and decoration (I'm taking a Kantian position here).

5. What I have called "High Primitive Art" (the sort of thing one finds in the Rockefeller Wing of the Metropolitan), controversial in the first decades of the twentieth century, had become an established, indeed mummified, category by the century's end. Consequently, when dams and roads are built, unearthing artifacts in the process, and when mounds covering pyramids are excavated to offer as new tourist attractions (events that occur as the nation-state, multinational corporations, and international tourism penetrate more broadly and more intensively into new terrain), new archaeological finds are being uncovered yearly. They are pronounced art almost as soon as they are unearthed.
6. Finally, masses of artifacts produced by hand for the market as souvenirs, functional items (placemats, glasses, frames for mirrors), wall hangings, jewelry, figurines, and anything else, are more and more being described as "art" or "artistic," and their makers as "artists" or at least as "artisans" (rather than craftsmen or souvenir-makers, say). (Check out, for instance, Novica.com, a commercial craft site done in association with National Geographic.)

You may think this is a good thing: we honor the human spirit by calling all beautifully crafted hand-made

> things "art," and you approve of people making a living so harmlessly, particularly given the fact that political violence and the Structural Adjustment Programs perpetrated on the world by the IMF and the World Bank in the 1980s and 1990s deprived many people of their former gainful employment. (Or, you may own stock in The Container Store or Stacks and Stacks.) You may think this is a bad thing: all this broadening of our appreciation flattens it, or confuses hierarchies by mislabeling. (Or, you may not look forward to visiting, years hence, the Fifty-Year Retrospective Exhibit of the Jane Beaufort Doe and John Kingston Doe Collection of Tsotchkes.) But you cannot deny it is a real thing.

To summarize the trend in arts by elevation, arts by appropriation, and new arts by intention: The rhetorically constructed figure of the craftsman is disappearing, and the figure of the artist — the one touched with genius — is replacing it. The rhetoric of art appreciation is being applied to everything that is even vaguely plausible as art, that is, hand-made or partially hand-made, and generally useless. Eventually replicas will be made for museum shops and T-shirts for exhibitions; the new objects will have their own catalogs and ephemera (which are likely themselves to become collectibles some day) and they will have become art. The rest of NAH will follow eventually, if the trajectory is not interrupted.

Is Art History Globalizable Because It Is a Self-Fulfilling Prophecy?

If the powerful discursive force of the universal category "art" in the marketplace causes the production of more and more art, and if so many sorts of artifacts are elevated or appropriated into the category art, and if the material support system of the narrative of art's universality (dealers, collectors, exhibition spaces, art-writing) continues unabated, then NAH is not likely to lack subject matter anytime soon. Thus the question for the seminar should not be "can (Normal) Art History be globalized?" because it obviously can. The question, rather, is whether Normal Art History is capable of recognizing something that would, as Clifford Geertz once put it, "embarrass the categories" and tell us something new.

I presume the term "normal art history" was intended to echo, many decades later, Thomas Kuhn's term "normal science" in *The Structure of Scientific Revolutions*,[22] so it may be worth looking there for a possible analogy.

Kuhn did not denigrate normal science or consider it pedestrian. He considered it the basis of science, which he very much respected. Kuhn believed that scientific breakthroughs or "revolutions" occurred when scientists, working diligently within the paradigms or frameworks of accepted scientific practices (normal science), noticed a pile-up of too many anomalous cases that could not be explained comfortably using the current paradigm. For a while, these anomalies could be accommodated within the normal science's paradigm in various ways or by adding extra formulas (you could call it the additive strategy), but at some point a scientist, deeply steeped in normal science, would think of quite a different way of accounting for the anomalous phenomena, and would construct a new theory, a new "paradigm" of explanation. The whole practice of science would recognize the new paradigm's superior explanatory power and would eventually undergo a "revolution" or "paradigm shift." (One of Kuhn's examples was the Copernican Revolution.) It was people practicing normal science who produce scientific knowledge and who were capable of understanding what *was* an anomaly. Without normal science, breakthroughs and revolutions could not occur.

The difference between Kuhn's vision of normal science and the practice of normal art history, however, is this: can there be a breakthrough, a revolution, a rethinking in "normal" art history? Normal science, at least the kind that Kuhn wrote about, could recognize anomaly. Normal art history sometimes seems as if it is specifically designed not to. NAH is a powerful and robust rhetoric that can quite easily incorporate the most alien objects and artifacts into its purview. If something made in an alien culture or deep in the past is flattish and has marks that can be read as resembling something, it becomes a form of Painting. If something made or worked upon (incised, painted, and so on) in an alien culture or from the deep past is freestanding and you can walk around it or put it on a coffee table, it becomes Sculpture. If something is big enough to walk through and sleep in, it becomes Architecture.

Objects that do not conform to the schema of art in NAH can be ignored as non-art, thus cannot embarrass the categories. (The categories, confident of both their universality and their political correctness, have no shame, cannot be embarrassed.)

What is that schema? I have dealt with this topic elsewhere, and I won't rehearse it here except to say that iconic content is very basic to the identification of an object as "art." This very deep presupposition, laid out in a famous story by Pliny, informs and in my view puts blinders on NAH.[23]

The art historian Carolyn Dean provides an interesting example from the study of Inca art and landscape. Inca figurines have long been considered a form of Inca "art," but outcroppings of rock, as important or perhaps more important to the Inca than the figurines, have only recently been taken seriously by art historians; and even so, most focus has been on the carved monoliths.[24]

Two assessors touched on the subject of the self-fulfilling prophecy of a universalist definition of art in constructing exhibitions. Shigemi Inaga, commenting on the exhibition *Le Japon des avant-gardes* at the Centre Georges Pompidou in 1986–87, points out that "By systematically eliminating every domain of artistic creation where no equivalent can be found in Western avant-garde, this huge exhibition helped the French public form a firm but tautological conviction: everything recognizable as partaking of the avant-garde in Japan is a Western imitation; and everything original in Japan does not fall into the category of avant-garde." Matthew

Rampley's example of an exhibit of Islamic art in Tehran is too complex to summarize here, but worth noting for this discussion.

The take-home point I want to make in using examples from these three authors is that it can be difficult to come to grips with real difference, for a variety of intellectual and institutional reasons.

Globalizing Art History

The question the Seminar and assessors were asked to consider was "How can art history be globalized while not losing its current recognizable shape?" Phrased like that, the question is ambiguous. If it means whether "normal art history" can be globalized, it would be a nonstarter. I think it can, just as my priest-acquaintance in Papua New Guinea could conjugate Austronesian verb-roots. And I think it will continue to be, because the material-support apparatus of this narrative form will continue to exist in the foreseeable future. Creating an art history that aspires to be worldwide or global in a nontrivial sense, however, requires something different from simply adding other nations' or traditions' arts to a story that unfolds within the abstract medium of unidirectional time from Lascaux to installation art. The additive strategy — what anthropologists call the "fill-a-gap" or "another country heard from" method — is not the answer.

The term "global" in the question probably does not help. Its virtue is to be provocative, which was good in the context of this seminar. But it tended to provoke hostility. Matthew Rampley says of a global art history, Who needs it? Who wants it? –even though, he wrote, the question is worth asking. Indeed, one could reasonably ask, Who besides The Teaching Company and the publishers of textbooks needs a global story? Nearly everyone in the roundtable identified it with the same old progressivist march through time culminating in the "modern," identified largely with Europe and North America, with the hegemony of European or North American models of art history (even if it is "new art history," maybe even published in *October*), with the structure of textbooks that virtually everyone despises and either doesn't use (or, very intelligently, uses to teach the lesson on the lesson), and with the hegemony of the English language in worldwide scholarship. The term "world" probably won't do, either, as there is something in art history called "world art" which, like "world music," evokes, in my mind at least, digital sampling from various traditions to put into a narrative or track created in the West.

I myself wonder further, if we did get a global or worldwide way of telling stories of art that was not reductionist in the same ways that NAH can be, why should we expect it to retain a recognizable shape compatible with the most conservative existing modes of art history? The cultural anthropology of today, for instance, in which we study and reflect upon our subject-positions, natter on about narrative, do multisited ethnography, study commodity-chains, and so forth, would not be recognizable to Radcliffe-Brown, but who cares? (Indeed, in the case of Radcliffe-Brown, in my opinion that is a good thing.)

The question posed to the seminar could also be whether the center of gravity of the discipline of art history can, or should, move away from NAH to live in the visual and communications environment of the present. Many participants and assessors have considered these issues, or something like them, and chose to write on them. Suppose one did want a way of conceptualizing art history's subject matter, scope, and narrative strategies in the early twenty-first century that would retain a certain recognizability as a discipline, an approach, a set of methods? Is such an art history possible? What might it look like? Several make the point that art history has changed a great deal already (see Hans Dam Christensen especially on this point), even if the empirically discovered center of gravity of art history may well be NAH. Many reflect on what a nontrivial "global" art history would require.

Hans Dam Christensen suggests abandoning an essentialist notion of what counts as art history and instead borrowing an idea based on "Wittgenstein's well-known game model, [for which it is] tempting to note that there need not necessarily be any essential commonality between all that is called 'art history.' Instead, and from various positions, one could speak of family resemblance."

A world or global art history would require translation in several senses. Frank Vigneron (a French voice from Hong Kong) and Suzana Milevska (from the Balkans) are particularly funny and ironical discussing dilemmas and paradoxes of translation.

The complexity of an art history that did justice to global connections and multiple translations is presented serio-comically in a delightful assessment by Vigneron — as a "prowling hypertextual edifice, useless and decidedly utopian," but I am not so sure. He was not aiming for a prowling hypertext, but Shigemi Imaga's complex, scholarly, humorous, and clear-headed comments on translation, narrratives, universalisms, and reciprocal influences stand as a model and warning of what an art history that really was global would have to cope with.

Many assessors have ideas about how to envision "art" and "art history" in a way that could be used nontrivially (that is, not as a tautologous or self-fulfilling prophecy) to understand arts made outside the usual subject matter. A nontrivial global art history would give up the hierarchy of fine arts, as Barbara Stafford suggests, and admit any sort of images.[25] Doing that would solve many of the problems of tautology I (and others quoted) have mentioned. That strategy would, of course, embrace "visual culture," which in the minds of some is the specter that haunts art history. It would also admit hybrid objects and not imagine that influence in either art objects or art history is or should be in only one direction. I see that as a good thing. Matthew Rampley briefly discusses indexicality rather than iconicity as a way objects can mean, borrowing from the work of the anthropologist Andrew Gell. David Summers, referred to throughout this seminar many times, takes a very different tack, suggesting "spatial arts" rather than visual arts should be the basic metaphor (or perhaps paradigm or model) of how art historians might orient themselves. Both Barbara Stafford and

Ladislav Kesner suggest absorbing information from cognitive sciences. Although I have my doubts about the relevance of cognitive science for what I want to know, at least, until it passes through the brain and hand of Barbara Stafford (whose work is always fascinating), I very much like the notion that art historians would focus not just on the object but on the trained sensibilities, within cultural or art-making traditions, that viewers and users bring to the objects — the "period eye," if you like. As Clifford Geertz wrote in his only article on art, "art and the ability to grasp it are made in the same shop."[26]

And suppose one did want a way of imagining the narratives of art history as worldwide but neither Eurocentric, essentializing nor reductionist? One would need an image, a metaphor, or a model of the kind of bigness or big-story-ness[27] that suggests expansiveness and circumstances of interconnections and of voice that is neither the voice-over of a BBC or PBS series on the unfolding of art, nor a point of view, subject-position, or location for storytelling that is like the "view from nowhere" in so many textbooks. I suggest that such an image of big-story-ness would probably look less like a line of time than like a web of connections.

Such a way of imagining the histories of arts (and the meanings, uses, productions, and materials of artifacts) is easier said than done, easier proposed than imagined. Nonetheless, other disciplines — history, literature, anthropology — came out of the same Eurocentric narrative that art history did, and have lived to tell the tale. Their journeys from 1960 have left them bloody, bowed, and blurred,[28] but recognizable, distinct enough to each claim a "method," or, *faut de mieux* and bottom line, to live in departments and grant Ph.D.s.

Historians, for instance, have been massively reimagining their discipline since the last quarter of the twentieth century. The *Journal of World History*'s first volume was published in 1990 — a date fraught with globalist associations. "Devoted to historical analysis from a global point of view," says its blurb on the Web, "the *Journal of World History* features a range of comparative and cross-cultural scholarship and encourages research on forces that work their influences across cultures and civilizations." Not putting Europe as the peak and central agent of the story of art does not mean the discipline of history is required to ignore itself. Contributors to this journal write on particular events and processes located in time (they are historians, after all), but no single voice or point of view or a single direction of history or influence is assumed *a priori*, and no single part of the world stands as the agent of history.

Except that the scope is worldwide rather than a single nation-state and of course is not focused on art, the sorts of articles that appear in the *Journal of World History* do not sound so different in spirit to me from the description Andrea Giunta gives of art history in Argentina. Art historians there, she writes, tends to concentrate on particular issues (rather than try to tell global narratives), on case studies such as "the function of history and landscape painting in the constitution of nation-states ... the function and power of images in relation to the public, the church, and the state ... the development of zones of contact; and the emergence of different regional maps." Accounts of dense interconnections among images (which "have the power to inaugurate and configure"), artifacts, nationalisms, media of representation, would be precisely the sort of thing that counts as global history in the *Journal of World History*. And, just as it is for historians, not putting Europe at the peak and central agent of the story of art does not mean the discipline of art history as practiced in Argentina is required to ignore itself. As Andrea Giunta, who firmly rejects general and universal art histories, wrote, it "seems useless to pretend that it is necessary for a history of art to be constructed outside the parameters of (Western) art history."

Another discipline that reinvented itself in the late twentieth century is comparative literature. "World literature" in university departments was once additive, and there was a tendency to proliferate programs of this or that ethnicity's or nation's literature on the model of an essentializing multiculturalism and identity politics. But that was then and this is now — we hope. Now, Suman Gupta, in this volume, suggests that various ideas from comp lit, such as those in David Damrosch's *What Is World Literature?* could be relevant to imagining what a "global" or "world" art history might look like.[29] Gupta writes that Damrosch "emphasizes the circulation of literature in formulating world literature; all texts cross and are received beyond their culture of origin. His analysis reflects on the relationship of circulation to national literatures, on the centrality of translation … and on the conditions of reading."

This sort of model, I think, provides a way of talking about, for instance, the translation of Wölfflin into Chinese — something that came up several times in the seminar and assessments — not as a "belated" event but as a text that arrived in a particular place at a particular time in particular intellectual and institutional circumstances and commodity or idea flows, and that will be read with or against what is already being read, there, by the Chinese scholars or students, with their own reading strategies and own agendas for the text. It would not assume that "we" know what the Chinese will make of it, or that they are "behind." For that matter, it could be art objects as well as texts that are understood thus.

Normal Art History and inexorably linear (albeit periodized) time may indeed be statistically the center of the discipline of art history; but I believe the intellectual center of the discipline may be at its margins — professionals deeply versed in and knowledgeable about the conventional, who push and pull it from within to new insights, perhaps using unusual subject matter. These practitioners may be considered excessively eclectic, or interesting but unsound, or to be writing something only marginally within the boundaries of art history proper, in spite of their unimpeachable training and deep knowledge. Their widely read excursions into unusual topics or their unconventional ways of construing an issue may be viewed as exceptions to their own more mainstream and therefore praised-as-serious writings. *Their* books are the ones I do not give a sigh about and put down, because they are making the familiar strange, or the strange even stranger, doing what the most exhilarating art historians can do with visible culture: revealing an unfamiliar way of seeing or signifying, or giving the reader a new way of construing a topic or imagining an artifact's meanings — providing an insight that opens the door to a world. That ability to recognize when received categories do not fit, an openness at, and to, the margins of art, at the same time deeply and imaginatively informed by historical particulars, could produce an art history I would hope would be extended around the globe — imagine a Baxandall writing on *Schemata and Experience in Eighteenth-Century Tibet: A Primer on Perceptual Styles and Thangkas*, or a Belting, writing on *Unlikeness and Presence: The Uncarved Holy Boulders of the Inca*…

Notes

1. Many thanks to James Elkins, whose lively and opinionated answers to my many questions about art history and art historians increased my pleasure in writing this piece immeasurably. Thanks to Larry Silver for conversation on related topics. Thanks to John Gillis for a historian's view of how to imagine global history. And thanks to my colleagues at U.C.S.C. for reading and commenting on an early draft: Carolyn Dean, Jennifer Gonzalez, and Donna Hunter of the History of Art and Visual Culture, and Carolyn Martin Shaw of Anthropology.
2. See Shelly Errington, *The Death of Authentic Primitive Art and Other Tales of Progress* (Berkeley: University of California Press, 1998).
3. How humans in various cultures have construed the past is a deeper and more complex topic than this paragraph seems to indicate. On genealogies, see E.E. Evans-Pritchard on "Nuer Time Reckoning," *Africa* 12 (1939): 189–216. On the landscape as nodes for memory, a topic that has gained ground in the last fifteen or twenty years, see Renato Rosaldo, *Ilongot Headhunting, 1883–1974: A Study in Society and History* (Stanford CA: Stanford University Press, 1980); see also an early and nicely crafted article by Edward L. Schieffelin, "Mediators as Metaphors: Moving a Man to Tears in Papua, New Guinea," in *The Imagination of Reality*, edited by A.L. Becker and Aram Yengoyan (Norwood NJ: Ablex Publishing Company, 1979), 127–37. Many works mention Australian Aborigines' "tracking" their ancestors' movements through the landscape in songs and stories; see Nancy Munn, "Totemic Designs and Group Continuity in

Walbiri Cosmology," in *Aborigines Now*, edited by Marie Reay (Sydney, Australia: Angus and Robertson, 1964). The notion of "time" or lack of it in Java and Bali has been a theme in Western scholarship at least since the 1930s. For a very interesting and clear read of it as expressed in Javanese *wayang kulit* see A.L. Becker, "Text-Building Epistemology and Aesthetics in Javanese Shadow Theater," in *The Imagination of Reality*, edited by A.L. Becker and Aram Yengoyan (Norwood NJ: Ablex Publishing Company, 1979), 211–43.

4. Ernest Gellner, *Thought and Change* (Chicago: University of Chicago Press, 1964) and Dipesh Chakrabarty, *Provincializing Europe: Postcolonial Thought and Historical Difference* (Princeton NJ: Princeton University Press, 2000).
5. See "Three Ways to Tell the History of (Primitive) Art," chapter 1 in *The Death of Authentic Primitive Art and Other Tales of Progress* (Berkeley: University of California Press, 1998).
6. David Summers, *The Judgment of Sense: Renaissance Naturalism and the Rise of Aesthestics* (Cambridge: Cambridge University Press, 1987).
7. James Elkins, *Stories of Art* (New York and London: Routledge, 2002). A yet more recent survey of surveys (digitally published January 25, 2006), which explores the style and sensibilities of the authors of a wide range of art history textbooks as well as the structure of the stories they tell, is Larry Silver and David A. Levine, "Quo Vadis, Hagia Sophia?: Art History's Survey Texts," College Art Association, www.caareviews.org.
8. Ernest Gellner, *Thought and Change* (Chicago: University of Chicago Press, 1964), 27 ff.
9. See Renato Rosaldo, *Ilongot Headhunting, 1883–1974: A Study in Society and History* (Stanford CA: Stanford University Press, 1980) and Shelly Errington, "Some Comments on Style in the Meaning of the Past," *Journal of Asian Studies* 38 no. 2 (1979): 231–44.
10. See Paul Oscar Kristeller, "The Modern System of the Arts," in *Renaissance Thought II* (New York: Harper and Row, 1965), 165–227. A much shorter account, which also speculates on the sociology of travel, markets, and grand estates that enabled the change in the status of arts and crafts between the early and late eighteenth century, is M.H. Abrams, "Art as Such: The Sociology of Modern Aesthetics," *Bulletin of the Academy of Arts and Sciences* 38 no. 3, 8–33. See also Phillip Fisher, "The Future's Past," *New Literary History* 6 no. 3 (1975): 587–606.
11. Alex Potts, *Flesh and the Ideal: Winckelmann and the Origins of Art History* (New Haven CT: Yale University Press, 1994), 13.
12. This sad story is well known. On the iconography of the images, see Sander Gilman's "The Hottentot and the Prostitute: Toward an Iconography of Female Sexuality," reprinted in Kymberly N. Pinder, *Race-ing Art History* (New York: Routledge, 2002).
13. This Greek ideal of beauty is still very much with us in popular culture; note the features of the winners of beauty pageants in, say, Malaysia, or of dark-skinned fashion models in Milan, or the phenomenon of cosmetic surgery to widen the eye by lessening the epicanthic fold in Japan, or the

American TV show *Extreme Makeover*, and you will see what I mean. It is not that plastic surgery can make you look like Venus, but looking more like Venus and less like someone, say, Melanesian or Dravidian or African, is the direction of the goal.

14. See Germain Bazin, *The Museum Age*, translated by Jane van Nuis Cahill (New York: Universe Books, 1967).
15. James Clifford's well-known article on this topic uses Greimas's semiotic square to make the point about art and culture categories generating their opposites; Frances Connelly reveals the long relation between the primitive or grotesque and "ornament" in European thinking concerning art. See James Clifford, "On Collecting Art and Culture," in *The Predicament of Culture: Twentieth-Century Ethnography, Literature, and Art* (Cambridge MA: Harvard University Press, 1988), 215–81, and Frances Connelly, *The Sleep of Reason: Primitivism in Modern Art and Aesthetics 1725–1907* (University Park: Pennsylvania State University Press, 1995).
16. William Rubin, "Modernist Primitivism: An Introduction," in *"Primitivism" in 20th Century Art,* edited by William Rubin (New York: Museum of Modern Art, 1984), 1–71.
17. On Indian historical writing in this context, whose general outlines can be extrapolated to other new nation states, see Gyan Prakash's "Writing Post-Orientalist Histories in the Third World: Perspectives from Indian Historiography," *Comparative Studies in Society and History* 32 no. 2 (1990): 383–408.
18. A refreshing exception, and one with many implicit lessons, is John Clark's *Modern Asian Art* (Honolulu: University of Hawai'i Press, 1998).
19. See *Ethnic and Tourist Arts: Cultural Expressions from the Fourth World,* edited by Nelson Graburn (Berkeley: University of California Press, 1976), especially Graburn's "Introduction: The Arts of the Fourth World."
20. On Balinese painting, see Hildred Geertz, *Images of Power: Balinese Paintings Made for Gregory Bateson and Margaret Mead* (Honolulu: University of Hawai'i Press, 1994). On Dorothy Dunn and the Santa Fe School, see Bruce Bernstein and W. Jackson Rushing, *Modern by Tradition: American Indian Painting in the Studio Style* (Santa Fe: Museum of New Mexico Press, 1995). On Australian Aboriginal art, see Fred R. Myers, *Painting Culture: The Making of an Aboriginal High Art* (Durham NC: Duke University Press, 2002).
21. *Africa Explores: Twentieth Century African Art,* edited by Susan Vogel, assisted by Ima Ebong (New York: Center for African Art, 1991).
22. Thomas Kuhn, *The Structure of Scientific Revolutions* (Chicago: University of Chicago Press 1962).
23. For years I have been struggling to pinpoint where the iconic presupposition came from in the study of art. At a conference a few years ago, an art historian mentioned over coffee Pliny's story of the origins of (Greek) art. I was stunned. The story has everything: art is flat, it signifies iconically, and it is not as real as the world (it is merely a shadow). Alfred North Whitehead famously said that Western philosophy is a footnote to Plato. It struck me that Plato's view of art, and art history's definition of art, is a footnote to Pliny's story. Since my conversation, several art historians

have assured me that the story is well known. Thanks to Hans Belting for generously sharing the story and reference, which is Plinius, *History of Nature* book 35.15 and 35.151, and referred to in Rosenblum, "The Origin of Painting," *Art Bulletin* 39 (1957): 279ff.

24. See Carolyn Dean, "The Trouble with (the term) Art," *Art Journal* (forthcoming, summer 2006).
25. In the history of European and American arts, I presume that what Stafford suggests here would promote the kinds of topics she herself deals with, and social histories of various stripes. For an appreciative account of hybrid arts that rejects the hierarchies of high and low, ritual versus commercial, see Ruth Phillips's *Trading Identities: The Souvenir in Native North American Art from the Northeast, 1700–1900* (Seattle: University of Washington Press, 1998).
26. Clifford Geertz, "Art as a Cultural System," in *Local Knowledge: Further Essays in Interpretive Anthropology* (New York: Basic Books, 1983).
27. I borrow this way of phrasing the issue from an unpublished paper by the anthropologist Anna Tsing called "Subcontracting et al."
28. Clifford Geertz, "Blurred Genres: The Refiguration of Social Thought," in Geertz, *Local Knowledge.*
29. David Damrosch, *What Is World Literature?* (Princeton NJ: Princeton University Press, 2003).

Notes on Contributors

Carol Archer teaches at the University of Macau. She recently completed a doctoral dissertation on paintings by Judy Watson, Cai Jin, and Marlene Dumas at the University of Hong Kong. Archer's mixed-media artworks have been exhibited in Australia, Japan, Italy, Hong Kong, and Macau. Her work may be found on the sites of Macau Art Net (www.macauart.net), Creative Macau (www.creativemacau.org.mo), and Imaginal Regions, a collaborative art/text project (www.imaginalregions.co.uk).

Leonard Bell is Associate Professor and Head of the Department of Art History at the University of Auckland. His research and writing focus primarily on cross-cultural interactions and representations in Australasia and the Pacific from the mid–18th century to the present, and on the works and careers of traveling, migrant, and refugee artists, photographers, architects, and art-writers. Many publications have resulted, in books, periodicals, and exhibition catalogs in New Zealand, Australia, Great Britain, the U.S., the Czech Republic, and Germany. He is the author of *Colonial Constructs: European Images of Maori 1840–1914* (Auckland University Press & Melbourne University Press, 1992). His most recent publication, on the complexities and problematics of photography in colonial Samoa, was included in *Tropical Visions* *in an Age of Empire*, edited by Felix Driver and Luciana Martins (Chicago: Chicago University Press, 2005).

Charlotte Bydler teaches in the Departments of Art History at Södertörn University College and at Stockholm University, Sweden. Her publications include *The Global Art World, Inc.: On the Globalization of Contemporary Art*, Figura Nova Series 32, diss. (Uppsala, Sweden: Acta Universitatis Upsaliensis, 2004); catalog essays for Carin Ellberg, Ingrid Falk and Gustavo Aguerre (FA+), Shirana Shahbazi, and others; and reviews in *Art & Text, Bidoun, NU: The Nordic Art Review, Tema Celeste,* and others. (charlotte.bydler@sh.se)

David Carrier is Champney Family Professor, a position divided between Case Western Reserve University and Cleveland Institute of Art. A philosopher who writes art criticism, he has published books on Poussin's paintings, Baudelaire's art criticism, and the abstract painter Sean Scully. His book on the museum is forthcoming from Duke University Press. He is at work on a multicultural art history. (dxc89@po.cwru.edu)

Hans Dam Christensen works with visual media, art history, visual culture, and museology at the Department of Cultural and Media Studies at the Royal School of Library and Information Science, Denmark. His publications include *Forskydningens kunst. Kritiske bidrag til kunsthistoriens historie* (Copenhagen, 2001) and "A Sign of the Times?: Art History as/vs. Cultural History," in *Images of Culture: Art History as Cultural History*, edited by Mikkel Bogh et al. (Copenhagen, in press), 1–20. (hdc@db.dk, www.db.dk/hdc)

Craig Clunas works at the Department of Art and Archaeology at the School of Oriental and African Studies, London. His publications include *Superfluous Things: Social Status and Material Culture in Early Modern China* (Cambridge, 1991); *Art in China* (Oxford, 1997); *Pictures and Visuality in Early Modern China* (London, 1997); *Elegant Debts: The Social Art of Wen Zhengming 1470–1559*

(London, 2004). (Department of Art and Archaeology, SOAS, Thornhaugh Street, Russell Square, London WC1H 0XG, U.K.; cc13@soas.ac.uk)

Ekaterina Degot is an art historian, art critic, and curator based in Moscow. She has worked as a senior curator at the State Tretiakov Gallery, an art columnist at *Kommersant Daily* (Moscow), and a curator of special exhibition projects in the Central House of Artists, Moscow. She has taught at the European University, St. Petersburg; and at the Institute of Contemporary Art, Moscow; and has been a guest professor at universities in the United States and Europe. Her books include *Terroristic Naturalism* (1998), *Russian Twentieth-Century Art* (2000), and *Moscow Conceptualism* (with Vadim Zakharov, 2005). She has curated a number of exhibitions including Body Memory: Underwear of the Soviet Era; (City Historical Museum, St. Petersburg, Russia);Moscow-Berlin 1950–2000 (Martin-Gropius Bau, Berlin, Germany); and Soviet Idealism (Liège, Belgium). (e.degot@mail.ru)

James Elkins teaches at the University College Cork, Ireland, and at the School of the Art Institute of Chicago. His most recent books include *Visual Studies: A Skeptical Introduction* (New York, 2003), *On the Strange Place of Religion in Contemporary Art* (New York, 2004), and *Master Narratives and Their Discontents* (New York, 2005).

Shelly Errington is a professor of (cultural) anthropology at the University of California at Santa Cruz, where she teaches courses emphasizing art, museums, visual media, and multimedia. Indonesia and Mexico are the major sites of her fieldwork and research focus, and early in her graduate career she spent a year doing fieldwork in Papua New Guinea. Her book most relevant to this seminar is *The Death of Authentic Primitive Art and Other Tales of Progress* (University of California Press, 1998). She is currently working on a book on the effects of globalization on the production and marketing of folk arts, as well as on a video about three artisans in Morelia, Mexico. She was one of the first MacArthur Prize Fellows, and she has been a Fellow at the Institute for Advanced Study in Princeton, New Jersey, and at the Center for Advanced Study in the Behavioral and Social Sciences in Stanford, California.

Andrea Giunta teaches in the Facultad de Filosofía y Letras, Universidad de Buenos Aires. She is the editor of *Leon Ferrari Restrospective 1954–2004* (2004); *Latin American and Chicano/a Art Criticism since the 1940s: Between Modernity and Globalization 2002-03; Jorge Romero Brest: La revista Ver y Estimar (1948–1955);* and *Cultura y política en los años '60* (1997). She is the author of *Avant-Garde, Internationalism and Politics: Argentinean Art in the Sixties* (2006 [2001]), as well as many articles. (agiunta@filo.uba.ar; agiunta@sinectis.com.ar)

Atreyee Gupta is a Ph.D. student at the Department of Art History, University of Minnesota. Her Ph.D. project studies the reception and display of modern Indian art both in the subcontinent and in Europe from the late nineteenth century to the contemporary. She completed her B.A. in Art History from M.S. University, Vadodara, before joining the University of Minnesota for an M.A. in 2003.

Suman Gupta is Senior Lecturer in Literature at the Open University, UK. He is also Principal Coordinator of the international collaboration Globalization, Identity Politics and Social Conflict (GIPSC). He is the author of seven monographs and numerous papers in literary studies, cultural studies, political philosophy, and current affairs. In March 2005 he made a presentation in a Tate Modern event on the theme *Art and Globalization.* (S.Gupta@open.ac.uk)

Shigemi Inaga 稲賀繁美 works at the International Research Center for Japanese Studies 国際日本文化研究センター in Kyoto. His publications include『絵画の黄昏 エドゥアール・マネ没後の闘争』*Le crépuscule de la peinture, la lutte posthume d'Édouard Manet* (Nagoya, 1997); 『絵画の東方 オリエンタリズムからジャポニスムへ』 *L'Orient de la peinture; de l'Orientalisme au Japonisme* (Nagoya, 1999), both published in Japanese. He edited *Crossing Cultural Borders: Beyond Reciprocal Anthropology* (IRCJS, 2000) in English as well as "Depiction and Description: Morphology of Modern Visuality and Marketplace in Transition—Methodological Reflections," in the special issue of *Art History Forum*, no. 20 (guest editor, Center for Art Studies, Korea, 2005). Other essays include "Cognition Gap in the Recognition of Masters and Masterpieces in the Formative Years of Japanese Art History (1880–1900), Historiography in Conflict," in *Japanese Hermeneutics: Current Debates on Aesthetics and Interpretation,* edited by Michael Marra (Honolulu: University of Hawaii Press, 2002), 115–26; "Un destin de pensée, l'impact d'Okakura Kakuzô (Tenshin) sur le développmenet de l'histoire de l'art en Inde et au Japon au début du XXe siècle," in *Approches critiques de la pensée japonaise du XXe siècle*, edited by Livia Monnet (Montréal, 2002), 329–48. (I.R.C.J.S. Kyoto 610–1192, Japan, inagas@nichibun.ac.jp)

George Intsiful works at the Department of Architecture at Kwame Nkrumah University of Science and Technology, Kumasi, Ghana. His publications include "Housing and Urban Development as a Means Towards the Alleviation of Poverty"; "Housing in the Cities of Kings: A Comparative Study of Housing Development in Kumasi, Ghana and Bulawayo, Zimbabwe"; and "Architectural Training and Practice in Ghana: Complexities in a Developing Country." (7 Buroburo Road, KNUST, Kumasi, Ghana; gwkintsiful@hotmail.com)

Dan Karlholm is Associate Professor at the Department of Art History, School of Arts & Media, Södertörn University College,

Stockholm. His main research interests include the history and theory of art history, modern visual culture, and museum studies. (dan.karlholm@sh.se)

Thomas DaCosta Kaufmann is professor in the Department of Art and Archaeology, Princeton University. His most recent books include *Toward a Geography of Art* (Chicago and London, 2004); *The Eloquent Artist: Essays on Art, Art Theory and Architecture, Sixteenth to Nineteenth Century* (London, 2004); *Central European Drawings in the Crocker Art Museum, Sacramento* (London and Turnhout, 2004); *Painterly Enlightenment: The Art of Franz Anton Maulbertsch, 1724–1796* (Chapel Hill NC, 2005); and *Time and Place: The Geohistory of Art*, introduction, and editor, with Elizabeth Pilliod (London, 2005).

Ladislav Kesner works at the Department of Art History at Masaryk University, Brno, Czech Republic and as a museum consultant. In 2006–7 he was a research fellow at the Internationales Forschungszentrum Kulturwissenschaften in Vienna. His most recent publications include *Marketing a management muzeí a památek / Marketing and Management of Museums and Heritage Sites* (Prague, 2005); "The Role of Cognitive Competence in the Art Museum Experience," in *Museum Management and Curatorship* 21 no. 1 (2006); and "Understanding Art as an Active Visual Hermeneutics," *Ars* 39 no. 1 (2006). (lkesner@cultropa.cz).

Suzana Milevska is a visual culture theorist and curator from Skopje, Macedonia. Her publications include "From a Bat's Point of View" in *Eduardo Kac*, edited by Peter Tomaz Dobrila and Aleksandra Kostić (Maribor, Slovenia, 2000), 47–58; *Capital and Gender,* edited by Suzana Milevska (Skopje, 2001); "The Readymade and the Question of Fabrication of Objects and Subjects" in *Primary Documents: A Sourcebook for Eastern and Central European Art since the 1950s* (New York, 2002), 182–91; "The Portrait of an Artist as a Young 'Strategic Essentialist'" in *Tanja Ostojić — Strategies of Success / Curators Series 2001–2003* (Belgrade, 2004), 33–43; "Hesitations, or About Political and Cultural Territories" in *Cultural Territories,* edited by Barbara Steiner, Julia Schäfer, and Ilina Koralova (Köln, 2005), 31–43. (Ruzveltova 46 a I–5, Skopje 1000, Macedonia; suzanamilevska@yahoo.com)

Keith Moxey teaches in the Art History Department at Barnard College/Columbia University in New York. His recent publications include "Dialogue with Mark Cheetham and Michael Ann Holly," in *Journal of Visual Culture* 4 (2005), 75–90; "Gehry's Bilbao: Visits and Visions," in *Learning from the Guggenheim,* edited by Anna Guasch and Joseba Zulaika (Reno: University of Nevada Press, 2005), 173–84; "Impossible Distance: Past and Present in the Study of Dürer and Grunewald, *Art Bulletin* 86 (2004), 750–63; "Disciplines of the Visual: Art History, Visual Studies, and Globalization, *Genre* 36 (2003): 429–48.

Sandy Ng received her Ph.D. from the School of Oriental and African Studies, University of London. Her thesis on the twentieth-century artist Lin Fengmian is primarily concerned with how modernism and hybridity were reinvented in twentieth-century Chinese art. Her current research interests include the significance of color in arts and cultures and the construction of corporal representation. She teaches in the Department of Fine Arts at the University of Hong Kong. (ydnas@hkucc.hku.hk)

Chika Okeke-Agulu is an Assistant Professor of Art History at Penn State University. He has contributed to edited volumes, including *Reading the Contemporary: African Art from Theory to the Marketplace*; *The Nsukka Artists and Contemporary Nigerian Art*; and *The Grove Dictionary of Art.* His writings have also appeared in *African Arts; Nka: Journal of Contemporary African Art; Meridians: Feminism, Race, Transnationalism;* and *Glendora Review.* As an independent curator, he has coorganized and written catalog essays for the Nigerian Pavilion at the First Johannesburg Biennale, 1995; *Seven Stories About Modern Art in Africa* (Whitechapel Art Gallery, London, 1995); *The Short Century: Independence and Liberation Movements in Africa, 1945–1994* (Museum Villa Stuck, Munich, 2001); and The Fifth Gwangju Biennale, South Korea, and *Strange Planet*, Georgia State University Art Gallery (2004). He is the coeditor of *Nka: Journal of Contemporary African Art*.

Jorgelina Orfila is a Ph.D. candidate at the University of Maryland. Previously she was the head of education of the Museo Nacional de Bellas Artes in Buenos Aires, Argentina. She was professor of art history at the Universidad del Museo Social Argentino and has taught by invitation at other universities in Buenos Aires. Her recent publications include "Blague, Nationalism, and Incohérence," in *Nationalism and French Visual Culture, 1870–1914,* edited by June Hargrove and Neil McWilliam (Washington, 2005). (ojorgel@yahoo.com)

Sugata Ray, a Ph.D. student at the Department of Art History, University of Minnesota, is working on the nineteenth- and twentieth-century histories of Braj Bhumi, a pilgrimage site in north India. In addition to an M.A. in Art History from M.S. University, Vadodara, Sugata holds an M.Phil. from the Center for Studies in Social Sciences, Kolkata.

Barbara Maria Stafford is William B. Ogden Distinguished Service Professor at the University of Chicago and teaches in the Art History Department. Her publications include *Body Criticism* (Cambridge MA, and London, 1992), *Voyage into Substance* (Cambridge MA, and London, 1984), *Artful Science* (Cambridge MA, and London, 1994), *Good Looking: Essays on the Virtue of Images* (Cambridge MA, and London, 1996), *Visual Analogy: Consciousness as the Art of Connecting* (Cambridge MA, and

London, 1999), and the exhibition catalog, with Francis Terpak, *Devices of Wonder: From the World in a Box to Images on a Screen* (Los Angeles and Oxford, 2001).

Maria de los Ángeles Taberna is Chief of Department of "Escuela de Letras" at Universidad Catolica Andres Bello, Caracas, Venezuela, where she has been Professor of Art History I, II, and III since 1988. She was Professor at the Universidad Metropolitana in 1992 and 1993, and Professor at the Universidad Simon Bolívar from 1994 to 1995. Her publications include "Reflexiones sobre tres formas de Representación discursiva" in the *Boletin Universitario Escuela de Letras* (1996); *An Approach to a Visual Quixote: The Graphic Quixote* (2005); and various articles.

Romuald Tchibozo is Assistant Professor of Art History, University of Benin. The topic of his Ph.D. thesis is *l'Art et l'arbitraire: une étude de la réception de l'art africain contemporain en Occident: le cas Allemand de 1950 à nos jours* (Berlin: Humboldt Universität zu Berlin, 2003). It is based on international cultural relations and demonstrates how ideologies influence the production and reception of African contemporary art. His most recent publication is a catalog called *Harmattan 2005,* about certain Beninese contemporary artists. (tchibozoromuald@hotmail.com)

Humberto Valdivieso works at the School of Literature at the Universidad Católica Andrés Bello, Caracas, Venezuela. His curatorial projects include Santiago Pol in the 51 Biennale of Venice. His publications include *Colore, amore e calore della picccola Venezia: Disegni venezueliani di Santiago Pol* (Venice, 2005); "Desocupado lector, mi semejante, mi hermano," in the brochure of the exposition *El Quijote Gráfico*, edited by UCAB (Caracas, 2005); and "La plástica en el origen del diseño gráfico contemporáneo en Venezuela," *Revista de Investigaciones Literarias* (Universidad Central de Venezuela, 2005).

Heie Treier is editor-in-chief of *kunst.ee*, a quarterly magazine in Tallinn, Estonia. She is also a and part-time lecturer at the Estonian Academy of Arts. Her interests range from early modernist art (which was the topic of her thesis) to contemporary art. *Kunst.ee* was chosen to participate in the magazine project of documenta 12 in 2007. (heie@sirp.ee)

Frank Vigneron works at the Fine Arts Department of The Chinese University of Hong Kong. He specializes in Chinese painting theory and contemporary Chinese art. He teaches courses on Western art, Western art theory, the theories of modernism and postmodernism, and Chinese and Western comparative aesthetics. He is also a practicing artist, has held several solo exhibitions in Hong Kong, and has taken part in local and international exhibitions.

Kitty Zijlmans is Professor of Contemporary Art History and Theory at the Department of Art History, University of Leiden, the Netherlands. She is a member of the Steering Committee of the European Science Foundation's "Discourses of the Visible: National and International Perspectives" (2003–2006). Her publications include *Gesichtspunkte: Kunstgeschichte Heute* (Berlin, 1995) and "Pushing Back Frontiers: Towards a History of Art in a Global Perspective," *International Journal of Anthropology* 18 no. 4 (2003): 201–10. (c.j.m.zijlmans@let.leidenuniv.nl)

Index

D

E

M

Q

R

Y

Z